Economic and Social Survey of
Asia and the Pacific
2008

Sustaining Growth and
Sharing Prosperity

United Nations

New York, 2008   ECONOMIC AND SOCIAL COMMISSION FOR ASIA AND THE PACIFIC

ECONOMIC AND SOCIAL SURVEY OF ASIA AND THE PACIFIC 2008

Sustaining Growth and Sharing Prosperity

United Nations publication
Sales No. E.08.II.F.7
Copyright © United Nations 2008
All rights reserved
Manufactured in Thailand
ISBN: 978-92-1-120537-4
ISSN: 0252-5704
ST/ESCAP/2476

FOREWORD

This year marks the sixtieth anniversary of the publication of the *Economic and Social Survey of Asia and the Pacific*. The first issue, published in 1948, came against the backdrop of the devastation of the Second World War and set out to provide policy guidance for the recovery and reconstruction of the war-torn countries in the region. Since then, the *Survey* has presented an independent analysis of the region's socioeconomic developments, provided early warning signals and presented policy options and recommendations. Today, it is considered the most comprehensive annual review of economic and social development in Asia and the Pacific.

In this context, the *Survey* examines the region's key short- and medium-term prospects and challenges in macroeconomic and selected social areas, especially from the point of view of minimizing human suffering; be it from economic hardships or social instability. The *Survey* also explores critical long-term development issues relevant to all developing countries in the region.

As the 2008 *Survey* spells out that, having enjoyed the fastest growth in a decade in 2007, the developing economies in the region are expected to grow at a slightly lower but still robust rate of 7.7 per cent in 2008. The main short-term challenge to economic prospects comes from the still unraveling sub-prime crisis of the United States and its possible impact on the world economy. The *Survey* emphasizes that the region's solid macroeconomic fundamentals, painstakingly put in place and strengthened through the years, have prepared the countries of Asia and the Pacific to absorb and adapt to such external shocks.

Despite good economic performance and efforts by Governments to foster social development, there are a number of fault lines in the region. Over 600 million of the world's poor still live in Asia, nearly two thirds of the global total, and mainly in rural areas. Other statistics are equally staggering. Ninety-seven million children remain underweight. Four million children die before reaching age five. While the region is well prepared to ride the current turbulence in the global economy, even smaller economic shocks can severely affect the most vulnerable people. The long-term impact of these shocks in terms of poverty, unemployment and inequality is of deep concern, highlighting the need for sound policies to share prosperity and the fruits of high growth.

In this spirit, the 2008 *Survey* takes a closer look at agriculture as a critical factor for poverty reduction and rural development. Agriculture still provides jobs for 60 per cent of the working population in Asia and the Pacific, and shelters the majority of the poor. But neglect has undermined the sector's capacity to reduce poverty and inequality. Long-term development issues related to agriculture need to be addressed head-on. The *Survey* proposes a two-track strategy to ensure that agriculture is both economically and socially viable, so as to raise productivity and make real inroads against poverty.

I hope the findings of this 60th anniversary *Survey* will provide a basis for wider discussion among policymakers in Asia and the Pacific, and support the region in its endeavours to remain a leading engine of growth while achieving shared prosperity.

Ban Ki-moon
Secretary-General

February 2008

ACKNOWLEDGEMENTS

Under the general direction of the Executive Secretary of the Economic and Social Commission for Asia and the Pacific (ESCAP), Noeleen Heyzer, this report was prepared by a team under the overall guidance of Ravi Ratnayake, Director of the Poverty and Development Division. The core team, led by Shamika Sirimanne, included Amarakoon Bandara, Shuvojit Banerjee, Somchai Congtavinsutti, Eugene Gherman, Alberto Isgut, Anna de Jong, Nobuko Kajiura, Muhammad H. Malik, Vanessa Steinmayer and Amy Wong.

Many others within ESCAP provided inputs and helpful comments. Valuable advice was received from internal peer reviewers Tiziana Bonapace, Haishan Fu, Masakazu Ichimura, John Moon, Keiko Osaki and Ja-Kyung Yoo. Substantive contributions were made by Adnan Aliani, Jonh Gilbert and Neema Paresh Majmudar of the Poverty and Development Division; Tiziana Bonapace and Mia Mikic of the Trade and Investment Division; Keiko Osaki of the Emerging Social Issues Division; Sangmin Nam of the Environment and Sustainable Development Division; and Taco Bottema of the Centre for Alleviation of Poverty through Secondary Crops' Development in Asia and the Pacific. The statistical annex was prepared by the Statistics Division, with Eric Hermouet acting as the focal point (tables 10-28), and Somchai Congtavinsutti (tables 1-9) of the Poverty and Development Division. Other inputs were received from Ron Corben, Clovis Freire, Thelma Kay, Amitava Mukherjee, Hitomi Rankine, Marco Roncarati, Le Huu Ti, Ja-Kyung Yoo and staff members of ESCAP Pacific Operations Centre. Contribution from Susanna Wolf of Economic Commission for Africa for the section on Africa-Asia trading relations is highly appreciated. The comments of Bhakta Gubhaju, Aynul Hasan, Raj Kumar, Wei Liu, Hiren Sarkar, and Srinivas Tata are noted with thanks.

Written country inputs were provided by the following external consultants: Mushtaq Ahmad, Sonam Chuki, Ron Duncan, Mohammad Kordbache, Panom Lathouly, George Manzano, Biswajit Nag, Hang Chuon Naron, Prakash Kumar Shrestha and Vo Tri Thanh.

The team appreciates the excellent logistical support in processing and administration provided by Woranut Sompitayanurak. Support from Metinee Hunkosol on financial matters and Anong Pattanathanes on proofreading is appreciated. Research assistance was provided by Sansiree Kosindesha, Michelle Lum, Kiatkanid Pongpanich, Frank Ramirez, Jonathan Selter and Amornrut Supornsinchai.

The report benefited from the comments and suggestions of an external peer review meeting held in Bangkok. Participants in the meeting were a group of prominent Asian policymakers and scholars: G.K. Chadha, Economic Advisor to the Prime Minister of India; Stephen Y.L. Cheung, Professor (Chair) of Finance, City University of Hong Kong, Hong Kong, China; Saman Kelegama, Executive Director, Institute of Policy Studies, Sri Lanka; Shoaib Sultan Khan, Chairman, Rural Support Programme Network, Pakistan; Prabowo, Director of Programmes, Strategic Asia, Indonesia; Andrey E. Shastitko, Director-General, Bureau of Economic Analysis Foundation, Russian Federation; Chia Siow Yue, Senior Research Fellow, Singapore Institute of International Affairs, Singapore; Cid L. Terosa, Associate Professor, School of Economics, University of Asia and the Pacific, Philippines; Boonjit Titapiwatanakun, Assistant Professor, Department of Agricultural and Resource Economics, Kasetsart University, Thailand; P.K. Mudbhary, Chief, Policy Assistance Branch, FAO Regional Office for Asia and the Pacific, Bangkok; and Jean-Pierre A. Verbiest, Country Director, Thailand Resident Mission, Asian Development Bank.

Substantive editing of the manuscript was performed by Communications Development Incorporated, headed by Bruce Ross-Larson. The Editorial Unit of ESCAP, headed by Orestes Plasencia, edited the manuscript. The layout and printing were provided by TR Enterprise. Special thanks to Tjerah Leonardo, who contributed to the design of the cover.

Special thanks to Hak-Fan Lau, Chavalit Boonthanom, Ari Gaitanis, Thawadi Pachariyangkun and other members of the United Nations Information Services, who coordinated the launch and dissemination of the report.

EXECUTIVE SUMMARY

Healthy macroeconomic fundamentals to shield the region from global financial turbulence

After the fastest growth in a decade in 2007, the developing economies of the Asia-Pacific region are expected to grow at a slightly slower but still robust 7.7% in 2008. The region's developed economies are expected to grow at 1.6% in 2008, slipping from 2% in 2007. China and India, the region's economic locomotives, are expected to continue growing briskly in 2008, boosting the rest of the region. Commodity- and energy-exporting countries, particularly the Russian Federation, are expected to add to the momentum. The major drags on performance are the slowdown in the United States driven by the bursting housing bubble, the unfolding credit crunch in the United States and Europe, the appreciation of currencies in the region against the dollar and the high oil and food prices.

Although exports may suffer from the slower growth in industrial countries, strong domestic demand – driven by private consumption and investment in fast-growing countries and by fiscal accommodation – should cushion the blow. Export-dependent economies in East and South-East Asia will see exports contribute less to growth, but China's on-going expansion will continue to offer opportunities.

North and Central Asia will continue to benefit from consumption and construction, thanks to income from high energy prices. With economies traditionally driven by domestic demand, South and South-West Asia will benefit from strong private consumption and investment – and from expansionary fiscal policy in some countries. In the Pacific, Fiji and Tonga are expected to recover from economic contractions, while Papua New Guinea will enjoy rising consumption as the benefits of high commodity prices spill over to the rest of the economy.

The region's resilience lies mainly in its healthy macroeconomic fundamentals, enabling countries to adopt supportive fiscal and monetary policies. Government budget deficits have gradually declined and, in some countries, have turned to surpluses. There have been no signs of excessive current account deficits, as in the prelude to 1997. Countries have reduced their dependence on bank financing, addressed currency mismatches and improved the health of banking sectors. Large foreign reserves have added to the region's resilience.

Food inflation – the next big challenge: Inflation in the developing economies of the region is projected at 4.6% in 2008, down from 5.1% the previous year, with currency appreciation cushioning the impact of high oil and food prices. This projection, however, is subject to some uncertainty. The key question is how much last year's surge in prices will continue in 2008 and beyond. Oil prices are expected to decline from the record levels at the beginning of 2008 as the industrial economies slow, led by the United States. Food prices are likely to remain high, posing a greater inflationary risk because food accounts for a far higher proportion of consumer spending.

The rising food prices in 2007 were due in part to drought in Australia, flooding in China and dry weather in Europe. Added pressure came from the demand for biofuels. With the march towards biofuels apparently unstoppable, governments need to consider carefully the impact on the poor. ESCAP analysis shows that the poor have so far benefited little from the biofuel revolution despite its opportunities for lower income groups.

Currency appreciation to continue: Since 2006, major currencies in the region have risen against the dollar, a trend expected to continue in 2008, driven by the unwinding of large United States imbalances with the rest of the world and the turmoil in global financial markets. Currency appreciation sheltered the region's economies from high oil and food prices, but it dealt a blow to the competitiveness of exports. Countries whose currencies appreciated the most faced intensive competition from lower cost producers, surrendering market share, especially in price-sensitive, low-technology manufacturing, along with some agricultural commodities.

Downside risks to the 2008 outlook – navigating the subprime crisis

The subprime crisis in the United States is still unravelling, and a significant slowdown in the United States and further turmoil in financial markets cannot be ruled out. Often-fickle investor sentiment makes it difficult to predict when and how that turmoil might affect regional markets. Even so, countries can ensure that they are strong and flexible enough to absorb the shocks and adapt to any disruption in financial flows. Because economic shocks exact a heavy toll on poor and vulnerable people, efforts to mitigate the impacts are urgent.

So far, Asia-Pacific economies have remained fairly immune to the tighter credit conditions in the United States and the European Union. The region's corporate sector is generally cash-rich and not highly leveraged. The region is also reported to have little exposure to subprime or other vulnerable debt.

The main impact on the region will come through a downturn in exports. The United States has been cutting interest rates aggressively in response to slowing growth, fuelling further depreciation of the dollar. Countries in the region will face twin blows: reduced demand and less competitive exports to the United States. The possibility of substantial capital outflows from the region is another risk, whether triggered by external developments, concerns about the region's growth or reversals in the foreign exchange "carry trade".

In the worst case scenario of a recession in the United States and a deeper depreciation of the dollar, the impact in much of the region would be harsh. Most vulnerable will be the exporters of high-technology products, such as electronics, to the United States: Singapore, the Republic of Korea and Taiwan Province of China. The economy of China will remain reasonably resilient, as strong domestic demand should partly cushion the external shock. The impact is likely to be felt less in economies led largely by domestic demand, such as India.

To strengthen economies and to reduce the impact on the poor, countries must:

- **Solidify macroeconomic fundamentals – to maintain investor confidence and sustain economic growth**. Key policies are for moderate and stable inflation, low budget deficits and sustainable debt burdens – and more flexible exchange rates to absorb shocks.

- **Develop robust microeconomic foundations – to ensure efficient economic systems**. Clear property rights, overseen by a strong judiciary, allow companies and institutions to operate with confidence. Training programmes to improve labour mobility and measures to safeguard vulnerable segments of the working population are also important.

- **Ensure healthy financial sectors – to build confidence and benefit from capital inflows**. Financial markets need to be deepened by developing domestic and regional bond markets. Authorities must also keep pace with the greater diversity and complexity of new financial products.

- **Strengthen social safety nets – to support people facing hardship during economic downturns**. As such systems are difficult to set up during crises, the time to act is now. Safety nets should be large enough in scale and coverage to provide broad-based social protection.

- **Improve regional cooperation – to prevent crises and react to them**. More needs to be done across the region to share information about portfolio flows and to collaborate in regulatory activities. Also needed is action to provide an early warning system for potentially disruptive financial flows.

On the upside, the subprime crisis can bring new opportunities. Interest in Asia-Pacific assets may increase because of the strong growth projections for the region. Asia-Pacific investors have been instrumental in supporting developed countries through the recent turmoil, as sovereign wealth funds and State investment institutions from the region bolster weakened banking sectors in the United States and Europe. That shifting balance of financial power is also evident in the dramatic rise in the overseas investment of Asia-Pacific corporations.

Medium-term challenges to sharing prosperity across the region

The region is likely to weather the relatively short-term global uncertainty in 2008. Asia-Pacific countries, however, will continue to face critical medium-term social, economic and environmental challenges in ensuring inclusive and sustainable growth that reaches the poor. Climate change and international migration are two key issues.

Managing climate change: In Asia and the Pacific, all people face severe consequences from climate change – but especially the poor, both rural and urban, who typically lack the resources to insulate themselves against natural disasters. Globally, Asia-Pacific countries can actively contribute to climate change negotiations. Closer to home, they can take the lead in implementing mitigation and adaptation measures. A new regional framework for managing climate change should include measures to promote eco-efficiency, expand carbon trading, support technology transfers and manage waste efficiently.

Addressing the social dimensions of international migration: International migration, which continues unabated, affects both those involved and broader communities – impacting marriage, families and governance structures. These dimensions seldom receive enough attention. Alongside the economic aspects of migration, Governments need to assess fully the social implications of family separation and marriage migration, as well as the public health effects. Protecting migrant rights by ensuring equal treatment under the law in receiving countries should be high on the policy agenda.

Added to these regionwide issues are specific challenges confronting each subregion:

- **Addressing rising inequality:** East and North-East Asia has witnessed widening income disparities across most countries. To address differences in economic and human development among provinces and between rural and urban areas, China has enacted a host of regional development programmes. As a result of the "Go West" policy, there are preliminary signs of faster economic development in some western provinces than in coastal provinces, with benefits for China and its neighbours.

- **Navigating economic transition:** Social reforms in North and Central Asian economies are lagging behind economic reforms. Strategic investments are needed to reverse rising inequality and deteriorating educational and health-care systems. The challenge for the subregion is to finance and deliver services efficiently and equitably. Effective use of the subregion's large intellectual potential should be integral to economic and social cooperation, especially on education. By pooling resources, North and Central Asian countries can set up new organizational structures and procedures for joint activities. The private sector has a role in mobilizing finance.

- **Improving employment opportunities:** The Pacific island developing countries must provide employment for their citizens. The challenges: widespread underemployment in most countries, too many engaged in subsistence and small-scale cash-cropping, women left disadvantaged and underrepresented in formal employment, and high youth unemployment. Developing skills and updating labour legislation to respond to changing macroeconomic and business conditions are crucial.

- **Ensuring public debt sustainability:** Public debts in South Asia are generally high and must be lowered to enhance the flexibility in the use of macroeconomic policies and to make resources available to create jobs and reduce poverty. Making South Asia's public debt more sustainable requires controlling fiscal deficits, expanding government revenues and containing wasteful expenditures. Public expenditure should be directed more towards priority areas such as providing education, health, sanitation, housing and other basic services to promote pro-poor growth.

- **Gaining from greater integration:** Regional integration in South-East Asia has intensified through regional trade agreements, but the potential gains remain largely untapped. Greater regional integration could substantially reduce the number of people living on less than a dollar a day and improve overall welfare. Nonetheless, the gains from multilateral trade liberalization are substantially higher than those from regional trade agreements.

A long-term challenge to the region – addressing the neglect of agriculture

Over the long term, sharing prosperity means including the more than 600 million of the world's poor who live in Asia, nearly two-thirds of the global total. Living largely in rural areas, many of them depend on agriculture. Addressing the neglect of agriculture is crucial to reduce poverty and inequality.

Agriculture employs 60% of the working population in Asia and the Pacific and shelters a majority of the poor. Decades of neglect, however, have weakened the sector's capacity to cut poverty and inequality. Growth and productivity in agriculture have stalled, and the green revolution that boosted agricultural yields in the 1970s has bypassed millions. Farmers are now facing mounting pressure, evident in declining subsidies, rising input prices, intensifying protests over landlessness and an alarming number of suicides among the indebted.

Improving agricultural productivity could have a profound impact on poverty. Raising average agricultural labour productivity to the level in Thailand, for example, would take 218 million people – a third of the region's poor – out of poverty. Large gains in reducing poverty are also possible through comprehensive liberalization of global agricultural trade, which could lift another 48 million people out of poverty. Diversification into high-value crops, so far limited to a few countries, should be the policy focus over the coming decades. But agriculture alone will not raise the region's 641 million poor people out of poverty. Developing the non-farm sector is just as important.

A two-pronged strategy is required to make agriculture economically and socially viable, returning it to its place in reducing poverty and inequality:

- First, agriculture needs another revolution. A market orientation with a focus on quality and standards would be part of this strategy. Investments in research and development and human capital will increase agricultural productivity significantly. Also necessary is to revamp land policies, connect the rural poor to cities and markets and make credit instruments and crop insurance farmer-friendly.

- Second, facilitating migration out of agriculture should complement agricultural development – by empowering the poor, particularly women, with the skills to tap labour market opportunities and by promoting rural non-farm activities and regional growth centres.

CONTENTS

	Page
Foreword	iii
Acknowledgements	iv
Executive summary	v
Abbreviations	xxii
Chapter 1. Regional socio-economic developments and prospects	1
Growth to moderate in 2008 but remain robust	1
Larger economies to maintain dynamism	1
Japan's growth spurt stutters	4
Least developed countries – largely unaffected by global turbulence	4
Domestic demand – cushioning slower export growth	7
Infrastructure and environment – holding back fast growers?	8
Greater uncertainty for inflation	8
Food inflation – the next big challenge	10
Currency appreciation to continue	11
Measures to help exporters not effective	13
Reserves accumulate – at what cost?	14
Downside risks to the 2008 outlook – navigating the subprime crisis	17
Hit to Asia-Pacific exports	17
The threat of financial sector turmoil	19
Asia-Pacific investors to the rescue	20
Asia and the Pacific well prepared to navigate global instability	21
The need to build defences against subprime fallout – now	21
A global call to action to regulate new financial actors	24
Medium-term policy issues on the watch list	25
Benefiting from trade in services – the next frontier	25
Addressing the social dimensions of international migration	27
Managing climate change – how Asia and the Pacific can take the lead in mitigation and adaptation	31
References	38

CONTENTS *(continued)*

Page

Chapter 2. Subregional performance and medium-term challenges 41

Robust growth despite slowing exports 41

**East and North-East Asia: Growth supported by domestic demand and ties
with China** 44

Domestic demand fuelled growth 45

International commodity prices fuelled inflation 45

China's growth cushioned export impact 47

Medium-term prospects: coping with a marked United States slowdown 48

Inequality and poverty remain long-term challenges 48

Policy research feature 2.1: China's "Go West" policy to reduce inequality
among provinces – and its benefits for Asia-Pacific economies 50

North and Central Asia: Among the most dynamic in the region 58

Surging food prices accelerated consumer price inflation 59

High global commodity prices caused exports earnings to surge 60

Remittances had a significant macroeconomic impact 61

Foreign direct investment continued to help economies develop and modernize 62

High commodity prices and tax reforms stabilized some countries' fiscal positions 62

Higher remittances and foreign direct investment meant stronger currencies 62

Sound monetary policy and continued tax reforms will maintain robust
economic performance in 2008-2009 63

Policy research feature 2.2: Poverty, education and health challenges during
economic transition in North and Central Asia 65

Pacific island developing countries: Modest growth 70

Growth was stronger in Melanesia than in Polynesia or Micronesia 70

Difficult times for exports meant trade deficits 72

Political conditions affect economic growth in the Pacific............................ 73

Tourism, telecommunications and agriculture could drive future growth 73

Policy research feature 2.3: Improving employment opportunities in Pacific
island economies 75

South and South-West Asia: Strong growth continues 79

High international prices for commodities added to inflationary pressures 82

Fiscal deficits remained high 83

High oil prices pressured trade and current account balances 84

Strong economic growth is expected to continue in 2008 86

Policy research feature 2.4: Fiscal deficit and public debt sustainability in South Asia 88

CONTENTS *(continued)*

Page

South-East Asia: Domestic demand supports GDP growth despite a small decline in export dynamism 93

Inflation decelerated in most countries 95

Exchange rates appreciated and foreign exchange reserves accumulated 96

Solid macroeconomic fundamentals leave countries well prepared for a slowdown in export demand 97

Policy research feature 2.5: Can the least developed countries of Asia and the Pacific escape the vulnerability trap? 102

Developed economies: Continued growth heightens capacity constraints 108

Growth was supported by domestic demand 108

Wage growth stimulated household consumption 109

A tight labour market led to wage growth in Australia and New Zealand but not in Japan 109

Inflationary pressure remained a concern in Australia and New Zealand; production costs increased in Japan 109

The trade surplus increased in Japan, while Australia and New Zealand remained in deficit 110

Growth is expected to slow in 2008-2009 111

Policy research feature 2.6: How secure is retirement in Japan? 112

References 118

Chapter 3. Unequal benefits of growth – agriculture left behind 121

Diagnosing Asia-Pacific's waning agriculture 122

Poverty declines are slowing, and rural poverty remains stubbornly high: A lethargic agriculture? 122

The role of agriculture in creating jobs is diminishing in some subregions 123

Inequality is widening due to the neglect of agriculture 124

Agricultural labour productivity growth is declining, and productivity gaps remain wide 124

Land productivity has improved but remains well below European levels 127

Agriculture – a powerful driver of poverty reduction and social equity 129

Raising agricultural productivity can take 218 million people out of poverty 129

Comprehensive reforms going beyond Doha could take 48-51 million people out of poverty 130

Developing Asia-Pacific region to gain $3.3-3.5 billion under comprehensive agricultural trade reforms 131

CONTENTS *(continued)*

Page

What is holding back agriculture? 133

Inequality in land ownership weighs on productivity 133

Wide inequality in access to health and education has made agriculture
less productive 134

Lack of rural infrastructure hinders growth 134

Macroeconomic policy has been anti-agriculture 137

Credit markets discriminate against rural farmers 138

Limited spending on agricultural R&D and extension constrains productivity growth 138

Slow progress in agricultural trade liberalization hits the poorest hard 139

Declining international prices discourage producers of staple crops 140

Progress in crop diversification is slow and limited 140

Official development assistance for agriculture is declining 144

Two strategies to make agriculture socially and economically viable 145

Strategy 1: Revitalize agriculture 145

Strategy 2: Facilitate migration out of agriculture 150

References 152

Statistical annex 157

BOXES

Page

1.1. Sharing the benefits of growth 4

1.2. Biofuels: Friend or foe of the poor? 11

1.3. Fast-growing trade between Asia and Africa 15

1.4. The impact of a United States recession on Asian economies – a pessimistic scenario 18

1.5. How economic shocks impact the poor 23

1.6. Cash for wind – how clean energy can become a big business 34

1.7. Cash from trash – financing mitigation and adaptation through decentralized solid
waste management... 36

2.1. Regional development strategies elsewhere in Asia and the Pacific 57

2.2. Socio-economic impact of natural disasters in Bangladesh 81

2.3. Gains from greater regional integration 98

3.1. Growing farm debt, increasing distress in Indian agriculture 126

3.2. The nexus between poverty and health in rural areas... 135

3.3. Rural infrastructure making a dent in poverty in Thailand 135

3.4. Improving the efficiency of farmers through technology..................................... 145

3.5. Using family histories to understand the intergenerational transmission of poverty 146

3.6. Climate change likely to change the landscape of the region 148

TABLES

Page

1.1. Economic growth and inflation, 2006-2008 2

1.2. Global services location index, 2007 27

1.3. The gender composition of migration outflows varies widely 29

1.4. Governments in the ESCAP region that have adopted key United Nations legal
instruments on international migration, as of November 2007 31

2.1. Current account balance as a share of GDP in selected East and
North-East Asian economies, 2004-2007 47

2.2. External accounts in North and Central Asia, selected economies, 2006-2007 60

2.3. Export and import growth in North and Central Asia, selected economies, 2005-2007 60

2.4. Challenging times for human development in North and Central Asia 66

2.5. The government contribution to higher per capita spending on health, 2000-2004 68

2.6. Merchandise trade and current account balances in selected Pacific island
economies, 2004-2007 72

2.7. Rapid population growth in much of the Pacific: Forecast percentage population
change in selected Pacific island developing economies, 2004-2029 75

2.8. Only moderate employment growth expected: Forecast changes in formal sector
employment in selected Pacific island developing economies 75

2.9. Highly variable labour force participation rates in the Pacific islands, selected economies 76

2.10. Urban employment dominates in some Pacific island developing economies,
rural employment in others 76

2.11. Summary of external accounts for selected South and South-West Asian economies 85

2.12. Debt can weigh on government budgets: Costs to service the public debt in
South Asia, 2000-2006 89

2.13. Foreign exchange reserves accumulations mostly reflected surpluses in the current account 97

2.14. Wealth, human assets and vulnerability in the least developed countries in
Asia and the Pacific 102

2.15. Worst natural disasters in the low-income countries of the Asia-Pacific region, 1980-2003 105

2.16. Budget and current account balances in developed ESCAP countries, 2004-2007 111

2.17. Eligibility criteria for the livelihood assistance programme and basic pension benefits:
Two examples 116

3.1. Agricultural and non-agricultural growth rates 125

TABLES *(continued)*

Page

3.2.   Sectoral employment elasticities, 1991-2003   125

3.3.   Land productivity by continent   128

3.4.   Impacts of labour productivity in agriculture on poverty reduction in the Asia-Pacific region   129

3.5.   Impact of Doha and comprehensive reforms on poverty   130

3.6.   Estimated aggregate welfare effect of agricultural reforms   132

3.7.   Taxation of agriculture in Asia   138

FIGURES

Page

1.1.	Real GDP growth in developing ESCAP economies and in other regions	1
1.2.	GDP growth to slow in 2008	3
1.3.	Strong contributions of domestic demand to GDP	7
1.4.	Inflation in ESCAP subregions, 2007-2008	9
1.5.	Inflation in selected developing ESCAP economies, 2007-2008	9
1.6.	Nominal and real oil prices, 1970-2007	10
1.7.	Rising food prices	11
1.8.	Real effective exchange rates for selected developing ESCAP economies, 2006-2007	12
1.9.	Current account balance for selected developing ESCAP economies, 2007-2008	13
1.10.	Record foreign reserves in the Asian and Pacific region 2006-2007	16
1.11.	Growing liquidity in 2006-2007	16
1.12.	Stock markets higher in 2007, but volatile	17
1.13.	Booming outward investment, 2005-2007	20
1.14.	Budget balances have improved...	22
1.15.	...as have external balances	22
1.16.	Strong service exports for ESCAP developing economies in 2000-2006	25
1.17.	India and China leading service exports in the region	25
1.18.	Exports of other commercial services in 2005, selected countries	26
1.19	Rising remittances in Asia and the Pacific, 2006-2007	28
1.20.	New migrant source countries emerging	28
1.21.	Framework for managing climate change	33
2.1.	Rates of economic growth in the ESCAP region, 2006-2007	41
2.2.	Contributions of agriculture, industry and services to GDP growth in selected East and North-East Asian economies, 2006-2007	44
2.3.	A strong fiscal position for most governments in the subregion: Budget balance in selected East and North-East Asian economies, 2006-2007	44
2.4.	Inflation and money supply growth (M2) in selected East and North-East Asian economies, 2004-2007	46
2.5.	East and North-East Asian exchange rates against the United States dollar, 1996-2007	47

FIGURES *(continued)*

		Page
2.6.	Wide inequality in human development among provinces	50
2.7.	Faster per capita income growth in a majority of western provinces in 2005/2006	51
2.8.	The income gap is narrowing faster in the lowest income provinces	52
2.9.	Rural income gap narrowing for a few western provinces	52
2.10.	Government spending went more to poorer provinces in 2006	53
2.11.	Fixed-asset investment is increasing quickly in many provinces	54
2.12.	Final consumption growth is fast in a few provinces	54
2.13.	Research and development is growing faster in a few provinces	55
2.14.	Exports are growing rapidly in most provinces	55
2.15.	FDI is increasing markedly in a few provinces	56
2.16.	Rapid growth in North and Central Asia: Real GDP and sectoral growth in North and Central Asian economies, 2006-2007	58
2.17.	Rapid inflation across North and Central Asia, 2006-2007	59
2.18.	Exchange rates against the United States dollar for selected North and Central Asian economies, 1996-2007	63
2.19.	Turbulence during economic transition: Index of real GDP in North and Central Asian developing economies, 1991-2006	65
2.20.	Health spending in North and Central Asia is rising more quickly in some countries than in others: Per capita health spending at international dollar rates	68
2.21.	Real GDP and sectoral growth in selected Pacific island economies, 2005-2007	71
2.22.	Industry and services perform well: Economic growth rates and sectoral contributions in selected South and South-West Asian countries, 2006-2007	79
2.23.	Investment higher than savings, except in the Islamic Republic of Iran, 2007	80
2.24.	Inflationary pressure persisted in South and South-West Asian countries in 2006-2007	83
2.25.	Budget deficits remained a serious problem in South and South-West Asian countries in 2006-2007	83
2.26.	Differing shares of domestic and external debt as a share of GDP, 2006	88
2.27.	Central government budget deficit as a share of GDP, 2000-2006	91
2.28.	Economic growth remained robust in 2007	93
2.29.	Investment accelerated in the Philippines, Indonesia and Singapore in 2007	94

FIGURES *(continued)*

Page

2.30. Private consumption grew more rapidly in most South-East Asian countries in 2007 94

2.31. Inflation fell in most South-East Asian countries in 2007 95

2.32. Interest rates in 2007 were lower than in 2006 or stable 96

2.33. The nominal exchange rate continued appreciating against the United States dollar 96

2.34. Intraregional trade becoming more important for ASEAN countries 98

2.35. Export concentration for selected Asian and Pacific countries 103

2.36. Kiribati's export earnings were volatile over 1980-2000... 104

2.37. ...but Bangladesh's grew steadily 104

2.38. Remittances as a share of GDP in selected Asian and Pacific countries, 2004 106

2.39. Aid dominates economies in Afghanistan, Solomon Islands and Timor-Leste: ODA
receipts as a share of GDP, 2004 106

2.40. Economic growth in developed ESCAP countries, 2005-2007 108

2.41. Inflation in developed ESCAP economies, 2005-2007 110

2.42. Nearly half of Japan's elderly households are low income: Distribution of elderly
households by income quartile 112

2.43. Single-person households are often poor: Distribution of elderly households
by type and level of income 113

2.44. Income, savings and liabilities by age group 114

2.45. Single elderly people often depend on pensions.. 114

2.46. Single households with lower pension benefits have lower savings 115

2.47. Distribution of male pensioners by pension benefits and pre-retirement occupation 116

3.1. Slowing declines in poverty since the 1980s, with progress mainly in urban areas 122

3.2. Agricultural growth's contribution to poverty reduction has slowed since the 1970s 123

3.3. The changing share of agriculture in GDP and employment... 123

3.4. A declining share of agriculture's value added in GDP 124

3.5. Income inequality and its relationship with the change in agriculture's share in GDP 125

3.6. Labour productivity trends in agriculture, 1980-2005 127

3.7. Productivity gaps in agriculture, 2005 127

3.8. Land productivity in selected countries, 1961-1994 128

FIGURES *(continued)*

Page

3.9. Land Gini coefficient and its relationship with poverty, 1960-2000 133

3.10. Weighted average rural-urban gap in access to water and sanitation in
Asia and the Pacific, 1996-2004 134

3.11. High real lending rates, 1970-2004 137

3.12. Interest rate spreads on the rise, 1970-2004 138

3.13. R&D intensities for selected Asia-Pacific countries and developed countries, 1960-2000 139

3.14. Trends in poverty and prices for major staple foods, 1965-2006 141

3.15. Per capita production in key staple crops, 1961-2005 141

3.16. Rice, wheat, cereal and maize yields, 1961-2005 142

3.17. Per capita production in fruits, vegetables, meat and milk, 1961-2005 143

3.18. Fruit and vegetable yields, 1961-2006 143

3.19. Declining multilateral lending to agriculture, 1995-2006 144

EXPLANATORY NOTES

Staff analysis in the *Survey 2008* is based on data and information available up to the end of January 2008.

The term "ESCAP region" is used in the present issue of the *Survey* to include Afghanistan; American Samoa; Armenia; Australia; Azerbaijan; Bangladesh; Bhutan; Brunei Darussalam; Cambodia; China; Cook Islands; Democratic People's Republic of Korea; Fiji; French Polynesia; Georgia; Guam; Hong Kong, China; India; Indonesia; Iran (Islamic Republic of); Japan; Kazakhstan; Kiribati; Kyrgyzstan; Lao People's Democratic Republic; Macao, China; Malaysia; Maldives; Marshall Islands; Micronesia (Federated States of); Mongolia; Myanmar; Nauru; Nepal; New Caledonia; New Zealand; Niue; Northern Mariana Islands; Pakistan; Palau; Papua New Guinea; Philippines; Republic of Korea; Russian Federation; Samoa; Singapore; Solomon Islands; Sri Lanka; Tajikistan; Thailand; Timor-Leste; Tonga; Turkey; Turkmenistan; Tuvalu; Uzbekistan; Vanuatu; and Viet Nam. The term "developing ESCAP region" excludes Australia, Japan and New Zealand. Non-regional members of ESCAP are France, the Netherlands, the United Kingdom of Great Britain and Northern Ireland and the United States of America.

The term "Central Asian countries" in this issue of the *Survey* refers to Armenia, Azerbaijan, Georgia, Kazakhstan, Kyrgyzstan, Tajikistan, Turkmenistan and Uzbekistan.

The term "East and North-East Asia" in this issue of the *Survey* refers to China; Hong Kong, China; Mongolia; and the Republic of Korea.

The designations employed and the presentation of the material in this publication do not imply the expression of any opinion whatsoever on the part of the Secretariat of the United Nations concerning the legal status of any country, territory, city or area, or of its authorities, or concerning the delimitation of its frontiers or boundaries.

Mention of firm names and commercial products does not imply the endorsement of the United Nations.

The abbreviated title *Survey* in footnotes refers to the *Economic and Social Survey of Asia and the Pacific* for the year indicated.

Many figures used in the *Survey* are on a fiscal year basis and are assigned to the calendar year which covers the major part or second half of the fiscal year.

Growth rates are on an annual basis, except where indicated otherwise.

Reference to "tons" indicates metric tons.

Values are in United States dollars unless specified otherwise.

The term "billion" signifies a thousand million. The term "trillion" signifies a million million.

In the tables, two dots (..) indicate that data are not available or are not separately reported, a dash (–) indicates that the amount is nil or negligible, and a blank indicates that the item is not applicable.

In dates, a hyphen (-) is used to signify the full period involved, including the beginning and end years, and a stroke (/) indicates a crop year, fiscal year or plan year. The fiscal years, currencies and 2007 exchange rates of the economies in the ESCAP region are listed in the following table:

Country or area in the ESCAP region	Fiscal year	Currency and abbreviation	Rate of exchange for $1 as at November 2007
Afghanistan	21 March to 20 March	afghani (Af)	49.64[a]
American Samoa	..	United States dollar ($)	1.00
Armenia	1 January to 31 December	dram	305.33
Australia	1 July to 30 June	Australian dollar ($A)	1.13
Azerbaijan	1 January to 31 December	Azeri manat (AZM)	0.85
Bangladesh	1 July to 30 June	taka (Tk)	68.60
Bhutan	1 July to 30 June	ngultrum (Nu)	39.68
Brunei Darussalam	1 January to 31 December	Brunei dollar (B$)	1.45
Cambodia	1 January to 31 December	riel (CR)	4 002.00
China	1 January to 31 December	yuan renminbi (Y)	7.40
Cook Islands	1 April to 31 March	New Zealand dollar ($NZ)	1.30
Democratic People's Republic of Korea	..	won (W)	139.00
Fiji	1 January to 31 December	Fiji dollar (F$)	1.54[b]
French Polynesia	..	French Pacific Community franc FCFP)	81.15

Country or area in the ESCAP region	Fiscal year	Currency and abbreviation	Rate of exchange for $1 as at November 2007
Georgia	1 January to 31 December	lari (L)	1.62
Guam	1 October to 30 September	United States dollar ($)	1.00
Hong Kong, China	1 April to 31 March	Hong Kong dollar (HK$)	7.79
India	1 April to 31 March	Indian rupee (Rs)	39.68
Indonesia	1 April to 31 March	Indonesian rupiah (Rp)	9 103.00[b]
Iran (Islamic Republic of)	21 March to 20 March	Iranian rial (Rls)	9 302.00
Japan	1 April to 31 March	yen (¥)	110.30
Kazakhstan	1 January to 31 December	tenge (T)	120.87
Kiribati	1 January to 31 December	Australian dollar ($A)	1.13
Kyrgyzstan	1 January to 31 December	som (som)	34.69
Lao People's Democratic Republic	1 October to 30 September	new kip (NK)	9 457.60[b]
Macao, China	1 July to 30 June	pataca (P)	8.02
Malaysia	1 January to 31 December	ringgit (M$)	3.34[b]
Maldives	1 January to 31 December	rufiyaa (Rf)	12.80
Marshall Islands	1 October to 30 September	United States dollar ($)	1.00
Micronesia (Federated States of)	1 October to 30 September	United States dollar ($)	1.00
Mongolia	1 January to 31 December	tugrik (Tug)	1 169.97[c]
Myanmar	1 April to 31 March	kyat (K)	5.35
Nauru	1 July to 30 June	Australian dollar ($A)	1.13
Nepal	16 July to 15 July	Nepalese rupee (NRs)	64.05
New Caledonia	..	French Pacific Community franc (FCFP)	81.15
New Zealand	1 April to 31 March	New Zealand dollar ($NZ)	1.30
Niue	1 April to 31 March	New Zealand dollar ($NZ)	1.30
Northern Mariana Islands	1 October to 30 September	United States dollar ($)	1.00
Pakistan	1 July to 30 June	Pakistan rupee (PRs)	61.22
Palau	1 October to 30 September	United States dollar ($)	1.00
Papua New Guinea	1 January to 31 December	kina (K)	2.90
Philippines	1 January to 31 December	Philippine peso (P)	42.80
Republic of Korea	1 January to 31 December	won (W)	929.60
Russian Federation	1 January to 31 December	ruble (R)	24.35
Samoa	1 July to 30 June	tala (WS$)	2.56
Singapore	1 April to 31 March	Singapore dollar (S$)	1.45
Solomon Islands	1 January to 31 December	Solomon Islands dollar (SI$)	7.67[b]
Sri Lanka	1 January to 31 December	Sri Lanka rupee (SL Rs)	110.50
Tajikistan	1 January to 31 December	somoni	3.45
Thailand	1 October to 30 September	baht (B)	33.81
Timor-Leste	1 July to 30 June	United States dollar ($)	1.00
Tonga	1 July to 30 June	pa'anga (T$)	1.96
Turkey	1 January to 31 December	Turkish lira (LT)	1.17
Turkmenistan	1 January to 31 December	Turkmen manat (M)	5 200.00
Tuvalu	1 January to 31 December	Australian dollar ($A)	1.13
Uzbekistan	1 January to 31 December	som (som)	1 279.00
Vanuatu	1 January to 31 December	vatu (VT)	104.81
Viet Nam	1 January to 31 December	dong (D)	16 114.00[c]

Sources: United Nations, *Monthly Bulletin of Statistics* website, <http://unstats.un.org/unsd/mbs/mbssearch.asp>; and national sources.

[a] January 2008.
[b] October 2007.
[c] December 2007.

ABBREVIATIONS

ADB	Asian Development Bank
AFTA	ASEAN Free Trade Area
ASEAN	Association of Southeast Asian Nations
APEC	Asia-Pacific Economic Cooperation
CD-ROM	compact disk read-only memory
CIS	Commonwealth of Independent States
CPI	consumer price index
ECE	Economic Commission for Europe
EIU	Economist Intelligence Unit
EU	European Union
FAO	Food and Agriculture Organization of the United Nations
FDI	foreign direct investment
f.o.b.	free on board
GDP	gross domestic product
GMO	genetically modified organism
HIV/AIDS	human immunodeficiency virus/acquired immunodeficiency syndrome
ICT	information and communication technology
IFAD	International Fund for Agricultural Development
ILO	International Labour Organization
IMF	International Monetary Fund
ICT	information and communications technology
IT	information technology
M2	broad money supply
MDG	Millennium Development Goal
MFA	Multifibre Arrangement
NGO	non-governmental organization

ABBREVIATIONS *(continued)*

NPL	non-performing loan
ODA	official development assistance
OECD	Organisation for Economic Cooperation and Development
OPEC	Organization of Petroleum Exporting Countries
R&D	research and development
RTA	regional trade agreement
SAARC	South Asian Association for Regional Cooperation
SARS	severe acute respiratory syndrome
UNCTAD	United Nations Conference on Trade and Development
UNDP	United Nations Development Programme
UNFCCC	United Nations Framework Convention on Climate Change
UNICEF	United Nations Children's Fund
UNIFEM	United Nations Development Fund for Women
USAID	United States Agency for International Development
VAT	value added tax
WTO	World Trade Organization

CHAPTER 1.   REGIONAL SOCIO-ECONOMIC DEVELOPMENTS AND PROSPECTS

Growth to moderate in 2008 but remain robust

Developing economies in the Asia-Pacific region, having enjoyed their fastest growth in a decade, are expected to see it moderate to 7.7% in 2008, down from 8.2% in 2007 (figure 1.1 and table 1.1). Developed economies in the region are expected to grow at 1.6% in 2008, slipping from 2.0% in 2007. The major drags on performance are the slowdown in the United States driven by the end of the housing bubble, the unfolding credit crunch besetting the United States and Europe, and the appreciation of many of the region's currencies against the United States dollar. Nonetheless, China and India, the region's locomotives, are expected to grow at a brisk pace in 2008, boosting the rest of the region. Commodity- and energy-exporting countries, particularly the Russian Federation, are expected to add to the region's momentum.

Exports may suffer from the slower growth in industrial countries, but strong domestic demand, driven by consumption in fast-growing countries and by fiscal accommodation, should cushion the blow. Export-dependent economies in East and South-East Asia will see exports contribute less to overall growth in 2008, but China will continue to offer opportunities. These countries will also see more domestic demand, in both consumption and investment.

North and Central Asia will continue to benefit from consumption and construction, thanks to high energy prices. South and South-West Asia, with traditionally domestic-demand-driven economies, will benefit from strong private consumption and investment – and from expansionary fiscal policy in some countries. Bangladesh, Nepal, Pakistan and Sri Lanka, however, may become more vulnerable to political uncertainty. In the Pacific, Fiji and Tonga are expected to recover from economic contractions in 2007, while Papua New Guinea will see rising consumption as the benefits of high commodity prices spill over to the rest of the economy.

The region is entering a phase of heightened uncertainty in 2008. The subprime crisis in the United States is still unravelling, and a significant slowdown of the United States economy and further turmoil in financial markets cannot be ruled out. In 2007 the Asia-Pacific economies felt the effects of the global financial turmoil, largely through increased volatility in domestic equity markets and a measurable widening of the yield spreads on their external debts. But neither effect lasted long.

The region's resilience lies mainly in its healthy macro-economic fundamentals, enabling countries to adopt supportive fiscal and monetary policies amid significantly declining export growth, financial market volatility or inflationary pressures from high oil and food prices. Large foreign reserves have added to this resilience.

Larger economies to maintain dynamism

China, beset by an inability to rein in its supercharged economy, is forecast to have GDP growth moderate to 10.7% in 2008 from 11.4% in 2007 (figure 1.2). A

Figure 1.1. Real GDP growth in developing ESCAP economies and in other regions

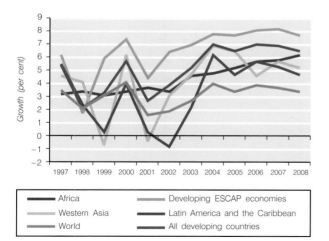

Legend:
- Africa
- Western Asia
- World
- Developing ESCAP economies
- Latin America and the Caribbean
- All developing countries

Sources: ESCAP, based on United Nations, *World Economic Situation and Prospects 2008* (United Nations publication, Sales No. E.08.II.C.2); and ESCAP calculations and estimates.

Note: Data for 2007 are estimates and those for 2008 are forecasts.

Table 1.1. Economic growth and inflation, 2006-2008

	Real GDP			Inflation[a]		
	2006	2007[b]	2008[c]	2006	2007[b]	2008[c]
Developing ESCAP economies[d]	8.1	8.2	7.7	4.4	5.1	4.6
East and North-East Asia	8.7	9.0	8.4	1.6	3.8	3.3
China	11.1	11.4	10.7	1.5	4.8	3.5
Hong Kong, China	6.8	6.1	5.7	2.0	1.8	3.4
Mongolia	8.4	9.0	8.0	5.1	9.0	..
Republic of Korea	5.0	5.0	4.9	2.2	2.6	3.1
Taiwan Province of China	4.7	5.5	4.7	0.6	1.8	2.4
North and Central Asia	7.6	8.6	7.1	9.7	9.4	8.2
Armenia	13.3	13.8	9.0	2.9	4.4	4.0
Azerbaijan	34.5	25.0	25.0	8.3	16.7	16.0
Georgia	9.4	11.0	9.0	9.2	9.2	8.0
Kazakhstan	10.6	9.0	9.0	8.6	10.8	8.0
Kyrgyzstan	2.7	8.2	7.0	5.6	10.2	5.0
Russian Federation	6.7	8.1	6.5	9.7	9.0	8.0
Tajikistan	7.0	7.8	6.5	11.9	21.5	10.0
Turkmenistan	9.0	10.0	10.0	8.2	6.5	9.0
Uzbekistan	7.3	9.0	7.0	14.2	12.2	9.8
Pacific island economies	3.1	2.7	4.8	2.8	2.8	3.1
Cook Islands	0.8	2.5	3.5	3.4	2.8	2.0
Fiji	3.6	−3.9	2.2	2.5	4.1	3.0
Papua New Guinea	2.6	6.2	6.6	2.3	1.8	2.9
Samoa	1.8	3.0	3.5	3.3	4.4	4.1
Solomon Islands	6.1	5.4	4.2	8.1	6.3	7.3
Tonga	1.3	−3.5	0.8	7.0	5.9	5.0
Vanuatu	5.5	4.7	4.6	2.6	2.5	2.5
South and South-West Asia[e]	8.0	7.4	7.4	8.3	7.9	7.0
Bangladesh	6.7	6.5	6.5	7.2	7.2	6.5
India	9.6	9.0	9.0	6.7	5.5	5.0
Iran (Islamic Republic of)	6.2	5.8	5.0	13.6	17.0	16.0
Nepal	2.8	2.5	4.0	8.0	6.4	6.0
Pakistan	6.6	7.0	6.5	7.9	7.8	7.5
Sri Lanka	7.7	6.7	7.0	10.0	15.8	10.0
Turkey	6.1	5.0	5.5	9.6	8.6	6.8
South-East Asia	6.0	6.2	5.8	6.7	3.7	4.4
Cambodia	10.8	8.5	7.0	4.7	3.0	3.0
Indonesia	5.5	6.2	6.2	13.1	6.3	6.4
Lao PDR	8.3	7.4	8.1	6.8	4.0	5.0
Malaysia	5.9	5.7	5.8	3.6	2.0	2.8
Philippines	5.4	7.0	6.7	6.2	2.7	3.5
Singapore	7.9	7.5	4.9	1.0	1.8	3.0
Thailand	5.1	4.5	4.9	4.7	2.3	3.3
Viet Nam	8.2	8.4	8.2	7.7	7.9	7.7
Developed ESCAP economies	2.4	2.0	1.6	0.6	0.2	0.6
Australia	2.7	4.2	3.2	3.5	2.4	3.1
Japan	2.4	1.8	1.4	0.3	0.0	0.4
New Zealand	1.8	3.1	2.3	3.4	2.4	2.6

Sources: ESCAP, based on national sources; IMF, *International Financial Statistics* (CD-ROM) (Washington, D.C., 2007); ADB, *Key Indicators of Developing Asian and Pacific Countries 2007* (Manila, 2007); website of the Inter-State Statistical Committee of the Commonwealth of Independent States, <www.cisstat.com> (3 December 2007 and 5 February 2008); and ESCAP estimates.

a   Inflation refers to changes in the consumer price index.
b   Estimate.
c   Forecast.
d   Based on data for 38 developing economies representing more than 95% of the population of the region (including the Central Asian republics). GDP figures in market prices in United States dollars in 2004 (at 2000 prices) have been used as weights to calculate the regional and subregional growth rates.
e   Fiscal year 2005/06 is 2005 for India and the Islamic Republic of Iran and 2006 for Bangladesh, Nepal and Pakistan.

Figure 1.2. GDP growth to slow in 2008

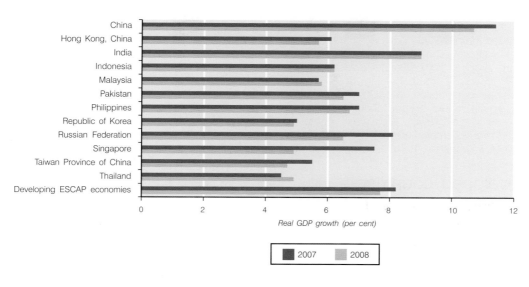

Source: ESCAP forecast.

Notes: There are 38 developing ESCAP economies (including the Central Asian countries). Calculations are based on the weighted average of GDP figures in United States dollars in 2004 (at 2000 prices).

slowdown in exports and the government's measures to cool the economy are the main reasons for the moderation. As government spending increases in rural areas and social sectors, domestic demand will provide more support to growth. Investment will continue to be the main demand component of GDP, as policy measures to rein in spending in overheating sectors face obstacles from buoyant liquidity. With inflation rising to a 10-year high in November 2007 and the Shanghai stock market doubling in value, the need to cool the economy has become more pressing.

> *The last few years have seen the Russian Federation emerge as an economic force in the region*

India, largely insulated from weaknesses in the international environment, is projected to maintain growth at 9.0% in 2008 – unchanged from 2007. Investment in booming manufacturing and services will remain the main driver. Private consumption will also remain healthy. Government spending is likely to be high in 2008 because of new demands on the exchequer, including a public-sector wage increase. Going forward, the drivers of growth may be under strain.

Cheap credit may evaporate as global financial markets lose their appetite for risk. Exports of price-sensitive software and information technology services are being trimmed by an appreciating currency and a slowing United States economy. While inflation has been brought under control, underlying supply constraints may still pose challenges.

GDP growth in the Republic of Korea should remain unchanged. The slowdown in the United States will hurt exports, but China will continue to offer opportunities. In 2007, sales to China offset the slowing United States economy and an appreciating currency. Exporters will also benefit from the free trade agreement with the United States in 2008, subject to its ratification by the United States Congress. Private consumption will remain strong, having recovered from the bursting of the household credit bubble. Consumer confidence is high, with rising household incomes, a buoyant stock market and unemployment at its lowest since 1997.

Growth in the Russian Federation has exceeded 6% per year since 2003 and is set to grow at 6.5% in 2008. Having boosted its share of world output by 20% in the last 10 years, it is now the world's eighth-largest economy in purchasing power parity terms. With the high energy prices, exports will remain strong, as will consumption. Manufacturing and services will expand to feed the growing domestic demand, but appreciation of the currency from energy exports threatens other exports.

Japan's growth spurt stutters

Japan's growth slowed in 2007 because of weak exports. Domestic demand will provide some support in 2008. Residential investment will gradually recover from the sharp drop in 2007. Capital investment, an important GDP driver at the beginning of 2007, will make a moderate contribution in 2008. Private consumption will remain muted if tight labour markets do not translate into wage growth. With weak domestic demand and slower external demand, growth in 2008 is expected to slow further to 1.4%.

Least developed countries – largely unaffected by global turbulence

Least developed countries in Asia and the Pacific, having grown at 6.5% in 2007, are expected to have growth slow to 6.4% in 2008. Cambodia grew at 8.5% in 2007, followed by the Lao People's Democratic Republic (7.4%), Bangladesh (6.5%) and the

Solomon Islands (5.4%). High oil prices pose major challenges to oil-importing least developed countries, but they also increase demand for foreign workers in some of the oil-rich countries in Western Asia. Remittance-dependent Bangladesh and Nepal will thus benefit from remittances to sustain their economies, and non-oil commodity exporters may benefit from high commodity prices.

Asian and Pacific least developed countries have been largely unaffected by the United States subprime meltdown because they have little exposure to the global financial system. A significant slowdown in the United States, however, could be damaging, particularly for Cambodia and its apparel exports.

For some least developed countries, especially Afghanistan, peace and stability will be the keys to economic growth and development. Others need to sustain and deepen ongoing reforms – maintaining macroeconomic stability, improving the business environment and investing more in infrastructure and human capital development, all crucial to promoting private investment to kickstart their economies.

Box 1.1. Sharing the benefits of growth

The Asia-Pacific region's unprecedented growth over the past decade has lifted about 300 million people out of extreme poverty since 1990, with China accounting for the largest share. Still, 641 million people in the region – two thirds of world's poor – live on less than $1 a day (see figure).

Another concern is widening income inequality: the rich are becoming richer faster than the poor are becoming less poor. The Gini coefficient, a popular measure of inequality, shows that inequality has increased over the past 10 years in 15 of 21 countries with data available (ADB, 2007). So, high economic growth does not always benefit the poor proportionately (see table).

Economic growth was highly pro-poor only in the Republic of Korea, with most other countries experiencing weakly pro-poor growth. So, while the poor benefited from high growth, the non-poor benefited even more. For example, Thailand's growth of almost 10% per year in 1988-1992 did not proportionately benefit the poor. And in 1996-2000, the financial crisis was extremely detrimental to the poor. Per capita welfare declined by an annual rate of almost 1%, while poverty increased sharply from 11.4% in 1996 to 16.2% in 2000 – making the overall pro-poor growth index weakly pro-poor (Son, 2003). Those areas showing only modest growth in per capita income, such as Bangladesh and rural India, brought poverty down, as illustrated by the pro-poor growth index.

The overall pro-poor index is created for a country for the entire period under study. But there are some important lessons from breaking down the index into different periods. During the early 1980s, China's agriculture-led development strategy was highly pro-poor. But when it shifted to a development strategy oriented towards exports and foreign direct investment, growth became less pro-poor and poverty reduction slowed (Pasha, 2002).

(Continued on next page)

Box 1.1 *(continued)*

Figure. People living on less than $1 a day in the ESCAP region

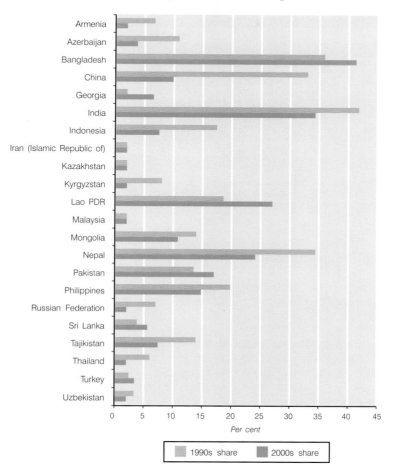

Source: United Nations Statistics Division.

Note: Data for earliest and latest years refer to 1996 and 2003 for Armenia and Georgia; 1995 and 2001 for Azerbaijan; 1992 and 2000 for Bangladesh; 1990 and 2004 for China; 1993 and 2004 for India; 1993 and 2002 for Indonesia; 1990 and 1998 for the Islamic Republic of Iran; 1993 and 2003 for Kazakhstan, Kyrgyzstan and Uzbekistan; 1992 and 2002 for the Lao People's Democratic Republic and Thailand; 1992 and 1997 for Malaysia; 1995 and 2002 for Mongolia; 1996 and 2004 for Nepal; 1999 and 2002 for Pakistan; 1991 and 2003 for Philippines; 1996 and 2002 for Russian Federation; 1990 and 2002 for Sri Lanka; 1999 and 2003 for Tajikistan; and 1994 and 2003 for Turkey.

In Viet Nam, too, growth had more benefits for the extremely poor in 1992, after the government introduced reforms known as *doi moi*. These reforms dismantled collective farms, redistributed land to peasant households through long-term leases and abolished price controls on goods and services. This paved the

(Continued overleaf)

Box 1.1 *(continued)*

Table. Growth not pro-poor across the board

	Pro-poor growth index	Nature of growth	Period
Bangladesh	0.39	Moderately pro-poor	6 observations (1983-2000)
China	0.28	Weakly pro-poor	21 observations (1981-2001)
India: rural	0.77	Pro-poor	12 observations (1977-2005)
urban	0.35	Moderately pro-poor	12 observations (1977-2005)
Indonesia	0.10	Weakly pro-poor	7 observations (1987-2002)
Lao PDR	0.21	Weakly pro-poor	6 observations (1992-1998)
Nepal	0.23	Weakly pro-poor	4 observations (1984-2003)
Republic of Korea	2.13	Highly pro-poor	13 observations (1990-2003)
Thailand	0.13	Weakly pro-poor	9 observations (1988-2006)
Viet Nam	0.15	Weakly pro-poor	4 observations (1992-2004)

Sources: ESCAP estimates based on the methodology developed in Kakwani and Pernia (2000) (see note 1 at the end of the chapter). For the Republic of Korea and Thailand, national data are from the Korea National Statistical Office and the National Economic and Social Development Board. All other data are from the PovcalNet database, <http://www.worldbank.org/lsms/tools/povcal>, retrieved October-November 2007.

Note: Poverty head count data from the PovcalNet database are derived by applying $1 a day poverty line to national survey data. For Viet Nam, the data are derived applying the $2 a day poverty line to national survey data.

way for spectacular growth in the 1990s, reducing poverty (Kakwani, Khandker and Son, 2004). But growth in 1998-2002 was less pro-poor: an increase in per capita income of 1% reduced poverty less than in 1993-1998 (World Bank, 2003).

So, it is not only the overall growth that determines how much poverty is reduced – it is also the pattern of growth. Growth has to direct resources to areas where the poor live, to sectors in which poor people work, to the factors of production they possess and to the products they consume. Because the majority of the poor live in rural areas, work in agriculture, have little education, provide unskilled labour and consume mostly basic necessities such as food, policies that address these fundamentals well are likely to be pro-poor.

Promoting agricultural development, particularly food production and generally rural development that promotes off-farm employment, can make the biggest contribution to reducing poverty in the Asia-Pacific region. As for China and Viet Nam, agricultural development has been a common feature in countries that have reduced poverty. Their agricultural development did not sacrifice growth – it drove growth. Rural prosperity spurred farm and non-farm enterprises that boosted employment and incomes, creating a virtuous cycle of growth and poverty reduction (chapter 3).

ESCAP analysis shows that some poverty-related indicators may not be responsive to economic growth (ESCAP, forthcoming). Health indicators do respond, but primary and secondary enrolments and completion rates do not. So, more targeted policy interventions and programmes may be needed. For example, mid-day meals in Bangladesh and India have improved schooling outcomes and health indicators (ADB, 2006).

Some policies to address inequalities may be politically difficult (for example, land reform) while targeted measures to address poverty may require significant fiscal resources, best initiated in a growing economy. With the region's unprecedented growth, it is time to take decisive steps to share the prosperity – and end poverty and inequality.

Domestic demand – cushioning slower export growth

In 2008, domestic demand will continue to sustain growth as exports decline. Robust private consumption and investment growth, supported by fiscal policy accommodation, are the keys. The strong fiscal position of many countries is likely to enable accommodative policies that compensate for weak external sectors. And the accumulation of foreign reserves has curtailed a more effective use of savings in the region. Redirecting foreign reserves from low-yielding foreign assets to financing domestic infrastructure could increase productive capacity. Policymakers may want to make a conscious effort to sustain the rise in domestic demand in order to reduce their economies' dependence on the external sector, which is becoming increasingly unpredictable.

Although all economies in East and North-East Asia, except China, saw a marginal slowdown in 2007, the better than expected performance over the year was due mainly to robust domestic demand (figure 1.3). Hong Kong, China; Taiwan Province of China; and the Republic of Korea all saw higher consumption and investment during 2007.

South Asian countries have enjoyed strong domestic demand and saw their merchandise trade deficits widening in 2007 due to increased imports of energy and consumption goods. North and Central Asia benefited from heightened activity in domestic consumption-led sectors as a consequence of the buoyant energy prices in recent years.

South-East Asia's highly export-dependent economies would be especially affected by a slowdown in the United States. Nevertheless, they will see an increased contribution from domestic demand, through both consumption and investment in 2008. Indonesia is expected to see strong investment due to lower interest rates, the new investment law, and government infrastructure spending plans. The Philippines is expected to see robust private consumption as a result of booming remittances. Consumption in Singapore is likely to remain high, with rising wages, high property prices and low unemployment. Thailand is expected to experience a significant increase in GDP growth following elections held at the end of 2007.

Figure 1.3. Strong contributions of domestic demand to GDP

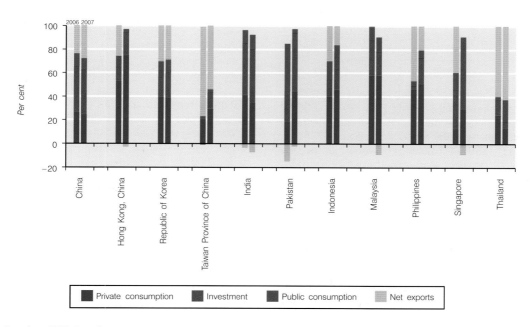

Sources: Based on CEIC Data Company Ltd; and EIU, *Country Forecasts* (London, 2007), various issues.

Notes: Data for 2007 are estimates. Investment refers to gross fixed investment.

Infrastructure and environment – holding back fast growers?

India's nearly 7% growth in the last decade is straining its ailing infrastructure, while China's 10% growth has degraded the environment.

India's growth created a large middle class with an appetite for consumer goods and services. In a fairly closed economy, its domestic manufacturing and services have strained to fill demand. Energy shortfalls have become evident in blackouts, with the peak electricity deficit rising to nearly 14% in 2007, the highest in eight years (Morgan Stanley, 2007). The power utilities suffer network losses of about 40%, and transport infrastructure is lagging. The national road building programme slowed to 500 kilometres of roads in 2006, down from 2,500 kilometres in 2005 (Financial Times, 2007). Airports struggle to cope with low-cost airlines, which increased domestic passenger numbers by more than 30% in 2006. Ports were at 93% capacity in 2006. And deficits in water supply, solid waste management and housing for low- and middle-income residents are growing.

> *India and China, with their breakneck growth, see first-hand that infrastructure and environment problems could jeopardize their economic growth – a lesson for other countries*

India needs to spend $320-$410 billion in 2007-2012 to finance its infrastructure needs (RIS, 2007). ESCAP analysis shows that annual financing requirements in energy infrastructure alone amount to about $25 billion for 2001-2031 (ESCAP, 2006a). Given the already stretched fiscal position, innovative private-public partnerships will have to bridge the gap. The groundwork has recently been laid with legal and regulatory changes for private-public partnerships in power, transport and urban infrastructure. Even so, government investment will remain paramount for rural roads and irrigation. As ESCAP proposes, regional cooperation mechanisms for infrastructure financing are worth exploring.

For China, the destabilizing effect of growth on the environment is becoming more apparent. Air pollution, especially in large cities, is increasing the incidence of lung diseases. Water pollution is causing growing

levels of cancer – and diarrhoea among children under 5 (World Bank, 2007a). The country has lost 8 million hectares of its arable land – 6.6% – to manufacturing and construction in the past decade (China Daily, 2007). In 2007, the country experienced one of its biggest environmental disasters, with Taihu, the third-largest freshwater lake, affected by toxic algae from the emissions of factories and farms along its shores.

The government has pledged to eliminate export tax rebates for 553 highly energy-consuming and resource-intensive products, such as cement, fertilizer and non-ferrous metals.

The rest of Asia and the Pacific faces infrastructure constraints and environmental degradation. But India and China, with their breakneck growth, see first-hand that infrastructure and environment problems could jeopardize their economic growth – a lesson for other countries.

Greater uncertainty for inflation

Inflation in the developing ESCAP economies was 5.1% in 2007, up from 4.4% the previous year. Currency appreciation in most economies moderated the impact of high international oil and food prices. With the exception of East and North-East Asia, all ESCAP subregions had lower inflation in 2007 than in 2006. Monetary policy has varied accordingly. China, India, the Republic of Korea and Taiwan Province of China tightened the monetary stance in 2007, while Malaysia kept its interest rates steady. In contrast, Indonesia, the Philippines and Thailand eased rates.

Inflation is projected at 4.6% in 2008 for the developing economies of Asia and the Pacific, with currency appreciation cushioning high oil and food prices (figures 1.4 and 1.5). Inflation is expected to edge up in 2008 in South-East Asia and the Republic of Korea. But it should moderate in China; Hong Kong, China; India; and the Russian Federation. Monetary policy in India and China is expected to remain cautious as they continue to manage the threat of overheating.

Monetary authorities face a dilemma this year. Restrictive policies may be required to counter inflationary pressures, but permissive policies may be called on to manage any significant slowdowns in GDP growth. Countries with credible monetary policies and lower inflationary expectations should ride out inflation in 2008.

Figure 1.4. Inflation in ESCAP subregions, 2007-2008

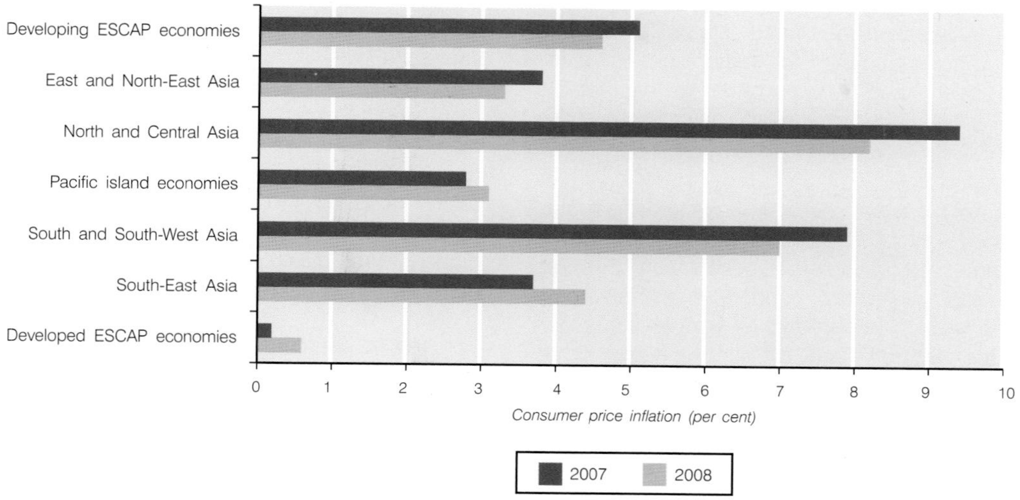

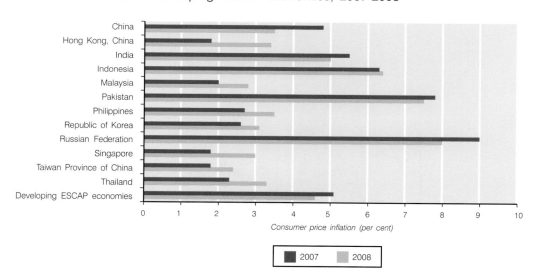

Source: ESCAP forecast.

Notes: Data for 2007 are estimates and those for 2008 are forecasts. Inflation rates refer to changes in the consumer price index. There are 38 developing ESCAP economies (including the Central Asian countries). Calculations are based on the weighted average of GDP figures in United States dollars in 2004 (at 2000 prices).

Figure 1.5. Inflation in selected developing ESCAP economies, 2007-2008

Source: ESCAP forecast.

Notes: Data for 2007 are estimates and those for 2008 are forecasts. Inflation rates refer to changes in the consumer price index. There are 38 developing ESCAP economies (including the Central Asian countries). Calculations are based on the weighted average of GDP figures in United States dollars in 2004 (at 2000 prices).

The key challenge is to decipher how much of last year's surge in oil and food prices might continue in 2008 and beyond. The price of Brent crude hovered at $70 a barrel for most of 2007 but surged to near $100 in November and hit $100 in January 2008 (figure 1.6). A weakening United States dollar and geopolitical tensions close to major oil-production areas have been, and will continue to be, factors outweighing those of demand in determining price movements.

Some pressure on oil prices may ease as the industrial economies, led by the United States, slow down. Recent oil price rises also reflect speculation. Supplies have some room to grow, especially as new fossil fuels become viable, investments in remote areas and deeper waters pay off, and oil sands, heavy crude and coal to oil conversions are developed.

Food inflation – the next big challenge

Food prices are likely to remain high. The rapid rise in 2007 was partly the result of drought in Australia, flooding in China and dry weather in Europe. Added pressure came from biofuels. With grains and oil seeds the key feedstuffs for biofuels, the oil price rise exerted a strong push on agricultural commodity prices in 2007, which enjoyed their best performance for almost 30 years. As oil hit $100 per barrel in January 2008, soybean prices jumped to a 34-year high, corn prices approached their recent 11-year high, wheat prices were just below their recent all-time high, rapeseed prices rose to record highs, and palm oil futures hit a historic high (figure 1.7). With the march towards biofuels apparently unstoppable, the region has to prepare for imported inflation through higher food prices. Governments need to carefully consider the impact of biofuels on the poor (box 1.2).

For many countries in the region, food prices are a bigger inflationary concern than oil prices. Why? Because food accounts for a far higher proportion of consumer spending. In the Philippines, food accounts for 50% of the consumer price index (CPI), far more than the 7% for energy. In India, food represents 46% of the CPI, in Indonesia 42%, and in China 33%. Food price inflation hits low-income households, so governments may need to target the poor with food stamps and cash.

Figure 1.6. Nominal and real oil prices, 1970-2007

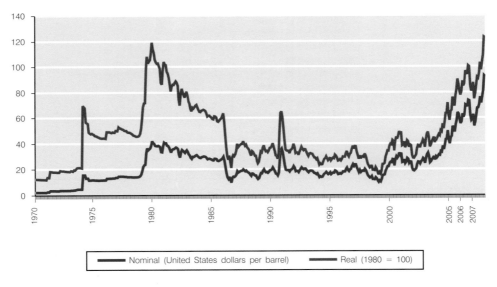

Nominal (United States dollars per barrel) ▬▬▬ Real (1980 = 100)

Sources: IMF, *International Financial Statistics* (CD-ROM) (Washington, D.C., 2007); PTT Public Company Limited; CEIC Data Company Ltd.; and ESCAP calculations.

Notes: Oil prices are for Brent crude. Real oil prices are calculated to December 2007. The consumer price index (all commodities) of the United States was used as the deflator for the nominal price of Brent oil.

Currency appreciation to continue

The currencies of the region have appreciated dramatically over the last two years on a tide of huge global liquidity. Since 2006, all major currencies in the region have risen against the dollar, a trend expected to continue in 2008, driven by the unwinding of large United States imbalances with the rest of the world and the turmoil in global financial markets. Of concern is the variation across countries. The Korean won rose by 7.3% against the dollar between 2006 and November 2007, and the Thai baht about 17%.

But currencies have not appreciated solely against the dollar. Many currencies have risen against the Japanese yen. Of particular relevance is the appreciation against the Chinese yuan, since China competes in third-country markets with the other economies of the region.

Figure 1.7. Rising food prices

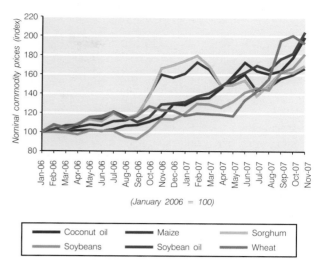

(January 2006 = 100)

▬ Coconut oil	▬ Maize	▬ Sorghum
▬ Soybeans	▬ Soybean oil	▬ Wheat

Source: IMF, *International Financial Statistics* (CD-ROM) (Washington, D.C., 2007).

Box 1.2. Biofuels: Friend or foe of the poor?

Under some projections, global demand for biofuel could rise from 10 billion gallons per year in 2005 to 25 billion gallons in 2010, or 20% per year.

The United Nations projects that biofuels will be "one of the main drivers" of projected food price hikes of 20-50% by 2016 (OECD-FAO, 2007). Higher food prices will most hurt the urban poor and the rural poor who are net food consumers, for whom food is usually the biggest expenditure item.

But biofuels do offer some potential for reducing poverty:

- Rural farmers benefit from higher demand for agricultural products. Sugarcane for ethanol has become more attractive for developing-country farmers. Many developing countries already grow or could grow other energy crops, such as soybeans, rapeseed and oil palm. Biofuels can increase the number of jobs and markets for small farmers and provide cheap renewable energy for local use.

- Biofuels can hold down oil prices. If biofuels reduce oil prices, this would provide relief for the poor and poor countries. Of the world's 50 poorest countries, 38 are net importers of petroleum and 25 import all their petroleum. Some now spend up to six times more on fuel as on health, while others spend twice what they allocate to poverty reduction (UN-ENERGY, 2007). If the gains from lower import bills can be spent by governments on poverty reduction, the effects of higher food prices can be mitigated.

- New biofuel inputs promise to hurt the poor less and help the environment more. Palm oil and sugarcane, some of the main crops of choice in developing countries, raise environmental concerns due to deforestation. One long-term possibility is cellulosic ethanol, which uses low-value wood chips, wood

(Continued on next page)

Box 1.2 *(continued)*

waste; fast-growing grasses; crop residues; such as corn stover, and municipal waste. Production is currently more expensive than food-based biofuel inputs, but the extraction technology is improving. Jatropha is a fast-growing crop that can be planted in poor soil and extremely arid conditions without any need for irrigation and that produces high yields for biodiesel. India has been particularly active in exploring Jatropha for its fuel needs (Reuters India, 2007).

Much of the crop-based fuel production is now concentrated in the United States and Western Europe. By subsidizing their domestic agriculture and their biofuel industries, however, many developed countries are distorting the opportunities for biofuel production and trade by developing countries.

So far, poor rural farmers have not seen the benefits of biofuel production. They lack the wherewithal to extend their land and adapt to new crops. And the impetus for large-scale farming can push the poor off their land, excluding them from biofuels. For example, sugarcane requires good land and large amounts of irrigation water, difficult for poor farmers to obtain. And the poorest rural dwellers live in areas often too dry for sugarcane (ICRISAT, 2007). With the demand for biofuel seemingly unstoppable, governments need to carefully consider the impact on the poor.

The relentless currency appreciation sheltered the region's economies from high oil and food prices, but it dealt a blow to the competitiveness of exports. Movements in real effective exchange rates, the best measure to gauge competitiveness, show that all large economies except Indonesia and Republic of Korea have experienced appreciations since 2006 (figure 1.8), ranging from 2.4% for Singapore to 20% for the Philippines. So, countries have lost export competitive-ness not only to the United States but also to their other trading partners.

Countries with the greatest appreciation in real effective terms since 2006 – especially Thailand and the Philippines – have already seen the impact on their export earnings. Thailand's export growth in dollar terms fell in the fourth quarter of 2007 (11.6% year on year) after rising in the third (11.6% year on year).

Figure 1.8. Real effective exchange rates for selected developing ESCAP economies, 2006-2007

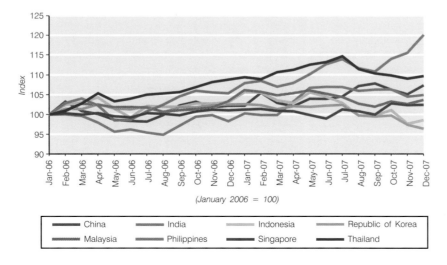

(January 2006 = 100)

Source: Based on online data from *Bank of International Settlements Databases* (accessed on 17 January 2008).

Export growth in the Philippines turned negative in November 2007 (2% year on year), after a rise of 10.5% the previous month.

These countries have faced intensive competition from lower cost producers, surrendering market share, especially in price-sensitive, low-technology-intensive manufacturing and sectors with a low import content, such as agriculture and commodities. In Thailand, local currency export earnings for garments, jewellery, furniture and rubber have been flat since 2006. And in the Philippines, textiles, furniture, bananas and pineapples have been most affected.

Measures to help exporters not effective

Countries throughout the region are expected to have weak merchandise exports in 2008. The current account balances would deteriorate slightly as a result (figure 1.9). Commodity exporters will be somewhat shielded, though some prices may ease from their highs in 2007. Indonesia and the Philippines will continue to receive support from the booming remittances of their overseas workers.

Governments have reacted by introducing a host of measures. One is to offer direct assistance to exporters. India offered interest rate relief, adjustments of duty drawback rates and swifter reimbursements of past export claims. The Philippines established a $1 billion hedging fund to protect exporters against currency movements. Another is to increase local demand for dollars from individuals and enterprises to ease the pressure on domestic currencies. Thailand allowed companies to take funds abroad for investment, exporters to keep earnings in foreign currency for longer periods, companies and individuals to open foreign-currency accounts at local banks and local investment funds to invest abroad. India increased the limit on portfolio investments in foreign companies and enhanced the limit for overseas investment in joint ventures or wholly owned subsidiaries.

How effective are these measures likely to be? Direct assistance to exporters is only a short-term coping mechanism for the loss of earnings. Exporters must still maintain competitiveness in the face of rising prices in foreign currencies. So, such measures can help only if currency appreciations are temporary.

> *Rising incomes and burgeoning middle classes in India, China and other fast-growing economies open enormous opportunities to diversify away from traditional trading partners*

Similarly, encouraging holdings of dollars by domestic entities may not meet the intent of policymakers. A more convertible currency for outward investment is a

Figure 1.9. Current account balance for selected developing ESCAP economies, 2007-2008

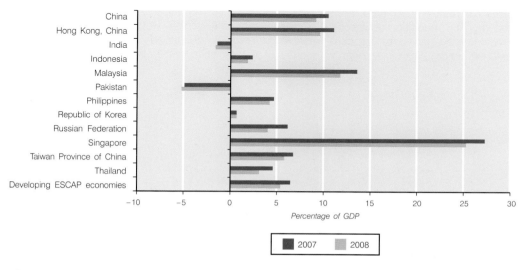

Percentage of GDP

■ 2007   ■ 2008

Source: ESCAP forecast.

Note: Data for 2007 are estimates, those for 2008 are forecasts.

sensible long-term measure for integrating into the global economy, but it is unlikely to have much effect in the near future. Investors will not be keen to make dollar investments when they see further dollar depreciations as likely.

In the long run, exporters will cope only by increasing the value added of their products through greater productivity and moving away from the low-value products most susceptible to price-based international competition. Trade in services is another area to focus on.

Countries should also diversify their markets. With the United States and European markets each receiving about 15% of developing Asia-Pacific exports, any severe downturn in these markets will still hurt the region. Rising incomes and burgeoning middle classes in India, China and other fast-growing economies open enormous opportunities. And other developing regions, particularly Africa, offer new trading opportunities (box 1.3). Exploring these new markets can help the region sustain exports as engines of growth while decoupling from cyclical downturns in the industrial markets.

Reserves accumulate – at what cost?

By October 2007, developing economies in the Asia-Pacific region had accumulated $3.4 trillion in foreign reserves, up from $2.7 trillion at the end of 2006 (figure 1.10). While reserves have been accumulated partly as a buffer against financial crises, the rapid increase has been the result of the fight against currency appreciation. Central banks have been conducting sterilization operations to mop up excess liquidity created by the build-up of reserves. Other measures have included increases in bank reserve ratios and interest rates. But increases in money supply aggregates over recent months indicate that liquidity continues to grow (figure 1.11).

> *While reserves have been accumulated partly as a buffer against financial crises, the rapid increase has been the result of the fight against currency appreciation*

Increasing liquidity has fuelled concerns about inflation. In November 2007, China witnessed its highest inflation in 10 years. India experienced a two-year high in January 2007 before aggressive tightening dampened prices. Beyond consumer price inflation, liquidity has been driving up the prices of other assets, sometimes unrealistically in view of underlying valuations. The price-earnings ratio for equities in China stands at 59 times 2007 earnings, by far the highest such ratio in Asia. In Indian urban centres, such as Bangalore and Mumbai, housing prices doubled during 2005 and 2006 (The Economist, 2007). The Republic of Korea has also seen a substantial rise in property prices in some urban areas.

Currency appreciation has also produced fiscal costs.[1] Foreign exchange reserves have been invested mainly in low-yielding United States government bonds. It has been estimated that India, which has comparatively high interest rates, faced a cost in fiscal year 2007 of 2% of GDP (ABN AMRO India, 2007). Another cost is the loss in the capital value of foreign reserve holdings, as the value of the dollar steadily declines. For example, China would suffer a capital loss on its reserves of around $50 billion as a result of a 5% depreciation in the United States dollar.[2]

---

[1] For background on this issue, see ESCAP (2006b), pp. 24-26.

[2] Calculation based on foreign exchange reserves of $1.4 trillion in October 2007, with roughly 70% held in United States dollars, according to estimates.

Box 1.3. Fast-growing trade between Asia and Africa

Between 2000 and 2006, exports from developing Asia-Pacific countries to Africa rose by an annual rate of more than 23%, from $17.7 billion in 2000 to $57.9 billion in 2006. Africa's exports to Asia more than tripled to $50.2 billion.

Among developing Asia-Pacific countries, China is the largest exporter to Africa, accounting for more than a third of the group's exports, or $26.4 billion in 2006. The Republic of Korea, Turkey, Thailand and Singapore follow. Together, these five countries accounted for 77% of exports during 2001-2006. Major exports are industrial and manufactured goods, except rice, which is the second-largest export item to Africa. The top exports are ships and boats; rice; cotton and man-made fabrics and knitted outerwear; telecommunication equipment; passenger motor vehicles, cycles and scooters and motor vehicle parts; vegetable oils; footwear; and electrical machinery and apparatus.

Africa's exports to developing Asia-Pacific countries are mainly petroleum and minerals, concentrated in Angola, South Africa, the Libyan Arab Jamahiriya, Algeria and Morocco. These five countries accounted for 75% of the total. Crude petroleum and natural gas, the largest export items, made up half the total in 2001-2006, followed by cotton; iron ore and base metals; pearls and semi-precious stones; wood; gold; copper; silver; aluminium; and cocoa. Again, China is the largest trading partner, receiving 45% of exports from Africa to developing Asia-Pacific countries, followed by Turkey, the Republic of Korea, Indonesia and Thailand. These five countries received 84% of Africa's exports to the developing Asia-Pacific region.

Stronger ties between Asia and Africa can benefit both regions. For Asia, stronger ties mean diversified markets and less reliance on the United States and Europe. For Africa based on current trading volumes, ESCAP analysis finds that a percentage point increase in the GDP of developing Asia and the Pacific will increase African exports by 0.5 percentage points. The impact will be greater if the rapid growth of trade between the two regions is taken into account.

So far, the increased demand for primary commodities and the net trade deficit for Asia in copper, iron ore, nickel and crude petroleum have favoured Africa with improvements in terms of trade. These exports are predicted to grow. The expected growth in per capita income in Asia will lead to higher demand for food products with high income elasticity – meat, fish and beverages – that will create further opportunities for African entrepreneurs.

There is concern that cheap goods from Asia will displace domestic producers in African economies. Jenkins and Edwards (2005) find that increased imports from China came at the expense of other exporters, with very little impact on domestic producers in Africa. Reisen (2006) notes, however, that Africa exporting primary commodities to Asia in return for manufactured goods could delay efforts by African producers to diversify away from traditional exports.

On whether Asia is a threat to Africa in third-country markets, Jenkins and Edwards (2006) find little similarity between exports from China and India and those from sub-Saharan Africa. Botswana's diamonds could face competition from India, and Lesotho's tobacco could face competition from China. But India exports cut and worked diamonds while Botswana exports raw diamonds. And Lesotho's and India's tobacco exports may go to different markets, with potentially little competition between them. The net effects are thus inconclusive.

Of greater concern are trends in textiles. There have been reports of job losses as textile plants closed across Africa after the 10-year phase-out of import quotas under the Multi-Fibre Arrangement. Kaplinsky and Morris (2006) show that African exports to the American market have declined substantially while those of China have increased. That decline went hand in hand with falling employment in southern Africa. Eichengreen and Tong (2005) note that the current threat from Chinese labour-intensive manufacturing exports may be but a taste of things to come. On the positive side, China becoming the centre of a rapidly growing global supply chain could attract FDI to countries that export raw materials to China.

Figure 1.10. Record foreign reserves in the Asian and Pacific region, 2006-2007

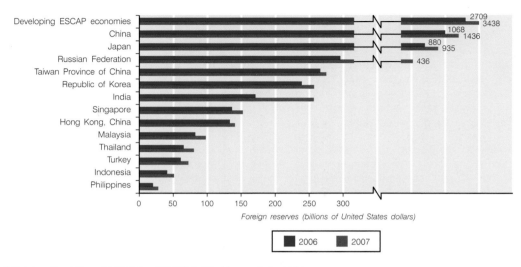

Source: IMF, *International Financial Statistics* (CD-ROM) (Washington, D.C., 2007).

Note: Foreign reserves exclude gold. Data for 2007 refer to October or the latest available month.

Figure 1.11. Growing liquidity in 2006-2007

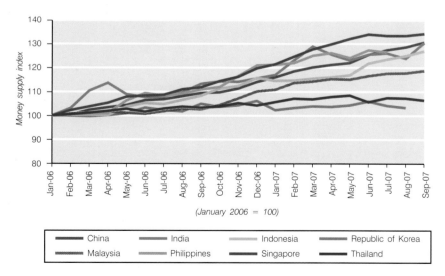

Sources: IMF, *International Financial Statistics* (CD-ROM) (Washington, D.C., 2007); and CEIC Data Company Ltd.

Downside risks to the 2008 outlook – navigating the subprime crisis

The major downside risk to the 2008 outlook comes from outside the region, from possible spillovers resulting from the downturn in the United States housing market. The fallout from the subprime crisis did not, however, have a significant impact on the region in 2007. The main effects were increased volatility in domestic equity markets and widening yield spreads on external debt. But stock markets recovered rapidly, ending the year with gains (figure 1.12).

But the broader impact of the subprime crisis on the United States is yet to be seen. Europe, where financial institutions were heavily invested in subprime-related products in the United States, has also been hit hard. Banks in the United States and Europe have accounted for some of the decline in their subprime investments, resulting in record losses for some. Even so, the spectre of further markdowns remains. The resulting credit crunch has raised borrowing rates and increased mortgage defaults. Finding it difficult to raise capital in the interbank market and to absorb losses in subprime investments, financial institutions have tightened lending conditions.

The collapse in the United States housing market has deflated its credit-led consumption boom, cutting growth projections for 2008. Europe faces a similar liquidity crunch. Looming contagion has forced central banks in the United States and Europe to step in as lenders of last resort. In December 2007, the United States Federal Reserve Bank made $20 billion available to commercial banks, the European Central Bank $500 billion, and the Bank of England GBP 10 billion. The United States has also moved to cut interest rates aggressively to ensure continued lending and consumption, with a reduction of 2.25 percentage points since September 2007. The subprime crisis now threatens to pull the United States into a severe downturn.

Hit to Asia-Pacific exports

The main impact on the region will come through its exports. The United States is likely to cut interest rates aggressively, fuelling further depreciation of the dollar. Countries in the region will face twin blows: lower demand and loss of competitiveness.

Figure 1.12. Stock markets higher in 2007, but volatile

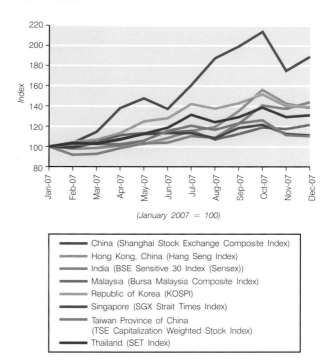

(January 2007 = 100)

──	China (Shanghai Stock Exchange Composite Index)
──	Hong Kong, China (Hang Seng Index)
──	India (BSE Sensitive 30 Index (Sensex))
──	Malaysia (Bursa Malaysia Composite Index)
──	Republic of Korea (KOSPI)
──	Singapore (SGX Strait Times Index)
──	Taiwan Province of China (TSE Capitalization Weighted Stock Index)
──	Thailand (SET Index)

Source: CEIC Data Company Ltd.

The sizes of the slowdown and of the decline in the dollar will shape the effects on Asia-Pacific economies. Intraregional exports have increased, but many such exports are inputs to final goods for developed-country markets. Exports to Europe are also up, with European Union countries, as a group, accounting for the same share of exports (16%) from Asian countries (except Japan) as does the United States. But the United States remains the largest single export market for nearly all countries in the region.

In a worst-case scenario – where the United States economy goes into a recession – the impact on much of the region will be deep, its size varying with the importance of exports for different countries (box 1.4). Due to its blistering pace, China's growth will be resilient but will slow. Some easing in exports will aid the Government's efforts to cool the economy. Other

Box 1.4. The impact of a United States recession on Asian economies – a pessimistic scenario

Using the assumptions of the pessimistic scenario in *World Economic Situation and Prospects 2008*, ESCAP has assessed the impact on the Asian economies of a hard landing in the United States. The report assumes virtually zero growth in the United States and its consumption sector, further depreciation of the dollar by 20%, and a fall in private investment due to the plunge in residential investment of 30%.

Recession in the United States and sharp depreciation of the dollar would curtail the country's import demand and hurt the export performance of Asia and the Pacific, where exports have driven growth. The reduction in United States import demand would be more pronounced for high-end products and capital goods, such as electronic products, high-value household goods, vehicles and machinery. Market volatility spurred by the sharp depreciation of the dollar would precipitate substantial losses for assets denominated in dollars and for investments in the United States. At the end of 2006, direct investment in the United States from Asia and the Pacific stood at an estimated $260 billion. Falling profitability and dim corporate earnings prospects for companies from the region would aggravate the turmoil. Through a negative wealth effect and pessimistic sentiment, the losses would depress consumption in the region. The subprime lending crisis would also choke off liquidity in the market, increasing interest rates in the region through higher risk premiums. Asia and the Pacific, which attracted capital on the back of low risk ratings, might face reversals as investors retreat to safe assets, such as United States Treasury bonds. The withdrawals would further jeopardize liquidity and hinder investment.

The impact would not be uniform (see table). Taiwan Province of China, Singapore and the Republic of Korea would feel the biggest effects, owing to their strong export orientations. Singapore's exports are almost 250% of GDP, and the countries' export mix is highly vulnerable to a sluggish United States. In the 2001 slowdown, when the economy weakened to 0.8% growth, United States import demand for consumer durables and their associated inputs, machinery and equipment contracted significantly. These goods are among the major exports of the three economies. More than a third of the exports of Taiwan Province of China are electrical machinery and equipment and parts of audiovisual appliances. Electrical machinery, apparatus and appliances represent about 30% of the exports of Singapore. Electrical machinery, road vehicles and

Table. Impact of a United States recession on Asian economies in a pessimistic scenario

Economy	Decline from baseline forecast (percentage point)
China	−3.3
Hong Kong, China	−1.7
India	−1.2
Indonesia	−4.0
Malaysia	−2.2
Philippines	−2.5
Republic of Korea	−6.6
Singapore	−5.2
Taiwan Province of China	−7.4
Thailand	−3.0

Source: ESCAP calculations.

(Continued on next page)

Box 1.4 *(continued)*

telecommunication equipment constitute almost 40% of the exports of the Republic of Korea. In the 2001 downturn, import demand for goods from Singapore and Taiwan Province of China fell by almost 20%, and those from the Republic of Korea by 13%. The blow to exports would reverberate into other sectors. Financial losses from investments in the United States would further reduce income. Consumption would contract. Possible capital reversals would batter the equity markets and exacerbate the situation.

A sharp downturn in the United States would also hit exports from Indonesia, Thailand, the Philippines and Malaysia, though less. The major exports of Indonesia are petroleum and fuels, which are expected, based on the 2001 experience, to be less sensitive to falling demand in the United States. For Thailand, the Philippines and Malaysia, the impact on consumption would be relatively light because the countries have lower exposure to global markets.

The GDP growth of China would fall significantly under the pessimistic scenario, but it would remain high in absolute terms. Strong domestic demand should cushion a portion of the external shock. The government is also expected to use macroeconomic policy to mitigate the crisis.

Hong Kong, China, would also be less affected because of its tight economic relationship with the mainland. And because of the linked exchange rate with the dollar, depreciation would enhance its competitiveness overseas. So, though consumption may fall, exports sector growth should ease the effects.

A relatively closed economy with an export-to-GDP ratio of only 13%, India would be resilient to a global downturn caused by a United States recession. Robust domestic demand and booming investment in manufacturing and services sectors would help contain shocks.

countries expanding at a slower pace will find the downward pressure more challenging, with the most risk for the more open and higher-end technology trading economies – Singapore, the Republic of Korea and Taiwan Province of China. The effects will come from lower demand for final goods from the United States and for intermediate goods from China. The smallest impact is likely to be in economies led largely by domestic demand, such as India.

The threat of financial sector turmoil

At present, Asia-Pacific economies remain relatively immune to the credit crunch in the United States and the European Union. The corporate sector is generally cash-rich and not highly leveraged. Companies, learning the lessons of the 1997 Asian crisis, have been conservative in their borrowing. Central banks are also well armed to supply liquidity to the financial sector, as has already been required in the United States and the European Union.

The region has, so far, had little exposure to subprime or other vulnerable debt. Banks in Japan, Singapore and China have revealed some losses, though the size is dwarfed by their capital bases. Some concerns remain, however, about the transparency of risky holdings by institutions in the region. Any unexpected disclosures would hamper interbank lending.

The region is feeling some tremors from the upheaval in the international financial sector. As of end January 2008, the Morgan Stanley Emerging Markets Asia index was down 14% for the year. Debt markets have also recently shown a spike in credit spreads in view of fears about the resilience of Asia-Pacific countries. The benchmark Markit iTraxx Asia Ex-Japan Series 8 Index of 70 borrowers rose to a record high of 205 basis points in January 2008 (Bloomberg News, 2008). If losses by large international financial institutions mount to substantial levels, investments in the region could be called in to rebalance portfolios and to mitigate the effect on trading profits. Countries that have received large short-term capital inflows in recent years are the most susceptible.

Policymakers also have to grapple with higher volatility in the carry trade, including periods of rapid and large reversals in inflows to economies in the region over the past few months. Investors' uncertainty about global interest rates and growth has spurred exits from popular carry-trade target countries, reflected in the appreciation of the Japanese yen, up more than 4%

on the dollar in 2008.[3] Large outflows from the region are possible as carry trades unwind.

Large capital inflows in the last few years have also contributed to significant increases in asset values in some countries – notably in equity and property markets – which may not be justified by underlying valuations. Global financial volatility threatens these values.

As of end January 2008, China and India have seen rises (year-on-year) in their main equity markets of 57% and 25%, respectively. Property prices in China have surged, with housing prices in 70 cities jumping by 10.5% in December 2007 compared with a year earlier. Major urban centres of India such as Bangalore and Mumbai saw a doubling of housing prices between 2005 and 2006. Viet Nam has recently witnessed dramatic increases in equity and property prices. The Republic of Korea has also seen a substantial rise in property prices in some urban areas.

These economies are resilient enough to withstand the spillover of a sharp fall in asset values. But such declines would be difficult for the burgeoning middle-class investors and for the companies that have cashed in on the boom. And declines in China and India, regarded by investors as markers for the region, would raise the spectre of contagion in other economies of the region. That danger was evident in the capital outflows from exchanges across the region in February 2007 after a sharp drop in the Shanghai stock exchange.

Figure 1.13. Booming outward investment, 2005-2007

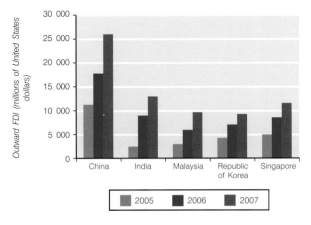

Source: EIU, Country Forecasts (London, 2008), various issues.

Note: Data for 2007 are estimates.

---

3   As of 31 January 2008.

The subprime crisis may bring new opportunities for the region. There may be increased interest in Asia-Pacific's assets due to the region's relatively strong growth projections. If investors regard markets in the region as having decoupled, at least partly, from the United States – through growth in exports to the European Union and Asia and stronger domestic demand – these markets may become attractive. Hope comes from the performance of Asia-Pacific markets over the past 12 months. As of end January 2008 while the S&P 500 witnessed a loss of 4.2% and the Dow Jones EURO STOXX 50 Index fell by 9.2%, the Morgan Stanley Asian Emerging Market Index gained 21%.

Asia-Pacific investors to the rescue

Asia-Pacific investors are playing a key role in supporting developed countries through the recent turmoil. Sovereign wealth funds and State investment institutions from the region have bolstered weakened banking sectors in the United States and Europe. Financial institutions have sought equity investment from investors in Asia and the Pacific to shore up their depleted capital bases. Notable purchases include equity stakes for the Government of Singapore Investment Corporation in Citigroup and UBS, for Korea Investment Corporation and Singapore's Temasek Holdings in Merrill Lynch, for the China Investment Corporation in Morgan Stanley and for Temasek Holdings in Barclays.

> *Asia-Pacific investors are playing a key role in supporting developed countries through the recent turmoil*

The shifting balance of financial power is also clear in the dramatic rise in the overseas investment of the Asia-Pacific corporate sector. Companies from the region, both private and State-owned, have benefited from blistering growth in their home markets and are using their wealth to acquire major enterprises in developed countries and in other developing regions. From 2005 to 2007, outward direct investments from India more than quadrupled, those from China more than doubled, and there were large increases in those from other major countries in the region (figure 1.13). Prominent Chinese acquisitions in 2007 included the China Development Bank's investment in Barclays Bank and the Industrial and Commercial Bank of China's purchase of a 20% stake in South Africa's Standard Bank. Recent deals by Indian enterprises included Tata's purchase of Anglo-Dutch Corus, Hindalco's purchase of Canada's Novelis and United Breweries purchase of the United Kingdom's Whyte and McKay.

Rising outward investment by State-owned institutions and private companies has generated controversy, provoking concerns about lack of transparency in strategies and portfolio composition. Regulators in target countries have been less than enthusiastic about foreign governments controlling national enterprises. In the United States and the European Union, calls arose in 2007 to mandate greater regulatory oversight of sovereign wealth funds.

To make target countries more welcoming of investments and to prevent a protectionist backlash, economies in the region with sovereign wealth funds can take proactive measures to foster disclosure and transparency:

- *Take the initiative to be more forthcoming about investment strategies.* Disclosure should include information on how the funds are incorporated into the overall investment strategy of the government, what types of assets are included in portfolios, how the assets are managed, where the responsibilities for their management lie, what investment and risk-management strategies are followed and how these elements can be changed.

- *Increase transparency through regular reporting on holdings and performance.* A good example is Norway's Government Pension Fund-Global, which provides the public with extensive information on its investment strategy and results on a quarterly basis, including month-by-month returns, and annually provides information on its holdings of the bonds and equities of individual countries and corporations.

Asia and the Pacific well prepared to navigate global instability

Asia-Pacific countries have made great progress since the Asian crisis of 1997 in reviving their economies. As a result, the region is equipped with strong fundamentals to navigate the global financial and economic instability.

- The region's GDP has doubled since 1997, with per capita incomes now significantly above their pre-crisis values.

- Countries have moved explicitly towards targeting inflation, rather than exchange rates. China and Malaysia widened their exchange rate bands in 2005, with significant currency appreciation since. The Republic of Korea, the Philippines and Thailand also saw large appreciations. Removing explicit exchange rate targets reduces the risk of

currency mismatches and encourages investors to hedge their currency exposure.

- Government budget deficits have gradually declined and, in some countries, have turned to surpluses. Concern for exploding public debts is thus limited, with public debt at its lowest since 2000 for most countries (figure 1.14).

- There have been no signs of excessive current account deficits, as in the prelude to 1997. Indeed, post-crisis East Asia now exports capital to the rest of the world. In 2007, current account surpluses in emerging Asian economies stood at 6.5% of GDP (figure 1.15).

- The ratio of foreign exchange reserves to short-term debt is high in all countries. Foreign exchange reserves in developing ESCAP member countries have increased sixfold since 1997, to $3.4 trillion as of October 2007. These reserves can smooth any sudden stop in capital inflows.

- There has been no excessive build-up of private domestic credit as a share of GDP, and the ratio of non-performing loans to total loans has declined significantly from the early 2000s. Banks' capital adequacy ratios are well above the international standard of 8%.

- Countries have reduced their dependence on bank financing. A positive development is nascent local-currency bond markets. Changes in perceived risk are reflected automatically through these markets, causing less systemic risk than foreign-currency-denominated loans.

The need to build defences against subprime fallout – now

With increasingly open capital markets, economies in the region are intimately linked to global financial flows. Investor sentiments are fickle and it is not possible to predict when and how financial sector turmoil will attack markets in the region. So, there is little countries can do to stop external financial sector shocks. Even so, countries can ensure that their economies are strong and flexible enough to weather shocks and adapt. Efforts to mitigate the financial shocks are critical because they exact a heavy toll on the poor (box 1.5). Because the poor are the least prepared to cope, they suffer the most from any income shock.

An effective defence includes macroeconomic measures to build resilience to shocks and socio-economic measures to reduce the impact on the poor:

Figure 1.14. Budget balances have improved...

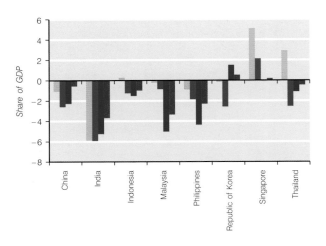

Figure 1.15. ...as have external balances

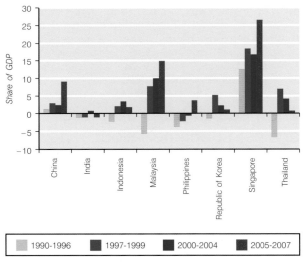

| 1990-1996 | 1997-1999 | 2000-2004 | 2005-2007 |

Sources: IMF, *International Financial Statistics* (CD-ROM) (Washington, D.C., 2007); ADB, *Key Indicators of Developing Asian and Pacific Countries 2007* (Manila, 2007); and ESCAP estimates.

Note: Data for 2007 are estimates.

- *Countries must ensure solid macroeconomic fundamentals to maintain investor confidence and sustain economic growth.* Key elements are moderate and stable inflation; sound fiscal policies that ensure low deficits and sustainable debt burdens; and more flexible exchange rates regimes that can absorb external shocks and reduce currency mismatches in borrowing.

- *Countries must develop healthy financial sectors to build confidence and benefit from capital inflows.* This requires well developed regulatory structures to prevent bad debt. Also necessary are independence and a competitive environment for banks to ensure efficient credit allocation and pricing. Authorities must keep pace with the great diversity of complex new products in financial markets in the region. Knowledge and risk management systems should be updated to ensure early warning of any adverse flows. Financial markets should be deepened by developing domestic and regional bond markets. These provide an avenue for investors, in times of uncertainty, to move away from equity and other domestic markets into another local-currency market – and thus reduce the risk of sudden capital flight. Local bond markets also create opportunities to keep regional savings close to home.

- *Countries must have robust microeconomic foundations to ensure an efficient economic system.* A basic requirement is clear property rights, overseen by a strong judiciary, that allow companies and institutions to operate effectively and transparently. The labour market should be robust enough to adjust to economic downturns through government provision of training and retraining and measures to safeguard vulnerable segments of the working population.

> *Social safety nets have to be improved to prevent people falling into hardship*

- *Social safety nets have to be improved to prevent people falling into hardship.* The interest in social safety nets just after the Asian crisis slowly diminished with the recovery, so adequate social protection mechanisms are lacking in most of the region. Most countries have some social protection system, but these programmes are ineffective due to limited coverage, insufficient funds, inadequate instruments and administrative bottlenecks. The systems cover only a portion of the formal

Box 1.5. How economic shocks impact the poor

The poor are hit the hardest by financial shocks that lead to economic downturns, clear in previous episodes within and outside the region.

Achievements in poverty reduction remain fragile in many developing countries, with many "near poor" living just above the poverty line and vulnerable to economic shocks. During the 1997 Asian crisis, 19 million Indonesians and 1.1 million Thais fell below the poverty line as real earnings slumped and jobs disappeared (World Bank, 2007b). The 2001-2002 financial crisis in Argentina increased the national poverty rate by 15 percentage points (Cruces and Wodon, 2003), and the 1998-1999 crisis in Ecuador increased poverty by 13 percentage points (Hall and Patrinos, 2005). Poverty rates rose among formal-sector workers through lower wages and job losses. And poverty deepens when workers switched from the formal sector to the informal, depressing the wages of those already in the informal economy.

Financial crises also have a strong impact on inequality. Poorer people are impacted more by a crisis than the rich because they have fewer buffers, and because the range and effectiveness of their buffers are inadequate. The poor lack assets, such as bank deposits and land, and have only restricted or expensive access to credit. Within the poor, the groups at greatest risk are marginal workers. In the last Asian crisis, these were youths, women and the less experienced and less educated. Lacking education and skills, the poor tend to be less mobile across sectors and regions than better educated workers, often leaving them unable to switch jobs and access other opportunities.

And the poor take much longer to recover from a reversal. Recovery in real wages and employment takes much longer than recovery in GDP. Many districts of Indonesia suffered from persistent poverty effects five years after the 1997 Asian crisis and three years after the country's rapid recovery in GDP (Lokshin and Ravallion, 2005). A review of financial crises in 80 countries over the past few decades finds that real wages take an average of three years to pick up again. Employment growth does not regain pre-crisis levels for several years after that (UNDP, 1999). Poor households facing rising vulnerability and insecurity are forced to respond with measures that keep them poor: reducing the number and quality of meals, postponing health-related expenditure and withdrawing children from school. These actions lead to lower future income-earning potential for current and future generations, resulting in persistent poverty. When the capacity of vulnerable households to protect themselves is very low, chronic poverty can result even from small, one-off shocks.

sector, often the wealthiest, and the instruments, often adapted from developed countries, may not be appropriate for the needs of developing countries. Because these systems are difficult to set up during crises, renewed and urgent actions are needed now. An effective safety net should be targeted towards the poor but should be large enough to provide broad-based social protection. Key areas to address are unemployment insurance, health care and pensions. Benefits should be ensured for the most vulnerable workers – youths, women and the less educated and less experienced. Because the poor often work in the informal sector, policies targeting this group should be different from those aimed at helping vulnerable groups in the formal sector. Social safety nets should be flexible so that they can adjust to changes in poverty.

• *Countries must improve regional cooperation to prevent and react to crises.* There have already been positive moves, such as the recent agreement by the ASEAN+3 countries to strengthen the Chiang Mai initiative by pooling some of their foreign exchange reserves to respond to crises. Converting the system of bilateral currency swaps to a multilateral pool will increase the speed and ease of response. The funds to be made available will be key because current resources are not a sufficient primary means to combat a crisis. It is also important to extend the country coverage of this new agreement to protect more Asia-Pacific countries. Much of the value of the initiative lies in its less heralded objectives. The ASEAN+3 economies are striving to share information about portfolio flows and collaborating in regulatory activities. More needs to be done in these areas across the region to provide an early warning system for potentially disruptive flows – and thus prevent the onset of crises.

A global call to action to regulate new financial actors

The subprime crisis has opened eyes to the failure of the international financial architecture to address the risks of new financial instruments. The old "buy and hold" model of bank lending has evolved into "originate to distribute". In the subprime crisis, banks in the United States originated loans and then repackaged and sold them to international investors, distributing risks throughout sectors and across the globe. Under this mechanism, banks have less incentive to monitor borrowers. They have switched from relying on soft information and long-term relationships with borrowers to model-based pricing. Another aspect is the unsatisfactory performance of ratings firms in evaluating new financial instruments without market values for illiquid products. Moving the loans off the books of banks to other financial investors transferred activity from regulated to unregulated investors, especially to international hedge funds and banks' off-balance-sheet special investment vehicles and conduits. These investors are not transparent and are sometimes highly leveraged. Some 9,000 hedge funds manage assets of about $1.6 trillion (Roth, 2007). Bank-sponsored conduits are estimated to hold assets worth about $1.4 trillion.

Action to regulate the new models of international finance must be global. Investment decisions in developed countries threaten financial disruption in developing countries, both in Asia and the Pacific and in other regions. Measures by developing countries to increase transparency are ineffective when the executing institutions are in other jurisdictions. And measures by developed countries acting independently are also often powerless when investments cross borders. The new pools of global capital are structured to avoid the scrutiny required of firms and financial institutions at the national level. Key measures are required through global cooperation among national supervisory institutions:

- Regulators need aggregate information on structured-finance-instrument holdings of financial institutions and on the concentration of risk to assist in the regulatory process.

- Major central banks must cooperate more closely in dealing with liquidity shocks, because the evaporation of liquidity may quickly cross borders.

- Banks should be required to explain the complex structured products they design to investors in sufficient detail, including information on underlying assets and their risk profiles.

- Regulators should standardize the valuation and risk-assessment methodologies used by credit rating agencies and clarify conflict-of-interest issues.

- Originators and arrangers might keep a certain portion of the underlying assets and the structured products, as incentives to examine and monitor more carefully the quality of the credits and the securitized products.

Medium-term policy issues on the watch list

The region's prospects, in both the short term and the long term, are shaped by many forces. Considered here are three issues for action in the medium term:

- Benefiting from trade in services

- Addressing the social dimensions of international migration

- Managing climate change

Benefiting from trade in services – the next frontier

Services, the fastest growing sector in the global economy, account for two-thirds of global output, one-third of global employment and nearly one-fifth of global trade. And since 1990, exports of services from developing countries have grown at an annual average of 8%, compared with 6% for developed countries (UNCTAD, 2007). World service exports accelerated from an annual average of 4.7% in 1995-2000 to 10.8% in 2000-2006. For ESCAP developing economies, service exports rose from 5% in 1995-2000, below Latin America and the United States, to 13.4% in 2000-2006, faster than in any other region (figure 1.16).

The ESCAP member country with the most spectacular growth in the services trade is India, whose average annual growth accelerated from 19% in 1995-2000 to 29% in 2000-2006. It quadrupled its share among ESCAP member countries between 1995 and 2006 to become the region's second-largest service exporter after China. China's growth in service exports has also been very fast, averaging 16% over 1995-2006. And service exports from the Russian Federation rebounded from an annual average decline of 6.5% in 1995-2000 to an increase of 21% in 2000-2006 (figure 1.17).

There are three main categories of services for which statistics are compiled: transportation, travel and other commercial. For 2006, the world exports of these categories were valued, respectively, at $630 billion, $745 billion and $1,380 billion. Over 2000-2006, the share of transport services remained stable at about 23%. Travel services fell from 32% to 27%. Other commercial services rose from 45% to 50% (WTO, 2007).

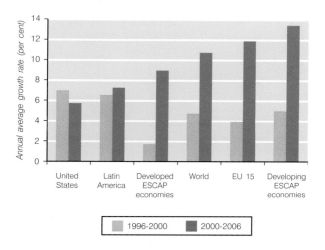

Figure 1.16. Strong service exports for ESCAP developing economies in 2000-2006

Source: ESCAP, based on data from WTO, *International Trade Statistics 2006* (Geneva, 2006), and *International Trade Statistics 2007* (Geneva, 2007).

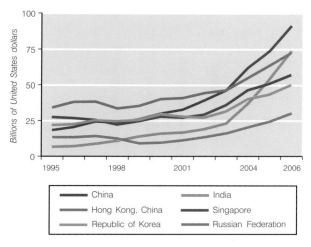

Figure 1.17. India and China leading service exports in the region

Source: ESCAP, based on data from WTO, *International Trade Statistics 2006* (Geneva, 2006), and *International Trade Statistics 2007* (Geneva, 2007).

In 2006, the top five exporters of transport services in the ESCAP region – the Republic of Korea; Hong Kong, China; China; Singapore; and the Russian Federation – were among the global top 10. Their exports that year amounted to $99 billion, or 16% of the world total. Of the top five exporters in the region, China had the best performance, growing at 34% per year over 2000-2006, faster than the world average of 10%. The Russian Federation and India, starting from lower bases, increased their exports of transport services at 19% and 26%, respectively. For travel services, China, Turkey and Thailand were ranked between third and eighth in 2006, with exports of $63 billion.

> *For ESCAP developing economies, service exports rose from 5% in 1995-2000 to 13.4% in 2000-2006, faster than in any other region*

Exports of other commercial services, the most dynamic category, grew at an annual average of 13% between 2000 and 2006. India; Hong Kong, China; China; Singapore; and the Republic of Korea, were among the top 10 in 2006, exporting $184 billion that year (figure 1.18). The exports of the Republic of

Korea and Hong Kong, China, grew at or slightly below the world average in 2000-2006, but those of China and Singapore grew above it, at 24% and 19% respectively.[4] The Russian Federation was the 13th largest exporter of other commercial services in 2006, with its exports growing at 31% per year over 2000-2006.

With $16 billion in earnings, India was the second-largest exporter of computer and information services in 2005, after the European Union. But other countries are emerging as competitors. The main one is China. With 12,000 software development companies employing nearly a million people, China had its exports increase at an annual rate of 40% after 2003, reaching $3 billion in 2006, when it became Japan's largest outsourcing location for computer and information services. Malaysia, now considered the third-most attractive site for outsourcing low-cost IT services after India and China, has been promoting the sector since 1996. With more than 1,100 international companies, Malaysia more than doubled its computer services exports in three years. The Russian Federation, now a base for outsourcing computer services for several European companies, increased its exports by 60% per year after 2003 (WTO, 2007).

ESCAP developing members are also becoming a prime location for offshoring services, with six countries ranked among the top 10 in 2007 (table 1.2).

> *The primary challenge in liberalizing services is balancing competition with such welfare objectives as universal access to health services*

Removing obstacles to market entry for domestic and foreign firms will create a more competitive environment, which in turn will foster domestic service firms able to compete in the international market (Findlay and Sidorenko, 2005). Reforms should emphasize a pro-competitive environment rather than changes in ownership: in other words, competition first and privatization second.

Figure 1.18. Exports of other commercial services in 2005, selected countries

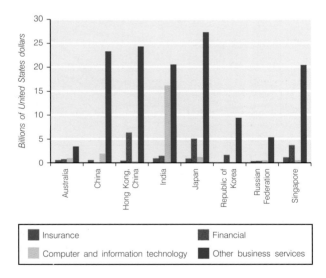

Source: ESCAP, based on data from WTO, *International Trade statistics 2007* (Geneva, 2007).

---

4 WTO (2007) does not report India's annual average growth rate of exports of other commercial services for 2000-2006, but it does report that India's growth rate for 2006 was 39%.

Table 1.2. Global services location index, 2007

Rank 2006 (rank 2005)	Country	Financial attractiveness	People and skills availability	Business environment	Total score
1 (1)	India	3.22	2.34	1.44	7.00
2 (2)	China	2.93	2.25	1.38	6.56
3 (3)	Malaysia	2.84	1.26	2.02	6.12
4 (6)	Thailand	3.19	1.21	1.62	6.02
5 (10)	Brazil	2.64	1.78	1.47	5.89
6 (13)	Indonesia	3.29	1.47	1.06	5.82
7 (8)	Chile	2.65	1.18	1.93	5.76
8 (4)	Philippines	3.26	1.23	1.26	5.75
9 (15)	Bulgaria	3.16	1.04	1.56	5.75
10 (17)	Mexico	2.63	1.49	1.61	5.73
11 (5)	Singapore	1.65	1.51	2.53	5.68

Source: A.T. Kearney, *Offshoring for Long Term Advantage: The 2007 A.T. Kearney Global Services Location Index*, <http://www.atkearney.com/res/shared/pdf/GSLI_2007.pdf> (accessed 18 January 2008).

The primary challenge in liberalizing services is balancing competition from improved market access for foreign providers with such welfare objectives as universal access to health services. Setting up an effective regulatory regime is essential for remedying problems of asymmetric information and market power where natural monopolies flourish, such as in energy and transport. But controlling market power and unseating large incumbents presents huge political challenges. Extensive evidence shows the huge political costs of mismanaging these elements of reform.

Addressing the social dimensions of international migration

There were 58 million international migrants in the Asian and Pacific region as of 2005, 53 million of them in Asia and 5 million in the Pacific (United Nations, 2006). The past few decades brought a marked increase in the cross-national mobility of the region's people. This trend continues unabated. Demographic imbalances and widening intercountry disparities in income and opportunities propel people to move in order to improve opportunities for themselves and their families. Technological transformations and economic links create new demand for skills and labour – demand often met by migrant workers. With more countries involved in migration streams, international migration has become a structural reality in the region.

Much of the migration debate centres around economics, especially capital inflows channelled through remittances. Recorded remittances to ESCAP developing

countries – the largest sources of external income in many poor countries – are estimated at $106 billion in 2007, 11% higher than in 2006. If unrecorded flows are taken into account, the size would be even larger. The region's five largest recipients of remittances in 2007 were India, China, the Philippines, Bangladesh and Pakistan, with remittances totalling $82 billion in 2007 (figure 1.19). Remittances are particularly important for smaller countries; in such countries as Armenia, Kyrgyzstan, Nepal and the Philippines, remittances contribute over 10% of GDP.

> *Much of the migration debate centres around economics, but migration is much more than flows of remittances*

International migration is about more than flows of labour and remittances, however. Migration affects the lives of those involved and the broader community – impacting marriages, families and governance. These dimensions often receive too little focus.

Changing patterns of labour migration in Asia and the Pacific

While the region continues to see outflows of people to the countries that traditionally admit migrants for permanent settlement – Australia, Canada, New Zealand and the United States – the mobility of people seeking temporary employment within the region has become more important.

Figure 1.19. Rising remittances in Asia and the Pacific, 2006-2007

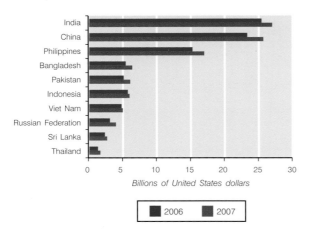

Billions of United States dollars

■ 2006 ■ 2007

Source: World Bank website <http://econ.worldbank.org/WBSITE/ EXTERNAL/EXTDEC/EXTDECPROSPECTS/0,,contentMDK:21122856~ pagePK:64165401~piPK:64165026~theSitePK:476883,00.html> (12 February 2008).

Note: Data for 2007 are estimates.

Figure 1.20. New migrant source countries emerging

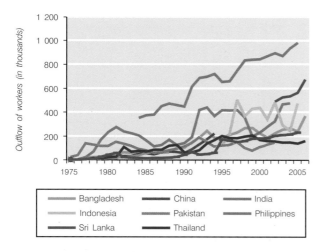

― Bangladesh	― China	― India
― Indonesia	― Pakistan	― Philippines
― Sri Lanka	― Thailand	

Source: ESCAP, Emerging Social Issues Division, *Database on International Migration.*

Two patterns have emerged. First, since the early 1970s, the oil – producing countries of Western Asia – Kuwait, Oman, Saudi Arabia and the United Arab Emirates – have attracted a large number of Asian workers. Second, since the 1980s, the newly industrialized economies of East and South-East Asia have become hubs for temporary migration. These include Japan, Brunei Darussalam, Malaysia, the Republic of Korea, Singapore and Thailand, as well as Hong Kong, China, and Taiwan Province of China. Their sustained growth, coupled with a limited supply of national workers resulting from low fertility, compelled these economies to seek manpower from neighbouring low-income, labour-surplus countries.

Meanwhile, new suppliers of workers have emerged, some of them officially promoting labour deployment. India, Pakistan and the Philippines have long histories of sending many workers abroad. By the mid-1990s, countries such as Bangladesh, China, Indonesia and Sri Lanka joined the group of migrant source countries, the shift evident in their official records (figure 1.20). The outflow of migrant workers abroad is likely greater, because unknown number of workers move without registering with national authorities.

As more women cross borders, feminization is also reshaping migration patterns. Women constitute a large majority of migrant workers from Indonesia, the Philippines and Sri Lanka (table 1.3). Migrant women in the region are engaged in a wide range of activities, predominantly in domestic work but also in health and entertainment. Demand for female migrants has been persistent in relatively affluent economies where local women are drawn into the labour force or the need for elderly care is on the rise due to ageing populations.

Challenges for family left behind

Temporary labour migration usually does not allow migrants to bring family members to the country of employment. Although migration can benefit families, there are concerns about potential costs to family cohesion, marital stability and children left behind.

Extended separation forces the family left behind to reshuffle an increased workload, to reallocate decision-making responsibilities and to fill the psychological emptiness generated by the absence. Extended families often fill the void and provide continuity in family-based care (Asis, 2008). Cheaper and faster communication has narrowed the distance between family members. Even so, marital instability and the break-up of the family unit are often mentioned as consequences of prolonged absence (Hugo, 2002).

Table 1.3. The gender composition of migration outflows varies widely

		Number of migrant workers deployed, annual average (in thousands)		Female share (per cent)
		Total	Female	
Indonesia	2000-2003	387	306	79.2
Philippines	2000-2002	266	188	70.5
Republic of Korea	2000-2002	226	80	35.5
Sri Lanka	2000-2003	195	129	66.1
Thailand	2000-2003	165	28	16.8

Source: ESCAP, Emerging Social Issues Division, *Database on International Migration*.

Note: Data for the Philippines refer to newly hired workers for overseas employment.

An estimated 3-6 million children have been left behind by Filipino parents working overseas, along with 1 million in Indonesia and half a million in Thailand (Bryant, 2005). The social cost to children left behind includes poor performance in school, violent behaviour, delinquency and psychological problems. The evidence in the Philippines and Sri Lanka, sources of large numbers of women migrants, suggests that families face more adjustments when mothers migrate than when fathers do so (Asis, 2008). When fathers migrate, mothers are likely to embrace their tasks and functions, but when mothers migrate, child care tends to be left to other female relatives.

> *The social cost to children left behind includes poor performance in school, violent behaviour, delinquency and psychological problems*

The potential consequences notwithstanding, migration does bestow benefits on families left behind. Families with migrant members tend to have better housing and higher ownership of consumer durables. Some families have adopted more modern ways of living, strengthening the family by using remittances to build houses or educate children.

"Marriage migration" on the rise

Migration to marry a foreign partner, known as "marriage migration", is on the rise in the region. Japan, the Republic of Korea and Taiwan Province of China have experienced a dramatic increase in international marriages, mostly involving foreign women and local men.

In the Republic of Korea, 14% of all new marriages in 2005 were between a Korean and a foreign spouse (Douglass, 2006). Foreign brides come to those countries mainly from neighbouring developing countries – China, the Philippines, Thailand and Viet Nam.

One factor behind this trend is the continuing urbanization in high-income economies, coupled with impending depopulation due to low fertility and ageing populations. In those societies, many men obligated to take charge of family farms are unable to find brides because local women prefer urban work and lifestyles (Douglass, 2006). Foreign brides are often sought through advertising services. In Japan and the Republic of Korea, some local governments have joined with farmers to sponsor searches for overseas brides in nearby countries.

For women, international marriage can be a chance for economic security and social mobility. Humbeck (1996) finds that Thai women who migrated to marry foreign men did so to escape poverty in rural Thailand, to help their families and to seek better jobs. Obtaining secure and legal residence, including status for work, in the host country was an important factor in international marriages between Japanese men and women from the Philippines, the Republic of Korea and Thailand (Piper, 1999).

The complexities are myriad. Brokers and agencies fostering marriage migration have raised concerns over fraudulent marriages and the trafficking of women. Facing restrictive policies, aspiring migrants may use marriage to gain residence in another country. Employers may also use marriage as a recruitment strategy. For receiving societies, foreign spouses and the children of internationally married couples raise questions about settlement, integration and the future of multiculturalism.

Migrant children more vulnerable

Although immigrant children may be with their parents, they confront serious institutional, social and psychological barriers, especially when parents occupy marginal positions in the destination country.

Legal identity, a problem faced by all migrants, is particularly difficult for children. Children born in Thailand to foreign parents, for example, generally do not qualify for Thai citizenship (Bryant, forthcoming). Children without identification documents are usually excluded from formal schooling, and it may be difficult for them to socialize and to create social networks because of language and cultural barriers.

In addition, migration puts unique stresses on children – from leaving a familiar social context and extended family network; from entering a new place, culture, and language; or from harsh conditions endured before or during the transition. The stress can be even more intense for adolescents. Migrant children who do not connect in some meaningful way with their peers, family or school are at an increased risk of suicide, substance abuse, school failure, drop-out, health problems and criminal activity (UNICEF, 2007).

Migrants more vulnerable to disease

The spread of HIV/AIDS and, more recently, the outbreak of SARS in East and South-East Asia have demonstrated the potential repercussions of human mobility and international migration for public health – and for the economy, international relations and tourism.

There is a close association between population mobility and the spread of HIV/AIDS. Migrants often become vulnerable to HIV during transit and after arrival, driven by such conditions as exploitation, separation from spouse and family and socio-cultural norms that guide behaviour. Migrants may have problems dealing with social and sexual norms in new environments and may not know how to protect themselves against sexual risks.

Migrants are also likely to have different risks for some illnesses than the host community. They may face higher risks because of differences in disease prevalence and the psychological and physical stress of moving to a new environment. Due to language, cultural and procedural barriers, migrants may have difficulties in accessing health services, or they may underutilize services, especially preventive services, such as prenatal care, dental care, immunizations and regular health examinations.

Both regular- and irregular-status migrants are at high risk of communicable diseases; those in irregular status may be more vulnerable. Irregular migrants may be reluctant to seek medical attention for fear of apprehension by the authorities. Migrants who have been trafficked and others in exploitative situations may have less access to curative and preventive health care. Migrant women in general – and those trafficked for sexual exploitation in particular – face risks of unwanted pregnancies, abortion, sexually transmitted diseases and HIV/AIDS, as well as mental and emotional disorders.

Protecting the rights of migrants – a policy priority

If governments are to formulate well balanced policies, the social implications of family separation, marriage migration, and the effects of migration on public health merit attention alongside the economic benefits of migration.

One key is protecting the rights of migrants by ensuring that they are treated equally under the law in the receiving country. Respect for these human rights is one of the most basic determinants of migrant's well-being – and essential to achieving greater social and economic development. Part of that is ensuring that migrants of all ages have access to affordable basic social and health services.

> *Less-skilled migrant workers are likely to face deception, discrimination, exploitation and abuse, so protecting the rights of migrants is crucial*

Many migrants enjoy positive experiences at their destination, but a significant number face hardships that erode their gains from migration. Informal work arrangements often disadvantage migrant workers through low wages, poor working conditions and lack of social protection and workers' rights. Less-skilled migrant workers are likely to face deception, discrimination, exploitation and abuse. Xenophobic sentiments and negative perceptions of migration are part of the explanation. Another part is the lack of enforcement of labour standards in host countries.

Despite the growth of international migration in Asia and the Pacific, protecting the rights of migrants remains on the fringes of discussion (Asis, 2008). A notable shortcoming in policy debates has been the rights of migrant workers. While there are bilateral agreements between some sending and receiving countries in the region, mostly through memoranda of understanding, these primarily regulate the movement of workers and have little impact on the treatment that migrant workers receive in the country of employment.

It is the sovereign right of States to regulate the entry of aliens and the terms and conditions of their stay. Even so, international human rights instruments call on States to abide by international principles when designing regulations and policies that affect the welfare of migrants. The countries in the region have made a significant step towards this objective by ratifying international conventions on the protection of migrants (table 1.4). The Protocol to Prevent, Suppress and Punish Trafficking in Persons and the Protocol against Smuggling, both adopted in 2000, have been ratified quickly, indicating the strong commitment of governments to combating such crimes. The pace of ratification of the 1990 Convention on the Protection of the Rights of All Migrant Workers and Members of Their Families has, however, been relatively slow in the region, enjoying support mostly from countries of migrant workers.

Managing climate change – how Asia and the Pacific can take the lead in mitigation and adaptation

At the Bali conference on climate change, Member States agreed on a road map of key issues to be negotiated by the end of 2009. These include adapting to the negative consequences of climate change, such as drought and floods; reducing greenhouse gas emissions; and widely deploying climate-friendly technologies and financing both adaptation and mitigation. With the Asia-Pacific region expected to be severely affected by climate change, it is imperative that the region contribute to these negotiations. The region does not have to wait for a global consensus, however; it can contribute to managing climate change in its own way.

The impact of climate change on the Asia-Pacific region could be immense. Rising temperatures could result in sea-level rise, melting of glaciers, water stress, land erosion, forest fires and diseases with devastating effects, particularly on the poor.

A regional framework for managing climate change

Almost 90% of global greenhouse gas (GHG) emissions come from five sources: energy (25.9%), industry (19.4%), forestry (17.4%), agriculture (13.5%) and transport (13.1%). Extensive use of fossil fuel, deforestation, agricultural practices, waste and other energy sources are responsible for much of global warming. The emission pattern of GHGs in the Asia-Pacific region is quite similar to that found at the global level, except that emissions from land use are much higher than the average and those from transport and industry are somewhat lower (World Resources Institute, 2007; Stern, 2006). Mitigating global warming requires targeting those sources.

> *Asking developing countries to cut their emissions and sacrifice growth is not equitable, but not including them in mitigating climate change will render the effort ineffective*

Climate change is a global threat. This means that both developed and developing countries should be involved in controlling GHG emissions. Left out of the

Table 1.4. Governments in the ESCAP region that have adopted key United Nations legal instruments on international migration, as of November 2007

Instrument	Year adopted	Entry into force	Number of countries ratified
Convention relating to the Status of Refugees	1951	1954	24
Protocol relating to the Status of Refugees	1967	1967	24
Convention on the Protection of the Rights of All Migrant Workers and Members of Their Families	1990	2003	7
Protocol to Prevent, Suppress and Punish Trafficking in Persons, Especially Women and Children	2000	2003	15
Protocol against the Smuggling of Migrants by Land, Sea and Air	2000	2004	15

Kyoto Protocol, developing countries should be included in climate change discussions and initiatives. While developing countries are low emitters, their growth will increase emissions. Asking these countries to cut their emissions and sacrifice growth is not equitable, but not including them in mitigating climate change will render the effort ineffective. The solution is to invest in carbon-reducing technologies. The Bali road map is only the beginning, and the task ahead in reaching an implementable agreement is huge.

Because the severest impacts of climate change will come in Asia and the Pacific, countries of the region need to take the lead in mitigation and adaptation. The measures needed will incur costs and will require the transfer of resources and technologies from developed to developing countries. Even so, governments in Asia and the Pacific can undertake several measures to mitigate the impact of climate change and prepare their countries for it – while spurring economic and social development.

To fully address climate change, governments need to better integrate their macroeconomic, social and environmental policies. Doing so includes measures to integrate economic and fiscal policies with industrial development, pollution control, energy use, urban planning and development, agricultural and water management, health and sanitation, and forestry and natural resource management.

A regional framework for managing climate change is depicted in figure 1.21. Creating a regional framework for managing climate change includes measures on several axes:

• Promote eco-efficiency

• Go carbon neutral

• Expand carbon trading

• Support technology transfers

• Green the land

• Manage waste efficiently

• Implement adaptation measures

The countries of the region, whatever measures they undertake, need to develop policies that reduce greenhouse gas emissions, encourage wide deployment of climate-friendly technologies and prepare the region for adaptation to the negative impacts of climate change.

Promote eco-efficiency. The core of "green growth" is to improve the eco-efficiency of rapid economic growth, so that it can be compatible with the limited carrying capacity of the region. Action to improve energy efficiency and promote a low-carbon economy is an important component. Oil prices have tripled from less than $30 per barrel in early 2004 to around $100 in early 2008, making investment in better energy efficiency more urgent and more economically feasible. Improving energy efficiency could have a triple dividend: enhanced energy security, a better local environment and less GHG emissions (box 1.6). This green growth approach was endorsed by the Fifth Ministerial Conference on Environment and Development in Asia and the Pacific in March 2005.

> *Governments can promote lifestyle and consumption changes by encouraging civil society organizations to take a more prominent role in advocating environmental sustainability*

Specific measures for green growth could include taxing older, less efficient vehicles; offering tax incentives to companies that invest in newer and cleaner technologies; lowering the taxes on low-energy consumption lights; and introducing more graded user charges on electricity. Governments can also promote lifestyle and consumption changes by encouraging civil society organizations to take a more prominent role in advocating environmental sustainability.

Go carbon neutral. In developed countries, more and more consumers are buying products and services from only those companies that purchase carbon offsets, and companies have started promoting their products as carbon neutral. A similar movement can be encouraged in Asia and the Pacific, particularly among the growing, globally connected and environmentally aware middle classes. This can be done through a partnership between governments and civil society organizations, particularly international environmental organizations, such as Greenpeace and the World Wildlife Fund. These partnerships could encourage producers in developed countries that sell products in Asia and the Pacific to go carbon neutral and induce demand for clean development mechanism (CDM) projects in the region.

Governments can encourage export-oriented firms to go carbon neutral and capture shares in this growing market by improving their efficiency and investing in

Figure 1.21. Framework for managing climate change

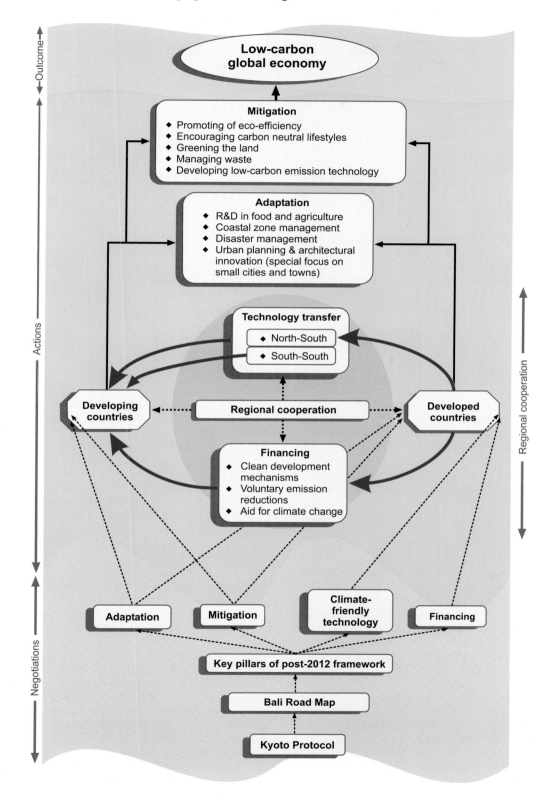

Box 1.6. Cash for wind – how clean energy can become a big business

Tulsi Tanti started by using wind power for his family textile business in Gujarat, India, in 1994 as a way to cut energy costs. Seeing the inadequate power supply and growing demand in India, Mr. Tanti perceived an opportunity. He founded Suzalon Energy, buying 10 turbines from Sudwind, a small German company, and setting up his first 3.5-megawatt wind farm for Indian Petrochemicals Corporation Ltd. When Sudwind went bankrupt in 1997, Suzlon hired its engineers and created an R&D centre in Germany, giving the company the technological capacity to produce its own turbines. The company also acquired a manufacturer of rotor blades in the Netherlands.

The company has grown exponentially. In the third quarter of 2007, it reported consolidated revenues of $916 million, 74% above the previous year. Today, Suzlon is ranked among the top five wind energy companies in the world, with a market share of close to 8%. Suzlon started selling in the United States in 2003 when it landed a contract with DanMar & Associates, a Minnesota development firm. Since then, the United States has become the firm's main export market, though China, Europe and Australia are also customers.

The company's success is due to its entrepreneurial, technological and managerial capacity, but its story also shows the profitability of investing in clean energies – and the role for policy. Indian investors in wind power have received an accelerated depreciation of 80% starting in the first year. Fostering these capabilities will go a long way towards mitigating climate change and supporting economic growth and development in the region.

Sources: Karmali (2006); Newindpress.com (2007); and Suzlon (2008).

carbon offsets locally. Such initiatives could be supported by removing distortional national energy subsidies, valued at around $250 billion per year globally, a sizeable share of that in Asia and the Pacific. Removing energy subsidies could reduce primary energy consumption and CO_2 emissions by a significant margin. Such a move could have short-term implications for inflation and growth, but it would ease the fiscal burden on governments, promote innovation in energy efficiency and help internalize the environmental costs of greenhouse gases. It would also promote growth and stability in the medium to long term.

An easy source of local carbon offsets are sanitation and urban solid waste management. This approach would induce demand for CDM projects in the region that trade in certified emission reductions (CERs) and in less stringent voluntary emission reductions (VERs). In 2006, the global CDM trading market was worth about $30 billion; the VER market, about $100 million. Both are growing rapidly.

Expand carbon trading. The CDM is designed to help industrialized countries reduce the costs of meeting their emissions targets under the Kyoto Protocol by achieving reductions at lower cost elsewhere. The mechanism allows developing countries to pursue carbon trading and reduces global emissions.

China and India dominate, with market shares of 61% and 12% respectively. Only a few other countries host CDM projects. Lack of awareness and capacity to develop CDM projects, and the relatively small size of the projects, prevents most developing countries from benefiting. Building awareness and improving national capacity could help. Clustering small projects and so avoiding high transaction costs could make smaller CDM projects more commercially attractive. Governments and regional institutions could assist countries in developing project-specific methodologies for carbon trading following the standard methodologies approved by UNFCCC.

As a precursor, developing countries could promote VERs. These reductions have a direct impact on GHGs and provide business opportunities to take advantage of the increasing VER demand that results from cost-effectiveness, less rigorous standards, speculative trading opportunities and marketing strategies linked to corporate social responsibility. Subregional and regional intergovernmental organizations, such as ASEAN, SAARC and ESCAP, can develop and promote regional or subregional over-the-counter markets for CERs and VERs. The region also need to strengthen the role of CDM by expanding the coverage (currently a few countries dominate CDM projects), scale and scope of projects and make it a major channel for coordinating action between developing and developed countries. CDM has significant potential as an incentive mechanism for non-Annex I parties to participate in GHG emission reductions by functioning as an efficient channel for financial resources and technology to developing countries. It is also necessary to make CDM projects a key instrument for bringing net reductions in global GHG emissions. Meeting such goals requires new operational rules, such as discounting CERs in accordance with the types and geographical locations of CDM projects. Any such approaches would need to be preceded by a comprehensive study on feasibility.

> *China and India could help other developing countries develop more practical and affordable climate-friendly technologies in energy efficiency, renewable energy and carbon capture and storage*

Foster South-South cooperation in technology transfer. A major barrier to developing countries addressing climate change is the lack of technology for domestic climate change monitoring, mitigation and adaptation. The most advanced and efficient technologies are in the private sector, mainly in developed countries. CDM is meant to assist the transfer of cleaner technologies to developing countries, but there is also a need to promote South-South cooperation within and across regions. China and India (and Brazil from outside the region) could help other developing countries develop more practical and affordable climate-friendly technologies in energy efficiency, renewable energy and carbon capture and storage.

Green the land. The region needs to take concrete measures for reducing emissions from deforestation and degradation as a key approach to mitigating carbon emissions in the post-2012 framework, including through strengthening and supporting ongoing efforts on a voluntary basis. Countries could do so by supporting capacity-building and undertaking efforts, including demonstration activities, to address the drivers of deforestation. This is important to address the needs of local and indigenous communities who depend on forests for their livelihoods.

Land-use emissions, driven mainly by deforestation, account for 17% of global GHG emissions. South and South-East Asia are losing over 28,000 square kilometres of land every year due to deforestation. If these trends continue, land-use emissions are likely to increase until 2050; much damage will already have been done by the time they start to recede. Reversing deforestation is thus critical. Moreover, this area requires minimal technology. Political will is needed to enact and implement regulations to stop to illegal logging and deforestation, particularly in rain forests. Countries in the region should also implement afforestation programmes by planting trees and greening 28,000 square kilometres of land every year to regain the green land lost in the past several decades. Afforestation will contribute to adaptation as well by reducing the impact of soil erosion and drought, protecting against floods, capturing and retaining groundwater, and increasing biodiversity and thus food security. Restoring coastal mangrove forests would help preserve the coastal environment, protect against typhoons and reduce the intrusion of seawater into coastal groundwater tables.

> *Reversing deforestation is critical and requires minimal technology*

Manage waste efficiently. Urban solid and liquid wastes emit methane, 21 times more potent as a GHG than CO_2. Converting urban solid wastes into compost and organic fertilizer not only reduces methane emissions but increases soil productivity and reduces the use of chemical fertilizers, keys for adaptation and mitigation (box 1.7). Methane from landfills and dumpsites can be captured and used as a fuel to generate electricity. The Peoples Committee of Ho Chi Minh City has entered into a partnership with a Korean company to generate 3 megawatts of electricity from the city's dump. The government of Andhra Pradesh, India, is providing 40-50% financing for projects that turn urban wastewater, particularly from slaughterhouses, into electricity. It also guarantees that the Andhra Pradesh State Electricity Board will purchase electricity generated from such plants at a set price (Nedcap.org, 2008). These revenues can be supplemented by selling CERs and VERs from the projects.

Implement adaptation measures. Adaptation is particularly important in poorer countries and poorer regions within countries due to their resource constraints. The adverse impacts of climate change on agriculture and food security reaffirm the importance of investing in research and development to create drought-resistant and heat-resistant seed varieties (see chapter 3 for details). Increased water stress necessitates changing farm practices to suit the changing environment. Behavioural changes will also make a

Box 1.7. Cash from trash – financing mitigation and adaptation through decentralized solid waste management

Under a business-as-usual scenario, by 2020 GHG emissions due to urban garbage will increase by at least 25%, even as municipal governments find it more difficult to collect and dispose of solid wastes. At present, most local governments use end-of-pipe solutions, focusing on collecting and disposing of wastes once they have been generated. These are capital- and technology-intensive – and thus costly. Solving the problem of solid wastes requires a new approach that minimizes methane emissions, treats both organic and inorganic wastes as resources, minimizes transportation of waste and provides regular incomes and better working conditions for waste pickers.

ESCAP identified such an approach, initiated by Waste Concern, an NGO in Bangladesh, and adapted and tested it in Matale, Sri Lanka, and Quy Nhon, Viet Nam. Under this approach, decentralized treatment plants, covering 1,000-1,500 households and treating 3-4 tons of wastes per day, are built in the neighbourhoods they serve. Waste is collected daily using hand carts and motorcycle-powered carts. Households are trained to separate wastes at source. Waste is then brought to the treatment plant, where it is sorted again. Recyclable materials (10-20% of the waste) are sold to junk dealers, organic wastes (70-80%) are composted, and rejects (5-10%) are collected and taken to the dump every one or two weeks. Strict quality control ensures optimum quality of compost. At present, raw compost is sold, but in the future some compost will be enriched with nitrogen, phosphorous and potassium to make designer organic fertilizer tailored to the requirement of local farmers. Each plant is designed as a profit-making public-private partnership with three main streams of income: collection fees from the users, sale of recyclables and sale of designer organic fertilizer.

An aerobic process that does not produce methane, composting considerably reduces GHGs. Because this approach uses motorcycle carts and hand carts and treats solid wastes within the neighbourhood, it minimizes transportation-related GHGs and fuel costs for the local government. ESCAP estimates that up-scaling could eliminate 7.5 million tons of CO_2 (equivalent) per year.

The approach also contributes to adaptation. Organic designer fertilizer is more cost-effective and beneficial for farmers than chemical fertilizer. Unlike chemical fertilizer, organic fertilizer returns organic matter to the soil, replenishing it, increasing its fertility and reducing the chemical fertilizer needed. Organic fertilizer also enables the soil to better retain water, conserving water. Increasing soil fertility and conserving water are key adaptation strategies for Asia and the Pacific recommended by IPCC (2007).

This approach works best in small and medium-size towns (populations 50,000-100,000) that are surrounded by agricultural areas and where the opportunity cost of land is relatively low. Scaling-up can be financed by selling VERs and CERs. Combining the sale of VERs and CERs with the revenues from user charges, sale of recyclables and sale of organic designer fertilizer can bring in potential revenues of up to $37 billion per year. Instead of spending resources on waste, local governments can make cash from trash.

difference, particularly in choices of food, transport and recreation. Sea level rise and the resulting climatic hazards will require greater efforts in early warning, sea defence construction and architectural innovation. Public policy should be redesigned to suit changing needs in health, water resources, disaster management, coastal zone management and agriculture and food security.

Natural disasters will be a particular challenge for smaller towns and cities, which have concentrated populations and poor urban planning. Lacking basic environmental and disaster-management infrastructure and services, these places have much laxer enforce-

ment of building control measures than do larger cities. Almost 50% of the region's urban population lives in such towns and cities. The need is not for additional resources but for improved governance structures and institutions. Governments, for example, could work with local NGOs and community-based organizations to develop local disaster management plans. Lessons from Bangladesh could be useful for other countries of the region.

Governments in Asia and the Pacific are likely to face eco-refugees from their own countries and elsewhere in the region, seeking shelter against short-term and long-term environmental catastrophes. These refugees are likely to head to cities and towns, so governments need to plan for this influx both in the short term, by providing emergency assistance, and in the long term, by accommodating those who have lost their livelihoods in rural areas.

A regional food bank is one measure that countries can adopt for mutual assistance. Greater emphasis will also need to go to housing the poor in cities and towns. The Baan Mangkong Programme of Thailand and the Khuda-ki-basti approach in Pakistan may provide useful lessons.

NOTE

1. Following Kakwani and Pernia (2000), the pro-poor growth index was calculated by decomposing the total change in poverty into (i) The impact of growth when the distribution of income does not change (η_g: growth [income elasticity of poverty]); and (ii) The effect of income redistribution when total income does not change (η_i: inequality elasticity of poverty).

Suppose η is the proportional change in poverty when there is a positive growth rate of 1%, where $\eta = \eta_g + \eta_i$, η_g is the pure growth effect (always negative), and η_i is the inequality effect (negative or positive).

Then the degree of pro-poor growth can be measured by an index: $\phi = \dfrac{\eta}{\eta_g}$.

Growth will be pro-poor when $\phi > 1$, meaning that the poor benefit proportionally more than non-poor. When $0 < \phi < 1$, growth is not strictly pro-poor (trickle-down growth). If $\phi < 0$, economic growth increases poverty.

References

ABN AMRO India (2007). "Does sterilization cost affect monetary instrument choice?", *The Knowledge Series* (New Delhi).

Asian Development Bank (2006). "Measuring policy effectiveness in health and education", in *Key Indicators 2006* (Manila, ADB).

_____ (2007). *Key Indicators 2007,* vol. 38 (Manila, ADB).

Asis, M. (2008). "Looking into Pandora's Box: The social implications of international migration in Asia", Asian Population and Social Studies Series (Bangkok, UNESCAP).

Bloomberg News (2008). "Asia-Pacific bond risk increases to a record on Citigroup loss", 16 January 2008.

Bryant, J. (2005). "Children of international migration in Indonesia, the Philippines and Thailand: a review of evidence and policies", Innocenti Working Paper No. 2005-05 (Florence, UNICEF, Innocenti Research Centre).

_____ (forthcoming). "Children and international migration", *Situation Report on International Migration in East and Southeast Asia,* report prepared by the UN Regional Thematic Working Group on International Migration, Bangkok.

China Daily, (2007). "Measures taken to increase arable land", 8 August 2007.

Cruces, G. and T. Wodon (2003). "Transient and chronic poverty in turbulent times: Argentina 1995-2002", *Economics Bulletin,* vol. 9, No. 3, pp. 1-12.

Douglass, M. (2006). "Global householding – the missing dimensions of transnational migration research and policy in Pacific Asia", paper presented at the Ritsumeikan Asia Pacific Conference, "Global Movements in the Asia Pacific", Beppu, Japan, 17-18 November.

Eichengreen, B. and H. Tong (2005). *Is China's FDI Coming at the Expense of other Countries?,* National Bureau of Economic Research Working Paper 11335 (Cambridge, Mass., NBER).

ESCAP (2006a). *Enhancing Regional Cooperation in Infrastructure Development Including that Related to Disaster Management* (United Nations publication, Sales No. E.06.II.F.13).

_____ (2006b). *Key Economic Developments and Prospects in the Asia-Pacific Region 2006* (United Nations publication, Sales No. E.06.II.F.3).

_____ (forthcoming). *Future within Reach* (Bangkok, ESCAP).

Financial Times (2007). "India infrastructure: A tether that keeps potential in check", 8 May 2007.

Findlay, C. and A. Sidorenko (2005). "Services: Importance of further liberalization for business and economic development in the region", presented at the Conference on Delivering on the WTO Round: A High-Level Government-Business Dialogue, Macao, China, October 2005.

Hall, G. and H. Patrinos (2005). *Indigenous Peoples, Poverty and Human Development in Latin America: 1994-2004* (New York, World Bank).

Hill, D. (2007). "Brazil, China, India, Russia, and Taiwan lead S&E article output of non-OECD countries", *Science Resources Statistics InfoBrief,* National Science Foundation, September.

Hugo, G. (2002). "Effects of international migration on the family in Indonesia", *Asian and Pacific Migration Journal,* vol. 11, No. 1, pp. 13-46.

Humbeck, E. (1996). "The politics of cultural identity: Thai women in Germany", in M. Garc□a-Ramon and J. Monk (eds.), *Women of the European Union: The Politics of Work and Daily Life* (London, Routledge).

ICRISAT (International Crops Research Institute for the Semi-arid Tropics) (2007). *Pro-Poor Biofuels Outlook for Asia and Africa: ICRISAT's Perspective* Working Paper.

Intergovernmental Panel on Climate Change (IPCC) (2007). "Climate Change 2007: Mitigation", contribution of Working Group III to the Fourth Assessment Report of the Intergovernmental

Panel on Climate Change, <http://www.ipcc.ch/pdf/assessment-report/ar4/wg3/ar4-wg3-frontmatter.pdf>.

Jenkins, R. and C. Edwards (2005). *The Effect of China and India's Growth and Trade Liberalisation on Poverty in Africa* (London, Department for International Development, DCP 70, DFID).

_____ (2006). "The economic impacts of China and India on sub-Saharan Africa: Trends and prospects", *Journal of Asian Economics,* vol. 17, pp. 207-225.

Kakwani, N. and E. Pernia (2000). "What is pro-poor growth", *Asian Development Review,* vol. 18, No. 1.

Kakwani, N., S. Khandker and H. Son (2004). "Pro-poor growth: Concepts and measurement with country case studies" (International Poverty Centre, UNDP).

Kaplinsky, R. and M. Morris (2006). "The Asian drivers and SSA: MFA quota removal and the portents for African industrialization", paper presented for the Conference on Asian and Other Drivers, St. Petersburg, 18-19 January.

Karmali, N. (2006). "India's 'wind man' is blowing strong", Forbes.com, 14 June.

Kox, H. and H. K. Nordas (2007). "Services trade and domestic regulation", OECD Trade Policy Working Paper No. 49, TD/TC/WP(2006)20/Final.

Morgan Stanley Global Economic Forum (2007). "Supply response: new hurdles are emerging", 2 April 2007.

Lokshin, M. and M. Ravallion (2005). "Lasting local impacts of an economy-wide crisis" (Washington, D.C., World Bank).

Nedcap.org (2008). "Tariff structure", <http://www.nedcap.org/index_files/Page2490.htm>.

Newindpress.com (2007). "The year of the billionaire", 29 December.

OECD-FAO (2007). *Agricultural Outlook 2007-2016.*

Pasha, H. (2002). "Pro-poor policies" (United Nations).

Piper, N. (1999). "Labor migration, trafficking and international marriage: Female cross-border movements into Japan", *Asian Journal of Women's Studies,* vol. 5, No. 2, pp. 69-99.

Reisen, H. (2006). "China and India: What's in it for Africa?", paper presented for the Conference on Asian and Other Drivers, St. Petersburg, 18-19 January.

Research and Information System for Developing Countries (RIS)(2007). *Regional Cooperation for Infrastructure Development in Asia: Towards a Regional Special Purpose Vehicle for Public-Private Partnership* (New Delhi).

Reuters India (2007). "India pins biofuel hope on jatropha, output to rise", 30 August 2007.

Roth, J.-P. (2007). "Highly leveraged institutions and financial stability: A case for regulation?", Speech to the Swiss National Bank, 29 June.

Son, H. (2003). "A note on pro-poor growth" (Washington, D.C., World Bank).

Stern, N. (2006). "The economics of climate change", HM Treasury, Government of the United Kingdom.

Suzlon Energy (2008). *Suzlon Energy website,* <http://www.suzlon.com>, accessed 9 January.

The Economist (2007). "Home truths", 5 July 2007.

UNCTAD (2007). "Globalization for development: opportunities and challenges", report of the Secretary-General of UNCTAD (TD/413), 4 July.

UNDP (1999). *Human Development Report 1999* (New York, Oxford University Press).

UN-ENERGY (2007). *Sustainable Bioenergy: A Framework for Decision Makers* (United Nations).

United Nations Children's Fund (2007). *Children and Migration* (UNICEF), <http://www.gfmd-fmmd.org/en/system/files/CHILDREN+AND+MIGRATION.pdf>.

United Nations, Department of Economic and Social Affairs (2006). *Trends in Total Migrant Stock: The 2005 Revision* (New York, United Nations), <http://www.un.org/esa/population/publications/migration/UN_Migrant_Stock_Documentation_2005.pdf>.

World Bank (2003). *Viet Nam Development Report 2004,* World Bank Poverty Reduction and Economic Management Unit East Asia and Pacific Region Report No. 27130.

_____ (2007a). *The Cost of Pollution in China* (Washington, D.C., World Bank).

_____ (2007b). *East Asia & Pacific Update – 10 Years after the Crisis* (Washington, D.C., World Bank).

World Resource Institute (2007). *Climate Analysis Indicators Tool,* <http://cait.wri.org/cait.php?page= gases> (Washington, D.C., World Resources Institute).

WTO (2006). *International Trade Statistics 2006* (Geneva, WTO).

_____ (2007). *International Trade Statistics 2007* (Geneva, WTO).

CHAPTER 2. SUBREGIONAL PERFORMANCE AND MEDIUM-TERM CHALLENGES

Robust growth despite slowing exports

In 2007 the Asia-Pacific region continued its robust growth of the year before, despite a slowdown in export demand due to a slower growing United States (figure 2.1). Domestic demand was increasingly important for sustaining growth in most of the region: both investment and private consumption grew faster in 2007 than in 2006. Rising prices for oil and other commodities benefited some countries – the Russian Federation, Kazakhstan, the Islamic Republic of Iran and Papua New Guinea – even as they had an inflationary impact on others, such as China.

Although exports slowed in most countries, the Asia-Pacific region continued to receive large inflows of foreign exchange thanks to current account surpluses and capital inflows. Central banks intervened in the foreign exchange market, accumulating foreign exchange reserves, but most domestic currencies continued to appreciate. In some countries, particularly in South-East Asia, currency appreciation was large enough to dampen the inflationary effect of rising commodity prices. Indeed, most South-East Asian countries saw inflation decelerate – allowing central banks to cut interest rates and stimulate domestic demand.

East and North-East Asia grew at 9% in 2007, despite slower growth in the United States and sluggish performance in Japan and the European Union. Domestic demand, largely from investment and private consumption, proved effective in taking up the slack from slowing exports. And China's strong growth fuelled demand for exports from other East and North-East Asian countries. Should external-sector weakness exert a stronger effect on growth in 2008, the strong fiscal position of most governments in the subregion will create room for public spending.

Most countries in East and North-East Asia faced a growing inflation threat during 2007, chiefly because of rising international prices for food and oil. In 2007, China's inflation was the highest in 10 years. Inflation

Figure 2.1. Rates of economic growth in the ESCAP region, 2006-2007

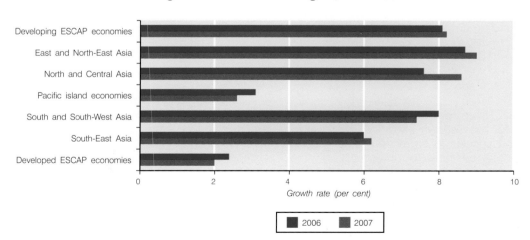

Sources: ESCAP, based on national sources; IMF, *International Financial Statistics* (CD-ROM) (Washington, D.C., September 2007); ADB, *Key Indicators of Developing Asian and Pacific Countries 2007* (Manila, 2007); website of the CIS Inter-State Statistical Committee, <www.cisstat.com> (18 December 2007 and 5 February 2008); and ESCAP estimates.

Notes: Data for 2007 are estimates. Developing ESCAP economies comprise 38 developing economies including the Central Asian countries and calculations are based on the weighted average of GDP figures at market prices in the United States dollars in 2004 (at 2000 prices).

there has also been stoked by a continuing injection of liquidity from the management of currency appreciation.

For the economies of North and Central Asia, 2007 marked another year of strong growth performance due to large external surpluses and increasing international reserves. As in other recent years, high oil and commodity prices were key. However, domestic demand was important in 2007, with retail turnover growing at double-digit rates on the back of higher remittances from migrants working in the Russian Federation and Kazakhstan. Robust economic expansion and surging hard currency inflows stoked strong money supply growth, which accelerated consumer price inflation in many North and Central Asian countries in 2007. Most countries in North and Central Asia, if not all, face two macroeconomic policy challenges in the short to medium term: to achieve durable and stable growth, and to improve fragile fiscal and current account positions.

> *Vanuatu and the Solomon Islands performed well, with growth rates around 5%*

Economic growth in the Pacific region was uneven in 2007. Papua New Guinea more than doubled its growth from 2.6% in 2006 to 6.2% in 2007, on the back of high petroleum and mineral prices. But civil unrest in Tonga in November 2006 and a coup d'etat in Fiji in December 2006, caused a decline in tourism to both countries during 2007, lowering their GDP growth. Palau, Vanuatu and the Solomon Islands performed well, with growth rates around 5%. Samoa, Tuvalu, Kiribati and the Marshall Islands grew at lower rates of between 1% and 3%.

South Asia's strong aggregate economic growth rate of 7.4% for 2007 was spearheaded by India, which grew by 9% and appears to be moving on to a new, high-growth phase as rates of investment in the economy rise sharply. Bangladesh, Pakistan and Sri Lanka continued their growth momentum and grew by more than 6.5% for the year. A sharp increase in domestic demand, particularly investment, is helping these countries to achieve high economic growth rates. Bhutan and Maldives maintained strong growth. Nepal was expected to pick up and grow at a higher rate following the cessation of hostilities among rival political groups, but the actual growth rate remained low at 2.5%, partly because of continued unrest in

some areas, and also because of low investment and adverse weather conditions that caused poor agricultural performance. The Islamic Republic of Iran, the only net oil exporter in the subregion, is expected to maintain robust economic growth at 5.8% due to rising oil prices.

Because of demand and supply pressures, inflation in most South Asian countries stayed high in 2007. Rising prices for oil and other commodities in international markets sustained those inflationary pressures. Food prices in general rose more rapidly than those of other items, imposing extra burdens on low- and fixed-income groups.

Strong domestic demand helped South-East Asia's economies continue their robust growth performance of 2006 into 2007. In all the South-East Asian countries with data available, except Thailand, domestic demand grew more rapidly in 2007 than in 2006. Investment accelerated most briskly in Indonesia, the Philippines and Singapore. In Indonesia, Cambodia, Singapore, and Malaysia, private consumption grew significantly more quickly in 2007 than in 2006. Strong domestic demand helped sustain South-East Asia's economic growth in the face of a weaker demand for exports from the United States and continued currency appreciation against the dollar.

> *All South-East Asian currencies, except the Indonesian rupiah, appreciated against the dollar in 2007*

All South-East Asian currencies, except the Indonesia rupiah, appreciated against the dollar in 2007 because of large foreign direct investment inflows and large surpluses in the current account, despite slowing exports. Central banks attempted to limit domestic currency appreciation by accumulating foreign exchange reserves. An increase in financial investments abroad, encouraged in some countries – such as Malaysia and Thailand – by regulatory changes, also contributed to limit exchange rate appreciation.

Among the developed economies of the region, Australia and New Zealand saw growth accelerating in 2007 compared to the previous year, while Japan grew at 1.8% down from 2.4% in 2006. Australia and New Zealand benefited from high commodity prices, while Japan's growth was largely attributable to export demand particularly from Asia. In all three countries, capacity constraints – in particular a tightening labour market – have become increasingly apparent. In Australia and New Zealand the increasing demand for labour pushed up wages, which supported household consumption while also putting inflationary pressure on production costs. These inflationary pressures remain a major concern, though strong currencies in both countries have cushioned the impact of high oil prices. In Japan the tight labour market has not been fully translated into wage growth. But increasing input prices and slow but steady wage increases have started to hurt business confidence, especially in small and medium-size enterprises.

East and North-East Asia: Growth supported by domestic demand and ties with China

The economies of East and North-East Asia faced two challenges in 2007, both emanating from abroad. The first challenge was a global economic slowdown mostly attributable to the United States – though growth was also sluggish in Japan and the European Union. This more difficult external environment noticeably affected the export performance of the subregion's outward-looking economies. The second challenge was a growing threat of inflation. Inflationary pressure spiked in most countries of the subregion, mainly because of rising international prices for two basic commodities: food and oil.

Countries across the subregion have withstood these twin challenges fairly well (figure 2.2), due to the growing importance of domestic demand and increasingly close trade links with China. While the overall exports of most economies have been hurt, robust growth has continued because domestic demand – largely from private investment and consumption – has proved an effective substitute. The continued strong demand for exports to China, where growth is strong, has considerably moderated the effect of slowing developed country markets. In all East and North-East Asian countries, exports to China have grown as a proportion of total exports. The strong fiscal position of most governments in the subregion (figure 2.3) also offers scope for public spending, should external sector weakness exert a stronger effect on growth performance in the coming year.

The enduring strength of China's economy continues to set records. Its growth rate accelerated in 2007 to 11.4%, the fastest for China in 13 years, despite the slowdown in the country's major export markets. Investment continues to be the main driver of growth, remaining resilient despite government cooling measures and with support from low real interest rates.

Private consumption in China also performed strongly, with urban wage growth boosting consumer confidence. Retail sales towards the end of the year were the strongest in a decade. Domestic consumption is likely to remain strong in 2008, as the government's "harmonious society" policy leads it to spend more on social welfare and as rural consumers increase their spending power. The external sector will likely weaken during the year ahead, as demand weakens, domestic costs rise, the export VAT rebate system is revised and the currency continues to

Figure 2.2. Contributions of agriculture, industry and services to GDP growth in selected East and North-East Asian economies, 2006-2007

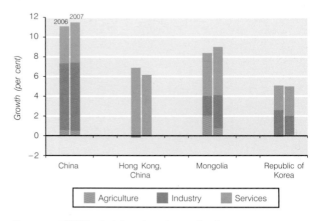

Source: ESCAP calculations based on national sources.

Note: Data for 2007 are estimates.

Figure 2.3. A strong fiscal position for most governments in the subregion: Budget balance in selected East and North-East Asian economies, 2006-2007

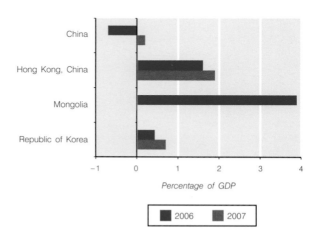

Sources: ESCAP calculations based on national sources; ADB, *Key Indicators of Developing Asian and Pacific Countries 2007* (Manila, 2007); IMF, *International Financial Statistics* (CD-ROM) (Washington, D.C., September 2007); and ESCAP estimates.

Notes: Data for 2007 are estimates. For Mongolia, budget balance includes grants.

appreciate. But resilient domestic demand will mostly mitigate the effects of a lower contribution from net exports.

Domestic demand fuelled growth

Strong domestic demand has enabled countries to overcome an increasingly difficult external environment. The highly export-dependent economy of Hong Kong, China, grew by 6.1%, with robust consumption and investment fuelled by lower interest rates (following lower United States rates under the territory's currency peg arrangement). Private consumption benefited from lower taxes and employment growth, while private investment was supported by high business confidence and large infrastructure projects. Growth in the Republic of Korea was stable in 2007 at 5%. Private consumption continued to grow steadily, having recovered strongly from the bursting of the household credit bubble in 2004. Consumer confidence was high, with household incomes rising – partly because of increased income from the rising stock market, and partly because unemployment in the Republic of Korea is at its lowest level since the Asian crisis of 1997.

> *Strong domestic demand has enabled countries to overcome an increasingly difficult external environment*

Growth in Taiwan Province of China increased in 2007, to 5.5%. Private consumption was an important driver of growth as unemployment fell and improved the health of the labour market. Firmer property prices and reduced political uncertainty also supported consumer confidence. Private investment also made a contribution, remaining robust due to healthy profits and continued economic expansion.

Mongolia's strong growth in 2007 was driven by strength in its mining sector. Growth in 2007 improved to 9.0%, with continued strong growth expected in the year ahead. The industrial sector has received strong inflows of foreign investment, particularly in mining – a result of the 2006 mining law. But the government still faces the need to clarify its approach to income from this potentially lucrative sector, as new investments are held up by uncertainty about the terms to be offered to investors. High growth in borrowing shows that business confidence is strong. The con-

struction sector has been boosted by government housing and infrastructure projects, as Mongolia attempts to use its strong finances to reduce its high poverty level.

Growth in Macao, China, has exploded as its gaming industry expands. Growth for 2007 stood at 30.1%, having increased rapidly during the year. Visitor arrivals were maintained as several major new gaming establishments opened, culminating in August with the inauguration of the territory's first mega-resort. Its retail sales have also grown strongly as it becomes a major shopping destination for mainland visitors. Investment has soared through major construction projects, both for gaming resorts and for transport infrastructure.

International commodity prices fuelled inflation

East and North-East Asia suffered in 2007 from the twin shocks of rising international oil and food prices, creating inflation pressures across all countries in the subregion (figure 2.4). Food prices rose in China, mainly for the staple goods of pork and eggs. Annual inflation in 2007 rose dramatically to 4.8% – the highest rate in 10 years and more than three times the 1.5% rate for 2006. Taiwan Province of China experienced increasing inflation in 2007, largely because of food and oil price increases. Inflation rose to 1.8% for the year – again, three times the 0.6% figure for 2006. And food prices in Hong Kong, China, exerted strong inflationary pressure towards the end of 2007, as produce from the mainland became more expensive. Wage growth also affected inflation over the course of the year, as did housing, the largest component of the territory's consumer price index.

> *East and North-East Asia suffered from the twin shocks of rising international oil and food prices*

Inflation in Mongolia rose to 9% for 2007 (up from 5.1% in 2006), primarily because of rising oil prices: oil-related increases in fuel, housing and utilities prices were the main driver of accelerated price increases. In the Republic of Korea, inflation accelerated in 2007 due to both rising global energy prices and strong domestic demand. Inflation rose to 2.6% for the year, driven by oil prices, rising utility bills and strong consumer spending.

Figure 2.4. Inflation and money supply growth (M2) in selected East and North-East Asian economies, 2004-2007

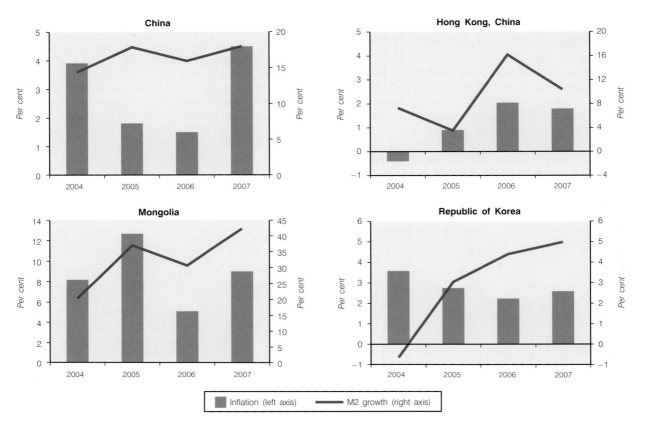

Sources: ESCAP, based on national sources; ADB, *Key Indicators of Developing Asian and Pacific Countries 2007* (Manila, 2007); IMF, *International Financial Statistics* (CD-ROM) (Washington, D.C., September 2007); and ESCAP estimates.

Notes: Data for 2007 are estimates. Inflation refers to changes in consumer price index. Money supply for 2007 refers to January-September for Mongolia.

The pace at which currencies appreciate in East and North-East Asian countries is influencing their inflation performance (figure 2.5). Weakness in the Hong Kong dollar (which is pegged to the United States dollar) is making imports more expensive in the territory. Similarly, fairly weak currency performance has contributed to import inflation in Taiwan Province of China. But inflation in the Republic of Korea remained under control as a result of the continued appreciation of the won.

Inflationary expectations in the Republic of Korea also remained low due to the strong policy stance of the country's central bank. Inflation for 2007 remained relatively moderate, within the bank's target range of 2.5 to 3%. The Bank of Korea has been aggressive in controlling inflationary pressures. In August 2007 its benchmark overnight interest rate reached 5%, its highest level in six years.

In China, inflation was stoked by a continued injection of liquidity from the management of currency appreciation. The money supply continued to expand strongly (see figure 2.4), fuelling asset price rises in the property and equity markets. The Shanghai A-Share index increased by more than 80%. Despite monetary policy tightening through interest rate increases, real interest rates on deposits remain negative. Interest rates were increased five times during the year, in September reaching a deposit rate of 3.87% and a lending rate of 7.29%.

The unattractiveness of bank deposits in China has drawn China's public to invest in the asset markets. To control high levels of bank lending during a time of fairly low interest rates, the government has tried various non-interest rate mechanisms such as reserve ratio increases for banks and reducing the spread between deposit and lending rates. Reserve ratios have been increased 10 times during the year, leading to the highest level, 14.5%, since the required reserves system was modified in 1998 (Hang Seng Bank, 2007). But the host of cooling measures still has not affected bank lending. How much China's economy overheats will depend on how effective these mechanisms prove. For China's government, interest-rate raises remain an unlikely main policy tool, given the risk of greater hot money inflows and the debt position of some state-owned enterprises.

China's growth cushioned export impact

China's continued strong market growth has supported exports from the subregion in the face of weak international markets. The current account for Hong Kong, China, remained buoyant (table 2.1) because of investment services for China and mainland tourist arrivals. With the continued liberalization of trade through the Closer Economic Partnership Agreement, the territory's economic ties to the mainland remain vital. The most recent round of measures (CEPA IV) will open up 11 new service areas to trade.

Exports from the Republic of Korea remained strong, as China's growth offset both domestic currency appreciation and weak demand from the United States. Another cushion has been the backlog in shipping

Figure 2.5. East and North-East Asian exchange rates against the United States dollar, 1996-2007

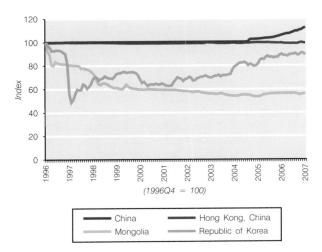

(1996Q4 = 100)

| —— China | —— Hong Kong, China |
| —— Mongolia | —— Republic of Korea |

Sources: IMF, *International Financial Statistics* (CD-ROM) (Washington, D.C., 2007); and *The Economist Databases.*

Note: Data for December 2007 are estimates.

industry orders, which surged in 2004, with exports likely to last for a number of years.

Exports from Taiwan Province of China to the United States and Japan were sluggish in 2007. But there was a strong increase in exports to China and Hong Kong, China, which expanded – to 40.7% – their share of total exports from Taiwan Province of China for the first 11 months of 2007 (Taiwan Headlines, 2007). Mongolia's export earnings were also supported in 2007 by buoyant demand from China (by far the country's major export market) as well as by strong copper prices.

> *Exports from the Republic of Korea remained strong, as China's growth offset both domestic currency appreciation and weak demand from the United States*

China itself experienced high export growth despite weakness in its main international markets. Growth in exports to the United States, China's second largest export market, fell steadily during 2007. But exports to the European Union took up much of the slack (Financial Times, 2007). Merchandise exports for Hong Kong, China – including re-exports from China – reflected the same trend, with growth in the European Union offsetting weakness in the United States. As export growth exceeded import growth, China's current account surplus widened.

The yuan has appreciated somewhat against the United States dollar. But depreciation against the euro

Table 2.1. Current account balance as a share of GDP in selected East and North-East Asian economies, 2004-2007

(Per cent)

	2004	2005	2006	2007
China	3.5	7.1	9.5	10.5
Hong Kong, China	9.5	11.4	10.8	11.1
Mongolia	3.9	4.0	11.4	11.1
Republic of Korea	4.1	1.9	0.7	0.7

Sources: ESCAP, based on national sources; ADB, *Key Indicators of Developing Asian and Pacific Countries 2007* (Manila, 2007); IMF, *International Financial Statistics* (CD-ROM) (Washington, D.C., September 2007); and ESCAP estimates.

Note: Data for 2007 are estimates.

is contributing to trade tensions with the European Union. Despite such concerns, it is not clear that China's currency management has been the major cause of its soaring trade surplus. The country's stellar productivity gains have done much to increase its competitiveness (Conference Board, 2007). And the government has actively tried to limit export growth – for example, by removing or reducing export rebates for many products. Growth in the surplus on the income account reflects China's rising earnings from foreign exchange reserves, as well as the income from rising outward FDI by Chinese enterprises.

Current account balances across the region were weighed down by the burden of high oil prices, which increased over the year. In Mongolia the price gains caused imports to rise: an effect amplified by government infrastructure projects and buoyant FDI. In Taiwan Province of China, rising imports – propelled, again, by the high oil prices and by strong domestic demand – squeezed the merchandise trade surplus. But the surplus on the income account remained higher thanks to repatriated profits and dividends from increasing outward FDI. Finally, high oil prices and strong domestic demand also ensured high merchandise imports to the Republic of Korea, where the services account balance remained negative in 2007 due to outbound tourism and royalty payments on overseas patents. But the income account stayed roughly neutral, as the outflow of profits from FDI was balanced by the rising stock of domestic residents' asset holdings abroad.

Medium-term prospects: coping with a marked United States slowdown

Should the United States economy slow down more than expected, countries in East and North-East Asia will not escape unharmed. In 2007, strong domestic demand helped the subregion weather the beginnings of a slowdown fairly well. But the evolving international outlook in 2008 will determine how well the subregion's economies can continue to cope.

Economies in the subregion are vulnerable because they remain highly export-dependent. Even though domestic demand can play a mitigating role in the short term, exports are still a high proportion of GDP in most East and North-East Asian countries. Sluggish export demand in the United States – a major market for all countries in the subregion – would significantly dampen subregional growth. No other country is expected to become a main export driver for the subregion during the year ahead. Its other chief export

markets, Japan and the European Union, are predicted to grow only sluggishly and will grow even more slowly in the event of a sharp United States slowdown. In Japan – where domestic demand has yet to recover – the export-dependent economy means that slowed United States consumption would further inhibit growth. Exports from the European Union will suffer from depressed United States demand and, more importantly, from any prolonged international credit crunch.

Inequality and poverty remain long-term challenges

Sterling growth performance across East and North-East Asia in 2007 masks the fact that most countries there are struggling to distribute the benefits of development. Inequality is a major challenge across most countries in the subregion (ADB, 2007). Governments seek policies that will spread growth more evenly across different population segments and across the different regions within countries.

> *Most countries are struggling to distribute the benefits of development*

Inequality in the higher-income economies stems from a skills gap among citizens. The Republic of Korea has seen rising inequality resulting from structural changes in the economy: the high-technology export sector has grown more important in recent years, widening the gap between skilled workers in the export manufacturing sector and less skilled domestic service workers (OECD, 2007a). Skills differences are also exacerbating inequality in Hong Kong, China, where the economy is increasingly service-driven. The territory's government is combating the skills gap by improving education to benefit less skilled workers. And in Macao, China, while the gaming industry provides jobs and fairly high wages for the young and talented, older workers face unemployment and lower wages in the non-gaming-related economy. The local government is seeking to respond by providing public housing and establishing a central provident fund.

Inequality in China stems from differences in economic and human development among its regions – particularly between rural and urban areas. In recent decades employment in China's export-led manufacturing industry has been highly concentrated in the country's coastal regions, prompting migration from rural and lagging areas to the coast. The result: unmanageable urbanization and a hollowing-out of the workforce in the rest of China. In response to this challenge the government has enacted regional development policies (see policy research feature 2.1). Other recent policies, such as the "new socialist countryside" policy of 2006, are directed specifically at the rural-urban gap.

Only Mongolia has seen a reduction in inequality over the past decade. But the country is confronted by a more basic problem: high poverty. Its recent strong growth performance has yet to significantly reduce the proportion of poor Mongolians. Growth is concentrated in the mining sector, which provides few employment opportunities. The government is trying to use new money from growing mining revenues to help the poor.

Policy research feature 2.1: China's "Go West" policy to reduce inequality among provinces – and its benefits for Asia-Pacific economies

China's income inequality is among the highest in the world, higher than all other Asian countries except Nepal in 2004 (ADB, 2007). A major part of China's income inequality is interprovincial inequality, mirrored by inequality in human development across economic and social indicators (World Bank, 2007a). Divisions are most pronounced between coastal and western provinces (figure 2.6).

In response, China introduced its western development strategy, "Go West", in 1999. Its priorities are infrastructure construction, environmental protection, industrial upgrading, human capital accumulation, science and technology research, and opening the provinces to foreign direct investment (FDI).

The Government has also enacted policies to reduce inequalities in the north-eastern provinces in 2003 and the central region in 2005. But the focus here is on the "Go West" policy, whose longer existence makes detecting the preliminary impact easier. The analysis compares the western provinces with the coastal provinces, generally regarded as China's most developed. The analysis focuses on 22 jurisdictions in 2006, the most recent year with data: the six western provinces of Gansu, Guizhou, Qinghai, Shaanxi, Sichuan and Yunnan; the five autonomous regions of Guangxi, Inner Mongolia, Ningxia, Tibet and Xinjiang; the municipality of Chongqing; and the 10 coastal provinces not covered by any regional development plan, Beijing, Tianjin, Hebei, Shanghai, Jiangsu, Zhejiang, Fujian, Shandong, Guangdong and Hainan.[1]

The picture is somewhat encouraging. In recent years, the gap in GDP per capita has shown some signs of closing. In 2005/2006, three-quarters of the western provinces experienced higher growth than the majority of coastal provinces. Rural income per capita, of the greatest concern given the rural-urban income divide, grew more than the majority of coastal provinces in

Figure 2.6. Wide inequality in human development among provinces

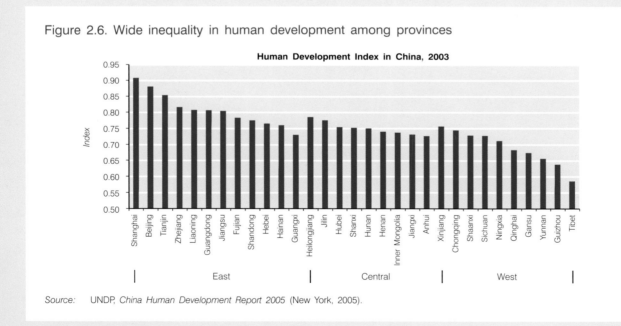

Human Development Index in China, 2003

Source: UNDP, *China Human Development Report 2005* (New York, 2005).

---

[1]   For simplicity, "province" is used in the rest of the feature to include provinces, autonomous regions and municipalities.

two western provinces. In 2006, government spending was higher in three-quarters of the western provinces than in the majority of coastal provinces. Fixed-asset investment grew relatively rapidly in three-quarters of the western provinces. Final consumption increased more in a quarter of the western provinces than in the majority of coastal provinces. Foreign direct investment, a focus of the "Go West" policy, increased substantially in a quarter of the provinces. Another focus, research and development spending, increased substantially in a third of provinces.

Some reduction in inequality in western provinces

There are preliminary signs of faster economic development in some western provinces than in coastal provinces. Average per capita GDP growth in 2005/2006 was higher in 8 out of 12 western provinces (Inner Mongolia, Chongqing, Guangxi, Sichuan, Shaanxi, Gansu, Qinghai and Guizhou) than in the majority of the 10 coastal provinces – narrowing the gap in income per capita (figure 2.7).

The narrowing income gap is evident in figure 2.8, which plots average province GDP per capita growth in 2005/2006 against average GDP per capita in 1998/1999. The downward-sloping trend line indicates convergence in the aggregate. Shanghai, with relatively low average income per capita growth in 2005/2006, supports the case for convergence. Guizhou does not. The province had the lowest average income per capita in 1998/1999 and did not exhibit relatively fast growth in 2005/2006.

There are preliminary signs of faster economic development in some western provinces than in coastal provinces

But despite faster comparative growth for many provinces in the aggregate, there appears to have been limited reduction in rural inequality in poorer provinces. Even within poorer provinces, urban areas are generally better off than rural areas. Tibet and Inner Mongolia are the only provinces with increases in rural income per capita in 2005/2006 greater than in the majority of the coastal provinces (figure 2.9).

Government spending helping poorer provinces

Government spending, the main instrument of the "Go West" policy, is showing signs of going more to western provinces. Data for 2006 show higher provincial government spending growth, as compared to the majority of coastal provinces, in 7 of the 12 western provinces (Xinjiang, Shaanxi, Qinghai, Sichuan, Gansu, Chongqing and Ningxia) than in the majority of coastal provinces (figure 2.10).

Provincial governments are responsible for most spending on health, education and welfare and some

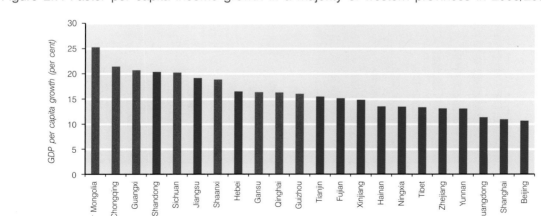

Figure 2.7. Faster per capita income growth in a majority of western provinces in 2005/2006

Sources: National Bureau of Statistics of China, *China Statistical Yearbook 2006* (China Statistics Press, 2006); and CEIC Data Company Ltd.

spending on infrastructure, making trends in central government transfers to provinces important – especially after China's 1994 tax sharing reform re-centralized revenues with the central Government but left expenditure responsibilities with local authorities. Central government direct spending on the provinces is largely on infrastructure.

Transfer funds for poorer regions, while growing rapidly, are lagging behind those for richer regions

Due to the country's method of fiscal decentralization, funds for poorer regions, while growing rapidly, are lagging behind those for richer regions. Analysis of absolute levels of central government transfers in 2004 shows a limited degree of relationship between transfers and the affluence of provinces (Shah and Shen, 2006). The lack of a stronger link between central government transfers and regional development is due to a relatively high proportion of transfers going to provinces as tax-related revenue sharing and tax rebates, which are regressive because richer provinces are returned more money. Progressive transfers to the regions have come mainly from equalization transfers and ad-hoc transfers, with ad-hoc transfers or "earmarked grants" accounting for the largest share.

Figure 2.8. The income gap is narrowing faster in the lowest income provinces

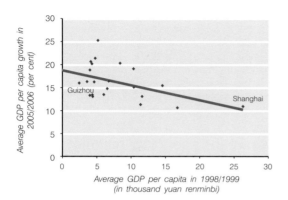

Sources: National Bureau of Statistics of China, *China Statistical Yearbook 2006* (China Statistics Press, 2006); and CEIC Data Company Ltd.

Figure 2.9. Rural income gap narrowing for a few western provinces

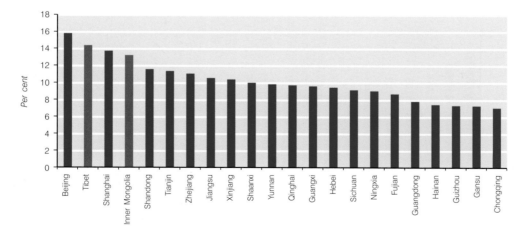

Sources: National Bureau of Statistics of China, *China Statistical Yearbook 2006* (China Statistics Press, 2006); and CEIC Data Company Ltd.

Figure 2.10. Government spending went more to poorer provinces in 2006

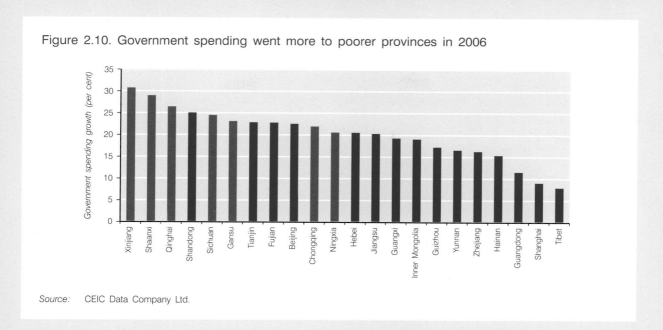

Source: CEIC Data Company Ltd.

These transfers are program-based and include funding for infrastructure construction and for assisting lagging regions.

Infrastructure investment, one focus of central government spending in the western provinces, is growing relatively quickly in many provinces. Provincial data for fixed-asset investment reflects a narrowing investment gap with coastal provinces in all provinces except Ningxia, Xinjiang and Gansu in 2006 (figure 2.11). On final consumption, three western provinces – Xinjiang, Inner Mongolia and Qinghai – grew more rapidly than the majority of coastal provinces (figure 2.12).

Research and development spending, another focus of the "Go West" policy, has grown more rapidly in 4 of the 12 western provinces (Ningxia, Tibet, Inner Mongolia and Xinjiang) than in the majority of coastal provinces (figure 2.13).

Particularly notable has been a more rapid rise in exports in most western provinces than in coastal provinces, albeit from a far lower base. Nine western provinces had an above-median increase in exports in 2006: Tibet, Qinghai, Gansu, Xinjiang, Sichuan, Ningxia, Guangxi, Chongqing and Yunnan (figure 2.14).

There has been modest improvement in FDI in western provinces, another objective of the "Go West" policy. Although the scale of the inequality in FDI inflows between the richest and poorest provinces remains enormous, there are signs of a rapid recent increase in FDI in Sichuan, Inner Mongolia and Shaanxi (figure 2.15).

Asia-Pacific countries benefit from trade with China's western provinces

The development of China's western provinces offers a comparative case study for other Asia-Pacific regional development policies (see box 2.1) as well as directly benefiting neighbouring countries. A particularly encouraging trend for China's neighbours is the relatively rapid export growth seen in many western provinces. The Government is encouraging this trend through extensive infrastructure projects to improve cross-border transportation.

A particularly encouraging trend for China's neighbours is the relatively rapid export growth seen in many western provinces

Sharing borders with Afghanistan, Kazakhstan, Kyrgyzstan, Mongolia, India, Pakistan, the Russian Federation and Tajikistan, Xinjiang is becoming China's gateway to Central Asia. The province's total trade with Central Asia has tripled since 2002, reaching a record $9 billion in 2006 (China View, 2007a). Most of Xinjiang's trade is with Kazakhstan, followed by Kyrgyzstan and Pakistan. The province exports its own products and is a conduit for products from the rest of the country.

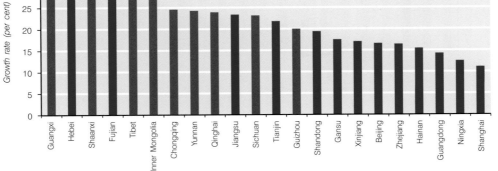

Figure 2.11. Fixed-asset investment is increasing quickly in many provinces

Source: CEIC Data Company Ltd.

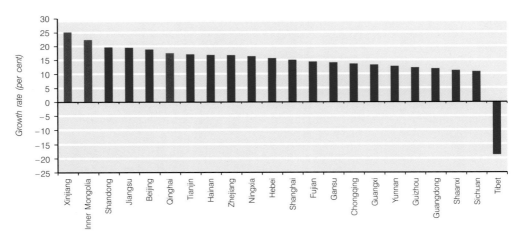

Figure 2.12. Final consumption growth is fast in a few provinces

Source: CEIC Data Company Ltd.

Figure 2.13. Research and development is growing faster in a few provinces

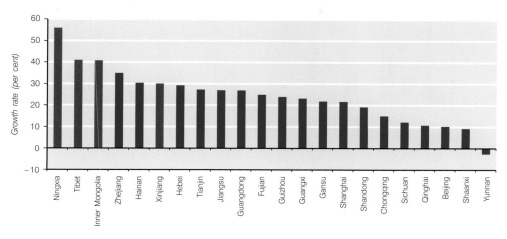

Source: CEIC Data Company Ltd.

Figure 2.14. Exports are growing rapidly in most provinces

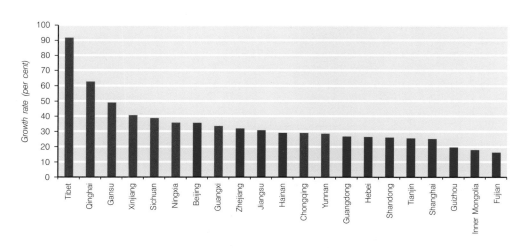

Source: CEIC Data Company Ltd.

Figure 2.15. FDI is increasing markedly in a few provinces

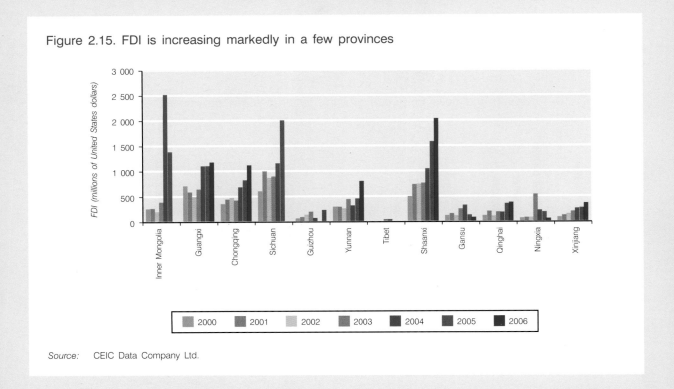

Source: CEIC Data Company Ltd.

Tibet, which borders India, Myanmar and Nepal, has also experienced rapid growth in trade with neighbouring countries. Trade grew by 60% in 2006 to reach $222 million (China View, 2007b). Trade with India is forecast to grow with the opening of border trade in 2007, and Tibetan goods can now reach the Indian port of Kolkata, four times closer than the closest port in China, more than 4,000 kilometers away in Tianjin.

Guangxi is rapidly boosting its cross-border trade with Viet Nam, currently Guangxi's largest trade partner. Trade grew by nearly 50% in 2006 to $1.8 billion, four times larger than in 2000. In 2006, trade with Viet Nam accounted for 80% of Guangxi's import-export turnover. Machinery and electrical appliances have been the major exports for Guangxi. Imports have been mainly raw materials and commodities, such as minerals, fruit, rubber, starch and cooking oil.

Yunnan has developed extensive trade links with its southwestern neighbours, the Lao People's Democratic Republic, Myanmar and Viet Nam, all of them members of ASEAN. Yunnan's ties with Viet Nam are expanding rapidly, with $500 million in trade in 2006 (Viet Nam, 2007). Myanmar has been the largest trading partner of Yunnan in recent years. Half of China's trade with Myanmar, nearly $700 million in 2006, passes through Yunnan (China View, 2007c).

Mongolia and the Russian Federation have rapidly increased trade with neighbouring Inner Mongolia. In 2006, Inner Mongolia's trade rose by 58% with Mongolia and by 31% with the Russian Federation (China.org.cn, 2007). Inner Mongolia now accounts for 40% of China's trade with Mongolia, with trade worth $580 million in 2006.

Development in China's western provinces ties in closely to similar initiatives in neighbouring countries to encourage development in lagging border regions through cross-country trading ties. India is promoting trade for its north-eastern states, which border Myanmar and Bangladesh and are close to Yunnan, China. As in China, a primary tool is infrastructure development. Plans have been outlined for a range of cross-country road and rail links passing through the north-eastern states.

Viet Nam is also trying to reduce interprovincial inequality, and increased ties with Guangxi are part of the country's strategy to develop its mountainous northern provinces. Viet Nam has also targeted infrastructure development as key to cross-border trade. Plans are under way for further improvement in road and rail links, both to connect to other parts of Viet Nam and for onward transport to other ASEAN countries.

Box 2.1. Regional development strategies elsewhere in Asia and the Pacific

As in China, many of the largest economies in Asia and the Pacific are grappling with regional inequality following rapid development. The characteristics of that inequality and the policy solutions pursued by governments, however, differ.

Economic liberalization in the Russian Federation, as in China, has resulted in uneven development within the country in response to business opportunities. Growth at the provincial level has been concentrated in a few locations – Moscow, Saint Petersburg and parts of the Urals and Siberia – in line with the development of the finance and energy sectors (Galbraith, Krytynskaia and Wang, 2004). Provinces that are primarily agricultural or industrial are in relative decline, with the growth gap particularly stark for southern regions.

As in China, the Russian Federation has instituted a far-reaching programme of financial transfers to lagging regions. The equalization effect is considerable: 70 regions of 88 receive net subsidies from the centre. Federal transfers to the regions rose to about a third of federal spending in 2005, up from 9 per cent in 1999 (Petrov, 2006). The central Government is striving to improve business opportunities in poorer regions by creating growth clusters and improving transport infrastructure.

The nature of the inequalities in India differs from that in China. While in China the division is between coastal and inland provinces, in India the gap is widest between southern and western states, on one hand, and northern states, on the other. Growth in India, dominated by services exports, has resulted in state-level development being tied to population skills, disadvantaging the north. The economy of China, in contrast, is led by manufactured exports, which ties provincial growth to the availability of transport linkages.

During India's reform, investment licensing was eliminated, and the Government lost control over the location of private investment, which then flowed to states with more skilled workers, good infrastructure and communications, and good governance. As in the Chinese experience, FDI and private corporate investment have been skewed towards a few states. The central Government has thus tried to improve state-level development resources through tax sharing and transfers from the centre. The country's effort to reduce its fiscal deficit at the central and state levels will, however, continue to hamper attempts to boost resources for lagging regions.

In Indonesia, poverty and inequality vary widely between the western provinces and the poorer eastern provinces. As in China, inequality in provincial income growth was driven by the geographic focus of export-led industrialization, concentrated in Java.

Indonesia recently embarked on a far-reaching system of fiscal decentralization. Under the new system, devolution of powers to local governments is accompanied by transfers of significant resources to poorer regions through the General Allocation Fund (Dana Alokasi Umum, or DAU). The fiscal transfer system has been highly redistributive. For example, the DAU increased by 64 per cent in 2006, with some of the poorest provinces, such as Aceh, Papua and Maluku, receiving more than 100 per cent increases in their allocation over the previous year (World Bank, 2007b).

As countries across the region face the common challenge of devising the appropriate mix of policies and financial resources to address spatial inequality, a cautionary note is that transfers to regional governments, while appearing highly equalizing, may not always be effective, as responsibility for long-term regional policies, such as infrastructure investment, may continue to lie with the central Government.

North and Central Asia: Among the most dynamic in the region

Most economies in North and Central Asia are expected to have expanded at double-digit rates in 2007 (figure 2.16). Azerbaijan's growth – at 25.0% of GDP in 2007 – remains among the most rapid in the world. Armenia's GDP grew by 13.8% in 2007.

The construction, agriculture and services sectors contributed most to GDP growth in Armenia and Azerbaijan. Growth in construction was strong, thanks to new investment in industrial production and to a boom in office and residential development. Kazakhstan's GDP grew by 9.7% in the first nine

Figure 2.16. Rapid growth in North and Central Asia: Real GDP and sectoral growth in North and Central Asian economies, 2006-2007

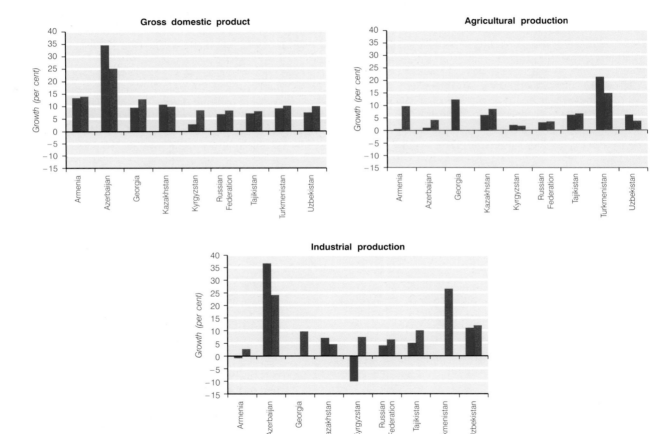

Sources: ESCAP, based on CISSTAT, *Database Statistics of the CIS* (Moscow, 2007 and 2008); and ESCAP estimates.

Notes: Growth rates for 2007 are estimates. GDP growth data for 2007 for Georgia, Kazakhstan and Uzbekistan refer to January-September. Agricultural production growth for 2007 for Turkmenistan refers to January-June while agricultural growth for Uzbekistan refers to January-September. Industrial growth rates for 2007 for Turkmenistan and Uzbekistan refer to January-October and January-September respectively while industrial growth for Georgia refers to January-June.

months of 2007, with a good wheat harvest at more than 20 million tons in 2007 – 3 million tons more than in 2006. And Kazakhstan's retail trade grew by 10.0% in 2007, as domestic demand advanced swiftly despite banking sector problems. The GDP of Turkmenistan is expected to grow by 10.0% in 2007 because of increased hydrocarbons production.

Economic growth remains impressive despite rising inflation

Domestic demand helped to speed GDP growth in the Russian Federation and Tajikistan. The GDP of the Russian Federation grew by 8.1% in 2007, mainly because of strong domestic demand and investment in construction. Household demand rose by 15.2%, and fixed investment by 21.1% in 2007. Tajikistan's GDP grew by 7.8% in 2007, with 9.9% growth in industrial production and 6.5% growth in agricultural output. Fuelled by rising household incomes and remittances, Tajikistan's retail trade grew by 5.2% in 2007.

The industrial sector was the main contributor to strong economic growth in Georgia, Kyrgyzstan and Uzbekistan in 2007. Georgia's GDP grew by 12.7% in the first nine month of the year, thanks to growth in industry and transportation services. But the financial and banking sectors were also major contributors to GDP growth in Georgia. In Kyrgyzstan industrial production grew by 7.3% in 2007. Both utilities and manufacturing showed strong growth. Along with a growing services sector and rising remittance inflows, Kyrgyzstan's expanding industrial output helped to fuel an 8.2% rate of growth in the country's GDP in 2007. Uzbekistan increased its industrial output by 11.9% in the first nine months of 2007. During the same period the country's GDP grew by 9.8% – the highest rate since the beginning of the 1990s – while agricultural production increased by 3.5% in 2007.

Surging food prices accelerated consumer price inflation

In 2007 all North and Central Asian countries experienced the highest inflation rates seen in recent years. Consumer prices rose by double digits in Azerbaijan, Kazakhstan, Kyrgyzstan, Tajikistan and Uzbekistan in 2007 (figure 2.17). In the subregion's many oil- and gas-producing countries, the rise in consumer price inflation can be traced partly to increasing government

expenditures and high inflows of foreign exchange from commodity exports. Other factors include rising prices for food, services and utilities.

Consumer price inflation was expected to rise in Tajikistan from 11.9% in 2006 to 21.5% in 2007, in Azerbaijan from 8.3% in 2006 to 16.7% in 2007. Tajikistan's especially high annual inflation was expected to exceed the government's target due to rising prices for imported gas, food and electricity. In Kazakhstan, annual consumer inflation was expected to rise from 8.6% in 2006 to 10.8% in 2007.

Consumer inflation in Georgia, after peaking at 9.2% in 2006, fell to 8.8% in the first 10 months of 2007. But rising gas prices and transportation costs could drive up the inflation rate to more than 9% by the end of the year. In Kyrgyzstan a surge in food prices raised the inflation rate from 5.6% for 2006 to 10.2% in 2007. Remittance flows into the country created additional inflationary pressure. In Armenia high import prices and rapidly expanding monetary aggregates helped raise inflation from 2.9% in 2006 to 4.4% in 2007.

In the Russian Federation, despite increasing food prices, inflation was expected to decelerate from 9.7% in 2006 to 9.0% in 2007. The government introduced price controls on foodstuffs in October 2007, both to lower food costs and to keep inflation in check.

Figure 2.17. Rapid inflation across North and Central Asia, 2006-2007

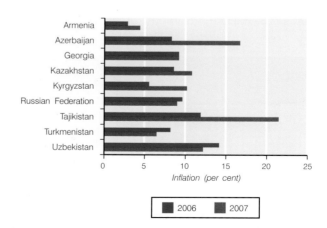

Sources: ESCAP, based on CISSTAT, *Database Statistics of the CIS* (Moscow, 2007 and 2008); and ESCAP estimates.

Notes: Inflation rates for 2007 are estimates. Inflation rates refer to percentage changes in the consumer price index.

High global commodity prices caused exports earnings to surge

Azerbaijan, Kazakhstan, the Russian Federation, Turkmenistan and Uzbekistan owed their substantial foreign trade surpluses for 2007 to rising volumes of oil and gas exports and high global hydrocarbon prices. These increased trade surpluses are expected to yield large current-account surpluses for 2007 (tables 2.2 and 2.3).

Azerbaijan ran a $408.4 million trade surplus in the first nine months of 2007 – lower than its $1.1 billion surplus for the first nine months of 2006, but still substantial. Oil and refined petroleum products accounted for the largest share of export earnings. Export revenue from non-oil sectors grew by about 11% in the first eight months of 2007. Merchandise imports rose in the first nine months of 2007 by 46.7% to $3.9 billion. Among the largest imports were food products and capital goods such as machinery, metals and transport equipment. Countries within the Commonwealth of

Table 2.2. External accounts in North and Central Asia, selected economies, 2006-2007

(Per cent)

	Exports (share of GDP)		Imports[a] (share of GDP)		Current account balance (share of GDP)	
	2006	2007	2006	2007	2006	2007
Armenia	15.9	11.3	30.0	25.9	−1.4	−2.5
Azerbaijan	65.6	67.2	26.5	20.0	18.6	25.7
Georgia	21.6	21.7	47.9	53.7	−16.1	−15.7
Kazakhstan	48.2	43.7	30.0	29.4	−2.2	−3.6
Kyrgyzstan	29.0	30.6	64.0	73.8	−14.8	−21.3
Russian Federation	30.9	28.2	16.7	17.8	9.7	6.3
Tajikistan	54.0	51.1	69.8	69.3	−2.9	−11.6
Turkmenistan	76.1	76.4	53.4	47.9	15.3	12.4
Uzbekistan	37.3	36.8	24.7	25.2	18.8	16.1

Sources: CISSTAT, *Database Statistics of the CIS* (Moscow, 2007); EIU, *Country Reports* (London, 2007), various issues; IMF, *International Financial Statistics* (CD-ROM) (Washington, D.C., September 2007), and *World Economic Outlook Databases* (Washington, D.C., 2007); and ESCAP estimates.

Notes: Data for 2007 are estimates.

[a] Import value in free on board.

Table 2.3. Export and import growth in North and Central Asia, selected economies, 2005-2007

(Per cent)

	Exports			Imports		
	2005	2006	2007	2005	2006	2007
Armenia	36.2	1.1	9.1	33.2	21.6	1.9
Azerbaijan	104.4	46.6	23.2	21.4	25.0	46.7
Georgia	34.8	14.8	26.5	33.8	47.8	39.4
Kazakhstan	37.4	37.3	22.9	30.1	36.5	45.2
Kyrgyzstan	33.3	18.2	38.6	98.7	56.0	50.3
Russian Federation	32.9	24.8	9.8	28.7	39.5	48.1
Tajikistan	15.9	53.9	8.9	97.0	29.5	35.5
Turkmenistan[a]	27.6	16.9	22.3	9.6	11.5	9.0
Uzbekistan[a]	11.6	19.6	16.5	8.1	13.9	20.4

Sources: CISSTAT, *Database Statistics of the CIS* (Moscow, 2007); and EIU, *Country Reports* (London, 2007), various issues.

Notes: All figures refer to January-September except in the cases of Turkmenistan and Uzbekistan, for which figures are whole year estimates.

[a] Import value in free on board.

Independent States (CIS) became Azerbaijan's main export partners in 2007 as it increased its exports to Georgia and the Russian Federation.

Kazakhstan recorded a $10.1 billion merchandise trade surplus in the first nine months of 2007 (compare with $11.9 billion for 2006). The surplus on trade in goods is expected to grow further in 2008-2009, to $16 billion, as a result of rising oil prices and growth in oil export volumes.

High oil prices sustained trade surplus

The foreign trade surplus of the Russian Federation was expected to exceed $100 billion in 2007. Its export volume rose by 9.8% in the first nine months of the year, to $242.8 billion. During the same period its expenditures on imports shot up by 48.1%, to $136.8 billion.

Turkmenistan was expected to record a trade surplus of $2.23 billion in 2007 thanks to high prices for its main export commodities, oil and gas. Export earnings were estimated to have grown by 22.3% in 2007, merchandise imports by 9.0%. Similar to Azerbaijan, capital goods accounted for 60-75% of Turkmenistan's total merchandise imports.

Uzbekistan was expected to record a trade surplus in 2007 because of high commodity prices and import controls. Export earnings were estimated to have grown by 16.5% in 2007, with increased exports of gas and cars to the Russian Federation and rising revenue from cotton fibre sales. Merchandise imports were expected to grow by 20.4% in 2007. Again, the growth in import spending remained high as capital goods, machinery and equipment were needed for large projects in the country's industrial sector.

Other North and Central Asian economies continued to have trade deficits in 2007, some showing slight increases over the corresponding figures for 2006 due to falling exports and rapidly rising imports. For example, weakened growth in Tajikistan's main export item, aluminium, kept export revenues down to $1.1 billion in the first nine months of 2007 – a growth rate of 8.9% (compared with 53.9% in 2006). Meanwhile its import expenditures rose by 35.5%, to $1.67 billion, chiefly because of higher fuel prices, strong domestic

demand and large infrastructure projects. The result: Tajikistan's merchandise trade deficit widened in the first nine months of 2007 to $577.5 million, or more than two and a half times its $214.6 million deficit for the same period in 2006.

Considerable remittances and FDI contributed to growth

Georgia's narrow export base and increasing merchandise imports caused its trade deficit to rise from $1.9 billion in 2006 to $2.7 billion in the first nine months of 2007. Export revenue grew by 26.5%, to $884.6 million, in the first nine months of 2007. But import expenditure grew in the same period by 39.4%, reaching $3.6 billion, propelled by rising prices for the economy's main import categories: gas, crude oil and petroleum.

Despite a 9.1% increase in Armenia's merchandise exports, the country's trade deficit widened considerably from $826 million in 2006 to almost $1.4 billion in the first nine months of 2007. Imports of mineral products, machinery and equipment for construction projects caused merchandise imports to rise by 1.9% during this period, to $2.2 billion.

In the first nine months of 2007, Kyrgyzstan showed a 38.6% increase in export earnings against a 50.3% rise in import expenditure, and the country narrowed its trade deficit to $860 million from $1.1 billion in 2006. But Kyrgyzstan's narrow export base and higher import prices for consumer and investment goods left it vulnerable to changes in the external economic environment.

Remittances had a significant macroeconomic impact

Remittances from migrants and temporary workers abroad have become a major source of money for Central Asia's economic development. Remittances to Armenia reached $424 million in the first half of 2007, accounting for 15% of the country's GDP, and were expected to grow to $1.35 billion by the end of the year. Remittances to Georgia grew by 57.5% in the first nine months of 2007, chiefly from migrants working in the Russian Federation. Remittance flows from the Russian Federation and Kazakhstan also benefited Kyrgyzstan, Tajikistan and Uzbekistan in 2007.

Foreign direct investment continued to help economies develop and modernize

FDI inflows continued to play a key role in developing and modernizing the economies of North and Central Asia in 2007. In the Russian Federation, with its strong market opportunities, FDI in the first half of 2007 reached $25 billion. FDI inflows in Uzbekistan doubled in the first nine months of 2007, after a new agreement was reached with the General Motors Corporation to build cars in that country. More than half of Georgia's FDI went to its banking, tourism and manufacturing sectors. Armenia's FDI inflows grew in the first half of 2007 by 33.0%, reaching $148 million. Most of the new foreign investment was directed towards financing the country's current-account deficit.

Foreign investment in Azerbaijan declined from $2.4 billion in the first six months of 2006 to $2 billion in the first half of 2007, as construction projects in the oil and gas sectors were completed. But these sectors continued to receive large FDI inflows. FDI in Tajikistan rose to $33 million in the first quarter of 2007 – still a low figure compared with those for other Central Asian countries.

High commodity prices and tax reforms stabilized some countries' fiscal positions

Budget revenues for oil- and gas-producing countries benefited in 2007 from high commodity prices. Energy-related earnings continued to buttress the Russian Federation's solid budget performance. Its federal budget surplus is expected to account for 3.0% of GDP in 2007.

In addition, many North and Central Asian economies continued to improve revenue collection and tax administration in 2007, stabilizing their fiscal positions. For example, when unexpectedly high revenues from oil export volumes brought Azerbaijan's state budget a surplus equal to 4% of GDP in the first eight months of 2007, taxes on corporate profits in construction and communications ensured that the rising prices resulted in higher government revenues. Azerbaijan's budget was expected, though, to revert to a deficit of 2% of GDP by the end of 2007, after increases to the minimum wage and to public sector salaries.

Georgia's budget deficit, caused by social welfare obligations, was expected to shrink in 2007 (from the 2.8% of GDP recorded for 2006) as the government

tried to reduce poverty and unemployment by tightening its fiscal policy – one of its main budget priorities for 2007. When the Government of Kyrgyzstan similarly tightened its fiscal policy in response to the 2007 surge in consumer price inflation, its budget deficit target for the year was revised down from 3.1% to 2.5% of GDP.

Kazakhstan was expected to have a small deficit in 2007 (0.8% of GDP) after increases to public sector wages, agricultural subsidies and government spending on regional development. Uzbekistan's 2007 budget performance was strong and its budget deficit was modest, thanks to high commodity prices (especially for gold and cotton).

Although countries in the subregion continued to reform their tax policies, working to ease tax burdens and to make tax structures conform better to a market-based system, the pace of such reforms slackened in 2007 and progress was uneven. Tajikistan was expected to have a budget deficit of 4.2% of GDP for the year because of the country's narrow tax base and its increased spending on health and education. To finance the deficit, the government has continued to depend (despite ongoing tax reforms) on external borrowing, international grants and credit from multilateral agencies.

Tax collection remained a serious problem in Armenia. After the government raised spending on social programmes, the state budget deficit for 2007 was expected to equal 1.5% of GDP – an amount to be covered by international financial institutions and government securities.

Higher remittances and foreign direct investment meant stronger currencies

The economies of North and Central Asia in 2007 had two key monetary policy targets: to curb rising inflation and to prevent excessive real exchange rate appreciation. Governments tightened their monetary policy by increasing bank and government deposits, and by periodically raising the benchmark interest rates and refinancing rates of the central banks.

The Central Bank of Armenia raised its refinancing rate to 5% and increased the use of domestic instruments, such as repo operations (sale-and-repurchase agreements), in 2007. To keep rising inflation under control, the national banks of Azerbaijan and Tajikistan raised their annual refinancing rates to 13%. But in these countries weak institutional capacity, low capitalization and an underdeveloped financial sector continued to constrain the use of sound monetary policy.

Georgia's monetary policy in 2007 was aimed at keeping inflation in the single digits and preventing real appreciation of the national currency, the lari. But an increase in FDI and remittance inflows led the lari's exchange rate to appreciate in both nominal and real terms in 2007 (figure 2.18). In both Kazakhstan and Uzbekistan massive foreign exchange inflows caused rapid growth in monetary aggregates. Uzbekistan's central bank continued to remove excess liquidity in 2007 as part of its drive to keep inflation in single digits. It resumed issuing bills, and it increased bank and government deposits, tightening monetary policy to slow expansion in the money supply – which is nonetheless expected to grow rapidly in 2008-2009, fuelled by higher commodity prices.

> *Kazakhstan was hit by the international liquidity crisis after a major growth in credit financed by foreign banks*

Kazakhstan was hit by the international liquidity crisis after a major growth in credit financed by foreign banks. The banking sector's liquidity problems drove up the people's demand for foreign currency. A growth of monetary aggregates, sparked by increased bank lending, in turn put upward pressure on prices. The government intervened quickly to stabilize the slowdown in banking sector credit growth, with a positive effect on prices. But tighter lending policies risked dampening growth in the non-oil economy, thereby jeopardizing the diversification targets identified in the government's published development strategy (Kazakhstan 2030). Growth in monetary aggregates was expected to slow in 2008 owing to increased reserve requirements for commercial banks.

The Russian Federation's monetary policy continued to focus on its exchange rate. A key policy issue for its central bank was to maintain a nominally stable rate of exchange for the ruble against a dual-currency basket, 55% of which would be United States dollars and 45% euros. But currency strengthening remained the best way to dampen inflation in the economy, and the inflationary pressures of 2007 forced the ruble to strengthen against its target basket in real effective terms. Meanwhile, as tighter global credit conditions sparked ongoing domestic liquidity concerns, the central bank cut its reserve requirements and expanded its refinancing operations to boost liquidity if needed.

Figure 2.18. Exchange rates against the United States dollar for selected North and Central Asian economies, 1996-2007

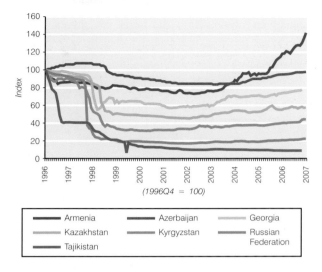

(1996Q4 = 100)

Armenia	Azerbaijan	Georgia
Kazakhstan	Kyrgyzstan	Russian Federation
Tajikistan		

Sources: IMF, *International Financial Statistics* (CD-ROM) (Washington, D.C., 2007); and *The Economist Database.*

Note: Data for 2007 are estimates.

In other North and Central Asian economies, national currencies were strengthened by large-scale foreign-exchange inflows and the weakening of the United States dollar on world markets. The Azerbaijan manat was stronger by 3% in real terms in November 2007 than it had been a year before. Kyrgyzstan's currency, the som, appreciated by almost 7% in the first eight months of 2007, reflecting robust remittance inflows and rising business activity in the country. In Tajikistan, continued growth in remittances from the Russian Federation and Kazakhstan allowed the somoni to remain stable in nominal terms against the United States dollar in the first half of 2007. Real appreciation of the national currency was a key concern for the National Bank of Tajikistan in 2007.

Sound monetary policy and continued tax reforms will maintain robust economic performance in 2008-2009

Food prices increased significantly throughout North and Central Asia in 2007, making sound monetary policy a main policy challenge for all countries in this subregion. The governments of Georgia and Tajikistan both faced the policy challenges of strengthening revenue collection and improving public expenditure policy. Georgia's government took measures to improve legislation and tax administration, to strengthen the financial, energy and health-care sectors and to implement privatization programmes. Tajikistan's state enterprises continued to run large tax arrears, which reached about $70 million in the first nine months of 2007. In Uzbekistan, the government sought to reinvigorate its privatization programme by undertaking preparatory measures to sell about 700 state-owned firms in the food, energy, chemical and automotive sectors. A new decree on privatization allowed the State to retain a 25% "golden share" in the privatized firms.

GDP growth in the economies of North and Central Asia in 2008-2009 will be closely linked to global commodity prices and to the economic performance of the subregion's largest investors and trading partners, such as the Russian Federation and Kazakhstan – the most important destinations for exports and migrants within the subregion. For example, increased investment in hydrocarbons and telecommunications from the Russian Federation and other Asian countries could push Uzbekistan's GDP up by about 7% in 2008-2009. High international prices for hydrocarbons should also drive economic growth in Azerbaijan, Kazakhstan, the Russian Federation and Turkmenistan.

> *Growth is expected to remain strong in 2008-2009*

Azerbaijan's GDP growth is expected to slow from an estimated 25% in 2007 and 2008 to about 10.5% in 2009 – still a vigorous rate, thanks to private consumption and investment spending. Kazakhstan 's growth is expected to slow from an estimated 9% in 2007 to 8.0% in 2009, with rising inflation and banking sector liquidity problems. Annual average consumer price inflation in Kazakhstan could decelerate to 8.0% in 2008 (from an estimated 10.8% in 2007), as demand-side pressures increase following public-sector wage hikes and rising social expenditures. Armenia's so-called second-generation reforms programme, intended to reduce poverty and ensure continued economic growth, envisages good governance and 9% GDP growth in 2008 and – in each of the next four years – an annual economic growth rate of at least 8%.

GDP growth is expected to slow to 6.5% in 2008-2009 in the Russian Federation, where tighter liquidity could dampen investment and consumption. In 2008, to improve budget planning and transparency, the government will begin operating on a three-year budget basis. Energy-related earnings will be separated from other revenue inflows. The federal budget surplus is expected to shrink in 2008-2009, with high growth in expenditure and a declining growth rate for energy earnings. High energy prices and fiscal loosening will prevent consumer price inflation in the Russian Federation from falling below 7.5% by the end of 2009. By that time, strong imports and moderate export growth could reduce the country's current account surplus.

Tajikistan's new country development strategy for 2008-2015 envisages balanced investment in energy, infrastructure and human development. To realize sustainable long-term gains, the government is expected to focus on ensuring external debt sustainability through a debt strategy with a manageable debt/GDP ratio as a ceiling, and through creating favourable private-sector development conditions that encourage both foreign investment and small and medium-sized enterprises. Two stated government priorities are gender equality (in both the public and private sectors) and a deepening of ongoing public administration reforms. Such reforms would ensure the delivery of basic services and offer aid donors the confidence they need to justify their financial support.

Kyrgyzstan has attained macroeconomic stability. Investment in its economy is growing. And its export potential is increasing. It has made the energy and transportation sectors priorities for increased foreign investment. Kyrgyzstan also has a new development strategy for economic reforms aimed at reducing poverty. The government will seek to reduce overall poverty from 41% to 30% over a three-year period. But it do this only with annual economic growth of 8% or 9% – and reduced gold exports are expected to lower Kyrgyzstan's GDP growth to 7% in 2008 and 4.5% in 2009.

Social reforms will present a central policy issue for North and Central Asian economies in 2008-2009. So far, such reforms have appeared to lag behind macroeconomic reforms. Although governments have taken many positive measures to channel the benefits of economic growth towards improved living standards, strategic investments are needed to reverse rising inequality and deterioration in the subregion's education and health-care systems (see policy research feature 2.2).

Policy research feature 2.2: Poverty, education and health challenges during economic transition in North and Central Asia

In the aftermath of the break-up of the former Union of Soviet Socialist Republics in 1991, the countries of North and Central Asia confronted new economic and social challenges, losing about half of their 1989 GDP. But since the mid-1990s, the achievements of transition have been considerable. By 2007, five economies of the subregion had grown beyond their 1989 GDP (figure 2.19), and the Russian Federation is expected to have done so by the end of 2007.

Economic improvements had a significant impact on poverty reduction

---

Achievements in education and health are impressive, with high literacy and high life expectancies. But the newly independent States of the former Soviet Union have grappled with complex social challenges. Compounding the collapse of the economic system were a deterioration in living conditions and sharply lower funding for social protection, education and health. No country was able to maintain the social infrastructure or the quality of education and health services inherited from the former Soviet Union.

Poverty's many dimensions in North and Central Asia

The transition to a market economy brought severe hardships for most people, and living standards collapsed in all of North and Central Asia. Over most of the 1990s, poverty sharply increased, the result of contracting GDP, galloping inflation, widening unemployment and falling real wages and incomes. Poverty incidence reached 62% in Azerbaijan (1995), 55% in Armenia (1998), 43.4% in Kazakhstan (1998), 64.1% in Kyrgyzstan (1999) and 83% in Tajikistan (1999).

As the economies of the North and Central Asia started to recover in the late 1990s, poverty came down. The proportion of people living below the national poverty

line fell to 29.3% in Azerbaijan (2005), to 34% in Armenia (2005), to 18.2% in Kazakhstan (2006), to 45.9% in Kyrgyzstan (2004), and to 64% in Tajikistan (2003). More impressive has been progress at reducing extreme poverty. In Kyrgyzstan, dollar-a-day poverty fell from 20.3% in 1996 to about 2% in 2003. In Tajikistan, it fell from 13.9% in 1999 to 7.4% in 2003.

Poverty is about more than income. Some social indicators in North and Central Asia remain impressive (table 2.4). Adult literacy rates are close to 100% in most countries. But life expectancy at birth decreased in Kazakhstan, the Russian Federation and Turkmenistan. The UNDP *Human Development Report 2007/2008* also shows declining human development for some North and Central Asian countries, the result

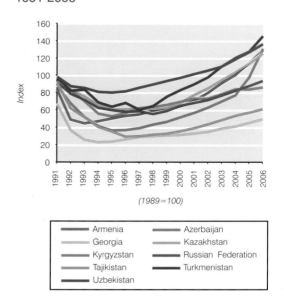

Figure 2.19. Turbulence during economic transition: Index of real GDP in North and Central Asian developing economies, 1991-2006

(1989=100)

Sources: ESCAP, based on website of the CIS Inter-State Statistical Committee, <www.cisstat.com> (28 November 2007); and ECE, *Economic Survey of Europe 2004,* No. 1 (United Nations publication, Sales No. E.04.II.E.7).

Table 2.4. Challenging times for human development in North and Central Asia

	Adult literacy rate (% ages 15 and above)	Life expectancy at birth (years)		Infant mortality rate (per 1 000 live births)		Human development index	
	2004	1990-1995	2000-2005	1990	2004	1992	2005
Armenia	99.4	68.7	71.4	52	29	0.739	0.775
Azerbaijan	98.8	65.6	66.9	84	75	0.696	0.746
Georgia	100.0	70.5	70.5	43	41	0.709	0.754
Kazakhstan	99.5	65.2	63.2	53	63	0.798	0.794
Kyrgyzstan	98.7	65.8	66.8	68	58	0.717	0.696
Russian Federation	99.5	66.8	65.4	23	17	0.849	0.802
Tajikistan	99.5	63.1	63.5	99	91	0.643	0.673
Turkmenistan	98.8	63.3	62.4	80	80	0.739	0.713
Uzbekistan	99.3	66.2	66.5	65	57	0.706	0.702

Sources: UNDP, *Human Development Report 2007/2008*; and ESCAP, *Economic and Social Survey of Asia and the Pacific 2007* (United Nations publication, Sales No. E.07.II.F.4).

of lower life expectancies and incomes. And though the region's economies continue to be classified as having medium human development, their rankings have fallen, with the Russian Federation ranked 67 of 177 countries, Kazakhstan 73, Uzbekistan 113 and Tajikistan 122 (UNDP, 2007).

Income inequality worsened in all of North and Central Asia after 1990, with initial improvements recorded only over 1996-1998. In Kyrgyzstan, the Gini coefficient (a measure of income inequality, with higher values denoting more unequal incomes) increased from 26.0 in 1988 to 40.5 in 1997. Only in 2003 did it come down to 30.3, still above the 1988 level. In Uzbekistan, the Gini coefficient rose from 25.0 in 1988 to 45.4 in 1998 before coming down to 36.7 in 2003. In the Russian Federation, the coefficient rose from 23.8 in 1988 to 46.2 in 1996 before dropping to 39.9 in 2002. If North and Central Asia is to make progress towards a full market economy, income inequality remains a major challenge.

Funding shortfalls in education

Since the transition to a market economy, education has been deprived of resources, and the standard of education has declined. In Armenia, spending on education was 6.6% of GDP in 1990, but by 2005 it plummeted below 3%. In Kazakhstan, spending fell from 3.9% of GDP in 1999 to 3.5% in 2005. In Azerbaijan, government spending on education fell to 2.7% of GDP in 2006 from 7.7% of GDP in 1990. In Kyrgyzstan, spending fell from 6.5% of GDP in 1995 to 3.5% in 2005. In Uzbekistan, spending dropped from 12% of GDP in 1992 to 6.3% in 2005. The Russian Federation is the exception. There, spending rose from

3.0% of GDP in 2000 to 3.7% in 2006. Significant attention was also given to teachers and academics, whose salaries had lagged behind the national average.

Funding shortfalls have led to a staffing crisis in most of North and Central Asia. The salaries of teachers were so low that many highly qualified teachers and university professors left the system for better paying jobs. Many school teachers in Central Asia supplemented their salaries by working in agriculture, raising animals or selling goods. Budget cuts have also reduced the funding for training teachers and purchasing textbooks.

Enrolment rates in pre-primary education have declined in all countries

The dramatic drop in education funding has made it difficult to maintain universal general education – and to meet the requirements of emerging market economies. From 1990 to 2005, enrolment rates in pre-primary education declined in all countries, and enrolment in basic education fell in Armenia and Turkmenistan. Upper secondary enrolment fell in Azerbaijan, Georgia, Kazakhstan, Kyrgyzstan, Tajikistan and Uzbekistan. During the same period, however, enrolment in higher education increased in most of North and Central Asia. Over 1990-2005, enrolment in universities increased from 18.7% to 44.7% in

Kazakhstan, from 12.9% to 37.2% in Kyrgyzstan, and from 24.6% to 47.2% in the Russian Federation.

The transition's challenges for health: funding and service quality

Post-independence economic conditions placed new demands on health systems – and revealed inefficiencies. In the mid-1990s, life expectancy dropped in all of North and Central Asia. Most economies ultimately recovered, but from 1990 to 2005, life expectancy dropped from 68.9 years to 65.5 in the Russian Federation, from 68.3 to 66.2 in Kazakhstan and from 69.2 to 67.4 in Uzbekistan. The patterns are the same for both male and female life expectancy.

Government health expenditure as a proportion of total budgeted expenditure rose slightly after 1999, but the rate of increase is limited and spending remains short of the pre-transition level. Per capita total health expenditures and per capita government health expenditures at international dollar rates over 2000-2004 have only slightly increased or have plateaued in Kyrgyzstan, Tajikistan and Uzbekistan. There has been a more significant increase in Armenia, Kazakhstan and the Russian Federation (figure 2.20).

Total expenditures on health rose by more than 188 international dollars in the Russian Federation over 2000-2004, by 94.6 dollars in Kazakhstan, by 75.7 dollars in Armenia, by 69.3 dollars in Georgia and by 15.3 dollars in Uzbekistan. In the Russian Federation, Kazakhstan and Uzbekistan, more than half the increase came from government sources (table 2.5). But in the other six countries, the increase was due largely to higher private health expenditure – indicating that out-of-pocket spending is rising in most of the countries and a sign that inequities in health services could continue to increase.

When the centrally planned system disintegrated, most of the formal hierarchy stayed in place but the quality of services and infrastructure plummeted. From 1990 to 2003, the number of physicians per 1,000 people fell from 4.9 to 4.1 in Georgia, from 3.4 to 2.6 in Kyrgyzstan, from 2.6 to 2.0 in Tajikistan and from 3.4 to 2.7 in Uzbekistan. In Central Asia, trained personnel in rural areas left their jobs to seek employment elsewhere, leaving a shortage of doctors. From 1990 to 2005, the number of hospital beds per 1,000 people declined from 9.8 to 3.8 in Georgia, from 12.0 to 5.1 in Kyrgyzstan, from 11.5 to 4.9 in Turkmenistan and from 12.5 to 5.2 in Uzbekistan. The ratio of physicians to people in the Russian Federation increased, however, owing to an expansion in private practitioners.

Policy issues and challenges

Lack of financial, human and institutional resources to support education and health hampers social development in North and Central Asia. Macroeconomic reforms to support the market transformation since 1991 have included measures to reduce poverty and to improve education and health care. Education and health have benefited from changed government expenditure priorities through new teacher training programmes, hospital renovations and more financing for primary health care:

- Tajikistan's draft budget for 2008 envisages a 41% increase in spending on education and a 44% increase on medical care, much of it earmarked for pay raises for medical personnel and teachers.

- Armenia is expected to increase spending on education and health care by 20% in 2008.

- The Russian Federation has made education a "national project" for priority government expenditure.

- Azerbaijan launched a 10-year education reform programme to address declining standards. With financial assistance from international organizations, the programme focuses on financing and budget reforms, enhancing the quality of the curriculum, increasing access to education for children from deprived areas and strengthening school management.

- Turkmenistan reinstated a compulsory tenth year of schooling and abolished the requirement for students to work before embarking on tertiary education.

Governments have promoted private schools and universities and encouraged parents to participate in financing their children's education, though the State continues to allocate resources for basic education. Private educational establishments have been set up in most of the subregion.

But challenges remain. Private education accounts for a small share and does not yet play a significant role. Enrolment in private institutions does, however, increase with the level of education. In the Russian Federation, private schools accounted for almost 40% of all higher education establishments in 2005.

From 2001 to 2005, health facilities became semi-autonomous and more responsible for their own financing. Regional and local health officials are responsible for national programmes and for enforcing

Figure 2.20. Health spending in North and Central Asia is rising more quickly in some countries than in others: Per capita health spending at international dollar rates

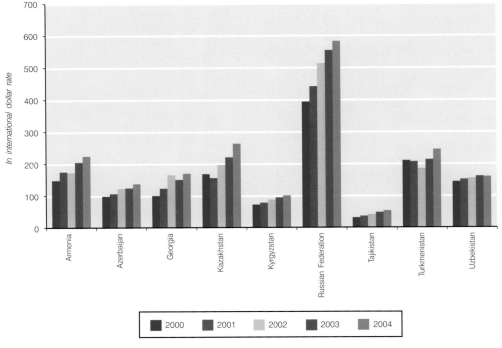

Source: World Health Organization, *Core Health Indicators,* <www.who.int/whosis/database/core/core_select.cfm>.

Table 2.5. The government contribution to higher per capita spending on health, 2000-2004

	Increase in per capita total expenditure on health at international dollar rate	Increase in per capita government expenditure on health at international dollar rate	Proportion of increase contributed by the government
Armenia	75.7	34.1	45.0
Azerbaijan	38.4	13.8	36.3
Georgia	69.3	20.0	28.9
Kazakhstan	94.6	74.6	78.8
Kyrgyzstan	28.5	6.4	22.4
Russian Federation	188.5	112.0	59.4
Tajikistan	21.5	4.1	19.1
Turkmenistan	34.3	12.4	36.2
Uzbekistan	15.3	9.5	62.1

Source: World Health Organization, *Core Health Indicators,* <www.who.int/whosis/database/core/core_select.cfm>.

policies and regulations. State health agencies are the principal public buyers of health services and handle State health-care funds. Some health facilities in Azerbaijan have been privatized, but the State remains the principal provider of health care, and the system is highly centralized. Georgia hopes to attract private investment in health care through the "100 New Hospitals" programme, launched in 2007. Through this programme, private funding is expected to make 7,800 more hospital beds available by 2009.

Unless addressed, inequality in access to health services could continue to increase

---

Kazakhstan, Kyrgyzstan, the Russian Federation and Turkmenistan have instituted compulsory health insurance plans. Tajikistan and Uzbekistan continue to rely mainly on government sources. Even so, insurance has been unable to increase health-sector revenues significantly, handicapped by the same limitations that affect tax collection. But social health insurance may change health systems in other ways, for example by introducing new provider payment systems and setting standards that may, in the long run, lead to better efficiency and quality.

Again, challenges remain. Introducing health insurance for a select group of people who would then have access to better health care risks excluding the poor and vulnerable from health services. The need is a funding system that protects everyone's interests while ensuring quality.

What will it take for progress on poverty, education and health? Macroeconomic performance is critical for reducing poverty and implementing policy reforms in education and health. With the countries of North and Central Asia becoming increasingly reliant on remittances, such inflows could contribute to resolving these problems. The inflow of remittances into Armenia increased by about 40% to $424 million, in the first half of 2007. Remittances accounted for more than 30% of GDP in Kyrgyzstan in 2006 and could reach a

new high in 2007. In Tajikistan, remittance payments increased by 57% – from $150 million in the first quarter of 2006 to $237 million in the first quarter of 2007.

Effective use of the region's large intellectual potential should be integral to subregional economic and social cooperation, especially on education. Since 1991, the countries of North and Central Asia have passed laws to change the content of training programmes and textbooks, widen the networks of high schools and universities to better respond to emerging skill needs, and introduce national languages in education. But the isolation of national educational systems creates difficulties in exchanging students and in establishing the equivalency of certificates, which affect the common labour market. A coordinated approach to these problems is needed.

Economic and social cooperation between countries in the subregion is necessary for making progress on the social agenda

---

Public health programmes remain underfunded in most economies. A major challenge everywhere is financing and delivering health services in an efficient and equitable way. Reforms in health-care systems are aimed at obtaining additional financing through non-budgetary sources, including insurance funds; reducing pressure on the national budget by decentralizing health-care financing to the regional and local levels; improving service delivery by restructuring it to favour primary care; promoting general and family medical practice; and eliminating unneeded hospital capacity.

Pooling financial and technological resources could help the subregion progress in education and health. To do this, the countries of North and Central Asia have to coordinate work and establish new organizational structures and procedures for joint activities. The private sector could also be important in mobilizing financial resources.

Pacific island developing countries: Modest growth

In contrast to Asia's robust economic growth, the island developing countries of the Pacific experienced an overall growth rate of less than 3% in 2007.

Growth was stronger in Melanesia than in Polynesia or Micronesia

In Melanesia, the economies of Papua New Guinea, Solomon Islands and Vanuatu, together with that of New Caledonia, continued to grow strongly at rates of around 5% or more. But a contraction was expected in Fiji in 2007. In Micronesia, only Palau showed strong projected growth, while Polynesia's island economies all grew modestly or contracted (figure 2.21).

Melanesia. Real GDP for Fiji was projected to fall by 3.9% in 2007. The coup d'etat in December 2006 created uncertainty, leading to declining tourist arrivals, worker layoffs, a fall in the wholesale and retail trades and a freeze on private-sector investment projects. Before this contraction, in 2006, Fiji's growth rate had been 3.6%. Growth in Fiji's real GDP is expected to recover to 2.2% in 2008.

Papua New Guinea continued to benefit from mineral and petroleum prices, which have been rising since 2003. The country's real GDP was estimated to have risen by 6.2% in 2007 – its highest rate since 2003, and twice the country's population growth rate (3.1%). The government has done a generally good job at managing this financial windfall. It has used new funds to strengthen public assets and reduce the public debt. Inflation has receded to historically low levels. The economic boom has spilled into the non-mining sector, which includes retail, construction, agriculture, forestry and fisheries. Growth in the non-mining sector rose from an estimated 3.7% in 2006 to 6.5% in 2007. Still, constraints on business – such as weak govern-ance, poor law and order, poor infrastructure and expensive and unreliable utilities – continue to limit interest in investment outside the mining and telecom-munication sectors. Real GDP was projected to grow by 6.6% in 2008.

Real GDP in Solomon Islands was estimated to grow by 5.4% in 2007, with increased logging and log exports. As logging continues at a rate estimated to be five times the sustainable rate, growth may suffer from any decline in this sector. An earthquake of magnitude 8.1 on the Richter scale struck Solomon Islands in April 2007. Despite the physical destruction it caused, international aid minimized the harm to economic growth.

Vanuatu's real GDP growth for 2007 is projected at 4.7%. Since 2002 its growth rate has consistently exceeded its annual population growth rate (2.6%), as construction and tourism-related services expand to meet growing demand from new tourist arrivals. But small-scale agriculture still supports two thirds of the island's people, and a recovery in the agricultural sector in 2006 was crucial to the country's economy. Vanuatu became the first recipient in the Pacific of the United States Millennium Challenge Account. It will receive a grant of nearly $66 million from 2006-2010.

> *Papua New Guinea grew at 6.2% in 2007 – highest since 2003*

Micronesia. Guam, Kiribati, Marshall Islands, Feder-ated States of Micronesia, Nauru, Northern Mariana Islands and Palau together comprise Micronesia. In these countries and territories the public sector ac-counts for a large share of GDP. In Kiribati projected real GDP growth for 2007 was 1.0%. Kiribati continues to be highly reliant on income in the form of fees for fishing licences. In the Marshall Islands real GDP is estimated to have grown by 2.5% in 2007, while economic growth in the Federated States of Micro-nesia was projected at 1.0%. The Marshall Islands and the Federated States of Micronesia both rely heavily on grants from the United States under the Compact of Free Association. But this support has started to decline and is expected to fall to zero by 2023. Under the Compact, trust funds have been established to ensure budgetary self-sufficiency in these countries and territories when their grants expire.

With the near exhaustion of phosphate reserves, the dependence of Nauru on mining is shifting to reliance on international assistance. After three years without any economic growth, real GDP rose in 2006 as a result of investments in phosphate mining infrastruc-ture. But negative growth is expected in 2007 and 2008.

Figure 2.21. Real GDP and sectoral growth in selected Pacific island economies, 2005-2007

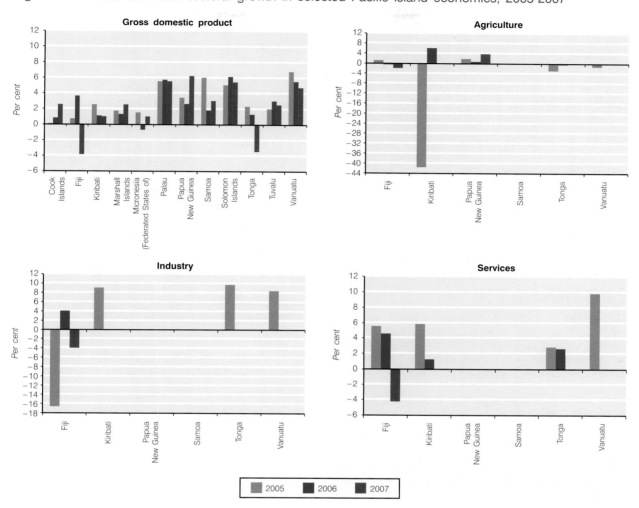

Sources: ESCAP, based on national sources; Department of Treasury and Planning, Papua New Guinea, *2008 National Budget* (Port Moresby, November 2007); Ministry of Finance and National Planning, *Republic of Fiji; Economic and Fiscal Update, Supplement to the 2008 Budget Address* (Suva, November 2007); ADB, *Key Indicators of Developing Asian and Pacific Countries 2007* (Manila, 2007), and *Asian Development Outlook 2007 Update* (Manila, 2007); IMF, *Samoa: 2007 Article IV Consultation Staff Report,* IMF Country Report No. 07/185 (Washington, D.C., June 2007); IMF, *Solomon Islands: 2007 Article IV Consultation Staff Report,* IMF Country Report No. 07/304 (Washington, D.C., September 2007); and IMF, *Tonga: 2007 Article IV Consultation Report,* IMF Country Report No. 07/297 (Washington, D.C., August 2007).

Notes: Growth rates for 2007 are estimates. Industry comprises mining and quarrying; manufacturing; electricity, gas and power, and construction.

In Palau, real GDP is estimated to have grown by 5.5% in 2007 and projected to grow by 4.8% in 2008, as tourism grows and as externally funded infrastructure projects are implemented. Like some other Micronesian countries, Palau depends heavily on assistance from the United States. Its long-term growth prospects are closely tied to future grants.

Polynesia. The small islands in the ESCAP region that comprise Polynesia are Samoa, Tonga and Tuvalu, together with American Samoa, the Cook Islands,

French Polynesia and Niue. Economic growth in Samoa is estimated to have risen to 3.0% in 2007, from 1.8% in 2006. The country's tourism and construction sectors grew, despite the scale-down of Yazaki Samoa (which produces automotive harness products for the Australian market) and a slow-down in the agricultural sector. One cause of growth was the Thirteenth South Pacific Games, which were held in Samoa in September 2007. Samoans living abroad sent home remittances equal to a quarter of GDP. Annual real GDP growth of 3 to 4% is projected in Samoa over the next three years.

Real GDP in Tonga was projected to fall by 3.5% in 2007, as a fire caused by civil unrest in Nuku'alofa in November 2006 severely damaged the business district. Both commerce and tourism fell sharply. These effects should be temporary, as reconstruction efforts will restimulate economic activity. But with weak growth of 0.8% forecast for 2008 in Tonga (and 1.3% for 2009), per capita income is still expected to continue its decline. A large inflow of remittances, equivalent to 45% of GDP in 2005, sustains the Tongan economy.

The economy of Tuvalu grew by 3% in 2006 and 2.5% in 2007, supported by the construction of the Funafuti power station and the upgrade of the Tuvalu Maritime Training Institute. Steady remittances continued to arrive from seafarers working on international vessels.

Difficult times for exports meant trade deficits

Imports of goods to Pacific countries often exceed exports because of their small and narrowly based economies (table 2.6). Some Pacific countries are seeking to improve market access for their exports.

For example, they are bringing commercial relationships into line with World Trade Organization rules, negotiating Economic Partnership Agreements with the European Union and discussing ways to ensure free trade with Australia and New Zealand.

Melanesia. Papua New Guinea is among the few countries in the Pacific with a trade surplus, estimated at $1.3 billion in 2007 – an effect of high commodity prices. Still, the current account surplus of $100 million in 2007 reflects a decline from 7.4% of GDP in 2006 to 2.5% of GDP in 2007. The account surplus decline resulted from net outflows in services and increased imports.

Fiji and Solomon Islands continued to have trade deficits in 2007. Fiji's commodity exports declined by an estimated 7.9% in 2007, while its imports declined by 5.4%. A World Trade Organization ruling against preferential sugar prices (formerly extended by the European Union) is expected to hurt Fiji's sugar industry. Exports of fish, lumber, fruits and vegetables, coconut oil and kava are expected to rise. Gold and garment exports are expected to fall.

Since log exports account for 10% of GDP, 15% of tax revenues and 70% of the Solomon Islands' total exports, export diversification is essential. Higher

Table 2.6. Merchandise trade and current account balances in selected Pacific island economies, 2004-2007

(Percentage of GDP)

	2004	2005	2006	2007
Merchandise trade balance				
Fiji	−20.6	−23.6	−28.0	−26.6
Papua New Guinea	19.0	16.3	26.1	23.8
Samoa	−35.8	−38.8	−44.0	−47.4
Solomon Islands	−9.2	−27.6	−38.8	−40.3
Tonga	−37.5	−40.7	−45.4	−45.7
Vanuatu	−21.0	−23.5	−26.3	−30.9
Current account balance				
Fiji	−11.0	−11.4	−21.1	−19.6
Papua New Guinea	2.2	3.8	7.4	2.5
Samoa	−1.6	−4.6	−6.1	−8.1
Solomon Islands	3.1	−24.2	−26.5	−40.0
Tonga	4.2	−2.6	−8.2	−10.5
Vanuatu	−7.3	−10.0	−8.0	−13.2

Sources: ESCAP, based on national sources; ADB, *Key Indicators of Developing Asian and Pacific Countries 2007* (Manila, 2007); ADB, *Asian Development Outlook 2007 Update* (Manila, 2007); Ministry of Finance and National Planning, *Republic of Fiji: Economic and Fiscal Update: Supplement to the 2008 Budget Address* (Suva, November 2007); Department of Treasury and Planning, Papua New Guinea, *2008 National Budget* (Port Moresby, November 2007); IMF, *Samoa: 2007 Article IV Consultation Staff Report*, IMF Country Report No. 07/185 (Washington, D.C., June 2007); IMF, *Solomon Islands: 2007 Article IV Consultation Staff Report*, IMF Country Report No. 07/304 (Washington, D.C., September 2007); IMF, *Tonga: 2007 Article IV Consultation Report*, IMF Country Report No. 07/297 (Washington, D.C., August 2007); and IMF, *Vanuatu: 2006 Article IV Consultation Report*, IMF Country Report No. 07/92 (Washington, D.C., March 2007).

Note: Data for 2007 are estimates.

prices for logs, fish and palm oil can partly explain why these products were increasingly exported in 2007. Imports rose in 2007, due to higher fuel prices and freight costs as well as a growth in domestic demand. The country's current account balance is projected to have deteriorated in 2007. But its overall balance of payments is expected to be positive, as a result of international assistance and investment inflow related to the Gold Ridge mine rehabilitation. Gold exports are expected to resume in 2008.

> *Solomon Islands is highly dependent on log exports for growth and tax revenues*

Vanuatu's exports increased in 2006 with a recovery in copra and cocoa exports and a rise in exported timber, beef and kava. But coconut oil exports declined to one fifth of their 2004 level. Imports increased, mainly because of an increase in construction and higher priced fuel, and the trade deficit showed a consequent slight increase. Kava exports may have suffered from an Australian ban on commercial kava imports in 2007 (following earlier bans by France, Germany and United Kingdom). Although Vanuatu's current account deficit increased in 2007, its overall balance of payments is expected to remain positive thanks to inflows from grants and FDI.

Micronesia. Because countries in Micronesia are small, dispersed and geographically isolated, there are few opportunities for import substitution or export diversification. Micronesian countries need to import most essential goods and are highly dependent on aid.

Kiribati's major revenue sources include fishing license fees along with fish, copra and seaweed exports. In the Federated States of Micronesia, exports have declined with the loss of textile trade preferences. Meanwhile, a decrease in international flights has hurt tourism. Nauru resumed its phosphate exports; reserves are expected to last at least until 2009. Although Nauru has no fishing industry of its own, fishing licence fees are an important source of foreign exchange for Nauru.

Polynesia. Polynesia's small island countries have a narrow export base. To cover the cost of imports these countries depend on aid, remittances and receipts from tourism.

Samoa increased its imports rapidly in 2007, driven by robust economic activity and a rise in public sector wages. Most exports declined. But fish exports are expected to rebound after modernized fishing facilities are completed. Tourism receipts and remittances contributed towards maintaining the balance of payments.

Exports from Tonga – chiefly products from fisheries and agriculture – have declined since 2004. Despite the large inflow of remittances, the current account deficit in 2007 was equal to 10.5% of GDP. In July 2007 Tonga acceded to the World Trade Organization and made commitments to liberalize its trade regime.

Political conditions affect economic growth in the Pacific

The private sector can drive economic growth, but this can only happen where investors confidently expect a stable macroeconomic environment. Recent events in the Solomon Islands (April 2006), Tonga (November 2006) and Fiji (December 2006) have once again shown that political uncertainties can inhibit long-term economic growth. To encourage private investment, some Pacific island countries need to address governance issues – in particular accountability – and to strengthen the legislative and regulatory environment (the rule of law).

Another urgent issue for investment in Pacific island countries is service quality – a critical factor affecting investment decisions. Most Pacific island countries have public monopolies in water and electricity supplies and port and inter-islands shipping services. The public and semi-public utilities (and other monopolies) are maintained with fiscal support. Even so, they are often inconsistent and expensive. To make the utilities more efficient, international donors and development agencies have often proposed privatization or international private participation, but such measures have yet to be introduced in most countries.

Tourism, telecommunications and agriculture could drive future growth

The countries of the Pacific could grow more rapidly through development in tourism, agriculture and telecommunications. In recent years tourism has led growth in several Pacific island countries. In Fiji this sector has been well-developed for many years. But tourism-related economic activity has become more important in the other countries only recently – a change facilitated by international air service liberalization in the Pacific.

A liberalized Pacific telecommunications market could lower service costs and mitigate the effects of geographic isolation. Both Papua New Guinea and Samoa have introduced competition into the mobile telephone market, causing prices to fall significantly. Such a move could create efficiencies for sectors that depend on these services, such as tourism and agriculture. And if the cost of telecommunications should fall to globally competitive levels, some countries might be able to develop viable industries in information and communication technology.

> *Liberalization of telecommunications could lower prices and improve services*

In Melanesia's fairly well-populated countries, a high proportion of the rural population is living at subsistence levels. These countries will experience a large "youth bulge" over the next 25 years. Without great changes most of these young Melanesians will be unable to find formal employment. For these large rural populations to be able to increase their incomes and living standards, agricultural productivity will have to increase significantly. Rising agricultural productivity, with its backward and forward linkages, could be an excellent basis for economic growth in these countries.

Pacific island developing countries face multiple challenges that have limited their economic growth. Such challenges include geographic dispersion, distance from major markets, small domestic markets, largely unskilled populations and – with the exception of Papua New Guinea – limited natural resource endowments. Limited labour markets present particular difficulties (see policy research feature 2.3). In addition, the high cost of petroleum has been a significant handicap for non-oil-producing countries in the Pacific in recent years. Some of the constraining factors, such as geography and a narrow resource base, cannot be changed. But others can – including poor governance, political uncertainties, costly and unreliable utilities, high transportation and telecommunication costs, rigid customary land tenure systems and an unwelcoming investment environment. To change these circumstances may be politically difficult. But it is not impossible.

Policy research feature 2.3: Improving employment opportunities in Pacific island economies

Demographic changes are pushing more people into the labour market in the Pacific island developing countries and territories. To ensure that new entrants into the labour market succeed, governments need to implement coherent macroeconomic and social policies to encourage growth in employment, especially in the private sector.

Fast-growing labour markets, limited employment prospects

Population growth in the Pacific will be rapid for the foreseeable future, except in countries with significant emigration. The implication will be more pressure on fragile ecosystems and the limited available land, as well as on infrastructure such as water supply and on public services such as education and health. There will also be greater difficulty in finding employment for the growing number of young and educated people with aspirations beyond village-based and family-oriented agriculture and fishing. These problems are of particular concern in the more populous countries of Melanesia, which, unlike most Micronesian and Polynesian countries and territories, do not enjoy historical migration outlets to other countries.

The populations of Papua New Guinea, Solomon Islands, Vanuatu, Kiribati and the Marshall Islands are forecasted to grow significantly by 2029 (table 2.7). In contrast, the population of Cook Islands is expected to contract because of high emigration rates. That of Tonga will experience relatively slow growth. Changes in migration patterns, mortality and fertility trends could affect the projections.

Formal sector employment prospects are poor, owing to the moderate economic growth expected (table 2.8).

Table 2.7. Rapid population growth in much of the Pacific: Forecast percentage population change in selected Pacific island developing economies, 2004-2029

(Per cent)

Melanesia		Micronesia		Polynesia	
Fiji	25.5	Kiribati	72.7	Cook Islands	−29.6
New Caledonia	37.5	Marshall Islands	82.4	French Polynesia	40.9
Papua New Guinea	72.2	Micronesia (Federated States of)	59.6	Samoa	24.5
Solomon Islands	75.3	Nauru	26.0	Tonga	9.2
Vanuatu	89.7			Tuvalu	32.2

Source: H. Booth, G. Zhang, M. Rao, F. Taomia and R. Duncan, *At Home and Away: Expanding Job Opportunities for Pacific Islanders through Labour Mobility* (Washington, D.C., World Bank, 2006).

Table 2.8. Only moderate employment growth expected: Forecast changes in formal sector employment in selected Pacific island developing economies

	2004	2015	Change (per cent)
Cook Islands	5 900	6 000	1.7
Fiji	122 000	145 880	19.6
Marshall Islands	10 480	11 270	7.5
Micronesia (Federated States of)	15 350	16 470	7.3
Papua New Guinea	205 870	226 460	10.0
Samoa	59 000	63 425	7.5
Solomon Islands	30 070	32 360	7.6
Tonga	35 820	37 610	5.0
Vanuatu	16 300	17 820	10.0

Source: H. Booth, G. Zhang, M. Rao, F. Taomia and R. Duncan, *At Home and Away: Expanding Job Opportunities for Pacific Islanders through Labour Mobility* (Washington, D.C., World Bank, 2006).

A 20% increase in employment in Fiji between 2004 and 2015 is plausible if tourism growth continues. But in the smaller countries, such as the Federated States of Micronesia and the Marshall Islands, the prospects for employment growth are weak. Public sector employment is not likely to grow much further against a backdrop of declining aid and public sector reforms, while private sector activity is limited. Formal sector employment growth will continue to be slow in Papua New Guinea, Solomon Islands and Vanuatu. Without substantial improvements in the investment environment in these countries, the prospects for private sector growth will remain slight.

Varied labour market characteristics

Labour force participation varies significantly among Pacific island economies and between men and women (table 2.9). Vanuatu has participation above 80% for both men and women. Male participation rates are comparatively high in Fiji and Solomon Islands. In contrast, participation rates are low in the Marshall Islands, particularly for women, and in the Federated States of Micronesia. However, much of the difference among countries may be due to measurement differences. Some countries include all people engaged in subsistence activities as economically active, while others only include those who indicate that they are working for cash. The treatment of women's activities also varies.

The labour force in most Pacific island developing economies has a large unskilled component, reflecting the dual nature of labour markets there. Most rural employment is informal or based on subsistence production and cash cropping. Formal sector employment, concentrated in urban areas, is dominated by the public sector. In the larger economies, there is substantial formal and informal employment in the private sector. The informal sector, often ignored, absorbs the unemployed and many who leave the rural agricultural sector. Papua New Guinea became the only Pacific island developing country to adopt legislation recognizing the contribution of the informal sector to employment growth when it adopted the Informal Sector Development and Control Act in 2004.

The urban-rural distribution of employment varies widely across the region (table 2.10). In Papua New Guinea, where the majority of the population is engaged in subsistence agriculture and small-scale cash cropping in the informal sector, about 90% of the 2.3 million workers are employed in rural areas. In contrast, in Fiji more than half of those employed are in urban areas.

Table 2.10. Urban employment dominates in some Pacific island developing economies, rural employment in others

	Total	Rural	Urban
American Samoa	12 902	..	..
Cook Islands	5 928	1 359	4 569
Fiji	219 314	107 853	111 461
Guam	54 980	..	..
Kiribati	39 912	21 505	18 407
Marshall Islands	10 141	3 218	6 923
Micronesia (Federated States of)	29 175	..	..
Niue	663	403	260
Northern Mariana Islands	42 753	3 530	39 223
Palau	9 383	1 213	8 170
Papua New Guinea	2 344 734	2 157 500	187 234
Samoa	50 325	37 933	12 392
Solomon Islands	57 472	..	..
Tokelau	542	..	..
Tonga	34 560	..	..
Tuvalu	3 237	1 816	1 421
Vanuatu	75 110	61 865	13 245
Wallis and Futuna	2 465	2 033	432

Sources: Compiled from the Secretariat of the Pacific Community, Pacific Regional Information System database, available at <http://www.spc.int/prism>; and the University of the South Pacific, Employment and Labour Market Studies Program database.

Table 2.9. Highly variable labour force participation rates in the Pacific islands, selected economies

(Per cent)

	Female	Male	Year
Cook Islands	61	76	2001
Fiji	55	83	2005
Guam	50	62	2002
Kiribati	56	72	2005
Marshall Islands	35	66	1999
Micronesia (Federated States of)	50	67	2000
Niue	49	75	2001
Northern Mariana Islands	78	85	1999
Palau	60	77	2005
Papua New Guinea	73	75	2005
Samoa	43	81	2005
Solomon Islands	56	83	2005
Tokelau	47	80	2001
Tonga	53	75	2003
Vanuatu	80	89	2005

Source: ADB, *Key Indicators of Developing Asian and Pacific Countries 2007* (Manila, 2007).

Unemployment, underemployment and migration

Reported unemployment varies considerably, in part because each country has its own criteria for determining who counts as unemployed. In Fiji, Papua New Guinea, Samoa and Solomon Islands, the unemployed are people in the labour force who are currently not working but are actively seeking work. In Tonga, the unemployed also include people not actively looking for a job. Because "unemployment" is hard to define in the rural areas of the Pacific, the region needs some agreed definitions in order to reflect the realities of rural life.

Underemployment is likely widespread in most countries, and many people are engaged in subsistence and small-scale cash-cropping activities.[2] Although many would be willing to take other income-earning opportunities, they are often hampered by lack of skills and access to high-quality education and training facilities.

Disadvantaged in Pacific labour markets, women are underrepresented in formal employment, except for occupations regarded as traditional for women. They are important in informal and cash-cropping activities in many countries. Lack of serious attention to gender issues in the labour market has often resulted in low labour force participation among women.

With 45% of the population in the 15-24 age group, the labour force in most Pacific island developing countries is young. Unemployment in this age group is widespread, and many youths are underemployed in subsistence work or the informal sector. In Solomon Islands and Vanuatu, youth unemployment is especially acute. In Fiji, 16,000 school graduates enter the labour market each year. Because opportunities for formal employment are limited, most have no choice but to join the informal sector.

The migration of skilled workers for permanent or temporary work overseas is a common feature of some Pacific island developing countries. Although generally leading to a greater inflow of remittances, such practices also reduce the pool of human resources. Many workers from Fiji, the Federated States of Micronesia, the Marshall Islands, Palau, Samoa and Tonga have used bilateral and preferential channels to migrate to such countries as Australia, New Zealand and the United States of America. Citizens of Kiribati and Tuvalu have a long-standing tradition of working overseas as seamen. Remittances now account for a high proportion of the gross national income in these countries.

Widespread unemployment among youth

The few migrants from three of the Melanesian countries (Papua New Guinea, Solomon Islands and Vanuatu) reflect the limited opportunities available to the many unskilled people in these countries, as well as cultural barriers to migration. The Pacific Island Countries Trade Agreement (PICTA) is designed to facilitate the free movement of goods within the subregion. But countries without substantial goods exports, such as Kiribati and Tuvalu, would benefit if labour was also included.

Policy issues and challenges

All Pacific island developing economies have legislation to frame labour market operations. But its reach tends to be restricted to the formal sector, which represents only about 10-15% of the labour force in most countries. The majority of the workforce is employed in the informal sector, not governed by workplace legislation. Except for Tonga, Pacific island countries have employment ordinances and legislation on trade unions. Those countries also usually have workmen's compensation acts that specify the definitions and conditions of various employee entitlements.

Fiji has recently passed new labour legislation to eliminate gender discrimination and workplace harassment

---

Many Pacific island developing economies are revising and updating their labour legislation and regulations to reflect changing labour market conditions. Fiji has recently passed new labour legislation, due to come into effect in 2008, that includes provisions to eliminate gender discrimination and workplace harassment.

Most Pacific island developing economies do not have social security arrangements or unemployment benefit

---

[2]   Underemployment refers to people who work fewer hours than they would be willing and able to work or are working in positions requiring less skill than they possess.

schemes.[3] Many have national provident funds, provided for by acts of Parliament, requiring employees and employers to contribute. But because these schemes cover only formal sector employees, most people working in the informal sector are not covered.

Some countries have recognized the need to improve labour market flexibility while maintaining adequate protection for workers. The institutional changes required to make the labour market more efficient, however, will require considerable political will. An additional difficulty is the lack of comprehensive and timely statistics on labour markets, which hampers informed discussion.

Economic structures have changed over the last decade. But skill development and training have often failed to adapt. Agricultural productivity and the contribution of the primary sectors to the gross domestic product have declined. The cost disadvantages for small Pacific island States in manufacturing and even agriculture mean that they must rely on services for growth and jobs (Winters and Martins, 2004). Tourism, one sector that has proved internationally competitive,

offers the greatest prospect for economic growth for Pacific island developing countries. But cost advantages could be eroded if skills needed by the tourism industry are not available and if overprotective labour market regulations slow growth.

Governments are vital in promoting efficient labour markets. Legislation for labour and employment needs to be reviewed and updated to respond to changing macroeconomic and business conditions. Critical issues include:

- Undertaking macroeconomic and structural reforms to boost economic growth.

- Cutting high rates of unemployment, especially among youth.

- Formulating policies for the informal sector.

- Addressing the lack of jobs for women and their low wages.

- Remedying skill mismatches and expanding training.

- Promoting key industries, such as tourism.

---

[3] Countries in the northern Pacific have generally established social security schemes, as have countries in the south that are in free association with New Zealand.

South and South-West Asia: Strong growth continues

The economy of India appears to have moved on to a new phase of high growth, with an average growth rate of 8.8% over the last five years as investment in the economy has risen sharply. India's 9.6% GDP growth rate for 2006 reflected double-digit growth in the industrial and services sectors. For 2007 the estimated growth rate was 9% (figure 2.22).

India's continued high growth in 2007 resulted from steady gains in the rate of savings and investment, consumption demand, addition of new capacity and the more intensive and efficient use of existing capacity. Strong growth in the industrial and services sectors supported the high overall rate, more than compensating for an agricultural slowdown.

The economy of Pakistan maintained its growth momentum in 2007, growing by 7%, slightly more than the 6.6% for 2006. Agricultural sector growth recovered sharply, from 1.6% in 2006 to 5% in 2007. Manufactur-

ing sector growth continued at 8.4% in 2007, slightly more moderate than the 10% for 2006. Services grew at 8% in 2007, down from 9.6% in 2006. Exports were sluggish in 2007; economic growth was driven mainly by strong domestic demand. Investment overtook consumption, helped by a surge in domestic private investment and record FDI flows. In 2007, investment in real terms increased by more than 20%.

Sri Lanka's GDP growth in 2007 remained strong despite high international oil prices and an unsettled security situation. The country's GDP is estimated to have grown by 6.7% in 2007, down from 7.7% in 2006. Growth in the industrial and services sectors slowed slightly, but these sectors still expanded by more than 7%. Agricultural growth decreased more sharply with adverse weather conditions. On the demand side, investment rose: it is estimated to have reached 29% of GDP in 2007, compared with 28.4% in 2006 (figure 2.23).

Figure 2.22. Industry and services perform well: Economic growth rates and sectoral contributions in selected South and South-West Asian countries, 2006-2007

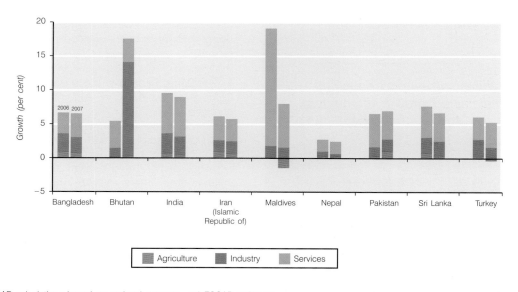

Sources: ESCAP calculations based on national sources; and ESCAP estimates.

Notes: Data for 2007 are estimates. The GDP growth rates for India, the Islamic Republic of Iran and Pakistan refer to real GDP at factor cost. The GDP growth rates for Bhutan refer to real GDP at purchasers' prices and GDP growth rates for Nepal refer to real GDP at producers' prices.

Figure 2.23. Investment higher than savings, except in the Islamic Republic of Iran, 2007

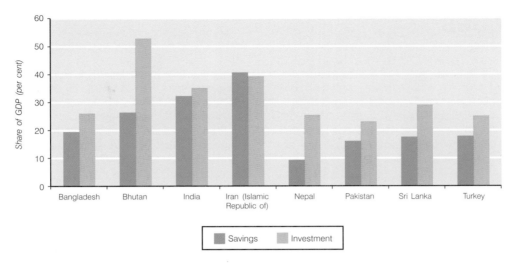

Sources: ESCAP, based on national sources; and ESCAP estimates.

Note: Data for 2007 are estimates.

In the Islamic Republic of Iran, GDP grew by 5.8% in 2007, slightly down from 6.2% in 2006. The country's GDP growth is set to remain fairly strong, supported by continued exceptionally high oil prices. Increased oil earnings will allow the government to press on with its expansionary fiscal policies. That in turn will increase private consumption. But the country faces constraints on future oil production, which cannot increase without massive investment in its ageing oilfields. Foreign investment has not been forthcoming - or else it has been slow to arrive.

> *Least developed countries maintained growth momentum amidst challenges*

Turkey's economy has experienced an impressive revival in recent years, supported by political stability, sound economic policies and favourable external conditions. The private sector has become more vibrant and the economy more open to foreign trade and investment. The main drivers of growth have been surging private consumption and investment, fuelled by declining real interest rates, rising capital inflows, rapid credit expansion and rising productivity. GDP is estimated to have grown by 5.0% in 2007, down from 6.1% in 2006. Consumer spending – especially for durables and fixed investments – has been adversely affected since mid-2006, when Turkey severely tightened its monetary policy to contain inflation.

Despite Afghanistan's security challenges and difficult political situation, its GDP is estimated to have grown by 13% in 2007, rising sharply from 7.5% in 2006. Since the economy is heavily dependent on the agricultural sector, the 2007 increase is attributed mainly to improved weather conditions that supported agriculture. Sustained growth in the construction and services sector has also been contributing to the rapid GDP growth.

In Bangladesh, despite the uncertain political climate, GDP grew by 6.5% in 2007 – a rate virtually unchanged from 2006. The 2007 expansion was propelled by higher growth in the manufacturing sector, which grew by 11.2%, and in services, which grew by 6.8%. Industrial growth was broadly led by continued domestic demand and buoyant external demand. Agriculture grew more slowly. The economy suffered losses from the severe floods of July-September 2007 (which caused considerable human distress, damage to infrastructure and immediate economic dislocation) and from a November 2007 cyclone (which killed several thousand people and damaged property and infrastructure in affected coastal areas; see box 2.2). But because the economy of Bangladesh has developed a resilience to such calamities, and authorities have improved their ability to respond to them, the overall macroeconomic impact will likely be modest.

Table 2.11. Summary of external accounts for selected South and South-West Asian economies

(Per cent)

	Exports/ GDP		Imports/ GDP		Current account balance/GDP	
	2006	2007	2006	2007	2006	2007
Bangladesh[a,b]	15.1	16.9	23.8	25.3	0.9	1.4
Bhutan[a,c]	33.9	31.2	46.8	43.9	−2.0	8.6
India[a,c]	13.9	15.7	20.9	23.7	−1.1	−1.4
Iran (Islamic Republic of)[a]	33.8	..	22.5	..	9.1	8.8
Maldives[d,e,f]	21.6	24.3	87.4	87.9	−39.8	−45.0
Nepal[a,c]	9.3	8.4	26.9	25.8	2.3	0.5
Pakistan[a,c]	13.8	12.5	24.0	22.5	−4.0	−5.0
Sri Lanka[f]	24.5	23.6	36.5	34.9	−4.7	−4.3
Turkey	21.3	..	34.7	..	−8.2	−7.3

	Growth rates					
	Exports			Imports		
	2005	2006	2007	2005	2006	2007
Bangladesh[a,b]	13.8	21.6	15.7	20.6	12.2	16.3
Bhutan[a,c]	34.5	47.2	64.5	75.5	−5.6	20.6
India[a,c]	23.4	22.5	24.3	33.8	27.8	24.4
Iran (Islamic Republic of)[a]	46.8	16.4	..	12.8	15.4	..
Maldives[d,e,f]	−10.7	39.4	15.5	16.1	24.4	13.0
Nepal[a,c]	13.0	2.2	3.6	13.8	15.8	13.2
Pakistan[a,c]	16.9	14.3	3.4	32.1	38.8	6.9
Sri Lanka[f]	10.2	8.4	10.0	10.8	15.7	8.9
Turkey[g]	14.6	18.9	24.8	19.7	19.5	21.5

Sources: Bangladesh Bank website <http://www.bangladesh-bank.org/pub/monthly/econtrds/econtrdsiv.html> (29 January 2008); Reserve Bank of India website <http://www.rbi.org.in/home.aspx> (20 November 2007); Maldives Monetary Authority website <http://www.mma.gov.mv/statis.php> (5 November 2007); Central Bank of Sri Lanka website <http://www.centralbanklanka.org/> (7 November 2007); Central Bank of the Republic of Turkey website <http://www.tcmb.gov.tr/yeni/eng/> (24 January 2008); IMF, *World Economic Outlook Database* (October 2007); and *International Financial Statistics* (CD-ROM) (Washington, D.C., 2007); national sources; and ESCAP estimates.

[a]   Data in fiscal year.
[b]   Exports and imports for 2007 are provisional.
[c]   Exports and imports for 2007 are estimates.
[d]   Imports value in f.o.b.
[e]   Exports and imports for 2006 are estimates.
[f]   Exports and imports for 2007 are projections.
[g]   Exports and imports for 2007 refer to the first 11 months.

In Sri Lanka in 2007, estimated export earnings rose by 10% and import earnings by 8.9%. Workers' remittances increased significantly and helped to contain the current account deficit, which is estimated to fall to 4.3% of GDP in 2007 (from 4.7% in 2006). FDI and financial flows to the government increased substantially, yielding a surplus in the overall balance of payments. Gross official reserves increased to $3.08 billion by the end of 2007, up from $2.53 billion at the end of 2006.

The Islamic Republic of Iran's current account surplus is expected to remain high in 2007 as rising global oil prices lift oil export earnings (and in spite of stagnat-

ing oil export volumes). In addition, the government's petrol rationing has curbed the demand for imported petrol, slowing import growth and further supporting the surplus.

Turkey has made good progress in achieving sustained high economic growth. But it still must struggle to contain inflation and its high current account deficit on the balance of payments. Because of strong private investment and increased energy prices, import growth has outpaced export growth. In 2006 and 2007 the current account deficit remained high, at more than 7% of GDP. The large capital inflows which have helped to finance Turkey's current account deficit have made its economy more and more dependent on such inflows, exposing it to sudden shifts in market sentiment. Turkey's government should maintain monetary and fiscal discipline and preserve the floating exchange rate as a useful shock absorber.

> *Large remittances from workers abroad provide cushion to balance of payments in Bangladesh and Nepal*

In 2007, large remittances from workers abroad contributed to current account surpluses in Nepal and Bangladesh. Exports from Nepal grew by 3.6% in 2007 – far more slowly than imports to the country, which grew by 13.2%. But thanks to large remittances, the country achieved a current account surplus of 0.5% of GDP (down from 2.3% in 2006). Bangladesh, by contrast, maintained rapid growth in both exports and imports in 2007. Exports grew by 15.7%, still relying heavily on the ready-made garment sector (an average 75% of total exports from the country in recent years). Imports grew by 16.3%. Workers' remittances rose to nearly $6 billion, and in 2007 Bangladesh exceeded slightly its 2006 current account surplus of about 1% of GDP.

Bhutan's trade balance improved in 2007, with large exports of electricity to India and much of the Tala hydropower project coming on stream. The country's current account balance turned to a surplus in 2007, and is expected to remain a surplus in the near future.

In Maldives, where the tourism sector has been recovering swiftly in the wake of the 2004 tsunami, the current account deficit widened in 2006 with rapid increases in imports related to tourism and construction. In 2007 it remained high, at about 40% of GDP. The country's dollar-pegged exchange rate regime caused its domestic currency to depreciate against other major currencies.

Strong economic growth is expected to continue in 2008

GDP growth for India over the next few years is projected to remain at between 8.5% and 9.5%. Concerns have been expressed about whether the country is growing beyond its growth potential thereby straining its labour force and capital stock, and engendering inflationary instabilities. The government has a strategy for maintaining high growth while keeping prices fairly stable: it will increase productivity, ameliorate skills shortages and add capacity through investments. Monetary policy will continue to play a critical role in maintaining price stability. But the sustainability of high economic growth with moderate inflation will depend critically on fiscal prudence and high investment levels. India could achieve and sustain a 10% growth rate by further improving the country's business environment, by developing its infrastructure and reforming the labour market.

Supported by all sectors, Pakistan's economic growth is expected to remain strong at 6.5% in 2008. In just a few years, sound macroeconomic policies have transformed Pakistan's consumption-led growth impetus to one in which investment-led growth can assume a more important role. But recent political uncertainty and violence related to the general election could slow the economy. Sri Lanka's GDP growth is expected to remain about 7% in 2008, with productivity improvements in all three sectors of its economy. Several large planned infrastructure projects would boost aggregate demand and output if speedily implemented. But the outlook for Sri Lanka remains vulnerable to any further escalation in the country's ethnic conflict.

The outlook for the Turkish economy remains positive, with GDP expected to grow by 5.5%. In the Islamic Republic of Iran, GDP growth is expected to fall slightly to 5.0% in 2008 as oil prices rise less rapidly and constraints on oil production consequently lowering export volumes. Should global oil prices fall, however, the economy will suffer markedly. And with economic sanctions related to the country's nuclear programme already in place, any intensification in the dispute over this programme could hurt future growth prospects.

Bangladesh, Bhutan, Maldives and Nepal are the least developed countries in South and South-West Asia. The Bangladesh government's target is to raise GDP growth to 7% in 2008. But with continuing political uncertainty, this target may prove elusive and GDP growth may remain at about 6.5%. The interim government's anti-corruption drive is expected to improve the country's business environment in the coming years, attracting FDI and helping the Bangladesh economy to grow. In Bhutan the construction of two new hydropower projects will help to sustain real GDP growth over the medium term. GDP is expected to grow at about 10% in 2008. In Maldives a further slowdown in the growth of the economy will continue in 2008, as reconstruction work in response to the 2004 tsunami nears completion. In Nepal, with the peace process moving forward, GDP growth is expected to increase to 4% in 2008. Tourism, services and transportation appear to be reviving. More government spending could support economic activity, as budgetary capital spending on rural infrastructure is expected to pick up. But since Nepal is still in transition politically, its economic situation remains vulnerable.

The main challenge for countries in South and South-West Asia is to sustain their growth momentum in the face of high oil prices. Should oil prices remain very high, they will compromise economic growth while putting pressure on budgets, inflation rates and the balance of payments in countries throughout the subregion. So, some measures must be taken to hedge the risk of continued high oil prices and – more importantly – to contain oil imports through selective energy conservation measures.

The current account deficit is already a serious problem in some South and South-West Asian countries. The abolition of the Multi-Fiber Arrangement (MFA) regime at the end of 2004 had a mixed effect on countries in the subregion. The MFA abolition might have further adverse medium-term effects as quota restrictions on Chinese exports are lifted in 2008, creating stiff competition from Chinese exports. To reduce the risk of depending too heavily on a single sector, export diversification should remain an important part of government strategies.

With large budget deficits accumulating, public debt is serious problem for many South and South-West Asian countries. And the share of domestic public debt in total public debt is on the rise (see policy research feature 2.4).

Policy research feature 2.4: Fiscal deficit and public debt sustainability in South Asia

Despite recent improvements, public debt remains a serious problem for most countries in South Asia. External debt is high, with domestic debt becoming a larger component of public debt. Domestic debt has received relatively less attention despite its serious economic implications. Excessive reliance on debt, whether domestic or external, carries macroeconomic risks that can hinder economic development.

High public debt constrains flexibility in the use of macroeconomic policies

---

In the presence of high public debt macroeconomic policies, including fiscal, monetary and exchange rate policies, can not be used freely and effectively to achieve desired objectives. For example, high public debt demand can increase the domestic interest rate, thereby crowding out private investment. Under such circumstances, it is extremely difficult for monetary authorities to lower interest rates in order to stimulate private investment. When a major share of budget is devoted to debt servicing, fiscal policy loses its flexibility, which hinders its capacity to promote macroeconomic stability, employment generation, poverty reduction and social development. An escalating external public debt stock increases the probability of default, causing creditors to raise their interest risk premium. In extreme cases, Governments can be forced into defaulting on public debt, which tarnishes a country's international reputation and makes further borrowing difficult. While defaulting on domestic debt can be avoided by printing money, it can lead to very high inflation, with serious economic and social consequences.

High public debt, with a growing domestic share

At 93% of GDP in 2006, the public debt in Sri Lanka was the highest in the subregion, the result of years of high fiscal deficits. When concessional foreign financing became scarce, government debt service ballooned and government reliance on shorter term domestic debt instruments increased. The debt-GDP ratio has come down recently, but this reflects fast nominal GDP growth rather than improved debt dynamics (IPS, 2007).

In India, high fiscal deficits increased the combined debt of the central and state governments from about 70% of GDP in 1990 to about 87% over 2002-2004. Public debt, on the decline more recently, is estimated at 82% for fiscal 2006. The central government share in public debt is much higher than that of state governments.

In Pakistan, debt growth during the 1990s was unprecedented. A credible debt reduction strategy and fast growth cut the public debt burden from 84% of GDP in 2000 to 57% in 2006. Pakistan reduced its external debt burden through rescheduling, a debt swap for social spending, debt cancellation and prepayment of expensive debt.

In Bangladesh, public debt has stabilized below 50% of GDP, estimated at 47% in 2006. Public debt in Nepal, coming down of late, stood at 56% of GDP in 2006.

The share of domestic debt in public debt has grown. In India, Pakistan and Sri Lanka, the share of domestic debt in public debt exceeds that of external debt (figure 2.26). In India, domestic debt made up 94% of public debt. External debt dominates in Bangladesh and Nepal.

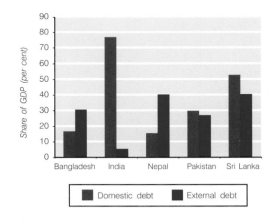

Figure 2.26. Differing shares of domestic and external debt as a share of GDP, 2006

Sources: Data for Bangladesh are from *IMF Statistical Appendix* (June 2007), and IMF Country Report No.07/229 (Washington, D.C., 2007); data for Sri Lanka are from Central Bank of Sri Lanka, *Annual Report 2006;* data for Pakistan are from State Bank of Pakistan, *Annual Report 2005-06;* data for India are from Ministry of Finance, *Economic Survey 2006-07;* and data for Nepal are from *IMF Article IV Consultations* (June 2007).

Domestic public debt includes internal borrowing through long-term bonds, short-term bills and loans from banking institutions, and small savings (mainly post office deposits and medium-term certificates) and provident funds. In Sri Lanka, 24.6% of domestic public debt in 2006 was held by the banking sector (8% by the central bank and 16.6% by commercial banks). The rest was held by provident and pension funds (31.8%), private businesses and individuals (25.2%) and savings institutions (11.3%). In Pakistan, the share of the banking sector in domestic public debt is rising, and commercial banks are becoming major players; in 2007, the share of commercial banks reached 65%, compared with 35% for the central bank.

Debt servicing – the real cost of debt

The real burden of public debt is in its servicing. In Sri Lanka, more than 90% of government revenues went to debt servicing in 2006 (table 2.12). In India, interest payments alone consumed more than 28% of the revenue of the central and state governments in 2005, more if repayments of principal are included.[4] The debt service ratio has substantially declined in Pakistan over 2000-2006, though about 30% of government revenues remain allocated to debt servicing. In Nepal, debt servicing stabilized at about 29% of total government revenues in 2006. In Bangladesh, interest payments consumed about 18% of government revenues.

Is public debt in South Asia sustainable?

Judging the sustainability of public debt is tricky, especially because defaults occur in countries with lower debt-to-GDP ratios, as well as in more indebted countries (IMF, 2003). On average, however, emerging market country defaulters since 1998 have a higher ratio of public debt to GDP, a higher debt-to-revenue ratio and a higher proportion of external debt in total public debt.

Table 2.12. Debt can weigh on government budgets: Costs to service the public debt in South Asia, 2000-2006

(Per cent)

	2000	2001	2002	2003	2004	2005	2006
Bangladesh							
Share of GDP	1.6	1.8	1.9	1.6	1.7	1.8	1.9
Share of government revenue	14.3	17.8	18.3	16.1	15.9	16.9	18.4
Share of government expenditure	11.0	12.6	13.8	12.3	12.0	13.0	13.7
India							
Share of GDP	5.8	6.2	6.3	6.4	6.0	5.9	..
Share of government revenue	31.2	32.8	31.9	33.1	30.0	28.1	..
Share of government expenditure	19.9	20.7	21.3	22.0	20.3	19.8	..
Nepal							
Share of GDP	..	2.5	2.9	3.7	3.5	3.7	3.5
Share of government revenue	..	21.9	25.1	31.0	28.7	28.6	28.7
Share of government expenditure	..	14.2	16.8	21.4	22.6	22.5	21.4
Pakistan							
Share of GDP	9.8	8.3	10.0	6.2	5.3	4.8	4.1
Share of government revenue	72.4	62.5	70.3	41.6	37.9	34.8	29.6
Share of government expenditure	52.3	48.1	53.1	33.3	31.4	28.0	22.7
Sri Lanka							
Share of GDP	14.0	12.7	17.9	19.6	14.8	14.3	15.9
Share of government revenue	83.2	76.4	108.6	124.6	96.5	91.0	93.1
Share of government expenditure	38.7	38.3	49.8	54.1	45.7	42.6	44.1

Sources: Data for Bangladesh are from *IMF Statistical Appendix* (June 2007), and IMF Country Report No.07/229 (Washington, D.C., 2007); data for Sri Lanka for 2003-2006 are from Central Bank of Sri Lanka, *Annual Report 2006;* data for 2001-2002 are from Central Bank of Sri Lanka, *Annual Report 2004;* data for Pakistan are from State Bank of Pakistan, *Annual Report 2005-06;* data for India are from Ministry of Finance, *Economic Survey 2006-07;* and data for Nepal are from *IMF Article IV Consultations* (September 2003, February 2006 and June 2007).

Note: For India and Bangladesh, public debt servicing includes interest payments only due to lack of data on repayment of principal.

---

[4] For India and Bangladesh, data on principal repayments are not readily available from published sources.

For Sri Lanka, the country with highest public debt in the subregion, IMF debt sustainability analysis shows that if GDP growth and primary balances continue at the average of the last decade, an already high debt-to-GDP ratio would continue rising – an unsustainable situation. But fiscal consolidation and improved growth can bring the debt ratio down to more sustainable levels. GDP growth of 7% over 2006-2010 and 6% through 2026, combined with sustained fiscal consolidation, could lower central government debt from 94% of GDP in 2005 to 74% in 2010 and 48% in 2026. This would cut the ratio of debt service to government revenue from 93% in 2006 to 68% in 2010 and about 50% in 2026.

If India's high GDP growth and fiscal consolidation continue, the debt-to-GDP ratio will fall by 10 percentage points over the next five years. If key variables (particularly GDP growth and primary balances) continue at the average level of the last decade, however, there will be no reduction in the debt-to-GDP ratio.

If Pakistan follows its historical growth path, its debt-to-GDP ratio will continue to decline over the next five years. But an upsurge in the primary deficit would slow the reduction. Because of a growing budget deficit, the improvement in the ratio of domestic public debt to GDP since 2001 appears to have bottomed out. The country is likely to face a higher external debt-servicing burden as repayments of the re-scheduled non-ODA Paris Club stock resume in 2008 and some foreign currency bonds mature. A sustained high current account deficit could also hurt the external debt-to-GDP ratio, which may start rising in the medium term.

If Nepal follows its historical growth path, no reduction in the debt-to-GDP ratio is expected in the medium term. Because external debt dominates public debt, the IMF found that the external debt-to-export ratio in 2005 was high and could remain so in the medium term under various scenarios, especially if growth is low and donor grant support inadequate.

> *Lower debt servicing means more funding for education, health and development*

The debt sustainability analysis by IMF shows that the ratio of public debt to GDP and the ratio of public debt service to government revenue can be reduced significantly over the medium term by promoting growth and adopting fiscal consolidation policies. In the case of Sri Lanka, which has high public debt, the ratio of public debt service to government revenue can be reduced by more than 20% within five years. The financial resources from lower debt servicing can be devoted to education, health or other development activities. An ESCAP analysis shows that a 20% decrease in the public debt service ratio in Sri Lanka can make resources available to raise development expenditure by 50%, expenditure on education by 114% or expenditure on health by 152% from the existing level.[5] In Nepal, a 20% reduction in the debt service ratio could raise spending on health by 50%. Pakistan increased its development expenditure from about 2% of GDP in 2001 to about 5% of GDP in recent years, mainly after the Government reduced its debt burden, partly due to external debt relief. A further 20% decrease in the debt service ratio could increase development spending by 24%.

Policy issues and challenges

Making South Asia's public debt sustainable requires three sets of actions:

*   Controlling fiscal deficits.
*   Expanding government revenues.
*   Prioritizing development spending on key areas.

Cutting deficits. Countries in the subregion are taking various measures, including the introduction of legislation, to bring fiscal deficits down to a sustainable level. India's Fiscal Responsibility and Budget Management Act, passed in August 2003, requires that the fiscal deficit of the central government not exceed 3% of GDP by 2007/2008 (later amended to 2008/2009). It also requires that the deficit on the revenue account be eliminated by the same date. The fiscal deficit of the central Government was 3.7% of GDP in 2005/2006 (figure 2.27) and is budgeted at 3.3% for 2007/2008. The target of 3% in 2008/2009 is expected to be met. The act requires that the central government not directly borrow from the Reserve Bank of India after 31 March 2006, though borrowing for ways and means advances is permitted. Similar fiscal responsibility acts have been implemented by India's highly autonomous states.

---

5   Financial resources released as a result of a reduction in the public debt service to government revenue ratio by 20% from the existing level in 2006 are computed first and then added separately to expenditure in 2006 on development, education and health. The results indicate the increase in expenditure that would be possible in each category alone, not all three collectively.

and Cambodia (from 26.9% to 16.8%). A weakened United States economy and local currency appreciation combined to inhibit the dynamism of electronic product exports from Malaysia and the Philippines. Cambodia's export growth is particularly fragile due to its concentration in the garment industry, where low-cost competitors from Viet Nam and India are gaining market share. The end of restraints on garment exports from China to the European Union (scheduled for the end of 2007) and to the United States (scheduled for the end of 2008) makes Cambodia's need to diversify its exports more urgent.

The deceleration of South-East Asian exports in 2007 is expected to continue in 2008, given the dollar's weakness and the prospect of growth in the United States continuing to slow down. So, the faster growth in domestic demand for the Asian and Pacific region in 2007 is encouraging: it suggests that the region's economies can keep up their robust growth performance despite an expected slowdown in external demand for 2008.

Inflation decelerated in most countries

Inflation fell in most South-East Asian countries during 2007 (figure 2.31). The drop in the inflation rate between 2006 and 2007 was particularly significant for Indonesia (from 13.1% to 4.7%), the Philippines (from 6.2% to 2.7%) and Thailand (from 4.7% to 2.3%). Inflation fell by about 2 percentage points in Cambodia, Malaysia and the Lao People's Democratic Republic, remained stable in Viet Nam, and increased slightly in Singapore (from 1% to 1.8%). The only country where inflation seems to have risen significantly is Myanmar, where prices increased at an annual rate of 37% in the first quarter of 2007 – up from an average rate of 25.7% in 2006 (and 10.7% in 2005). The August 2007 increase in subsidized fuel prices, which triggered large-scale anti-government protests and consequently a brutal crackdown, may have contributed to a further increase in inflation during the rest of the year.

> *Most South-East Asian currencies appreciated against the dollar, none against the Euro*

The reasons for the drop in inflation varied across countries. Good harvests helped to keep food price inflation down in Indonesia and the Philippines. Another inhibitor of inflation in the Philippines was appreciation in the peso, which restrained the prices of imported goods. And appreciation in the currencies of Malaysia, Thailand and the Lao People's Democratic Republic partly explains those countries' reduced inflation rates.

Figure 2.31. Inflation fell in most South-East Asian countries in 2007

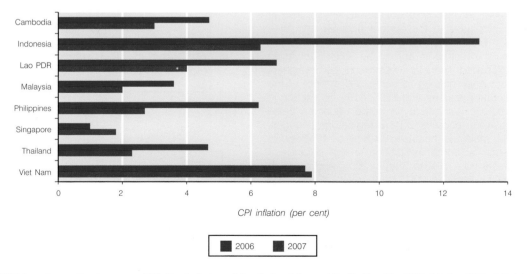

CPI inflation (per cent)

■ 2006 ■ 2007

Sources: ESCAP, based on national sources; ADB, *Key Indicators of Developing Asian and Pacific Countries 2007* (Manila, 2007); IMF, *International Financial Statistics* (CD-ROM) (Washington, D.C., September 2007); and ESCAP estimates.

Notes: Data for 2007 are estimates. Inflation refers to changes in consumer price index.

Subdued inflation rates allowed some countries' central banks to ease their monetary stances. Bank Indonesia cut its reference rate 13 times, for a total of 450 basis points, between May 2006 and July 2007. The Bank of Thailand cut its policy interest rate – the one-day repurchase (repo) rate – from about 5% in January to 3.25% in July 2007. Interest rates also fell in the Philippines and Singapore, and remained stable in Malaysia and Viet Nam (figure 2.32).

Exchange rates appreciated and foreign exchange reserves accumulated

In 2007 the currencies of South-East Asian countries continued to appreciate against the United States dollar, with the sole exception of the Indonesian rupiah (figure 2.33). The rate of currency appreciation since the start of 2007 was highest for the Philippines followed by Singapore, Malaysia, Thailand and the Lao People's Democratic Republic. Over the two-year period from January 2006 to November 2007, the cumulative appreciations of the Philippine peso and the Thai baht against the United States dollar were 22% (Phillipine peso) and 17% (Thai baht). For both the Malaysian ringgit and the Singaporean dollar this figure was around 12%. South-East Asian currencies appreciated somewhat less during these two years against the Japanese yen. In contrast, all the South-East Asian currencies depreciated against the euro which meanwhile appreciated 22% against the dollar.

Currency appreciation in the South-East Asia subregion during 2006 and 2007 reflected large inflows of foreign exchange. The largest contributions to these inflows came from surpluses in the current account and from FDI (table 2.13, columns 1 and 2). But during these two years, financial investments abroad by South-East Asian residents exceeded financial investments by foreigners in South-East Asia, helping to soften the impact of the current account surpluses and FDI inflows on exchange rates (table 2.13, column 3). In some countries these investments were encouraged by regulatory changes. For example, Malaysia increased its limit on holdings of foreign assets by some institutional investors and investment trusts from 10% to 30% in 2005, and again to 50% in 2007. And in 2007 the Bank of Thailand liberalized regulations on the holding of foreign assets by Thai individuals or businesses.

While increased financial investments abroad helped to counteract upward pressures on domestic currencies, central banks in South-East Asia continued to intervene in foreign exchange markets by accumulating international reserves (table 2.13, column 5). The cumulative increase in international reserves from the beginning of

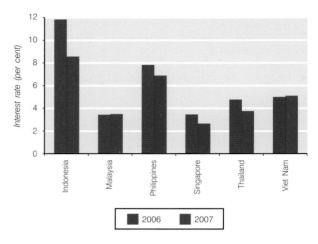

Figure 2.32. Interest rates in 2007 were lower than in 2006 or stable

Sources: ESCAP, based on data from Oxford Economics and Economist Intelligence Unit.

Note: Interest rate refers to the 14-day repo rate in Thailand, interbank call loan rate in the Philippines, one-month treasury notes in Indonesia, overnight interbank rate in Malaysia, three-month interbank rate in Singapore, and money market rate in Viet Nam.

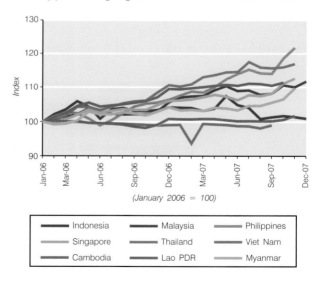

Figure 2.33. The nominal exchange rate continued appreciating against the United States dollar

(January 2006 = 100)

Source: IMF, *International Financial Statistics* (CD-ROM) (Washington, D.C., 2007).

Notes: Data for November to December 2007 are estimates for Indonesia and Malaysia. Data for 2007 are through November for Cambodia, Myanmar, Philippines, Singapore and Thailand. Data for 2007 are through October for Lao People's Democratic Republic. Data for 2007 are through September for Viet Nam.

Table 2.13. Foreign exchange reserves accumulations mostly reflected surpluses in the current account

(Billions of United States dollars)

		Current account balance [1]	Net foreign direct investment [2]	Increase in foreign financial liabilities minus foreign financial assets [3]	Net errors and omissions [4]	Accumulation of foreign exchange reserves [5]=[1]+[2]+[3]+[4]
Indonesia	2006	9.9	2.9	−3.9	−2.0[b]	6.9
	2007	10.2	2.7	−6.1[a]	..	6.8
Malaysia	2006	25.5	0.0	−11.9	−6.7	6.9
	2007	26.1	0.5	−7.9[a]	..	18.7
Philippines	2006	5.0	2.2	−2.9	−1.4[b]	2.9
	2007	7.2	2.1	−1.3[a]	..	8.0
Singapore	2006	36.3	15.6	−36.5	1.7	17.0
	2007	44.0	11.8	−38.4[a]	..	17.4
Thailand	2006	3.2	10.0	−2.1	1.6	12.7
	2007	8.7	10.0	−8.6[a]	..	10.1

Sources: ESCAP calculations based on IMF, *International Financial Statistics* (Washington, D.C., 2007); Economist Intelligence Unit; and Oxford Economics.

[a] Includes errors and omissions.
[b] Includes exceptional financing and use of the IMF credit and loans.

2006 to the end of 2007 was close to 60% for the Philippines and Cambodia, about 54% for Indonesia and Thailand, 38% for Malaysia and 27% for Singapore.

The fact that the exchange rates appreciated against the dollar in most South-East Asian countries, despite the accumulation of reserves, reflects a move towards a more flexible management of exchange rates. ESCAP (2007a), commented on the complications created for monetary policy when countries try to target the nominal exchange rate while inflows of foreign exchange are strong. Accumulations of foreign exchange reserves remained very important in 2007. But most countries allowed their exchange rates to appreciate, intervening less than would have been necessary to keep the rates fixed. Changes in regulations to facilitate financial investments abroad represent another step towards flexibility.

> *Regional trade integration is expected to support economic growth in the medium run*

Not all countries in the subregion have moved towards greater exchange rate flexibility. The Vietnamese currency has been held tightly by the monetary authorities at a target rate of about 16,000 dong/dollar since January of 2005. However, in 2007 Viet Nam's successful efforts to prevent the dong from appreciating were complicated by the country's large capital inflows. The State Bank of Viet Nam tried to sterilize those inflows by selling bonds. That caused a rise in domestic interest rates, which in turn attracted more capital inflows. Nonetheless, the bank did manage to keep the inflation rate in check in 2007.

Solid macroeconomic fundamentals leave countries well prepared for a slowdown in export demand

Countries in the region appear well prepared to face the slowdown in export demand that is expected to result from slower economic growth in the United States and other industrial countries. First, foreign exchange reserves are at very high levels, allowing countries to withstand a deterioration in their current accounts. Second, the importance of domestic demand growth increased from 2006 to 2007. Further domestic demand growth can help sustain GDP growth, should export demand continue to slow down during 2008. Third, lower inflation rates during 2007 allowed countries to lower interest rates in 2007. Continued monetary stability in 2008 will help to support investment and private consumption as increasingly important drivers of GDP growth. Finally, the growing importance of Association of South-East Asian Nations

(ASEAN) countries and China as destinations for ASEAN exports (figure 2.34), together with current efforts towards regional trade liberalization (see box 2.3), suggest that in the medium to long term regional trade will play an ever-larger role in supporting economic growth in South-East Asia.

Figure 2.34. Intraregional trade becoming more important for ASEAN countries

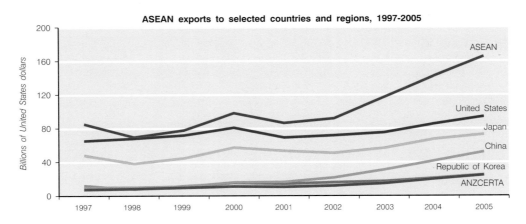

ASEAN exports to selected countries and regions, 1997-2005

Source: IMF, *Direction of Trade Statistics* (CD-ROM) (Washington, D.C., 2007).

Note: ANZCERTA is the Australia New Zealand Closer Economic Relations Trade Agreement.

Box 2.3. Gains from greater regional integration

Regional integration in East Asia intensified recently, reflecting a desire to strengthen economic cooperation after the economic crisis of 1997/1998; to increase bargaining power in multilateral negotiations with the North American and European regional blocs (Stubbs, 2002); to consolidate earlier gains through regional trade agreements (RTAs; Kawai and Wignaraja, 2007); and to spread the gains from economic prosperity to the region's least developed countries (ESCAP, 2007b).

A precursor was the ASEAN Free Trade Area (AFTA), signed in 1992 by the six members of ASEAN at that time – Indonesia, Malaysia, the Philippines, Singapore, Thailand and Brunei Darussalam (ASEAN 6) – and expanded in the second half of the 1990s to the new ASEAN members – Cambodia, the Lao People's Democratic Republic, Myanmar and Viet Nam (CLMV). AFTA aims at lowering rates to zero by 2010 for ASEAN 6 and by 2015 for CLMV. ASEAN has recently expanded its regional integration efforts through the ASEAN-China Free Trade Agreement, the ASEAN-Korea Free Trade Agreement, and the ASEAN-Japan Comprehensive Economic Partnership Agreement. These bilateral agreements could be consolidated into an ASEAN+3-wide RTA. A more ambitious proposal is to expand ASEAN+3 to Australia, India and New Zealand to form an ASEAN+6 RTA.

Do regional trade agreements improve welfare? Welfare gains from trade creation may be outweighed by losses from trade diversion, as members switch imports from more efficient producers outside the union to less efficient producers inside (Viner, 1950). Would this happen in East Asia? Consider an ESCAP simulation

(Continued on next page)

Box 2.3 *(continued)*

of two scenarios, ASEAN+3 and ASEAN+6, using the Global Trade Analysis Project (GTAP) model to estimate the welfare effects.[a]

In both, the effects are small (see figure below). The largest welfare improvement is for Malaysia under the ASEAN+6 scenario, where GDP is estimated to increase by 1.35%. The median improvement in GDP for the participating countries is only 0.4% under ASEAN+3 and 0.55% under ASEAN+6. But though small, the welfare effects of cutting tariffs are overwhelmingly positive, suggesting that trade-creation gains outweigh trade-diversion losses. The exceptions are the Philippines, with no gains under either scenario, China, with no gains under ASEAN+3, and India, with a small loss under ASEAN+6.[b] ASEAN+6 brings larger improvements in welfare to all countries except Thailand, India and Japan. The varying extent of welfare gains from these agreements could be due to many factors, including the complementarity of trade among the countries concerned and the level of existing tariff protection.

Figure. ASEAN+3 and ASEAN+6 are welfare-improving: Simulated welfare effects on selected countries

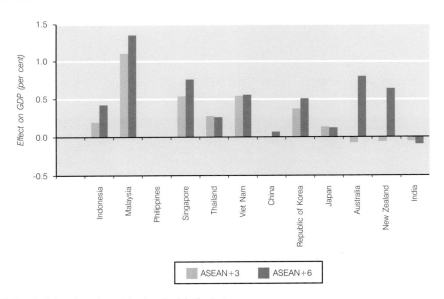

Source: ESCAP calculations based on data described in the text.

---

[a] The simulations assume that all the products of all the countries are transferred to the inclusion list. The GTAP model does not include Brunei Darussalam, Cambodia, the Lao People's Democratic Republic or Myanmar; so, for the purposes of the simulation, ASEAN comprises only Indonesia, Malaysia, the Philippines, Singapore, Thailand and Viet Nam. The assumption is that AFTA's tariff cuts are completed in the base case.

[b] Not surprisingly, Australia, India and New Zealand experience welfare losses under the ASEAN+3 scenario because they lose market access to China, Japan and the Republic of Korea.

(Continued overleaf)

Box 2.3 *(continued)*

Such simulations should be taken with great caution: differences in assumptions, databases, and scenarios can change the results. Compared with results for ASEAN+3 obtained by other researchers, those here, with a median-country welfare gain of 0.4% of GDP, are at the bottom end of the spectrum (table a). Kawai and Wignaraja's (2007) results, with a median-country welfare gain of 4.8% of GDP, are at the high end. The disparities can be partly explained by differences in the modelling assumptions. For instance, ESCAP's simulations capture just static gains from trade and are based on the assumption that only goods trade is liberalized through tariff cuts. In contrast, Kawai and Wignaraja's (2007) simulations allow trade to affect capital stocks through investment activities, assume that both goods and services trade is liberalized, and consider the impact of trade facilitation measures.[c] However, the other studies support the finding of welfare gains from ASEAN+3 and suggest that further gains are possible if liberalization beyond trade in goods and the removal of other forms of trade barriers are taken into account.

Does cutting tariffs reduce poverty? The answer depends on how trade liberalization affects incomes and prices in the consumption basket of the poor. ESCAP used the ratio of unskilled workers' wages to the prices of primary commodities and textiles as a rough measure of the real consumption of the poor, and consumption-to-poverty elasticities to estimate the final impact on headcount poverty ratios, following Anderson et al. (2006). The analysis suggests that ASEAN+3 could reduce the number of people living on less than a dollar a day by 9.3% (2.7 million people) in Indonesia, Malaysia, Philippines, Thailand and Viet Nam, with over 80% of the reduction in Viet Nam and Indonesia.

Table a. Simulations agree on welfare gains from ASEAN+3, disagree on the magnitude

(Per cent)

	Urata and Kiyota (2003)	Gilbert et al. (2004)	Mohanty et al. (2006)	Joint Expert Group (2006)	Plummer and Wignaraja (2007)	Kawai and Wignaraja (2007)	ESCAP	Median
Indonesia	4.9	0.4	1.8	1.7	0.4	2.6	0.2	1.7
Malaysia	2.2	0.4	1.9	5.8	4.6	5.5	1.1	2.2
Philippines	0.8		1.3	4.0	0.5	2.6		1.3
Singapore	3.7	2.5	3.1	4.2	1.5	4.8	0.5	3.1
Thailand	12.5	1.6	2.8	4.5	3.0	12.1	0.3	3.0
Viet Nam	6.6	3.1		2.8	3.3	7.4	0.5	3.2
China	0.6		0.6	1.7	−0.2	1.3		0.6
Japan	0.2	0.1	2.5	0.4	0.3	1.5	0.1	0.3
Republic of Korea	1.8	0.7	3.0	3.5	3.5	6.2	0.4	3.0
Median	2.2	0.7	2.2	3.5	1.5	4.8	0.4	2.2

Notes: Data for Mohanty et al. (2006) are based on ASEAN+4 (ASEAN+3 + India). For Plumner and Wignaraja (2007), China includes Hong Kong, China. Numbers below 0.1% in absolute value not shown.

---

[c] Another reason for the disparities is that ESCAP's baseline scenario is based on the latest tariff data, which includes reductions agreed under the Uruguay Round. With lower baseline tariffs, the gains from additional trade liberalization are diminished.

(Continued on next page)

Box 2.3 *(continued)*

ASEAN+3 is estimated to reduce the number of people living on less than 2 dollars a day in these countries by 3.5% (6.7 million people), suggesting that the impact of ASEAN+3 on poverty reduction is about three times greater than that of just completing AFTA. And ASEAN+3 is estimated to reduce the number of people living under a dollar a day in China by 1.2% (2.1 million people). Although ASEAN+6 is expected to slightly reduce India's GDP, ESCAP estimates that it would reduce the number of people living under a dollar a day by 1.2% (4.1 million people).

Should regional trade agreements be the end goal? Additional simulations show that the gains from global free trade are substantially larger than those from regional trade agreements. Overall, welfare and the potential for poverty reduction increase as economic integration expands from the completion of AFTA, to ASEAN+3, ASEAN+6, and global free trade (table b). This is true both for ASEAN countries, its new partners, and the world at large. Therefore, while the current efforts towards increased regional trade integration are steps in the right direction, multilateralization should continue, despite the difficulties of the Doha Round.

Table b. Global free trade gains exceed those from regional trade liberalization

	Completion of AFTA	ASEAN+3	ASEAN+6	Global free trade
Effects on welfare (millions of United States dollars)				
ASEAN	580	2 170	2 940	4 900
China, Republic of Korea, and Japan	−340	6 950	8 260	27 400
Australia, India, and New Zealand	−50	−510	2 830	3 900
World	−200	3 800	8 100	59 800
Poverty reduction (millions of persons living under $1/day)				
ASEAN	0.9	2.7	3.3	7.2
China	−0.1	2.1	2.5	17.3
India	−0.1	−0.2	4.1	6.6

Sources: ESCAP simulations based on GTAP model.
Note: ASEAN under effects on welfare excludes Brunei Darussalam, Cambodia, Lao People's Democratic Republic and Myanmar.

Policy research feature 2.5: Can the least developed countries of Asia and the Pacific escape the vulnerability trap?

Asia-Pacific, the world's most dynamic region, hosts some of the world's most vulnerable countries, vulnerable to climate change, imperiled by rising sea levels or unable to break the vicious circle of conflict and poverty.

There are enormous differences among Asia-Pacific's 14 most vulnerable – and least developed – countries. One group has successfully started transforming economic structures, some with the potential to become Asia's next newly industrializing countries. Another group is still in conflict or just emerging, leaving a weak and vulnerable economic base. A third group, the Pacific island countries, is wealthier but highly vulnerable, suffering from frequent shocks that imperil development.

How can economic vulnerability be measured?

Economic vulnerability, one criterion for classifying a country as least developed, is measured in the United Nations System by a "economic vulnerability index" that includes economic structures, such as export

concentration and the share of agriculture in GDP; population; remoteness from major markets; the number of people displaced by natural disasters and instability of agricultural production and exports of goods and services.

But the index has to be improved. Based on data with a time lag, it fails to portray the full threat of climate change. It does not distinguish between country-inherent vulnerability, such as geography, and structural vulnerability, which can be reduced through policy interventions (Briguglio, 2005). And the index does not capture internal vulnerability – civil war, political unrest, financial crises.

Of the region's least developed countries, Bangladesh is the least economically vulnerable. The Pacific island least developed countries have the highest vulnerability but the highest per capita incomes and human development (table 2.14). Incomes in the Pacific islands have frequent spikes and setbacks. In Kiribati, Solomon Islands and Vanuatu incomes were lower in 2004 than in 1980. Over the same period many other least developed countries have grown enormously. Empirical studies have also shown that countries with higher growth

Table 2.14. Wealth, human assets and vulnerability in the least developed countries in Asia and the Pacific

	Population 2004 (millions)	Per capita gross national income (United States dollars)	Human assets index	Economic vulnerability index
Afghanistan	29.9	122	11.5	60.3
Bangladesh	141.8	403	60.1	25.8
Bhutan	2.2	690	44.4	46.6
Cambodia	14.1	303	46	52.3
Kiribati	0.1	917	90.5	84.3
Lao PDR	5.9	350	54	57.9
Maldives	0.3	2 320	81.9	50.5
Myanmar	50.5	167	68.4	42.2
Nepal	27.1	243	56	37.4
Samoa	0.2	1 597	90.4	64.7
Solomon Islands	0.5	557	70.6	56.9
Timor-Leste	0.9	467	55.3	65.2
Tuvalu	0.01	1 267	89.7	91.9
Vanuatu	0.2	1 187	66	64.3

Source: Committee for Development Policy (2006), "Report on the eighth session", *Official Records of the Economic and Social Council, 1999, Supplement No. 13* (E/2006/33).

volatility tend to have lower long-term growth (Ramey and Ramey, 1995; Guillaumont, 1999 and 2006).

Geography traps: small, remote, sea-locked

The Asia-Pacific region hosts geographic extremes: six countries consist of small islands, four are landlocked. The geographic disadvantages of Pacific island countries are evident in their economic structures, skewed towards exports in vulnerable sectors, such as agriculture or tourism, leading to highly volatile export yields. The result is macroeconomic instability, with chronic trade deficits that can be sustained only by capital inflows.

Small size hinders economies of scale, which restricts development and makes public goods more expensive. The world's successful small countries have mitigated the negative impact by finding economic niches, harnessing the potential of surrounding economies or, if lucky, exploiting natural resources. The Pacific islands, however, are small, sea-locked, resource-poor and remote (Briguglio, 2004).

Pacific island States also have the highest export concentration-measured by the Hirshman-Herfindahl-Index of export concentration-among the region's low-income and lower middle-income countries, concentration that has barely decreased over time (figure 2.35). Empirical studies have found a correlation between export concentration and growth volatility (Jansen, 2004).

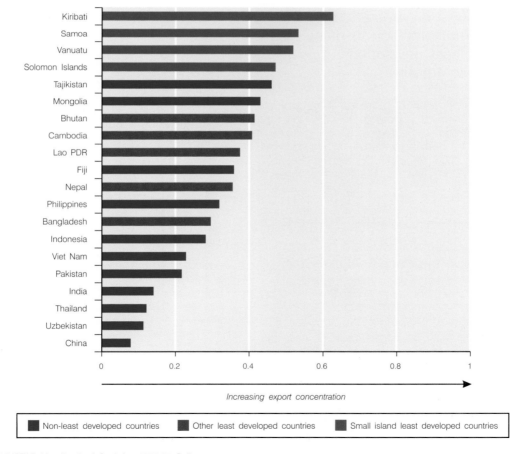

Figure 2.35. Export concentration for selected Asian and Pacific countries (Hirshman-Herfindahl-Index, average over 1980-2004)

Increasing export concentration

■ Non-least developed countries   ■ Other least developed countries   ■ Small island least developed countries

Source: UNCTAD Handbook of Statistics 2006-07 Online.

Note: Data are unavailable for Afghanistan, Maldives, Myanmar and Timor-Leste.

Export earnings have also been highly volatile in Pacific island States; in other countries, whether least developed or not, earnings tend to have grown consistently (figures 2.36 and 2.37).

The threat from climate change

Natural disasters are another source of vulnerability, their increasing frequency often attributed to climate change. Such disasters reduce growth and exports and undermine the balance of payments (Auffret, 2003; Crowards, 2000; Gassebner, 2006). Small countries, especially small islands, are hit harder by natural disasters. A major disaster in a large country will usually be confined to a relatively small area and affect only a fraction of its people. The cyclone that hit Samoa in 1990 inflicted damage equivalent to 100% of GDP, affecting nearly all its people (table 2.15). As both least developed countries and small island developing States, Pacific island countries need special attention and international support to tackle these threats.

Economic transformation in many Asia-Pacific least developed countries, but not all

Asia-Pacific least developed countries in general still have a higher share of agriculture to GDP than the comparator countries in the region, exposing them to weather conditions and dependence on world prices. Afghanistan, the Lao People's Democratic Republic, Myanmar and Nepal have a share approaching or exceeding 40%.

Economic transformation remains elusive in the Pacific, Afghanistan, Myanmar and Timor Leste

---

Many Asia-Pacific least developed countries have initiated an economic transformation over the last quarter-century, reducing the share of agricultural raw material in merchandise exports – from 48% in 1980 to 1% in 2004 in Nepal (World Bank, 2006). Economic transformation remains elusive in two groups of countries: Pacific island countries and Afghanistan, Myanmar and Timor-Leste.

The share of agriculture in GDP is relatively low in the Pacific islands, but economic transformation remains limited. Agricultural productivity has fallen, and output

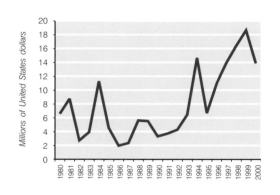

Figure 2.36. Kiribati's export earnings were volatile over 1980-2000…

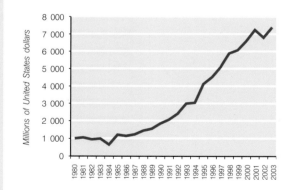

Figure 2.37. …but Bangladesh's grew steadily

Source: World Bank, *World Development Indicators Database.*

Table 2.15. Worst natural disasters in the low-income countries of the Asian and Pacific region, 1980-2003

		Event	Total persons affected		Estimated damage	
			Number (thousands)	Population affected (per cent)	Value (millions of United States dollars)	Share of GDP (per cent)
Samoa+	1990	Cyclone Ofa	170	100.0	200	105.5
Kiribati+	1999	Drought	84	95.0		..
Vanuatu+	1985	Cyclone Eric & Nigel	118	91.0	173	109.2
Samoa+	1991	Cyclone Val & Wasa[a]	85	52.8	278	150.1
Cambodia	1994	Drought	5 000	46.0	100	4.1
Bangladesh	1988	Flood[a]	45 000	42.9	2 137	7.9
India	1987	Drought	300 000	37.6	..	..
Fiji+	1998	Drought	263	33.0	..	..
Solomon Islands+	1986	Cyclone Namu	90	32.0	..	..

Sources: EM-DAT, *Emergency Disasters Database;* and World Bank, *World Development Indicators Database.*

Notes: Bold indicates a least developed country. A "+" indicates a small island developing country.

[a] Same disaster accounts for the highest percentage of the population affected and damage/GDP.

is volatile, with slow average growth over the last 20 years. The high agricultural volatility is closely related to natural disasters. And the overall contribution of agriculture to the economy is much higher than its share of GDP because most manufactured exports are based on processing agricultural goods.

The second group has barely transformed because of governance factors. Afghanistan's long conflict has not been fully resolved. Timor-Leste, also with a long history of conflict, has only recently gained independence. These are not economies where a manufacturing sector can be established. In Myanmar, the share of agriculture in GDP has increased from 46% in 1980 to 57% in 2000. In 1992, the last year with data, the share of agricultural raw material in exports was 35%, by far the highest share of Asia's low-income and lower middle-income countries (Hauff, 2007).

Remittances and aid can reduce vulnerability – or increase it

Inflows from aid or remittances can mitigate trade deficits and help balance the current account. But they can also be volatile, potentially increasing vulnerability. In Samoa, remittances are an important contributor to the economy and, in absolute numbers, have been stable over time. In Bangladesh, the Lao People's Democratic Republic and Nepal, remittances in absolute numbers and as a share of GDP are becoming more important (figure 2.38).

Whether remittances cushion economic shocks is debated. If remittances are driven by altruism, the diaspora may increase flows during a major economic shock. Empirical studies on Bangladesh, however, found little evidence that remittances rise in response to an internal economic shock (IMF, 2007). Remittances have, however, cushioned oil price shocks, perhaps driven less by altruism than by the fact that most Bangladeshi workers migrate to oil-rich Arab countries. In Nepal, remittances sustained the economy during the recent political crisis and prevented larger losses in growth. Nepal had GDP growth of -0.6% in 2002, but remittances sharply increased.

The major official development assistance (ODA) recipients in the region are Afghanistan, Solomon Islands and Timor-Leste, all of them conflict or post-conflict countries. ODA dependence in these countries also reflects their narrow economic base, and concerns about Dutch disease have already been raised (EIU, 2007). Although Pacific island countries receive high amounts of ODA per capita due to their small populations, ODA represents only about 10% of GDP, similar to Bhutan, Cambodia and the Lao People's Democratic Republic (figure 2.39).

Most least developed countries in Asia-Pacific that have initiated economic transformation are no longer dependent on ODA. In Bangladesh, the ratio of ODA to GDP is only 2.5%. ODA in these countries has been volatile, however, because of emergency aid after floods and cyclones.

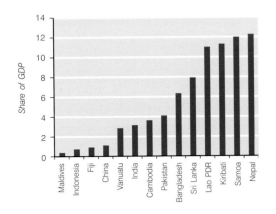

Figure 2.38. Remittances as a share of GDP in selected Asian and Pacific countries, 2004

Source: ESCAP calculations based on World Bank, *World Development Indicators Database.*

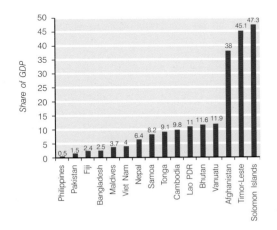

Figure 2.39. Aid dominates economies in Afghanistan, Solomon Islands and Timor-Leste: ODA receipts as a share of GDP, 2004

Source: ESCAP calculations based on World Bank, *World Development Indicators Database.*

Weak economic environments, persistent economic vulnerability

A capable State is better able to mitigate economic shocks and promote economic transformation, reducing vulnerability. Small countries may have advantages here: research has found that small countries tend to develop better institutions because enforcement is likely to be more effective (Fors, 2006).

The World Bank's Doing Business rankings, one indicator of the institutional environment, reveal that, among Asia-Pacific least developed countries, the institutional environment is most conducive in the Pacific islands. These countries have mitigated their geographic disadvantages by making it easier to do business. But there is still room for improvement. Timor-Leste, a conflict country until recently, ranks 174 of 175 countries surveyed. No survey has not been conducted for Afghanistan or Myanmar, but anecdotal evidence suggests a difficult security situation and widespread corruption in Afghanistan and a restrictive macroeconomic environment in Myanmar (Hauff, 2007).

Improving the business environment a key challenge for LDCs

Infrastructure and human capital are also essential for a conducive economic environment, necessary to kick-start an economic transformation – and to reduce vulnerability. Human assets, including health and education, are low in Afghanistan and Timor-Leste but disproportionately high in Myanmar (see table 2.14). The Pacific island countries have the highest human asset indicators in the group of Asia-Pacific least developed countries. Having improved the institutional environment within their control, they are trapped by geographic disadvantages.

Infrastructure – the road network, electricity supply and information and communications technology coverage – is particularly weak in Afghanistan, Myanmar and Timor-Leste. Afghanistan's road density is among the lowest in the region, as is its number of Internet users (0.9 users per 1,000 people). Myanmar has the second lowest number of Internet users in the region (1.3 users per 1,000 people) and by far the lowest share of mobile phone subscribers (1.8 users per 1,000 people) (World Bank, 2006).

Improving the business environment is among the key challenges for the large group of least developed countries that have embarked on economic transformation and that will likely find ways out of the vulnerability trap (Bhutan, for example, ranks 138). For the landlocked countries in the group, this will also mean improving integration with the global trade system and improving transportation.

The vicious circle of conflict and poverty

Some countries in Asia-Pacific, notably Afghanistan, have been hard hit by repeated conflicts and seem to be trapped in a vicious circle of conflict and poverty. The effects of civil wars and other conflicts can be similar to those of economic shocks and natural disasters, with growth reduced by 2.2% a year during conflict (Collier, 1999). And it can take much longer to recover from a civil war, as spending shifts from social to military, lowering human capital and increasing

poverty. Cambodia still suffers from the long-term loss of human capital under the Khmer Rouge regime (de Walque, 2004). Even after a conflict, the government priority is often physical infrastructure, leaving little room for social spending. If the problems that led to the conflict are not addressed, rising social tensions can lead to social mobilization and raise the spectre of a new conflict.

> *Economic transformation is impossible in conflict-torn LDCs*

Economic transformation is impossible in such circumstances. Establishing peace and security and making a commitment to equitable and inclusive development must therefore be the first step towards more sustainable – and less vulnerable – economies. Priority must also be given to reducing the risk of reigniting a civil war.

Developed economies: Continued growth heightens capacity constraints

After growing at 2.4% in 2006, the Japanese economy – the largest in the region – continued to grow modestly at 1.8% in 2007 (figure 2.40). Profit growth continued in the corporate sector, thanks to solid business sector growth and rebounding export growth from Asia in the third quarter. But Japan's economy also faced significant challenges. Household consumption decelerated in mid-year. And, starting in July 2007, a plunge in construction further deteriorated private investment.

> *The troubled US credit market did not slow investment demand growth in the developed economies in 2007*

A rapidly ageing society (see policy research feature 2.6), Japan faces the major policy challenge of making its social security system work despite massive public debt. The government had envisaged achieving a primary budget balance in 2007, but in fact the pressure on public finances remained intense and Japan's fiscal position got worse. The net public debt for 2007 stood at over 180% of GDP. Yet any attempt at fiscal consolidation might seriously damage fragile consumer confidence.

Figure 2.40. Economic growth in developed ESCAP countries, 2005-2007

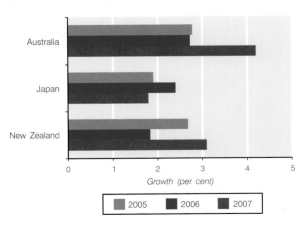

Sources: ESCAP, based on national sources; and ESCAP estimates.

Note: Data for 2007 are estimates.

Economic growth gained speed in Australia and New Zealand in 2007. The Australian economy recorded its 17th consecutive year of expansion, led by renewed strength in household consumption and by continued private investment growth. Its overall GDP growth rate was 4.2% in 2007, up from 2.7% in 2006. But strong growth in non-farm sector production was partly offset by a large drop in farm sector production, reflecting the drought. New Zealand, with nearly a decade of growth behind it, maintained strong growth momentum. Its GDP growth rate was 3.1% in 2007, up from 1.8% in 2006. As in Australia, household consumption – encouraged in New Zealand by continued wage growth and a tax policy on disposable income – led growth in domestic demand. Export demand also remained robust.

Growth was supported by domestic demand

The troubled United States credit market has not yet slowed investment demand growth in the developed economies. In Japan, continued corporate profit growth and a relatively optimistic view of future growth prospects encouraged further investment in 2007. With external demand still solid, the business sector, particularly large manufacturers, enjoyed strong profit growth and remained generally optimistic about their prospects. Investment growth was modest in 2007, however, compared with that of past years. The increasing cost of production has progressively squeezed profits in the business sector, especially for small and medium-sized enterprises, as competitive pressures prevent firms from passing on increased production costs to consumers. And private investment suffered a major setback after June 2007, when a revised building standards law took effect, precipitating a sharp decline in construction starts. In September 2007, non-residential construction dropped by 54% (though this is considered a temporary impact, and construction starts are expected to rebound in 2008). Finally, according to the Tankan Survey, a short-term economic survey of enterprises in Japan conducted by the Bank of Japan and released in December, uncertainty about the effect of the subprime loan crisis on the United States economy has eroded business confidence (Bank of Japan 2007).

In Australia, as commodity prices level out and investment opportunities in natural-resource-based sectors become increasingly scarce, a moderation in private fixed investment has resulted. In addition, credit conditions have tightened. The problem of the United States credit market has not directly affected business sector investment decisions, and strong profit growth still whets the appetite for investment in the non-mining sector. But tighter conditions in the global money market have led domestic banks to meet strong demand for credit by switching from external funding to domestic sources, pushing up the interest rate in the second half of 2007.

Wage growth stimulated household consumption

Household consumption supported growth in all three developed economies, though not by the same amount in each. In Japan, household consumption growth remained modest. But rising business profits have slowly increased household income through employment growth and dividend payments to shareholders. Private consumption therefore continued to grow moderately, though sluggish wage growth and high oil prices discouraged consumer confidence. As with non-residential construction, housing construction also dropped suddenly in July 2007 in Japan – with largest fall during September by 44%.

> *Household consumption supported growth in all three developed economies*

Australia's household consumption regained strength in 2007. A tax cut, and continued growth in employment and wages, drove disposable income up. The rise in disposable income outweighed consumption growth, yielding a modest rise in household savings. Factors that had militated against consumption growth in 2006 were absent in 2007, as increased housing prices added to household wealth while a strong Australian dollar cushioned the economy against the impact of high oil prices.

Despite wage growth in New Zealand, household consumption there is showing signs of slowing down. As the housing market cools, households find it increasingly difficult to balance expenditure with rising debt service costs. Household debt has risen with rising interest rates – from 100% of disposable income in 2003 to 160% in 2007. But continued growth in wages and employment has partly offset the problem.

A tight labour market led to wage growth in Australia and New Zealand but not in Japan

The tightening of labour markets has become a source of concern for all three developed economies. Japan's tight labour market has not caused wages to grow. Although the unemployment rate fell to a 10-year low, the demand for labour was largely met by an increase in the number of part-time workers, who earn much less than regular workers. More downward pressures have accompanied the retirement of the baby boomers, who typically earn much more than younger workers under Japan's chiefly seniority-based wage system. If Japan's tight labour market inspires more rapid wage growth in the coming years, consumer demand will grow along with it.

In Australia and New Zealand – unlike Japan – the tight labour market did prompt wage growth. Australia's labour shortage continued in 2007. Its unemployment rate reached 4.3% in the third quarter of 2007, a multi-decade low, and the labour participation rate was at a record high. Firms' intention to recruit remained high. Regions benefiting from the commodity price boom contributed most to the trend. In New Zealand, in the third quarter of 2007, the unemployment rate fell to a historical low of 3.5%. The business sector found it more difficult to find skilled and unskilled labour. But New Zealand's employment growth did not indicate a rise in full-time employment. Instead it reflected additions to the number of part-time workers, which outpaced a reduction in the number of regular workers.

The tightening labour markets in the three developed economies differed qualitatively in one respect: employment growth in Australia was associated with an increase in full-time employment, but only part-time employment increased in Japan and New Zealand.

Inflationary pressure remained a concern in Australia and New Zealand; production costs increased in Japan

Japan's corporate price inflation remained at about 2% in 2007, reflecting high oil prices and an increase in commodity prices combined with a weaker exchange rate. With tightening labour market conditions, the hourly wages of part-time workers have been increasing more rapidly than those of regular workers. Price increases at the producer level, however, were not passed on to consumers due to downward price pressures from market competition. Consumer price inflation in Japan continued to hover around 0% in 2007 (figure 2.41).

> *Inflationary pressure continued to cause concern for both Australia and New Zealand in 2007, leading to monetary tightening*

By contrast, inflationary pressure continued to cause concern for both Australia and New Zealand in 2007, leading to monetary tightening in both countries. At the end of the year consumer price inflation appeared to have been contained. Australia's consumer price inflation rate, after peaking at 4% in mid-2006, decelerated to 1.9% by the third quarter of 2007. Thus consumer price inflation in Australia fell from 3.5% in 2006 to 2.4% in 2007. Because the decrease largely reflected the price volatility of few items, such as oil and fruit, inflationary pressure remained a concern – particularly while the labour market was tight and capacity use was high – and the Reserve Bank of Australia continued to tighten its monetary policy in 2007, raising the official cash rate to 6.75%. New Zealand's consumer price index fell from 3.4% in 2006 to 2.4% in 2007, but the drop is likely a temporary effect of changes in government policy. Capacity constraints and high prices for inputs, such as oil and dairy products, drove output prices up. Gradually the increase was passed on to consumers. The Reserve Bank of New Zealand

Figure 2.41. Inflation in developed ESCAP economies, 2005-2007

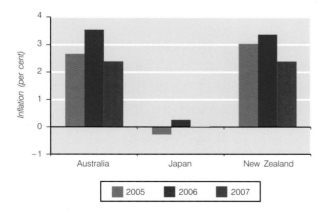

Sources: ESCAP, based on national sources; and ESCAP estimates.

Notes: Data for 2007 are estimates. Inflation rates refer to percentage changes in the consumer price index.

tightened its monetary policy four times during 2007, bringing the overnight cash rate to 8.25%.

The trade surplus increased in Japan, while Australia and New Zealand remained in deficit

Japan's trade surplus expanded in 2007. Strong export growth continued, but import growth slowed reflecting rising import prices and subdued growth in domestic demand. Although demand for Japan's exports weakened in the United States, demand from other parts of the world remained solid in 2007. By 2006 the share of export demand from Asia had already increased to 46%, led by rapidly growing demand from China. Whereas the share of demand for Japanese exports from China and Hong Kong, China, had stood at 12% in 2000, by 2006 this figure had risen to 20% – almost equal to the 22% share of export demand from the United States in 2006.

The sources of Japan's export growth have diversified in the past five years among China, other Asian countries and the European Union. While almost 30% of export growth was attributed to United States demand in 2000, this share had shrunk to less than 10% by 2006. So, the direct impact of the United States economic slowdown on Japanese exports has been partly offset by the growth of demand from other regions. But there is still uncertainty about the magnitude of the slowdown's effects, as it is likely to reduce United States demand for Asian products.

Australia's current account deficit has widened, as has its trade deficit (table 2.16). Import growth exceeded export growth. Export volumes continued to grow in all but rural sectors. From mid-2005 to September 2007, resource sector exports expanded by 22%. But their growth has still been constrained by production capacity – as was seen, for example, in mining production – though continued investment in recent years has gradually eased those constraints. Import growth in 2007 was supported by strong domestic demand and a strong exchange rate. All the major components of imports increased. Capital import was particularly strong, reflecting still-robust investment growth. The net income deficit remained high, at 4.5% of GDP, reflecting the high equity payments of foreign companies operating in Australia and the high interest payments due to a rising stock of net debt.

In New Zealand export growth exceeded import growth, reducing the current account deficit. The strong growth in exports reflected robust external demand. Moreover, export volume soared as dairy product prices increased. But the high exchange rate partly offset commodity price increases in domestic

Table 2.16. Budget and current account balances in developed ESCAP countries, 2004-2007

(Percentage of GDP)

	2004	2005	2006	2007
Budget balance				
Australia[a]	2.0	2.4	1.6	0.8
Japan	–6.2	–4.8	–4.1	–3.9
New Zealand[b]	4.6	5.7	5.0	2.9
Current account balance				
Australia	–6.0	–5.8	–5.5	–5.8
Japan	3.7	3.6	3.9	4.9
New Zealand	–6.6	–8.9	–9.0	–8.1

Sources: ESCAP, based on IMF, *International Financial Statistics* (CD-ROM) (Washington, D.C., September 2007) and *World Economic Outlook Databases* (Washington, D.C., October 2007); and ESCAP estimates.

Notes: Data for 2007 are estimates. Budget balance is the general government fiscal balance as a percentage of GDP. Current account balance is as a percentage of GDP.

[a] Data exclude net advances (primarily privatization receipts and net policy-related lending).
[b] Government balance is revenue minus expenditure plus balance of State-owned enterprises, excluding privatization receipts.

currency. Demand for imported capital goods was modest, while the higher exchange rate muted the value of the imports volume.

Growth is expected to slow in 2008-2009

Developed economies in the region are expected to grow more slowly in the coming years. A moderation of external demand is expected in Japan. In Australia and New Zealand, private consumption is expected to cool in response to tight monetary policy.

Japan's economy is forecast to slow to 1.4% in 2008, and to 1.3% in 2009, as external demand softens. Demand from China will become more moderate. And the United States economic slowdown may directly and indirectly moderate demand from other trading partners in Asia. Nevertheless, construction starts are expected to grow strongly in 2008, as plans that were delayed because of the 2007 construction law revisions are gradually implemented. And household expenditure will support domestic demand – if the tight labour market translates into wage growth.

In Australia, economic growth is expected to slow to 3.2% in 2008 and 2.8% in 2009. Private consumption, buoyed by disposable income growth from tax cuts and wage and employment growth, is expected to support overall economic growth – though a tighter

monetary policy would gradually decelerate consumption growth. Private investment is likely to slow down with tighter monetary conditions and fewer opportunities to invest in the mining sector.

New Zealand's economic growth is also expected to become more moderate, at 2.3% in 2008 and 2.7% in 2009. With tight monetary policy continuing and debt-laden households bearing a heavier burden of interest payments, household consumption will be subdued.

> *Despite the rising importance of China, Japanese economy still linked closely to the United States*

There are still considerable uncertainties over the magnitude of the slowdown in the United States economy, as it may gradually erode economic growth in these countries in 2008 through reduced demand for their exports and uncertainties in global credit markets, although the short-term impact on the three economies has been limited so far.

For instance, the increasing reliance of the Japanese economy on Asia, particularly China, has given rise to the notion that Japanese economy may be decoupling from the United States economy. Japanese export growth in the past five years is largely attributable to the demand from Asia, most notably from China. One-fifth of Japanese exports are destined to the United States markets, while another one-fifth goes to China and Hong Kong, China. Nonetheless, a significant amount of Japanese exports to Asia, particularly China, is likely to end up in the United States, as Asian countries process intermediary goods imported from Japan and export them to the United States. Thus the impact of the United States economy slowdown will be felt directly as well as indirectly through the reduced demand from Asia for Japanese products. ESCAP analysis shows that 1 percentage point reduction of United States GDP growth will reduce Japan's GDP growth by 0.3 percentage points, while it will reduce the growth of China by 1.2 percentage points. Still if China manages to withstand the United States slowdown and continues to accelerate its economic growth by 1 percentage point above the baseline projection, the impact on Japan would be negligible. It suggests that despite the rising importance of the Chinese economy for Japanese trade, prospects of the Japanese economy may be linked more closely with the United States economy. It should be noted, however, that the model may not fully capture the reactions of financial sector nor the impact of the shocks on consumers and business confidence.

Policy research feature 2.6: How secure is retirement in Japan?

Near the top of the list of countries with ageing populations, Japan faces monumental challenges in its public pension system. Despite low incomes, Japan's elderly seem, on average, to be able to maintain living conditions similar to those before their retirement. But averages can mislead. Disaggregated data show that a possibly significant proportion of elderly people experience difficulties in maintaining a minimum standard of living – particularly those unable to earn additional income beyond the basic pension.[7]

Socio-economic change has eroded the traditional family support system and increased the number of households with only one or two elderly people. Longer life expectancy means that elderly people must have the means to support themselves, either on their own or through institutional support, long after retirement. The public pension, including the universal basic pension, is an important source of income for elderly people and reduces the number of low-income households. But the basic pension alone is insufficient for an adequate living standard, and a large proportion of elderly people rely solely on it. Although a social safety net is in place, its stringent eligibility criteria discourage many from applying. While the heavy burden of social expenditure leads to the charge that current pensioners enjoy an affluent retirement life at the cost of future generations, there have been surprising reports on the "poverty" of elderly people.[8]

Income, consumption and savings among Japan's elderly

Elderly people tend to have lower incomes than the working age population because many of them withdraw from the labour market. Of Japan's elderly households, 45% belong to the lowest income quartile (figure 2.42). In 2002, more than 20% of elderly people in Japan had incomes below the poverty line, compared with 13.5% among the working age population.

In disposable incomes, however, elderly people as a group are not particularly worse off. Disposable in-

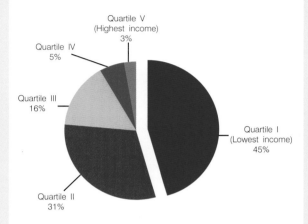

Figure 2.42. Nearly half of Japan's elderly households are low income: Distribution of elderly households by income quartile

Source: Calculations based on Ministry of Health, Labour and Welfare, *Comprehensive Survey of the Living Conditions of the People 2005* (Tokyo).

come tends to decline with age, but elderly people in Japan still have about 80% of the working-age disposable income. A disproportionate share of single-person households are in the low-income group (figure 2.43).

> *In 2002, more than 20% of elderly people in Japan had incomes below the poverty line*

Older couples maintain consumption similar to that of younger couples, if with different patterns. Older people spend significantly less on housing than younger people, reflecting the high rate of home ownership (Yamada and Casey, 2002). Almost 30% of elderly single-person households (65 and older), however, do not own a home; among larger households, home ownership exceeds 90%. The expenditure of single households without real estate is about the half the elderly average, suggesting financial constraints on their consumption.

Figure 2.43. Single-person households are often poor: Distribution of elderly households by type and level of income (over 65)

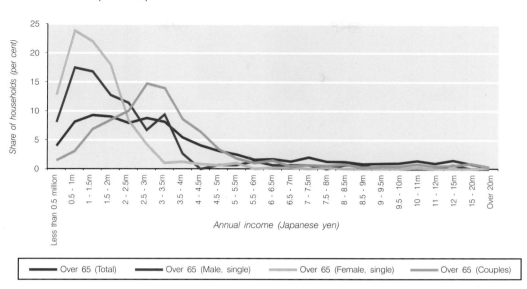

Source: Calculations based on Ministry of Health, Labour and Welfare, *Comprehensive Survey of the Living Conditions of the People 2005* (Tokyo).

Many elderly people maintain their consumption by using financial assets to supplement low incomes. With many employees receiving large lump-sum retirement payments, elderly households appear to have large enough savings to support themselves – at least as a group (figure 2.44). But the averaged data mask uneven distribution. A third of elderly households have savings over ☐20 million ($165,300), but another quarter have savings of less than ☐7.5 million ($62,000), less than twice the average annual earnings of regular workers. One survey indicates that as many as 20% of people older than 60 have no savings (Japan, 2005). And the savings rate among elderly households is declining – from over 20% in the 1990s to just over 10% in the early 2000s). A considerable proportion of elderly people appear to have insufficient funds to support themselves for their two decades of average expected life after retirement.

Income in old age – labour and pensions

A notable feature of elderly people in Japan is their long labour participation beyond retirement age, until age 69 on average (OECD, 2005). To supplement old-age pensions, many people (mostly men) continue to work at lower paying activities after retiring from their

main occupation. More than 70% of men ages 65-69 are employed or willing to work, but many of them have already retired (Japan, 2004a). Labour income is a major determinant of income inequality among the elderly in Japan, putting those without labour income at a disadvantage.

> *Many people continue to work after retiring from their main occupation*

Many people in their 60s stay in labour market. More people, however, cease earning income as they age and come to depend solely on pension benefits. Despite the labour income of "younger" retirees, the dependency of elderly people on pensions is significant. For almost three-quarters of pensioners over 65, pension benefits contribute more than 80% of income (figure 2.45).

The two major financial sources of support for elderly people who withdraw from the labour market are savings and pension payments. A high pension payment can supplement low savings and vice versa, but in reality, low pension earners tend to have smaller

Figure 2.44. Income, savings and liabilities by age group

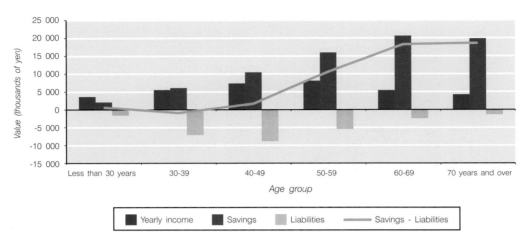

Source: Calculations based on Cabinet Office Statistical Bureau, *Household Savings Survey 2004* (Tokyo).

Figure 2.45. Single elderly people often depend on pensions

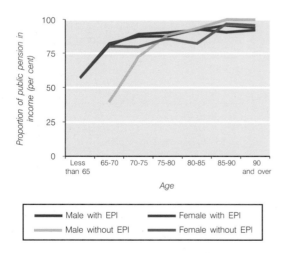

Source: Calculations based on Ministry of Health, Labour and Welfare, *Comprehensive Survey on the Public Pension System 2005* (Tokyo).

Note: EPI is the Employees Pension Insurance Scheme, a pension that covers some private sector workers. With higher contributions made during the working period, workers receiving this pension tend to be better off than those who do not at their retirement.

savings, partly due to the earnings-related public pension system (figure 2.46). More than 30% of the lowest public pension earners have no savings, while over 40% of high public pension earners have savings of more than ¥20 million ($165,300).

Japan's public pension system – and those it leaves behind

Pensions become the major source of income for "older-old" households. But the amount of benefit varies significantly under Japan's public pension structure.

How Japan's public pensions work. The Japanese public pension system has two tiers: the Employees Pension Insurance Scheme (EPI) for many private sector employees and the National Pension System (a basic pension), which consists mostly of self-employed people, farmers and many of the non-regular workers not covered under the EPI.[9] The EPI combines an earnings-related component and a flat-rate basic pension component. The National Pension System is a basic, flat-rate and universal scheme intended to cover all residents over 20 years old. Benefits are

---

[9] Public sector employees are covered by a mutual aid pension scheme, which is similar to the EPI scheme. Both schemes belong to the same group (Category II) in the public pension system.

Figure 2.46. Single households with lower pension benefits have lower savings

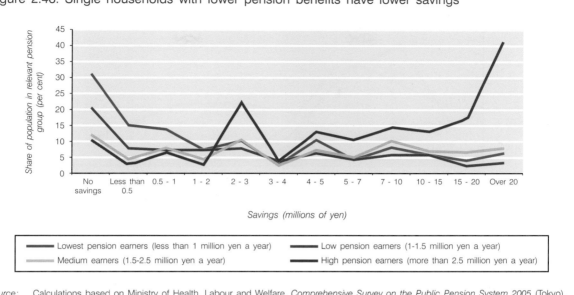

Savings (millions of yen)

| ——— Lowest pension earners (less than 1 million yen a year) | ——— Low pension earners (1-1.5 million yen a year) |
| ——— Medium earners (1.5-2.5 million yen a year) | ——— High pension earners (more than 2.5 million yen a year) |

Source: Calculations based on Ministry of Health, Labour and Welfare, *Comprehensive Survey on the Public Pension System 2005* (Tokyo).

paid from age 65 with a minimum of 25 years of contributions, but full benefits require more than 40 years. About a third of people are covered under the National Pension System.

The higher premium contribution under the EPI is reflected in pension payouts. Average employees under the EPI receive 59% of pre-retirement earnings (Japan, 2004b). Full basic pension benefits correspond to 14% of average earnings.

> *The basic pension does not promise a minimum standard of living*

The large earnings-related component of the EPI means that the public pension system is not very progressive and does not facilitate income redistribution from high- to low-income groups. The basic pension does, however, contribute to poverty reduction among households (Tachibanaki, 2006).

Under the EPI, pre-retirement income determines pension payouts. Employment status during working life makes a big difference in payouts, preserving the wage inequality between regular and non-regular workers. Despite significant variation in pension payouts among former regular workers, most receive

pension benefits well above the basic pension (figure 2.47). Pension receipts by people of other employment status are concentrated around   the basic pension payout.

Although the basic pension is the main source of income for many elderly and a big contributor to poverty reduction, it does not promise a minimum standard of living. As part of the social safety net, Japan has a livelihood assistance programme, designed to ensure a minimum living standard, that differs from the basic pension in scope, eligibility criteria and benefits (table 2.17). The basic pension alone does not guarantee sufficient income to support the minimum standard, particularly for single households. Failure to meet the requirement of 40 years of contributions further reduces payouts.

Because livelihood assistance is meant for the poor, the system is difficult for normal households to use. Eligibility requires stringent means and asset tests.[10] Compounded by the stigma of the scheme, this means that only a small portion of those eligible apply.

---

[10]   The applicant must use all available resources, including assets, ability to work and family support. Land, houses and farms must be sold, and those who are considered capable of working may not be eligible for the assistance, given only to those who have exhausted all these possibilities (National Institute of Population and Social Security Research, 2007a).

Figure 2.47. Distribution of male pensioners by pension benefits and pre-retirement occupation

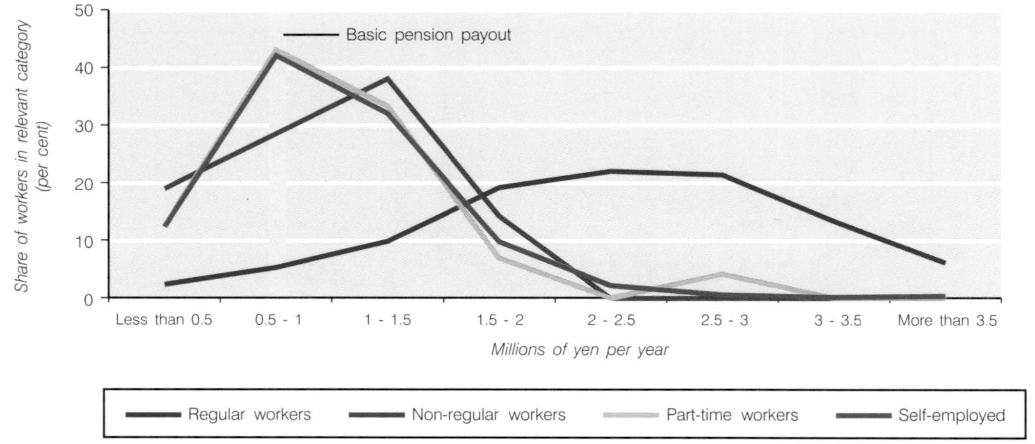

Source: Calculations based on Ministry of Health, Labour and Welfare, *Survey of Old Age Pensioners: Distribution of Pensioners by Pension Benefit Level and by Type of Pre-retirement Employment Status* (Tokyo).

Table 2.17. Eligibility criteria for the livelihood assistance programme and basic pension benefits: Two examples

(Japanese yen per month)

Type of household	Threshold income for livelihood assistance programme (example)		Basic pension payment (full payment)
	Urban areas	Rural areas	
Single person, age 68	80 820	62 640	66 000
Couple, ages 68 and 65	121 940	94 500	132 000

Sources: Social Insurance Agency website <http://www.sia.go.jp/e/np.html>; and Ministry of Health, Labour and Welfare website <http://www.mhlw.go.jp/bunya/seikatsuhogo/seikatuhogo.html>.

Note: Because threshold for livelihood assistance is determined by age, the size of the household and location, the information here is for comparison only.

> *The pension system has created pockets of population that are excluded from benefits*

In 2001, about 5% of the elderly population received livelihood assistance (National Institute of Population and Social Security Research, 2007b). A much larger elderly population has income meeting the eligibility criteria – 28% of elderly single households and 11% of elderly couples by some estimates (Tachibanaki and Urakawa, 2006).

Who the public pension system leaves behind. The public pension system is meant to be universal. In theory, anyone older than 20 who is not part of the EPI is covered under the basic pension (Abe, 2003). But the system has created pockets of the population that, for one reason or another, are wholly or partly excluded. First, people who do not meet the minimum requirement of 25 years of contributions receive no pension. Second, people who are granted an exemption from contribution payments receive a reduced pension if the exemption is too long (the exemption period counts for only a third of a paid period). As of 2005, 25% of those under the contributory basic pension scheme (category I) were exempted from contribution payments. While the exemption is given to disadvantaged groups and those in temporary financial difficulties, the design penalizes them in payouts. Third, more people are defaulting on their premium payments. As of 2004, the default rate of the basic pension – the portion of the expected monthly payment not collected – was 36.4% (Social Insurance Agency, 2007). In a survey of defaulters, almost two-thirds across all age groups cited economic difficulties as the reason for defaulting. For many basic pension participants, exemptions and defaults are temporary, but they run the risk of having little or no entitlement to a basic pension benefit on retirement.

The need to define the role of social insurance

Countries in the region would be able to draw lessons from the Japanese experience in creating a universal pension scheme and the challenges it faced in developing a coherent and effective social insurance scheme. For example, a clear definition is needed of the role and the target group of the public pension system for poverty reduction, income redistribution and compulsory old-age savings. If the basic pension is to ensure a minimum living standard for all, it will need change. The current system has created pockets of people who, for one reason or another, are wholly or partly excluded. For instance, if affordable, New Zealand's far less complicated system, New Zealand Superannuation (NZS), may be one to consider. A flat-rate basic pension provided regardless of other pension income, NZS is an entitlement for everyone older than 65 who satisfies the residential requirement, without asset or income tests. A contribution is not required for eligibility. Benefits are affected only by marital status. The result is that poverty among older generations has been eliminated (OECD, 2007b).

References

Abe, A. (2003). "Low-income people in social security systems in Japan", *Japanese Journal of Social Security Policy,* vol. 2, No. 2, pp. 59-70.

Anderson, K., W. Martin and D. Mensbrugghe (2006). "Global impacts of the Doha scenarios on poverty", World Bank Policy Research Working Paper No. 3735 (Washington, D.C.).

Asian Development Bank (2007). *Key Indicators of Developing Asian and Pacific Countries 2007* (Manila, ADB).

Auffret, P. (2003). "High consumption volatility: the impact of natural disasters", World Bank Working Paper No. 2962 (Washington, D.C., World Bank).

Bank of Japan (2007), The Tankan Survey December 2007, <http://www.boj.or.jp/en/theme/research/stat/tk/index.htm>.

Briguglio, L. (2004). "Economic vulnerability and resilience: concepts and measurements", presented at the International Workshop on Vulnerability and Resilience of Small States, organized by the Commonwealth Secretariat at the University of Malta, University Gozo Centre, Malta, 1-3 March 2004.

_____ (2005). "Small island developing States and their economic vulnerabilities", *World Development,* vol. 23, No. 10, pp. 1615-1632.

China View (2007a). "Silk road center returns to past glory as trading post", 22 November.

China View (2007b). "Tibet's rate of economic growth highest for a decade", 8 February.

China View (2007c). "Chinese Ruili municipality delegation visits Myanmar", 29 March.

China.org.cn (2007). "Inner Mongolia witnesses growing foreign trade", 9 August.

CISSTAT (Interstate Statistical Committee of the Commonwealth of Independent States) (2007). Database statistics of the CIS (Moscow, CISSTAT), <http://cisstat.com/eng/index.htm>.

Collier, P. (1999). "On the economic consequences of civil war", Oxford Economic Papers No. 51, pp.168-183.

Committee for Development Policy (2006). "Report on the eighth session" (20-24 March 2006), *Official Records of the Economic and Social Council, 1999, Supplement No. 13* (E/2006/33).

Conference Board (2007). "Can China's growth trajectory be sustained?", Report No. 1410, 3 December (New York).

Crowards, T. (2000). "Comparative vulnerability to natural disasters in the Caribbean", Staff Working Paper No. 1/00 (St. Michael, Barbados, Caribbean Development Bank).

Economist Intelligence Unit (2007). *Country Reports,* various issues (London, 2007).

ESCAP (2007a). *Economic and Social Survey of Asia and the Pacific 2007* (United Nations publication, Sales No. E.07.II.F.4).

_____ (2007b). *Ten as One: Challenges and Opportunities for ASEAN Integration,* ESCAP Series on Inclusive and Sustainable Development.

Financial Times (2007). "US slowdown threatens Chinese export growth", 15 November 2007.

Fors, H. (2006). "Island status, country size and institutional quality in former colonies", Economic Studies No. 157 (Department of Economics, School of Business, Economics and Law, Goeteborg University).

Galbraith, J., L. Krytynskaia and Q. Wang (2004). "The experience of rising inequality in Russia and China during the transition", *European Journal of Comparative Economics,* vol. 1, No. 1, pp. 87-106.

Gassebner, M., A. Keck and R. Teh (2006). "The impact of disasters on international trade", Staff Working Paper ERSD-2006-04 (World Trade Organization).

Gilbert, J., R. Scollay and B. Bora (2004). "New regional trading developments in the Asia-Pacific region", in Shahid Yusuf, M. Anjum Altaf, and Kaoru Nabeshima (eds.), *Global Change and East Asian Policy Initiatives* (Washington, D.C., World Bank), pp. 121-190.

Guillaumont, P. (1999). "On the economic vulnerability of low income countries", Working paper prepared for the International Task Force on Commodity Risk Management in Developing Countries (World Bank).

Guillaumont, P. (2006). "La vulnérabilité économique, défi persistant à la croissance africaine", 17 novembre 2006 (mimeo).

Hang Seng Bank (2007). *China Economic Monitor* (Hong Kong, December).

Hauff, M. (2007). "Economic and social development in Burma/Myanmar", Marburg.

International Monetary Fund (2003). "Public debt in emerging markets: Is it too high?", Chapter *3 in World Economic Outlook: Public Debt in Emerging Markets,* September 2003 (Washington, D.C.).

_____(2007). "Bangladesh: selected issues", IMF Country Report 07/203, June 2007, (Washington, D.C.).

Institute of Policy Studies (2007). *Sri Lanka State of the Economy 2007* (Colombo, IPS).

Japan (2004a). "Employment survey", Ministry of Health, Labour and Welfare, Tokyo.

_____(2004b). "Review of the financial status of the public pension scheme", Tokyo.

Japan (2005). "White paper on the national lifestyle", Cabinet Office, Tokyo.

Jansen, Marion (2004). *Income Volatility in Small and Developing Economies: Export Concentration Matters* (Geneva, World Trade Organization).

Joint Expert Group (2006). "Towards an East Asia FTA: modality and road map", Report by Joint Expert Group for a Feasibility Study on EAFTA.

Kawai, M. and G. Wignaraja (2007). "ASEAN+3 or ASEAN+6: Which way forward?", ADB Institute Discussion Paper No. 77, September.

Kopits, G. (2007). "Fiscal responsibility framework: international experience and implications for Hungary", Occasional Paper 62, Magyar Nemzeti Bank (Budapest, Central Bank of Hungary).

Mohanty, S.K., S. Pohit and S. Sinha Roy (2004). "Towards formation of close economic cooperation among Asian countries", RIS Discussion Paper No. 78, September (Delhi, Research and Information Systems for the Non-Allied and Other Developing Countries).

National Institute of Population and Social Security Research (2007a). *Social Security in Japan,* Tokyo, <www.ipss.go.jp>.

_____(2007b). "Data on the Livelihood Assistance Programme", <http://www.ipss.go.jp/s-info/j/seiho/seihoH19.xls>.

Organisation for Economic Cooperation and Development (2005). *Society at a Glance 2005* (Paris, OECD Publishing).

_____(2007a). *Economic Survey of Korea* (Paris, OECD Publishing).

_____(2007b). *Economic Survey New Zealand* (Paris, OECD Publishing).

Petrov, N. (2006). "The budget nomenklatura", Carnegie Endowment for International Peace-Carnegie Moscow Center, <http://www. carnegie.ru/en/pubs/media/74914.htm>.

Pinto, B. and F. Zahir (2004). "India: Why fiscal adjustment now?", World Bank Policy Research Working Paper No. 3230 (Washington, D.C.).

Plummer, M. and G. Wignaraja (2007). "The post-sequencing of economic integration in Asia: trade as a complement to a monetary future", Asian Development Bank Series on Regional Economic Integration No. 9 , May.

Ramey, G. and V. A. Ramey (1995). "Cross-country evidence on the link between volatility and growth", *American Economic Review,* vol. 85, No. 5, pp. 1138-1151.

Shah, A. and C. Shen (2006). "The reform of intergovernmental transfer system to achieve a harmonious society and a level playing field for regional development in China", Policy Research Working Paper WPS4100 (Washington, D.C., World Bank).

Social Insurance Agency (2007). "Overview of the social insurance programme in 2005", <http://www.sia.go.jp/infom/tokei/gaikyo2005/gaikyo.pdf>.

Stubbs, R. (2002). "ASEAN plus three: emerging East Asian regionalism?", *Asian Survey* vol. 42, No. 3, pp. 440-455.

Tachibanaki, T. (2006). "Inequality and poverty in Japan", *Japanese Economic Review,* vol. 57, No. 1, pp. 1-27.

Tachibanaki, T. and K. Urakawa (2006). *A Study on Poverty in Japan* (Tokyo, University of Tokyo Press).

Taiwan Headlines (2007). "Exports seen to hit record high of $250b in 2007", 13 December.

United Nations Development Programme (2007), *Human Development Report 2007/2008: Fighting Climate Change: Human Solidarity in a Divided World* (New York, Palgrave McMillan, 2007), <http://hdr.undp.org/>.

Urata, S. and K. Kiyota (2003). "Impacts of an East Asian FTA on foreign trade in East Asia", NBER Working Paper No. 10173 (Cambridge, National Bureau of Economic Research).

Viet Nam (2007). "State president talks up trade with China's Yunnan province", Ministry of Foreign Affairs, 21 May.

Viner, J. (1950). *The Customs Unions Issue* (New York, Carnegie Endowment for International Peace).

Walque, D. (2004). "The long-term legacy of the Khmer Rouge period in Cambodia", World Bank Policy Research Working Paper No. 3446 (Washington, D.C.), November 2004.

Winters, L. and P. Martins (2004). "When comparative advantage is not enough: business costs in small remote economies", *World Trade Review,* vol. 3, No. 3, pp. 347-383.

World Bank (2006). *World Development Indicators 2006* (CD-ROM) (Washington, D.C.).

_____ (2007a). "Annual World Bank Conference on Development Economics: Beyond Transition 2007" (Washington, D.C.).

_____ (2007b). "Spending for development making the most of Indonesia's new opportunities", *Expenditure Review 2007,* Jakarta, July, <www.publicfinanceindonesia.org>.

Yamada, A. and Bernard Casey (2002). "Getting older, getting poorer? A study of the earnings, pensions, assets and living arrangements of older people in nine countries", Income Study Working Paper Series, Working Paper No. 314 (Luxembourg), <http://www.lisproject.org/publications/liswps/314.pdf>.

CHAPTER 3. UNEQUAL BENEFITS OF GROWTH – AGRICULTURE LEFT BEHIND

Rapid economic growth and good macroeconomic fundamentals are hallmarks of the Asia-Pacific region. The share of people living on less than $1 a day fell from 29% in 1990 to 18% in 2004, and more than 300 million people have escaped poverty since 1990. But despite this success, fault lines are apparent. Of the world's poor, 641 million still live in Asia-Pacific – nearly two-thirds of the global total, mainly in rural areas. Based on recent estimates, countries in South Asia are either slow or regressing in pursuing the Millennium Development Goal of reducing the number of people living on less than $1 a day by 2015 (ESCAP/ADB/UNDP, 2007). The rural poor account for around 70% of the poor in the Asia-Pacific region, and agriculture is their main livelihood.

> *Agriculture appears neglected, despite providing jobs for 60% of the working population in the region*

Another worrisome trend: the gap is widening between the rich and the poor, because the benefits of growth are not shared equally by different sectors, regions or income groups. Agriculture appears neglected, even though it still provides jobs for 60% of the working population in Asia-Pacific and generates a quarter of the region's GDP. Growth and productivity in agriculture are slowing, and the green revolution has bypassed millions. The mounting pressure on farmers is evident in declining subsidies, rising input prices, protests over landlessness and an alarming number of suicides among the indebted.

This chapter diagnoses Asia's waning agriculture and assesses the impact of agricultural productivity growth on poverty. Raising average agricultural labour productivity in the region to that in Thailand could take 218 million people out of poverty, a third of the poor. Large gains are also possible through comprehensive liberalization of global agricultural trade, with the region poised to take another 48 million people out of poverty.

The chapter next analyses agriculture's role in reducing poverty and inequality. It finds that agriculture has been static for many years since the green revolution. Diversifying into high value crops, so far confined to a few countries, is something the region could bank on in coming decades. But agriculture alone will not lift Asia-Pacific's 641 million poor people out of poverty. Developing the non-farm sector is equally important.

The chapter then proposes a two-pronged strategy to make agriculture economically and socially viable, returning it to its place reducing poverty and inequality.

- First, agriculture needs another revolution. A market orientation with a focus on quality and standards would be part of this strategy. Investments in Research and Development and human capital will increase agricultural productivity significantly. Also needed are revamping land policies, connecting the rural poor to cities and markets, and making credit instruments and crop insurance farmer-friendly.

- Second, facilitating migration out of agriculture should complement agricultural development – by empowering the poor, particularly women, with the skills to tap labour market opportunities and by promoting rural non-farm activities and regional growth centres.

Public policy should support both tracks by levelling the playing field for poor and rich.

Diagnosing Asia-Pacific's waning agriculture

The Asia and Pacific region is at the forefront in reducing poverty, cutting the number of poor living on less than $1 a day from 1.25 billion in 1981 to 641 million in 2004 – a decline of around half. Compare that with a reduction of 2% in Sub-Saharan Africa and an increase of 20% in Latin America. Asia-Pacific's success is attributable mainly to China, where the poverty rate fell from 63.8% in 1981 to 9.9% in 2004, taking more than a half billion people out of poverty.

Figure 3.1. Slowing declines in poverty since the 1980s, with progress mainly in urban areas

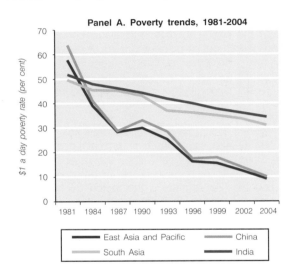

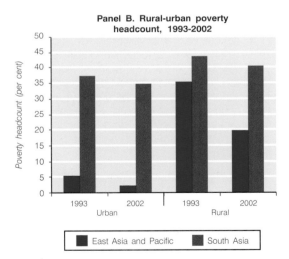

Source: Based on data from S. Chen and M. Ravallion, "Absolute poverty measures for the developing world", World Bank Policy Research Working Paper No. 4211 (Washington, D.C., World Bank, 2007).

Poverty declines are slowing, and rural poverty remains stubbornly high: A lethargic agriculture?

The decline in poverty has slowed since the late 1980s (figure 3.1, panel a). In China, half the aggregate decline was in the first half of the 1980s (Ravallion and Chen, 2007). In India, only 6 million people were taken out of poverty after 1999, a period of rapid economic growth.

The reductions have been mainly in urban areas (figure 3.1, panel b). In East Asia and the Pacific, urban poverty fell by almost 50% during 1993 and 2002, rural poverty by 44%. In South Asia, urban and rural poverty each fell by a meagre 7%. Growth has been concentrated in cities and regions where infrastructure and basic service delivery are superior. In Sri Lanka, half the GDP is generated in the western province, indicating a huge regional disparity (Central Bank of Sri Lanka, 2007). In China, most growth is in the eastern coastal belt, while contributions from the central and western regions are substantially lower (Ravallion and Chen, 2007).

The slowing poverty reduction is a result of the neglect of agriculture, which is the focus of the rural sector. Agriculture's lethargy has broken agricultural growth's historically strong contribution to reducing poverty.

Growth in agricultural value added had the largest impact on poverty reduction in Asia in the 1970s and 1980s. That impact has since been waning (figure 3.2). Consider this: a 1% increase in agricultural value added growth in Asia led to a nearly 0.6% reduction in poverty in the 1970s, compared with a 0.1% reduction by manufacturing value added growth and −0.1% by services growth. But agriculture's impact declined to around 0.1% in the 1980s and 1990s, about the same as manufacturing's.

What drives this outcome? One factor is the low productivity of agricultural labour.

Productivity in industry and services increased more rapidly. And the number of people whose livelihood depends on agriculture did not decline as rapidly as the share of agriculture in GDP (figure 3.3). So, less income in agriculture had to be shared by more people. In addition, the land Gini coefficient is high in many developing countries of the region, implying that the income generated in agriculture is not shared equitably.

> *The share of agriculture in GDP is declining fast – as is policy attention*

The share of agriculture in GDP has declined due to low productivity (figure 3.4). Low product prices and high input prices have also made agriculture less attractive. The result: low growth in agriculture and lower incomes for the people dependent on it (table 3.1). In South Asia, growth in agricultural output dropped from 3.6% in the 1980s to 3.0% in 2000-2003. Underlying this trend are India's low crop yields, the result of limited investment in research and extension beyond the early green revolution years. Growth in agriculture dropped even more rapidly in East Asia and the Pacific, from 4% in the 1980s to a mere 0.1% in 2000-2003. The benefits of green revolution technologies have largely been exploited, with little room for further gains without new technological infusions (FAO, 2006a).

The role of agriculture in creating jobs is diminishing in some subregions

Although agriculture is still the largest employer, its capacity to generate new employment is falling. In East Asia, South-East Asia and the Pacific, it now has less employment potential than industry or services (table 3.2). In South Asia, it has the highest potential for generating employment, but even there the employment elasticities in agriculture have plunged in recent years.[1]

---

[1] Except in Bangladesh, employment elasticities in South Asia declined from the 1980s through 2004 (SAARC, 2005).

Figure 3.2. Agricultural growth's contribution to poverty reduction has slowed since the 1970s

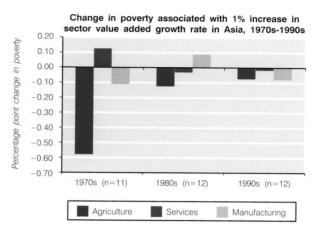

Source: N. Majid, "Reaching Millennium Development Goals: how well does agriculture productivity growth reduce poverty?" Employment Strategy Papers, No. 2004/12 (Geneva, ILO, 2004).

Note: Based on ordinary least squares regression with Sala-i-Martin poverty data. *n* refers to the number of countries in the sample.

Figure 3.3. The changing share of agriculture in GDP and employment

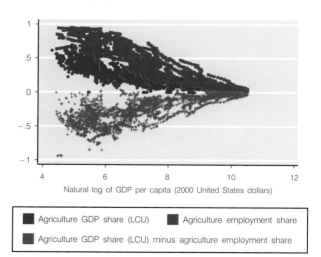

Source: C.P. Timmer, "Agriculture and pro-poor growth: An Asian perspective", Center for Global Development, Working Paper No. 63 (Washington, D.C., CGD, 2005).

Figure 3.4. A declining share of agriculture's value added in GDP

(Per cent)

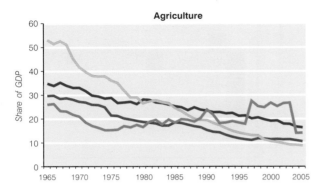

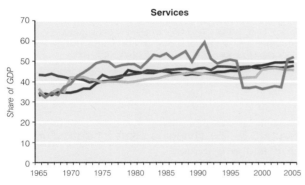

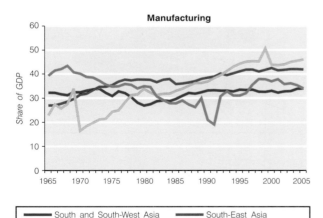

| South and South-West Asia | South-East Asia |
| East and North-East Asia | Pacific island economies |

Source: Based on data from World Bank, *World Development Indicators 2007* (CD-ROM) (Washington, D.C., World Bank, 2007).

Structural changes in production – in response to productivity gains and opportunities from globalization – appear to have hurt agriculture. Value addition in industry and services is several times that in agriculture. So, agriculture's share in GDP fell from 53% in 1965 to 9% in 2004 in East and North-East Asia, from 35% to 17% in South and South-West Asia, and from 30% to 11% in South-East Asia.

Inequality is widening due to the neglect of agriculture

The region's impressive gains in economic growth and poverty reduction came with a sharp increase in inequality since the 1990s. Only Thailand, Malaysia and Indonesia reduced income inequality, while most countries experienced sharp increases (figure 3.5, panel a). The main reasons? Low and stagnant agricultural productivity, lack of rural infrastructure, incomplete land reform, poor basic service delivery and limited alternative income-generating activities – and thus low incomes for the majority of the rural workforce. Moving away from agriculture is associated with widening income inequality (figure 3.5, panel b). Such inequality may impede growth and threaten social cohesion by leaving people's skills idle.

With limited resources, farmers depend on borrowed money to purchase seeds and other inputs and to farm their land (box 3.1). A drop in their farm income could lead to indebtedness. In India, for example, the distress in rural areas is reflected in the high number of suicides by farmers: 86,922 during 2001-2005 (Government of India, 2007). Sharma (2004) puts the blame on a shift towards commercial agriculture and more liberal imports. Farm debts and suicides are also reported in China (BBC News, 2007), Sri Lanka (MONLAR, 2005) and Thailand (Asian Farmers Association for Sustainable Development, 2007).

Agricultural labour productivity growth is declining, and productivity gaps remain wide

Asia-Pacific's average annual agricultural labour productivity growth of 2.5% in the 1980s dropped to 2.2% in the 1990s and to 1% during 2000-2002. The main culprits were stagnating productivity growth in South-East Asia, after it reaped the benefits of the green revolution in the 1970s and 1980s, and South Asia's slow progress in catching up. Even within Asia-Pacific, productivity gaps remain wide (figures 3.6 and 3.7). On the back of China's rapid technological progress in

Table 3.1. Agricultural and non-agricultural growth rates

(Average annual percentage, 1960-2003)

	Agriculture					Non-agriculture				
	1960s	1970s	1980s	1990s	2000-2003	1960s	1970s	1980s	1990s	2000-2003
South Asia	2.9	1.7	3.6	3.2	3.0	5.7	4.7	6.4	6.2	5.9
East Asia and Pacific	4.0	3.2	3.0	1.7	0.1	7.7	7.4	4.9	5.1	5.0
Europe	1.2	1.7	2.0	1.7	−0.8	6.0	3.5	2.6	2.5	2.3
North America	..	−0.3	3.2	2.7	−1.8	..	3.7	2.7	2.7	3.2

Source: Based on data from L. Christiaensen, L. Demery and J. Kuhl, "The role of agriculture in poverty reduction", World Bank Policy Research Working Paper No. 4013 (Washington, D.C., World Bank, 2006).

Table 3.2. Sectoral employment elasticities, 1991-2003

	Agriculture		Industry		Services	
	Elasticity	Value added growth	Elasticity	Value added growth	Elasticity	Value added growth
East Asia	0.23	3.7	0.06	12.5	0.50	8.8
South-East Asia and Pacific	0.20	2.1	0.68	5.4	0.99	4.6
South Asia	0.71	2.9	0.37	5.9	0.36	6.9

Source: Based on data from ILO, *Key Indicators of the Labour Market 2007 Database, 5th Edition* (Geneva, ILO, 2007).

Figure 3.5.   Income inequality and its relationship with the change in agriculture's share in GDP

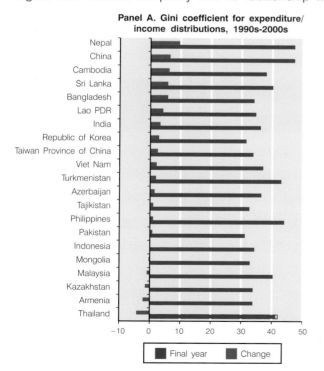

Panel A. Gini coefficient for expenditure/income distributions, 1990s-2000s

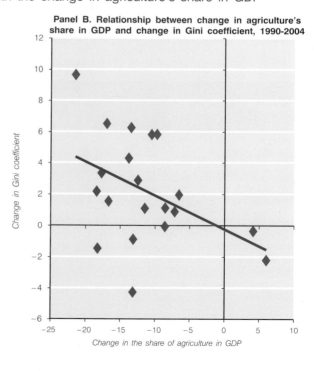

Panel B. Relationship between change in agriculture's share in GDP and change in Gini coefficient, 1990-2004

Sources: Based on data from ADB, *Key Indicators of Developing Asian and Pacific Countries 2007* (Manila, ADB, 2007); and World Bank, *World Development Indicators 2007* (CD-ROM) (Washington, D.C., World Bank, 2007).

Box 3.1. Growing farm debt, increasing distress in Indian agriculture

Rising farm debt and its tragic consequences are major concerns in many developing countries in the region. Perhaps India is the best example where this phenomenon has been studied in depth and brought to the attention of senior policymakers.

According to a recent report (Government of India, 2007), Indian agriculture faces a crisis from debt, especially since the mid-1990s, evident in the large number of farmer suicides in some regions. Of the estimated 89.3 million farmer households in 2003, 43.42 million (48.6%) were indebted (Government of India, 2005). The average outstanding debt was 12,585 rupees ($320) per farmer household and 25,902 rupees ($660) per indebted farmer household (Government of India, 2007).

Farmers' indebtedness varies by state, low in less developed states and high in agriculturally developed states (see table). In 2003, indebtedness was higher in states that had input-intensive and diversified agriculture, as in Andhra Pradesh (82%), Tamil Nadu (74.5%), Punjab (65.4%), Kerala (64.4%), Karnataka (61.6%), Maharashtra (54.8%) and Haryana (53.1%). In at least four states, a large proportion of the debt went to productive purposes. More than half the indebted farmers took loans for capital or current business expenditures, accounting for 58.4% of outstanding loans.

The sources of that debt make a big difference. At one end of the spectrum is Maharashtra, where institutional credit accounted for most of the indebtedness. But in Andhra Pradesh, local moneylenders dominate the scene. Across India, more than two-fifths of debt is owed to non-institutional agencies. Of that non-institutional debt, 37.5% carries an interest rate above 30%. Interest rates for home and car loans are lower than those for farm loans. And even banks and microfinance institutions charge 18-24% on farm loans (Indian Express, 2007). Formalization of debt will thus reduce the debt burden on farmers, but other measures are also essential.

Also evident is some relationship between farm debt and suicides. In all states that reported suicides among farmers, debt incidence and debt per farmer household were high. During 2001-2005, 86,922 farmers committed suicides – 54% from Andhra Pradesh, Karnataka, Kerala and Maharashtra. Driving the distress were declining profitability, growing production and marketing risks, an institutional vacuum and lack of alternative livelihood opportunities.

Table. Farmer indebtedness in major Indian states, 2003

State	Estimated number of indebted farmer households	Share of farmer households indebted (per cent)	Average loan per household (rupees)
Andhra Pradesh	49 493	82.0	23 965
Tamil Nadu	28 954	74.5	23 963
Punjab	12 069	65.4	41 576
Kerala	14 126	64.4	18 135
Karnataka	24 897	61.6	18 135
Maharashtra	36 098	54.8	16 973
Haryana	10 330	53.1	26 007
Rajasthan	27 828	52.4	18 372
Gujarat	19 644	51.9	15 526
Madhya Pradesh	32 110	50.8	14 218
West Bengal	34 696	50.1	10 931
Orissa	20 250	47.8	5 871
Uttar Pradesh	69 199	40.3	7 425
Himachal Pradesh	3 030	33.4	9 618
Bihar	23 383	33.0	4 476
Jammu and Kashmir	3 003	31.8	1 903
Assam	4 536	18.1	813
All India	434 242	48.6	12 585

Source: Based on data from National Sample Survey Organization, "Situation assessment survey of farmers, 2003", as reported in Government of India, *Report of the Expert Group on Agricultural Indebtedness* (New Delhi, Ministry of Finance, 2007).

agriculture, agricultural productivity growth accelerated in East Asia after 1980.

The potential gains from higher productivity in agriculture are large. Christiaensen and others (2006) suggest that a percentage point of additional growth in agricultural GDP per capita in South Asia would reduce the poverty headcount 3.85 times more than an additional percentage point growth outside agriculture. In the region as a whole, the figure is 2.63 times.

Low labour productivity in agriculture reflects slow progress in technological adaptation and innovation in farm practices due to low literacy among the rural poor; low mechanization rates; inability to produce on a mass scale because of restrictions on land ownership; and limited knowledge of the quality aspects of production, distribution and marketing.

For example, access to high-yielding varieties of grain by the poor is limited in remote communities, and illiterate farmers do not have the knowledge to use them. Illiteracy among the rural poor, particularly women, is high in Asia, particularly in South Asia. Female illiteracy was 46% in India in 2001, and 72% among rural females (NLM, 2001). Illiteracy among rural females in Balochistan (Pakistan) was 98% (Rehman, 1998).

Slow progress in mechanization also contributes to low agricultural productivity. Agricultural tractor use in developing countries of the region in 2001 was 40% of that in the rest of the world (8.4 tractors per 1,000 hectares in Asia and the Pacific, against 20.7 in the rest of the world). Per capita agricultural land holding in developing countries in Asia and the Pacific was only 0.27 hectares, against 1.41 hectares in the rest of the world. A large portion of Asia's agricultural produce is lost during transportation to markets. For example, nearly 40% of India's agricultural produce is wasted because of a lack of post-harvest facilities for handling, storage and transportation (India Research, 2006).

Land productivity has improved but remains well below European levels

Asia has recorded the largest land productivity gains anywhere since 1961. Output per hectare increased by 284% during 1961-1994, faster than the United State's 186% and Europe's 169%. But its land productivity, although ahead of North America's by a large margin, was 24% lower than Europe's in 1994 (table 3.3). It

Figure 3.6. Labour productivity trends in agriculture, 1980-2005

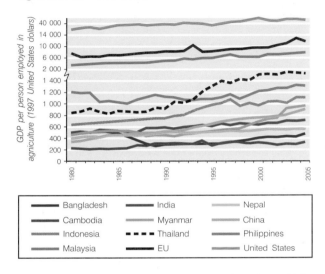

Source: Based on data from ILO, *Key Indicators of the Labour Market 2007, 5th Edition* (Geneva, ILO, 2007).

Figure 3.7. Productivity gaps in agriculture, 2005

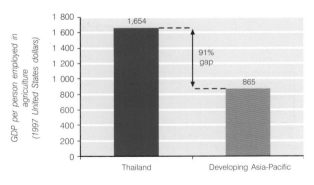

Source: Based on data from ILO, *Key Indicators of the Labour Market 2007, 5th Edition* (Geneva, ILO, 2007).

Table 3.3. Land productivity by continent

	Asia	Europe	North America
Output per hectare (United States dollars)			
1961	370.6	815.04	374.79
1994	1 051.18	1 374.48	697.37
Productivity growth (per cent)			
1961-1994[a]	8.5	0.8	5.6[b]
1994/96-1998/00	3.5	1.1	2.3
2000-2003	2.1	−0.8	−0.3
Annual productivity gap vs. Europe			
1994			
United States dollars per hectare	323.3	-	677.11
Per cent gap	23.5	-	49.3
2003			
United States dollars per hectare[c]	126.7	-	707.5
Per cent gap	9.9	-	102

Sources: Data for 1961-1994 from FAO, AGROSTAT Database (Rome, FAO, 2007); data for 1998-2000 from FAO, Compendium of Agricultural-Environmental Indicators 1989-1991 to 2000 (Rome, FAO, 2003); data for 2000-2003 based on World Bank, World Development Indicators 2006 (CD-ROM) (Washington, D.C., World Bank, 2006).

[a] Simple annual average growth.
[b] Includes Central America.
[c] Estimates.

Figure 3.8. Land productivity in selected countries, 1961-1994

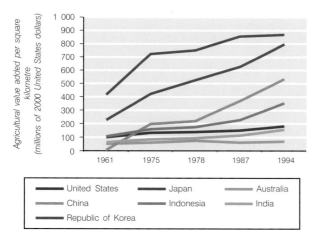

Sources: Data based on D. Lee and L. Zepeda, "Agricultural investment and productivity in developing countries" (Rome, FAO, 1997) and FAO, AGROSTAT Database (Rome, FAO, 2007).

improved further since then, if at a declining pace. Even with the improvement, it is estimated to be 10% lower than Europe's.

Land productivity gains in Asia are spearheaded by China, with an 87-fold increase since 1961 (figure 3.8), but other developing countries are catching up. Land productivity in India and Indonesia lags far behind Japan, Republic of Korea and China. China's success is due partly to land reforms, mechanization and higher input use. Its fertilizer use is on a par with Japan and New Zealand. Fertilizer use in India, by contrast, is less than half that. While land irrigation had a greater impact on agricultural productivity in the 1960s through the 1980s, its impact has been declining due to the scarcity of water and the resulting slow growth in irrigated land, which now comes mostly from groundwater development, putting pressure on its sustainability.

Agriculture – a powerful driver of poverty reduction and social equity

Faster economic growth is only one part of reducing poverty. The regions and sectors of growth also matter. Poverty in India responds far more to rural economic growth than to urban (Ravallion and Datt, 1996). Differences in initial conditions related to rural development and human resource development also lead to different outcomes (Ravallion and Datt, 1999). And agricultural productivity and public expenditure on rural development are important determinants of poverty (Ravallion and Datt, 2002).

Raising agricultural productivity can take 218 million people out of poverty

Agricultural labour productivity also has a significant impact on poverty reduction. ESCAP estimates show that a 1% increase in agricultural productivity would lead to a 0.37% drop in poverty in the Asia-Pacific region (table 3.4).[2] Given the large agricultural labour productivity gaps among countries in the region, the potential gains appear substantial. Raising the region's average agricultural productivity to Thailand's, the benchmark for this chapter, can take 218 million people out of poverty.[3,4] India has the most to gain from a productivity drive, with nearly two-thirds of the region's poor and a large agricultural productivity gap.

Investment, literacy and agricultural productivity reduce income inequality. Increases in agricultural value added are more effective in reducing income inequality because of their disproportionate effect on the lowest income groups (World Bank, 2007). ESCAP estimates that raising agricultural productivity to the level of Thailand could reduce inequality, measured by the Gini coefficient, by 6%.

> *Agricultural development promotes equality*

Agricultural R&D, education of the rural population and rural infrastructure, particularly electricity and roads, are key determinants of labour productivity and have a major impact on poverty reduction (Fan and others, 2003). Additionally, there is strong evidence of the greater impact of human capital development on agricultural total factor productivity (Majid, 2004; Rao, Coelli and Alauddin, 2004). ESCAP estimates a significant positive impact on agricultural productivity from life expectancy (elasticity of 0.20), literacy (0.70) and economic openness (0.40). These estimates indicate that both economic and social conditions – particularly health and education – affect agricultural productivity.

---

[2] This is consistent with estimates by others. Fan and others (2003) estimated the agricultural labour productivity elasticity of poverty to be at −0.417 for Thailand. Rao and others (2004), using Sala-i-Martin data, found an elasticity of −0.87.

[3] Thailand was taken as the benchmark for several reasons. First, it is one of the few countries in the region that has achieved most of the Millennium Development Goals. Second, agriculture has contributed much towards these targets. Third, the productivity levels in better performers (such as Malaysia, Singapore and the Republic of Korea) are either relatively high or not representative.

[4] The impact of agricultural productivity growth could be highest on the poorest. For example, Ligon and Sadoulet (2007) found that a 1% increase in GDP originating in agriculture increased the expenditures of the poorest half of the population on average by 3.7%, far more than growth originating in the rest of the economy.

Table 3.4. Impacts of labour productivity in agriculture on poverty reduction in the Asia-Pacific region

Results		Reduction in the number of poor (millions)
Agricultural labour productivity (long run) elasticity of $1 a day poverty line: −0.37	Due to 1% increase in agricultural labour productivity	2.37
	By raising the agricultural labour productivity to the benchmark level	218.3

Source: ESCAP estimates.

Note: Pooled least squares estimation for 46 developing countries for 1975-2000.

Liberalizing trade in agricultural products and its impact on developing economies have long been contentious in international trade negotiations, including the Doha development round. Developing countries have so far been cautious in multilateral agricultural trade reforms – because of possible harm through preference erosion, rising agricultural prices for small food-importing economies and adverse effects on food security and poverty.

A study by ESCAP on the impact of agricultural trade liberalization shows poverty reductions in some countries but increases in others (table 3.5). The region could take 5 million people living on less than $1 a day out of poverty through Doha agricultural trade reforms in the short run, possibly increasing to 7 million in the long run. China appears to gain the most, reducing the number of poor people by 10 million, mainly in rural areas, due to an increase in unskilled workers' real wages. Thailand and Viet Nam

would also reduce the prevalence of poverty, as would Indonesia and the Philippines.[5] Poverty would increase, however, in Bangladesh, India, the Russian Federation and Sri Lanka in both the short and long runs. India would suffer the most, with 7.2 million new poor due to the negative impact on the real wages of unskilled labourers.[6]

Comprehensive reforms going beyond Doha could take 48-51 million people out of poverty

If the world goes beyond the Doha reforms and undertakes comprehensive agricultural liberalization – eliminating all tariffs, export subsidies and domestic support for agricultural and food products – the Asia-Pacific region could take 48 million people out of poverty in the short run, increasing to 51 million in

Table 3.5. Impact of Doha and comprehensive reforms on poverty

(Based on $1 a day poverty line)

	Under Doha reforms		Under comprehensive reforms	
	Short run headcount (Δ *millions*)	Long run headcount (Δ *millions*)	Short run headcount (Δ *millions*)	Long run headcount (Δ *millions*)
Bangladesh	0.4	0.3	−2.5	−2.4
China (rural)	−10.3	−11.5	−24.7	−27.3
China (urban)	−0.1	−0.1	−0.2	−0.3
India (rural)	5.9	5.9	−10.2	−10.0
India (urban)	1.3	1.3	−2.2	−2.1
Indonesia	−0.9	−1.2	−3.2	−3.8
Malaysia	0.0	0.0	0.0	0.0
Mexico	−0.1	−0.1	−0.4	−0.3
Philippines	−0.6	−0.8	−2.1	−2.4
Russian Federation	0.0	0.0	−0.5	−0.5
Sri Lanka	0.0	0.0	0.1	0.1
Thailand	−0.4	−0.5	−0.6	−0.6
Viet Nam	−0.2	−0.2	−1.4	−1.4

Source: ESCAP estimates.

[5] Estimates by Cororaton and others (2006) indicate that Doha reforms could lead to a slight increase in poverty in the Philippines due to a deterioration in the terms of trade that could result in a larger increase in the prices of consumption goods than in household nominal incomes.

[6] Annabi and others (2006) find similar results for Bangladesh.

the long run. All countries except Sri Lanka would see a reduction. Rural China would see nearly 25 million people come out of poverty, and India 12 million.

Many other studies find a positive impact from agricultural trade reform on developing economies (see, for example, Anderson and Martin, 2005). The results also suggest that the largest increases in welfare would accrue to rural households. The size of the effect varies. In China, the urban-rural income ratio declines under global trade liberalization scenarios, but not significantly (Hertel and Zhai, 2006). In Indonesia too, the impact on inequality would be negligible, but rising incomes would boost a small number of people out of poverty (Robilliard and Robinson, 2006).

> *The largest increases in welfare due to trade reforms would accrue to rural households*

ESCAP estimates of the aggregate welfare effects under Doha show modest annual gains of $4.6 billion globally in the short run, increasing to $5.2 billion in the long (table 3.6). Two-thirds of the total gains would accrue to Asia, with Japan gaining the most. Developing countries in Asia would gain a modest $365 million (8% of the total) in the short run, rising to $640 million (12%) in the long run. The Republic of Korea, Thailand and India appear to gain the most from agricultural trade liberalization under Doha, due mainly to gains in the terms of trade. China, which stands to gain the most in poverty reduction under Doha, appears to lose in overall absolute welfare gains. Many others will also lose, though marginally, mainly

due to a terms-of-trade shift. The small aggregate gains reflect the relatively small degree of reform anticipated if the proposal on agriculture remains in its current form.

Similar results are found in Annabi and others (2006). According to that study, Doha reforms could result in aggregate welfare losses for Bangladesh due to an adverse terms-of-trade effect. In India, the welfare of the poorest households could fall while the richest could gain.

Developing Asia-Pacific region to gain $3.3-3.5 billion under comprehensive agricultural trade reforms

Under comprehensive agricultural trade reforms, both regional and global welfare gains increase several times. Global welfare gains exceed $23 billion in the short run, increasing to $37 billion in the long run. Developed economies in Asia and the Pacific as a group – Japan, Australia and New Zealand – gain the most under Doha and comprehensive reforms. Developing country gains in the region also increase nearly 10 times to $3.3 billion in the short run, rising to $3.5 billion in the long run. Many countries that could suffer welfare losses under Doha reforms turn out to be net gainers under the comprehensive reforms, with China, Bangladesh and the Philippines the exceptions.

The Republic of Korea, Malaysia, Thailand and India would gain the most in absolute terms. Malaysia and Sri Lanka would turn losses under Doha into gains under the comprehensive reforms, of 1.5% and 0.7% of GDP, respectively.

Table 3.6. Estimated aggregate welfare effect of agricultural reforms

	Under Doha reforms				Under comprehensive reforms			
	Short run		Long run		Short run		Long run	
	Welfare effect (millions of United States dollars)	GDP share (per cent)	Welfare effect (millions of United States dollars)	GDP share (per cent)	Welfare effect (millions of United States dollars)	GDP share (per cent)	Welfare effect (millions of United States dollars)	GDP share (per cent)
Developing Asia-Pacific economies								
Bangladesh	−39.9	−0.09	−27.7	−0.06	−46.1	−0.10	−19.0	−0.04
China	−477.4	−0.04	−441.0	−0.04	−976.5	−0.08	−918.6	−0.08
Hong Kong, China	−15.8	−0.01	−3.7	0.00	1 64.2	0.10	201.3	0.12
India	66.2	0.01	94.6	0.02	351.3	0.07	844.2	0.18
Indonesia	−64.3	−0.04	−53.8	−0.04	101.8	0.07	−25.8	−0.02
Malaysia	−30.0	−0.03	−22.6	−0.03	1 346.4	1.53	830.6	0.94
Philippines	−31.5	−0.04	−38.4	−0.05	−27.9	−0.04	−73.1	−0.10
Republic of Korea	818.3	0.19	955.0	0.22	1 741.1	0.41	2 113.1	0.49
Singapore	−15.7	−0.02	22.5	0.03	6.1	0.01	16.6	0.02
Sri Lanka	−0.4	0.00	3.9	0.02	105.5	0.66	116.0	0.73
Thailand	130.7	0.11	156.0	0.14	508.4	0.44	415.9	0.36
Viet Nam	−6.3	−0.02	−13.3	−0.04	46.9	0.14	43.5	0.13
Developed Asia-Pacific economies								
Australia	856.9	0.24	755.2	0.21	1 242.5	0.35	2 145.6	0.60
New Zealand	390.4	0.77	324.6	0.64	529.8	1.05	506.1	1.00
Japan	1 514.7	0.04	2 117.2	0.05	8 067.9	0.19	17 614.1	0.42
Other								
Canada	90.0	0.01	70.8	0.01	314.0	0.04	442.3	0.06
Mexico	−188.7	−0.03	−143.9	−0.02	−177.6	−0.03	−125.6	−0.02
Russian Federation	−344.4	−0.11	−273.5	−0.09	3.2	0.00	108.7	0.04
United States	1 213.9	0.01	1 483.2	0.01	2 179.0	0.02	2 691.6	0.03
European Union	1 716.2	0.02	1 196.6	0.01	5 405.9	0.07	7 587.6	0.09
South and Central America	607.4	0.04	465.6	0.03	578.4	0.04	263.2	0.02
Rest of the world	−1 617.5	−0.07	−1 415.7	−0.06	1 886.6	0.08	2 340.0	0.09

Source: ESCAP estimates.

Note: Welfare effect is based on equivalent variation. Changes in GDP share are as a percentage of base GDP.

What is holding back agriculture?

Structural constraints, anti-agriculture policy bias and external factors are behind the slow growth in agricultural productivity.

- Structural constraints include inequality in land ownership, lack of human capital development due to limited access to health and education, and inadequate rural infrastructure.

- Policy constraints include anti-agricultural macro-economic policies, failure in agricultural credit policies and lack of promotion of R&D and extension services.

- External factors include limited progress in liberalizing agricultural trade, agricultural price instability and declining official development assistance (ODA).

Inequality in land ownership weighs on productivity

Inequality in asset ownership, particularly land, remains high in the region, holding down agricultural productiv-

ity. The land Gini coefficient remains high in many developing countries in the region (figure 3.9, panel a). The distribution of land is often skewed towards the rich and the middle class, with the poorest left out. In China, however, the household responsibility system, introduced in the 1980s, has had a significant impact on agricultural growth and poverty reduction (figure 3.9, panel b; Lin, 1992).

> *Agriculture is not being widely used as an effective channel for redistributing income*

Redistribution policies will not reduce poverty without economic growth, but, combined with growth, they can reduce poverty more than growth that leaves the distribution unchanged. Progress in distributional change will – in addition to the one-shot effect on

Figure 3.9. Land Gini coefficient and its relationship with poverty, 1960-2000

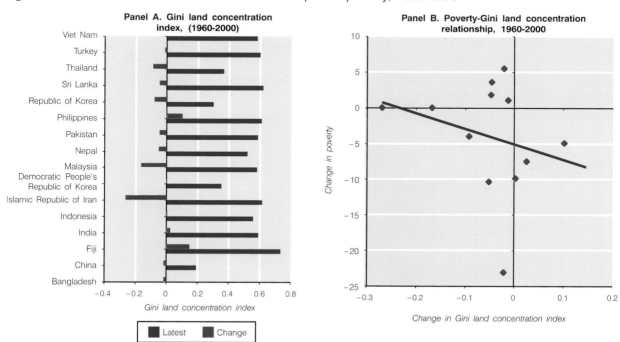

Panel A. Gini land concentration index, (1960-2000)

Panel B. Poverty-Gini land concentration relationship, 1960-2000

Sources: Calculations based on data from IFAD, *The Rural Poverty Report 2001* (Rome, IFAD, 2001); and World Bank, *Millennium Development Goals Database* (Washington, D.C., World Bank, 2007).

Note: The Gini land concentration index measures the inequality of land holding, with numbers closest to 1 indicating greater inequality.

poverty from pure redistribution – have a long-run effect by increasing the sensitivity of poverty to growth (World Bank, 2005). But despite agriculture's potential, many Asia-Pacific countries are not using it as a channel for redistributing income.

Wide inequality in access to health and education has made agriculture less productive

Inequalities in access to health and education are common. The urban-rural gap in access to safe drinking water is 19% in the Asia-Pacific region. Nearly a quarter of the rural population does not have access to safe drinking water, against 7% in urban areas. The gap in access to improved sanitation is worse, at 52% (figure 3.10). Fewer than a third of people in rural areas have access to improved sanitation, compared with 70% in urban areas.

> *Lack of rural infrastructure is a major bottleneck for growth in agriculture and for poverty reduction*

The inequality in access to water and sanitation is reflected in health indicators as well. Infant mortality was 12% higher in rural areas in China in 1995 (Zhang

and Kanbur, 2003), and in India 68% higher (Ravi, 2003), mainly the result of disparities in basic services (box 3.2). In China, the number of hospital beds per 1,000 people was more than five times higher in urban areas than in rural areas; in India, it was 15 times higher. Equally large are the disparities in health-care personnel and births attended by a skilled health professional. A similar disparity is seen in education. In China, 116 million adults, mainly in rural areas, were illiterate in 2005 (Washington Post, 2007). In India, rural female literacy rate was 47% in 2001 (India, 2001).

Inequality in access to health, education and other services makes poverty reduction difficult and retards growth. By increasing strength, endurance and cognitive power, better health would mean higher worker productivity. And better education boosts productivity by increasing workers' ability to adopt and adapt to new technologies.

Lack of rural infrastructure hinders growth

A lack of rural roads, electricity and telecommunication constrains rural farmers. In South Asia, 35% of the rural population lives more than two kilometres from an all-weather road (ESCAP, 2006b). More than a billion people in Asia and the Pacific did not have access to electricity, the majority of them rural poor. In South Asia alone, 57% of the population did not have electricity, and in Nepal 85%. Better access to electricity can clearly reduce poverty (box 3.3; Fan, Jitsuchon

Figure 3.10. Weighted average rural-urban gap in access to water and sanitation in Asia and the Pacific, 1996-2004

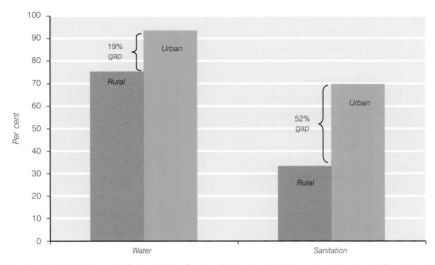

Source: Based on data from United Nations, *A Future Within Reach: Reshaping Institutions in a Region of Disparities to Meet the Millennium Development Goals in Asia and the Pacific* (United Nations publication, Sales No. E.05.II.F.27, 2005).

Box 3.2. The nexus between poverty and health in rural areas

Poverty is often compounded by a lack of access to quality health care. And that, in turn, is partly the result of relatively low investment in health. India has three times more physicians in urban and high-income areas than in rural areas. The situation is similar in many other Asian developing countries and in the Pacific (Durairaj, 2007).

Reinforcing the vicious cycle of poverty and ill health in rural areas are low levels of education (especially for women and girls), widespread landlessness and unemployment, poorly developed financial institutions, and limited negotiating experience and collective organizations. People in rural areas lack basic services, such as safe water, sanitation and electricity. Environmental issues are also important, with rural areas prone to flooding, drought and desertification. Added to these are diseases such as malaria, which remain entrenched in rural areas of the Pacific, South Asia and South-East Asia.

In the larger countries of Asia-Pacific, 80-90% of poor people live in rural areas. Bangladesh, China, India, Indonesia and Pakistan alone have more than two-thirds of the world's people living in rural areas without access to sanitation (ESCAP, 2007). For most such people, out-of-pocket expenditures are the main way to finance heath care. Such expenditures can become catastrophic. In some instances, household spending on health is more than 40% of income after subsistence needs are paid for. Out-of-pocket payments increased the rate of poverty by 33% in Viet Nam, 19% in China, 17% in Bangladesh and 12% in India (Durairaj, 2007).

The lesson is the need for greater investment, both in the health sector and in other sectors related to rural health and poverty. Improvements in health and economic growth are mutually reinforcing, especially if policies are pro-poor. One example is suitable and effective health insurance systems that pool risks and subsidize health care for those least able to pay. And addressing the social determinants of health, which include gender equity and education, can have far-reaching benefits for the rural poor.

Box 3.3. Rural infrastructure making a dent in poverty in Thailand

In the last quarter century, rural infrastructure in Thailand has improved immensely, connecting the rural economy to markets. Rural road lengths increased on average by 11% per year, increasing the rural road density from 12 kilometres per 1,000 square kilometres of geographical area to 124 kilometres. Rural telephone lines have increased by 23% per year, raising the number of telephone lines per 1,000 rural residents to 37 in 2000 from 0.5 in 1977. Finally, a 17% annual increase in rural electricity access raised the share of the rural population with access to electricity from 7% in the early 1970s to 97% in 2000. The result has been a tremendous increase in agriculture's productivity.

Improvements in rural roads and electricity have had a positive effect on human capital by providing opportunities for education (figure a). The impact of such improvements on the poorest is very high. Rural infrastructure has enabled the rural poor, mostly in agriculture, to generate more income and reduce poverty. Human capital development had an even larger impact on poverty reduction (figure b).

(Continued on next page)

Box 3.3 *(continued)*

Figure a. Positive effect of rural roads and electrification on education, 1975-2000

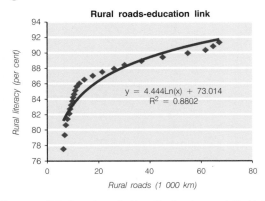
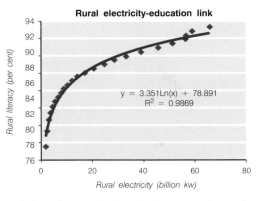

Source: Data based on S. Fan, S. Jitsuchon and N. Methakunnavut, "Impacts of public investments on poverty reduction in Thailand", International Food Policy Research Institute (Washington, D.C., IFPRI, 2003).

Figure b. Rural infrastructure helped reduce poverty over 1975-2000

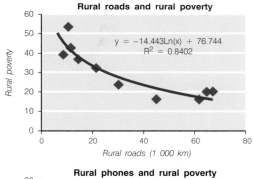
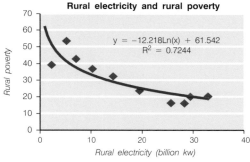

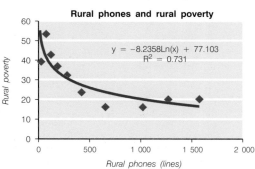
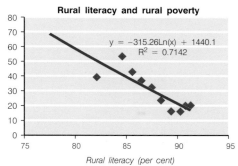

Source: Data based on S. Fan, S. Jitsuchon and N. Methakunnavut, "Impacts of public investments on poverty reduction in Thailand", International Food Policy Research Institute (Washington, D.C., IFPRI, 2003).

Note: Rural poverty refers to percentage of rural population living below the poverty line.

and Methakunnavut, 2003). Poor telecommunications also deprive farmers of vital information on agricultural product prices. In India, only 4 of 100 farmers had a fixed telephone line in 2004, and another 4 a mobile phone.

Macroeconomic policy has been anti-agriculture

Macroeconomic policies have both direct and indirect effects on the agricultural poor. Inflation – a regressive and arbitrary tax on incomes and assets – has a disproportionate impact on the purchasing power of the poor. High interest rates reduce the borrowing capacity of small-scale farmers, curtailing investment and farm cultivation. High inflation and interest rates also discourage private investment, reducing growth, the single most important factor influencing poverty (IMF and World Bank, 2001). A low-yielding agricultural sector could bear the brunt of inflation-induced investment cuts. Maintaining macroeconomic stability is therefore a key policy in agricultural growth and poverty reduction.[7]

Inflation in the developing countries of Asia and the Pacific rose from a low of 3% a year in the 1960s to more than 10% in the 1970s and 12% in the 1980s and 1990s. Rates have since come down to about 6%, but they remain high in Pakistan, Sri Lanka, the Lao People's Democratic Republic, Samoa and Tonga.

> *Taxing agriculture pushes people into poverty*

Higher inflation tends to produce more poverty – and lower inflation, less. Research has found that macroeconomic stability has a positive impact on poverty reduction, notably by avoiding inflationary shocks (Chen and Ravallion, 2007). The inflation-poverty nexus signals the macroeconomic policy implications, particularly in South Asia and Central Asia, which have higher inflation than East, North-East and South-East Asia.

The real lending rate climbed to a historical high exceeding 8% in the mid-1990s and remains high even now (figure 3.11). North and Central Asia, the Pacific islands and South Asia have had higher real interest rates than East, North-East and South-East Asia. Interest spreads are on the rise, indicating the pressure of inflation (figure 3.12).

Direct and indirect taxation of agriculture was common in many countries from the 1960s to the 1980s, reaching 40% in some countries and slowing both agricultural growth and overall growth. In Asia, as in other regions, indirect taxation on agriculture is more than twice direct taxation, such as through price intervention

Figure 3.11. High real lending rates, 1970-2004

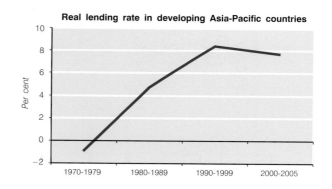

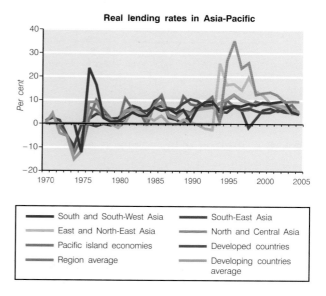

___

[7]   Other elements of macroeconomic stability, such as exchange rates and debt, also affect the poor.

Source: Based on data from World Bank, *World Development Indicators 2007* (CD-ROM) (Washington, D.C., World Bank, 2007).

(table 3.7). Agricultural taxation comes mainly through exchange rate policies and industrial protection, but because the poor depend heavily on agriculture, they lose most.

Credit markets discriminate against rural farmers

Access to finance by rural farmers has also been curtailed, particularly since the structural adjustment programmes of the 1980s and the phasing out of subsidized credit schemes. With the changes in monetary policy, the agricultural refinance schemes operated by central banks have ceased. Price stability has become the main objective. Many central banks now set rediscount rates and avoid directly supporting specific sectors.

Commercial bank lending for agriculture is naturally limited due to the low returns and lack of collateral. Many countries – such as Indonesia, Malaysia, Thailand and Viet Nam – tend to use voluntary savings for financing agriculture. Thailand and Viet Nam have issued bonds for agricultural finance, while Pakistan has used equity issues in recent years, but the amounts remain small (FAO, 1999).

Although the region is resource-rich, the financial resources available for agriculture could be curtailed if global recessionary fears materialize. If the subprime crisis spills over to Asia-Pacific, it could compel financial institutions to be cautious in lending to risky areas such as agriculture, unless governments step in to guarantee such loans or make special arrangements to mitigate the adverse effects.

Figure 3.12. Interest rate spreads on the rise, 1970-2004

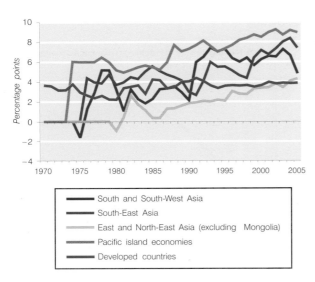

Source: Based on data from World Bank, *World Development Indicators 2007* (CD-ROM) (Washington, D.C., World Bank, 2007).

Note: Interest rate spread refers to lending rate minus deposit rate.

Limited spending on agricultural R&D and extension constrains productivity growth

Agricultural R&D is one of the main sources of productivity growth, amply evident in the green revolution. While expenditure on R&D in the Asia-Pacific region has gradually increased, in some countries it either declined or remained stagnant. In China, it fell from 0.57% of agricultural value added in the early 1960s to 0.4% in 2000. In Thailand, it has remained more or less stagnant, at 0.4-0.5% since the 1970s, with a small recent improvement. India recently increased its R&D expenditure from 0.18% of agricultural value added to 0.34% (figure 3.13).

Table 3.7. Taxation of agriculture in Asia

(Period averages, per cent)

	Period	Indirect tax	Direct tax	Total tax
Malaysia	1960-1983	8.2	9.4	17.6
Pakistan	1960-1986	33.1	6.4	39.5
Philippines	1960-1986	23.3	4.1	27.4
Republic of Korea	1960-1983	25.8	−39.0	−13.2
Sri Lanka	1960-1985	31.1	9.0	40.1
Thailand	1962-1984	15.0	25.1	40.1

Source: M. Schiff and A. Valdes, "Agriculture and the macroeconomy", World Bank Policy Research Working Paper No. 1967 (Washington, D.C., World Bank, 1998).

Figure 3.13. R&D intensities for selected Asia-Pacific countries and developed countries, 1960-2000

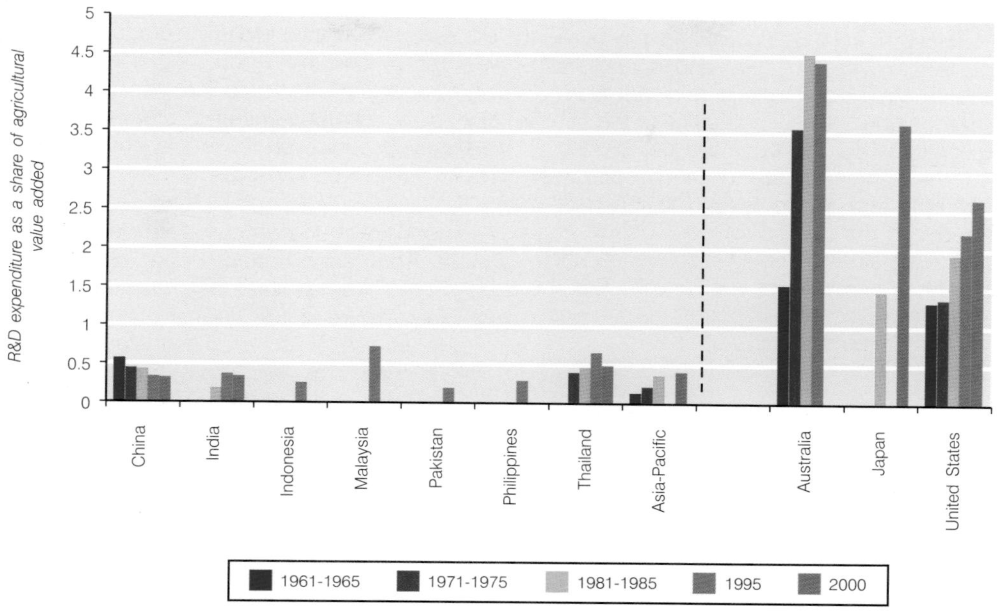

Source: Based on data from World Bank, *World Development Report 2008* (Washington, D.C., World Bank, 2007).

Despite a gradual increase in R&D spending for agriculture in the region, it remains much lower than in developed countries, a possible constraint on productivity growth. Why the slow growth? First, private participation in R&D in the region is limited. In 2000, the share of private agricultural R&D was 8.1% of total R&D expenditure. Although this is somewhat higher than the developing-country average of 6.3%, it is far below the 54% of developed countries. Among the reasons for the lethargic participation of the private sector are issues related to patents, plant breeder rights and other forms of intellectual property.

> *Private participation in agricultural R&D is limited*

Second, the drop in donor support for agricultural R&D since the mid-1990s curtailed R&D. For example, USAID support for the region closed in 1996, when it shifted funds to global research. World Bank funding of agricultural R&D also declined.[8] Third, public financing of agricultural R&D is constrained by fiscal pressure and low motivation for innovation. As the contribution of agriculture to growth has dwindled, public policy priorities have shifted from agriculture to industry and services.

Slow progress in agricultural trade liberalization hits the poorest hard

The impact of agricultural trade liberalization on poverty is unclear, particularly for the poorest, who produce mostly non-tradable goods. Trade liberalization affects multiple actors, markets and institutions in the economy, some positively, others negatively (Winters, 2002). The impact can also vary depending on infra-

---

[8] World Bank lending in 1998 was an exception, with large research components under which China ($68 million) and India ($136 million) were able to borrow for agricultural R&D.

structure, type of commodity and social structures (such as inequality of land ownership).

International trade can have a positive impact on the poor through changes in relative prices and the availability of goods. Net exporters of food and agricultural products (Indonesia, Malaysia, Thailand and Viet Nam) could benefit from higher agricultural prices, the impact becoming larger when the poor are net producers. In Viet Nam, the poorest quarter of the people are net producers of rice, and export liberalization is estimated to have reduced the number of poor people by 5% (FAO, 2006b). Liberalization could also benefit the poor by making food available at low prices. But it could harm the poor in net importers, such as Bangladesh and the Philippines.

> *The full benefits of globalization and international trade are not reaching the poor*

Another channel for trade liberalization to affect agriculture and poverty is the greater availability of farm inputs and the resulting increase in agricultural productivity. In Bangladesh, liberalizing trade in irrigation equipment and fertilizer markets in the early 1990s produced structural changes in agriculture and a significant increase in rice productivity. The resulting increase in output reduced rice prices by 25%, benefiting the poor, who are the main consumers of rice (Klytchnikova and Diop, 2006).

For trade to have a greater impact on growth requires not just a supportive macroeconomic policy environment but effective institutions and good governance. In most developing countries in the region, however, institutions and governance structures are weak, and liberalization is incomplete. Facing stiff resistance from both developed and developing countries, agricultural trade liberalization has been limited. So, the full benefits of globalization and international trade are not reaching the poor.

Declining international prices discourage producers of staple crops

The share of staple foods in the food basket of the population is falling with rising incomes, but the decline in international prices to historical lows brings mixed blessings. The low prices benefit the landless poor the most by increasing their purchasing power, with the trend in poverty quite close to that of grain prices (figure 3.14). But low and unstable prices could cut competitiveness and discourage producers. People with the means (both poor and non-poor) could diversify production into more lucrative higher value crops. But poor farmers' income dropped, reducing their purchasing power, so those just above the poverty line could have fallen into poverty.

Average growth in production of the main staple crops in the Asia-Pacific region – rice, wheat and cereals – has been low in the last decade, at around 1% annually (figure 3.15). In per capita terms, average growth in production of these staples remained low: 2% for rice, 1% for wheat and cereals. Yields increased by 2-3% (figure 3.16). Production declined gradually from a peak in the late 1990s before recovering in 2003. In China, production of rice, wheat and cereals dropped by 12%, 20% and 12%, respectively, during 1999-2003. A similar trend was seen in India, with drops in rice and cereal production of 19% and 12%, respectively, during the same period.

However, production of rice, wheat and cereals has increased by 12-13% since 2002-2003 due to recoveries in China and India and production increases in Bangladesh, Indonesia, Myanmar, Thailand and Viet Nam. Rice production increased by 10% during the past decade. While wheat production declined marginally, cereal production increased by 11% over the period, and maize production, by 41%.

> *The increases in staple prices create an opportunity to correct agricultural policies*

Recent increases in the production of staple crops could reflect higher demand generated by their increased use in biofuels. The price increases could bring opportunities for the rural poor to raise their incomes – and enable governments to remove distortionary agricultural subsidies as the sector becomes commercially viable.

Progress in crop diversification is slow and limited

The driving force behind the revival of agriculture in some Asia-Pacific countries, particularly China and

Figure 3.14. Trends in poverty and prices for major staple foods, 1965-2006

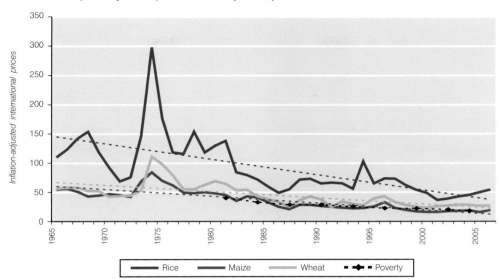

Sources: IMF, *International Financial Statistics* (CD-ROM) (Washington, D.C., IMF, 2007); and World Bank, *Millennium Development Goals Database* (Washington, D.C., World Bank, 2007).

Figure 3.15. Per capita production in key staple crops, 1961-2005

(Metric tonnes per capita)

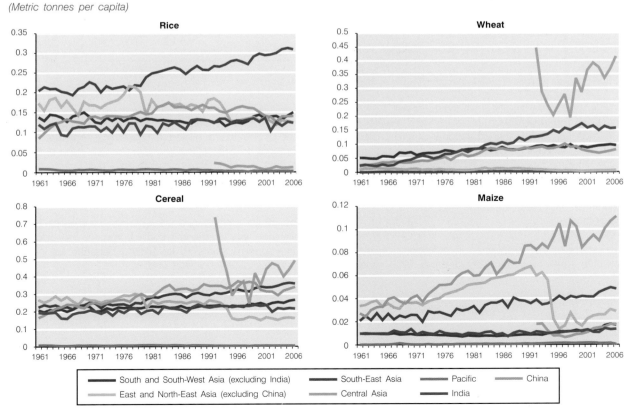

Source: Based on data from FAO, *State of Food and Agriculture 2003-04 Database* (Rome, FAO, 2004).

Figure 3.16. Rice, wheat, cereal and maize yields, 1961-2005

(Kilograms per hectare)

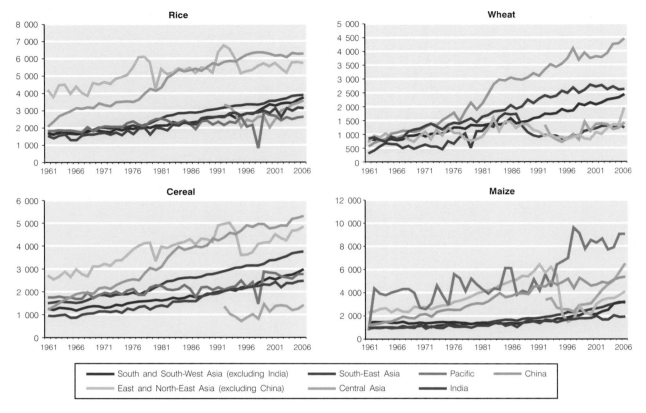

Source: Based on data from FAO, *State of Food and Agriculture 2003-04 Database* (Rome, FAO, 2004).

India, is the emergence of crops and livestock that are more profitable than traditional staples. Globalization and changing dietary patterns across regions have made diversifying into high value crops and livestock feasible and financially rewarding. The changing structure of production in major agricultural products indicates consumer appeal and producer response.

For example, fruit production in developing Asia-Pacific countries grew by 5.3% per year since 1990, more than doubling total production, much higher than 2.3% in the rest of the world (figure 3.17). China registered phenomenal growth of 345%, and India 59%. The picture is similar for vegetables, meat and milk, with growth substantially exceeding that of the rest of the world, due in part to higher yields (figure 3.18).

The recent shift towards non-staple crops is an important step in generating more income for the poor, but the impact appears to be limited because only a few countries have benefited from it.

Figure 3.17. Per capita production in fruits, vegetables, meat and milk, 1961-2005

(Metric tonnes per capita)

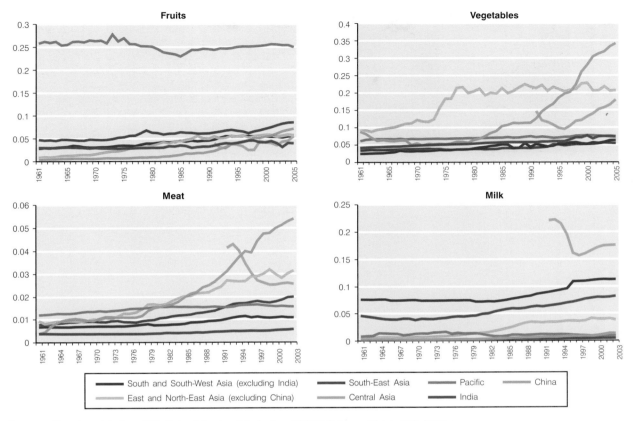

Source: Based on data from FAO, *State of Food and Agriculture 2003-04 Database* (Rome, FAO, 2004).

Figure 3.18. Fruit and vegetable yields, 1961-2006

(Kilograms per hectare)

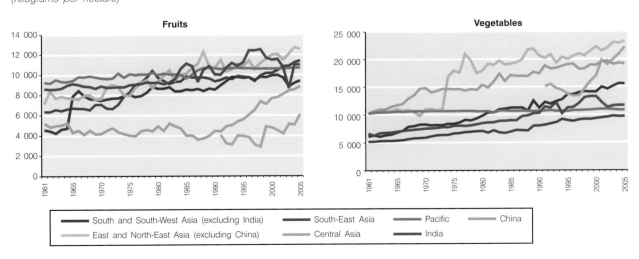

Source: Based on data from FAO, *State of Food and Agriculture 2003-04 Database* (Rome, FAO, 2004).

Figure 3.19. Declining multilateral lending to agriculture, 1995-2006

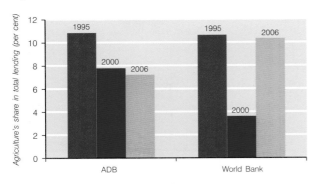

Sources: ADB, *Annual Report 2006* (Manila, ADB, 2006); and World Bank, *Annual Report 2006* (Washington, D.C., World Bank, 2006).

Official development assistance for agriculture is declining

Between 1983-1987 and 1998-2000, official development assistance for agriculture fell by 57% to an annual average of $5.1 billion (Anriquez and Stamoulis, 2007). Lending for agriculture by multilateral lending agencies, such as the World Bank and the Asian Development Bank, also trended downwards. The World Bank's free-standing agricultural credit dropped from a peak of more than $1 billion in 1983 to less than $200 million in 1995. The share of agriculture in total lending to the Asia-Pacific region declined from 11% in 1995 to about 4% in 2000 before increasing to 10% in 2006 (figure 3.19). Lending for agriculture by the Asian Development Bank also declined, with the share dropping from more than 10% in 1995 to about 7% in 2006.

Two strategies to make agriculture socially and economically viable

Because most of the poor live in rural areas and depend heavily on agriculture for their survival, a policy priority should be to revitalize agriculture. Some of the poor will remain in agriculture and continue to make farming their primary livelihood. Others, however, will shift from agriculture to industry and services, which offer them a better chance of escaping poverty. Policies should be put in place to make this transformation easy. Public policy could thus adopt a two-pronged approach, taking both aspects into account: revitalizing agriculture while facilitating the migration of excess labour from agriculture to industry and services.

> *Attacking poverty head-on requires both reviving agriculture and facilitating migration out of agriculture*

Strategy 1: Revitalize agriculture

Revitalizing agriculture requires connecting the poor to markets by improving rural infrastructure, improving agricultural technology, increasing the capacity to adapt technologies, and speeding diversification and commercialization. It also requires improving the distribution of land and the access to agricultural credit and extension – and making macroeconomic policy friendlier to agriculture, all enabling the poor to make a dent on poverty by themselves.

Connect the rural poor to cities and markets to alleviate poverty

Connecting the rural poor to cities and markets is vital to reducing costs and risks and exploiting new opportunities. Information and communications technology could give them easier access to information on the prices of inputs and products (box 3.4). Rural roads would enable them to sell their products in the marketplace and obtain better prices. Better information would also give them a sense of market demand and of seasonal variations in produce and prices so that they can adjust their production.

Electricity and water supply appear to have the highest payoffs for the poor. Electricity could generate a multiplier effect on poverty reduction through mechanization,

---

Box 3.4. Improving the efficiency of farmers through technology

Telecentres called e-Choupals – established by ITC Ltd., an Indian company – have a computer with Internet access, operated by an ITC-trained local farmer. The operator facilitates the farmers' access to good practices in agriculture and to market prices for commodities. Better market information helps farmers to decide when and where to sell (in the local market or to ITC). By purchasing directly from the farmers, ITC made the channel more efficient and created value for both the farmers and the company (Bowonder, Gupta and Singh, 2003). Farmers benefit from more accurate weighing, faster processing and prompter payment. By 2007, more than 6,500 e-Choupals were operating in about 31,000 villages (Sahay, 2007).

In Malaysia's remote Bario district, telecentres (e-Bario) have improved livelihoods through education and tourism. The once-isolated community now communicates with potential tourists directly through email and confirms bookings for accommodations online. More youths are staying in Bario to run the tourist accommodation and tourist activities (ESCAP, 2006a).

Another example is the Beijing Academy of Agriculture and Forestry Science, which runs a distance education system to train farmers on the outskirts of Beijing and in the rural areas of Xinjiang and Tibet. Since 2002, its centres have provided more than 600,000 farmers with remote education by satellite (Jianxin, Sun and Luo, 2005).

The Indian Space Research Organization also uses satellites to provide remote health services for the rural poor. The medical history of the patient in rural areas is sent to specialist doctors, who study and provide diagnosis and treatment during videoconferences with patients. More than a million patients in rural areas have received health services through this system (Satyamurthy and Murthy, 2007).

entrepreneurship and human capital development. In Bangladesh, rural electrification increased study time by two hours per day and raised women's involvement in their children's education. Literacy and school enrolment were much higher in electrified areas, and service delivery was better (Songco, 2002).

Improve service delivery to boost the health and education of the rural poor

Human capital, an important ingredient in production, can help the poor acquire and adapt new technologies in agriculture. Providing education for young and adult men and women would provide some insurance against poverty. Timmer (2005) points out that expanding public spending on education had a disproportionately positive effect on the poor in Indonesia. In particular, it enabled girls to catch up with boys, virtually eliminating the gender bias. Education helps the poor raise their agricultural productivity and thus their income. It also helps them acquire the skills to move into industry and services. Better health service delivery in rural areas can add to productivity gains.

Public spending on health and education should be increased sharply, especially targeting rural areas. In addition, there should be a conducive policy and institutional environment for the private sector to engage in service delivery. This would relieve pressure on the government budget and increase flexibility in allocating funds.

Human capital development should go hand in hand with providing opportunities for employment in rural and urban areas. Establishing links with the rural non-farm sector can provide employment in both the agricultural and non-farm sectors. Special programmes could target needy poor families for skills development by providing education and employment opportunities. These initiatives could have an intergenerational effect on poverty (box 3.5).

Diversify and commercialize agriculture to tap new markets and opportunities

Diversifying and commercializing agriculture is the key to raising incomes, particularly in a globalized world where tastes and quality matter. This transformation is already under way in China, India and Thailand, but many poor developing countries are lagging. Increasing the production of rice, wheat and maize will be a focus of antipoverty programmes in many parts of Asia, but tapping highly competitive retail food markets and supermarkets, with higher quality and safety standards, will require investments in skills development and technology, including R&D and extension services.

Box 3.5. Using family histories to understand the intergenerational transmission of poverty

The retrospective family life history approach focuses on individuals and households within a larger kinship network, particularly on descendants of a common ancestor, to identify determining factors in the long-term dynamics of rural poverty. Rather than looking in detail at one or two points in time, histories generate a long-term perspective. This allows researchers to study and explain changes in time in ways that household surveys cannot (Moore, 2001). Life history interviews can register important elements in the history of individuals, even across generations, by focusing on downward and upward mobility; ownership and control of assets; inheritance; accumulation strategies; strategic decisions, such as sending children to school or migrating to other areas; and life crises and shocks leading to downward mobility (Quisumbing, 2007).

A study in the progress of families over three generations by Centre for Alleviation of Poverty through Secondary Crops' Development in Asia and the Pacific (Bottema, Siregar and Madiapura, 2007) finds that:

- Every pathway consists of sequential components: agriculture, migration, local trade, local services and agriculture again.

- The number of rural-born people returning and residing in their area of origin is very high, over 95% in the current explorative research.

- People and families have a true long-term view of how to improve their lives. This offers huge scope for local livelihood improvements and participatory methods.

The region could also benefit from agricultural biotechnology for food crops. Asia and the Pacific has so far been cautious and selective in the use of genetically modified organisms in agricultural production, due to safety concerns, but it may be worthwhile to explore their use with strict safeguards in place. Organic farming represents another possible lucrative venture, given the rising consumer demand for organically produced food products.

Don't forget staples

Staple foods have historically had a large effect on poverty reduction. In countries where a single staple dominates consumption, the production of that staple has reduced poverty more than any other. Despite the potentially large multiplier effects, market failures and political biases have undermined the agricultural sector. As a result, the productivity of most staple crops is stagnant, the area under cultivation declining, and investment in R&D for staple crops falling.

Country experiences indicate that a balanced approach could be more effective in reducing poverty. Where poverty is acute, opportunities for crop diversification may not be readily available to the poorest. For these groups, staple crop production will still have a larger impact on poverty. In Bangladesh, India, the Lao People's Democratic Republic and Nepal, an emphasis on staple crops could be the most effective route to reducing poverty among the poorest because staples dominate consumption.

Redouble investment in agricultural R&D and extension

Traditional staples and the new agriculture require upscaling R&D. The benefits are simply too large to be neglected. In the poorest region of China, 140 people can be brought out of poverty with each 100,000 yuan of extra R&D investment, against the national average of 30 people (Fan, Zhang and Zhang, 2002). Productivity increases in staples will reduce poverty. Higher value crops will enhance access to markets, both national and international. The adverse effects of climate change on agriculture will require heavy investments to develop seeds that are not only more drought-resistant, heat-resistant and flood-tolerant but scale-neutral so that the poor can benefit. According to the Intergovernmental Panel on Climate Change (2007), the rising temperatures in the coming decades could reduce South Asia's agricultural productivity by 30% by the mid-21st century (box 3.6).

> *The benefits of R&D are simply too large to be neglected*

Investments in R&D can also be lucrative. Of all public investments in rural agricultural R&D had the highest cost-benefit ratio (12.62), several times higher than any other (Fan, Jitsuchon and Methakunnavut, 2003). National R&D in agriculture should be redoubled at a time when ODA for agricultural research is declining and most research is governed by commercial interests. An investor-friendly environment has to be created for private engagement in R&D by resolving issues related to patents, plant breeder rights and other intellectual property.

Focus on irrigation and water management to avoid overexploitation

North-west India and the North China plain are two places where the scarcity of water has affected wheat production (FAO, 2006a). Water scarcity will also be a major issue for most other Asian countries in the near future, particularly as competition from industrial, and municipal use increases. Output increases based on irrigation will therefore be very limited, and good, effective water management will be critical. Requiring greater policy attention are water conservation, water pricing, diversions from surplus to deficit areas, and establishing and restoring water management structures and institutions. Shifts to more diversified agricultural production, with less water-intensive higher value crops, would ameliorate the impact of growing water scarcity on agricultural production.

Remove institutional bottlenecks to sustain agricultural productivity and growth

Institutional bottlenecks hinder growth in agriculture, and the disproportionate impact of weak institutions on the poor widens inequality. Providing new institutions to support agriculture and improving the efficiency of defunct or inefficient institutions can revitalize agriculture. Productivity gains, however, are possible and sustainable only if proper institutions are in place and efficiently run. Well functioning institutional structures are required in rural finance, agricultural insurance, input and output markets, land titling and leasing, agricultural R&D and extension, irrigation and water management, and health and education.

Box 3.6. Climate change likely to change the landscape of the region

With many in Asia-Pacific dependent on agriculture for their livelihoods, the impact of climate change is of great significance. If business continues as usual, the region will be reshaped by climate change:

- The world's average temperature could rise by as much as 6 degrees Celsius by the end of the century, with devastating economic and social implications. Water and agriculture are particularly likely to be affected.

- Sea levels could rise by as much as 40 centimetres by the end of the 21st century, causing landward erosion and more frequent climate-related hazards. Livelihoods, particularly of those dependent on tourism, could be affected. Some of the small island States in the Pacific could disappear. Asia is likely to lose most in aquatic ecosystems: around 30% of Asia's coral reefs could disappear during the next 30 years, compared with 18% globally.

- Increased water stress will hit 185 million to 1 billion people in South and South-East Asia. Ingress of sea water in costal areas could make the subsurface water saline in many countries where ground water is subject to overexploitation.

- Himalayan glaciers could shrink by 80% by 2030, increasing river run off, floods and avalanches. As a result, the fresh water and water for irrigation for downstream agriculture could become unsustainable.

- Floods will affect 13-94 million people in low-lying areas of South, South-East and East Asia. Bangladesh, China, India and Viet Nam will be among the most affected. Asian mega-delta regions could be under threat of intense flooding from both seas and rivers.

- Agricultural productivity is estimated to decrease by 5-30% by the 2050s compared with 1990, increasing poverty and hunger. Central and South Asia, in particular, could face crop yields lower by as much as 30% by the mid-21st century.

- Health consequences could come from a higher risk of dengue fever, particularly in China and India, where transmission rates are 50%. Other insect-borne diseases, including malaria, schistosomiasis and other viral diseases, could spread widely. Heat stress and smog-induced cardiovascular and respiratory illnesses could become common, as could water-borne diseases such as cholera and diarrhoea with the contamination of drinking water.

- Forest fires could become more frequent and intense in northern Asia and South-eastern Australia.

These effects will be felt more acutely by the poor, both rural and urban, who live and work in settlements on marginal lands and do not have the resources to insulate themselves against natural disasters and other adverse effects of climate change.

Source: IPCC, "Climate change 2007: mitigation", Contribution of Working Group III to the Fourth Assessment Report of the Intergovernmental Panel on Climate Change, <http://www.ipcc.ch/pdf/assessment-report/ar4/wg3/ar4-wg3-frontmatter.pdf>.

Recognize that sound macroeconomic policy is always pro-poor

A sound macroeconomic policy environment promotes growth and has a direct, positive impact on the poor. Low inflation is necessary to keep the prices of basic consumption goods low and affordable. Artificially high interest rates in most Asia-Pacific countries, indicating inefficient financial systems, can reduce investment and lead to more defaults. Maintaining positive real interest rates is a must for raising savings, but lending rates should not be kept artificially high. Exchange rates have to be stable and aligned to macroeconomic conditions. All taxes on agriculture, except sector development-oriented cesses, should be removed in view of efficiency and welfare gains.

Be fair, that's all farmers want

Create farmer-friendly credit markets

The structural adjustment policies of the 1980s removed impediments to the interest rate structure and improved monetary management, but they have not been accompanied by micro-arrangements to counter the negative impact on agricultural credit markets in most countries. Furthermore, there is still a wide communication gap between bankers and poor farmers. As a result, the poor in rural areas have to depend on informal lenders at high rates.[9] If the debt is paid in kind (a portion of the harvest), the effective rate could be 200-300% per year.

Local credit institutions (such as cooperatives or regional rural banks with limited scope) could bridge the gap between credit institutions and farmers. Crop insurance could defend against agricultural loan defaults. Commercial bank branches could also be expanded to rural areas. Group lending along the lines of Grameen Bank could be viable for sustainable financing of agriculture, particularly through existing cooperative institutions and NGOs. Improving land ownership and entitlements and enabling the poor to use such entitlements as collateral would be the keys here. Also needed are more savings opportunities for the poor, innovative substitutes for collateral and flexible borrowing arrangements.

---

[9] In Cambodia, the effective lending rate in the informal market, where the majority of the rural poor borrow, exceeds 180% per year.

Urgent policy attention needed on farm debt

Governments must be prepared for eventual intervention to ensure the flow of credit to the agricultural sector if the subprime crisis spills over to the region and curtails institutional credit.

Introduce crop insurance to mitigate crop failures and price declines

Most farm-related suicides occur because of and debts from crop failure or price declines. Many countries have crop insurance to cover crop failures, but few cover losses from price declines. Extending crop insurance to cover price declines below a cut-off could help farmers avoid extreme hardship. Rent-seeking by field officers and other malpractices have to be eliminated for the full benefits of such schemes to reach poor farmers. A positive step would be providing farmers with information on commodity prices, perhaps by establishing commodity futures markets.

Revamp land policy for socially inclusive growth

Many countries have undertaken extensive land reforms. In China, they led to significant gains in agricultural productivity and reductions in poverty. Yet for many others, the reforms are incomplete and inadequate. For example, India's land reform mainly changed tenure but not ownership. Half of India's arable land therefore remains in the hands of large landowners.

Improving efficiency in land records and administration can eliminate rent-seeking and corruption. Governments could impose ceilings on land ownership and distribute public land, but these steps would require political commitment at the highest levels. Another option is to adopt innovative mechanisms for land use, particularly in land leasing and renting. Community organizations in Pakistan lease land from landlords or the State at scale, negotiating good terms. They then lease these lands to the landless poor. As an intermediary, they fill gaps in land ownership. Removing regulatory barriers to leasing and renting land could thus help the landless poor.

Pursue fiscal decentralization to gain extra resources to meet local needs

In regions where agriculture is the major economic activity, local governments have a narrow revenue base, and the resources for development are very limited.[10] Fiscal decentralization could also affect the central government's redistributive power.[11]

To reduce the large disparities in local revenue and spending, it is necessary to widen the tax base. Increased transfers are important for equalizing revenue, and better fiscal management would reduce rent-seeking and corruption. Close coordination among local and central authorities is required to implement a national agricultural policy at local levels to achieve the desired outcomes.

Promote social mobilization to influence agricultural policy

Social mobilization puts poor people at the centre of their own development initiatives and organizes them into forums for microplanning. The potential of people in agriculture could be built on the three elements of social mobilization. First, the poor in the agricultural sector are brought into an organized fold through social mobilization. Second, the skill base of the poor – managerial, productive, technical and cooperative skills – is enhanced. Third, a financial or capital base is built to move the poor towards greater self-reliance.

Rural support programmes specialize in mobilizing the poor, something that governments are not equipped to do. As intermediaries between the government and the people, they can advocate for communities to influence public policy.

Strategy 2: Facilitate migration out of agriculture

Farmers can leave agriculture for non-farm activities in rural areas or for work in urban areas. The first requires creating opportunities in the non-farm sector – the second, urban planning. Both require better oppor-

tunities for skills development and strategies for raising overall economic growth.

Empower the poor to enter labour markets

Finding work in the non-farm sector in rural and urban areas requires skills. So, providing basic education to all can facilitate outmigration. Increasing the opportunities for technical education can build the entrepreneurial skills of young people for self-employment and wage employment. Social barriers that restrict women's access to education and participation in the labour market need to be eliminated, and better access to health care can enhance the productivity of the poor by supplementing the gains in education.

Improve urban planning

Concentrations of economic growth and opportunities for employment in cities make rapid rural-urban migration inevitable. Good urban planning and development are therefore essential to help people out of agriculture. If not properly planned and managed, urbanization could add to congestion, ill health, environmental damage and unmet demand for basic services.

Promote the rural non-farm sector

One way of managing rural-urban migration while promoting poverty reduction is to promote the rural non-farm sector, enabling the poor to diversify their income sources and insure against shocks to their agricultural income (McCulloch, Weisbrod and Timmer, 2007). Rural infrastructure is the key. Because the non-farm sector is competitive and requires better skills, the work force needs to be healthy and educated. Technology transfers and finance are also important. A little effort could bring a large reward. In Indonesia, for example, non-farm income is more than 50% higher than agricultural income. And people who migrate to non-farm jobs in urban areas earn 60% more than those in the rural non-farm sector.

Promote regional growth centres

Regional growth centres, acting as "multi-hubs" to develop peripheral communities, could become production centres and end-markets for rural products. Promoting them would address regional growth disparities – and reduce the push factors that drive the rural poor to big cities.

---

[10] See Zhung (2006) for a discussion on this issue in China.

[11] For example, fiscal decentralization in China has reduced the central government's redistributive power (see Zhang and Kanbur, 2003).

Go beyond Doha agricultural trade liberalization to reap immense benefits

The benefits of comprehensive agricultural trade liberalization flow to all countries in the region, a far better option than piecemeal approaches that benefit only a few. In countries such as India, where Doha agricultural trade reforms could increase poverty, comprehensive reforms would include rationalizing subsidies and removing regulations restricting trade. Under the Doha agricultural reforms, such countries could redistribute welfare gains to the poor through progressive income taxes.

Liberalizing manufacturing and services would add to the benefits of agricultural trade liberalization, if accompanied by better facilitation. Promoting international trade can raise the net returns to farmers if post-harvest operations attract more attention. Post-harvest losses of vegetable and fruits are high. Better packaging, quality control, transport and marketing could slash these losses, enabling rural producers to increase their net incomes by about 30%.

References

Anderson, K. and W. Martin (2005). *Agricultural Trade Reform and the Doha Development Agenda* (Washington, D.C., World Bank).

Annabi, N., B. Khondker, S. Raihan, J. Cockburn and B. Decaluwe (2006). "Implications of WTO agreements and unilateral trade policy reforms for poverty in Bangladesh: short vs. long run impacts", in K. Anderson and W. Martin (eds.), *Agricultural Trade Reform and the Doha Development Agenda* (Washington, D.C., World Bank).

Amnesty International (2007). "The state of the world's human rights", <http://thereport.amnesty.org/eng/Regions?Asia-Pacific>.

Anriquez, G. and K. Stamoulis (2007). "Rural development and poverty reduction: Is agriculture still the key?", ESA Working Paper No. 07-02 (Rome, FAO).

Asian Development Bank (2007a). *Inequality in Asia* (Manila, ADB).

_____ (2007b). *Key Indicators 2007* (Manila, ADB).

Asian Farmers Association for Sustainable Development (2007). "Proceedings of the regional consultation workshop on farmers' situation: Responding to major difficulties faced by farmers in Asia", June 12-15 2007, Quezon City, Philippines, <http://asianfarmers.org/?p=315>.

Baird, S., J. Friedman and N. Schady (2007). "Infant mortality over the business cycle in the developing world", Policy Research Working Paper No. 4346 (Washington, D.C., World Bank).

BBC News (2007). "Rural China's suicide problem", 4 June, <http://news.bbc.co.uk/2/hi/asia-pacific/6711415.stm>.

Bottema, T., M. Siregar and H. Madiapura (2007). "Family life history as a tool in the study of long-term dynamics of poverty: an exploration", paper prepared for International Poverty Conference, UNDP, PM Office, 11-13 December, Kuala Lumpur, Malaysia.

Bowonder, B., V. Gupta and A. Singh (2003). "Developing a rural market e-hub: The case study of e-Choupal experience of ITC", Planning Commission of India, <http://planningcommission.gov.in/reports/sereport/stdy_ict/4_e-choupal%20.pdf>.

Cardoso, A.R. and D. Verner (2007). "School drop-out and push-out factors in Brazil: the role of early parenthood, child labour and poverty", Policy Research Working Paper No. 4178 (Washington, D.C., World Bank).

Chang, H. and L. Zepeda (2001). "Agricultural investment and productivity in developing countries", Economic and Social Development Paper 148 (Rome, FAO).

Chen, S. and M. Ravallion (2007). "Absolute poverty measures for the developing world", Policy Research Working Paper No. 4211 (Washington, D.C., World Bank).

Christiaensen, L., L. Demery and J. Kuhl (2006). "The role of agriculture in poverty reduction", Policy Research Working Paper No. 4013 (Washington, D.C., World Bank).

Cororaton, C.B., J. Cockburn and E. Corong (2006). "Doha scenarios, trade reforms, and poverty in the Philippines: A CGE analysis", in T. Hertel and L.A. Winters (eds.), *Poverty Impacts of a WTO Agreement* (Washington, D.C., World Bank).

Dhall, R.K. and A.S. Dhatt (2002). "Horticulture: have quality, will export", <http://www.tribuneindia.com/2002/20020819/agro.htm>.

Dollar, D. (2007). "Poverty, inequality and social disparities during China's economic reform", Policy Research Working Paper No. 4253 (Washington, D.C., World Bank).

Dollar, D. and A. Kraay (2002). "Growth is good for the poor", *Journal of Economic Growth,* vol. 7, No. 3, pp. 195-225.

Durairaj, V. (2007). "Enhancing equity in access to health care in the Asia-Pacific region: Remediable inequities", report prepared for the United Nations Regional Thematic Working Group on Health, May, Bangkok, WHO and UNFPA.

ESCAP (2005). *A Future Within Reach: Reshaping Institution in a Region of Disparities to Meet the Millennium Development Goals in Asia and the Pacific* (United Nations publication, Sales No. E.05.II.F.27).

_____ (2006a). "Guidebook on developing community e-centres in rural areas: based on the Malaysian experience", <http://www.unescap.org/icstd/applications/projects/Malaysia_CeC/docs/guidebook.pdf>.

_____ (2006b). *Enhancing Regional Cooperation in Infrastructure Development including that related to Disaster Management* (United Nations publication, Sales No. E.06.II.F.13).

_____ (2007). *Development of Health Systems in the Context of Enhancing Economic Growth towards Achieving the Millennium Development Goals in Asia and the Pacific* (United Nations publication, Sales No. E.07.II.F.12).

ESCAP/ADB/UNDP (2007). *The Millennium Development Goals: Progress in Asia and the Pacific 2007* (ST/ESCAP/2465) (Bangkok, ESCAP/ADB/UNDP).

Fan, S., S. Jitsuchon and N. Methakunnavut (2003). "Impacts of public investments on poverty reduction in Thailand" (Washington, D.C., International Food Policy Research Institute).

Fan, S., L. Zhang and X. Zhang (2002). "Growth, inequality and poverty in rural China: the role of public investments", Research Report 125 (Washington, D.C., International Food Policy Research Institute).

FAO (1999). "Agricultural finance revisited: sources of funds for agricultural lending" (Rome, FAO).

_____ (2004). *State of Food and Agriculture 2003-2004 Database* (Rome, FAO).

_____ (2006a). "Rapid growth of selected Asian economies; lessons and implications for agriculture and food security: China and India", Policy Assistance Series 1.2 (Rome, FAO).

_____ (2006b). *The State of Food and Agriculture in Asia and the Pacific* (Rome, FAO).

Hanushek, E. (1995). "Interpreting recent research on schooling in developing countries", *World Bank Research Observer,* vol. 10, No. 2, pp. 227-246.

Hertel, T. and F. Zhai (2006). "Impacts of the Doha development agenda on China: The role of labour markets and complementary education reforms", in T. Hertel and L.A. Winters (eds.), *Poverty Impacts of a WTO Agreement* (Washington, D.C., World Bank).

IFAD (2001). *The Rural Poverty Report 2001* (Oxford, Oxford University Press).

ILO (2007). *Key Indicators of the Labour Market, 5th Edition* (Geneva, ILO).

IMF (2007). *International Financial Statistics* (Washington, D.C., IMF).

IMF and World Bank (2001). *Macroeconomic Policy and Poverty Reduction* (Washington, D.C.).

India (2001). *Census Statistics of India 2001* (New Delhi, Office of the Registrar General and Census Commissioner).

_____ (2005). "Press Note on indebtedness of farmer household (January-December, 2003)" (New Delhi, National Sample Survey Organization, Ministry of Statistics and Programme Implementation).

_____ (2007). *Report of the Expert Group on Agricultural Indebtedness* (New Delhi, Banking Division).

India Express (2007). "Panel on farmers distress to miss budget deadline, report in May", 27 February.

India Research (2006). "Processed food: adding value to the farmers' harvest", <http://www.indiaindustryreports.com/info.aspx?sid=3&id=17&doc=Articles-Business-17.htm>.

IPCC (2007). "Climate change 2007: Synthesis report", Fourth Assessment Report of the Intergovernmental Panel on Climate Change, <http://www.ipcc.ch/ipccreports/ar4-syr.htm>.

Jianxin, G., S. Sun and C. Luo (2005). "Transformation digital divide into digital opportunities for rural population – research and practice of rural distance education and information service in Beijing", US-China Education Review (United States).

Klytchnikova, I. and N. Diop (2006). "Trade reform, farm productivity, and poverty in Bangladesh", Policy Research Working Paper No. 3980 (Washington, D.C., World Bank).

Kremer, M. (1995). "Research on schooling: what we know and what we don't: A comment on Hanushek", *World Bank Research Observer,* vol. 10, No. 2, pp. 247-254.

Ligon, E. and E. Sadoulet (2007). "Estimating the effects of aggregate agricultural growth on the distribution of expenditures", paper prepared for the *World Development Report 2008* (Washington, D.C., World Bank).

Lin, J. (1992). "Rural reforms and agricultural growth in China", *American Economic Review,* vol. 82, pp. 34-51.

Madiapura, H. and M. Siregar (2007). *Studies in Progress* (Bogor, CAPSA).

Majid, N. (2004). "Reaching Millennium Development Goals: How well does agricultural productivity growth reduce poverty?", Employment Strategy Papers No. 2004/12 (Geneva, ILO).

Masuy-Stroobant, G. (2001). "The determinants of infant mortality: how far are conceptual frameworks really modeled?", Working Paper No. 13 (Louvain, University Catholique de Louvain).

McCulloch, N., J. Weisbrod and C.P. Timmer (2007). "Pathways out of poverty during an economic crisis: an empirical assessment of rural Indonesia", Policy Research Working Paper No. 4173 (Washington, D.C., World Bank).

MONLAR (Movement for National Land and Agricultural Reform) (2005). "Movement for National Land and Agricultural Reform: Lessons of farmers' hunger strike in Polonnaruwa, Sri Lanka August 2000", paper presented at the La Via Campesina Human Rights Committee Human Rights Training, 23-29 September, Sarawak, Malaysia.

Moore, K. (2001). "Framework for understanding the intergenerational transmission of poverty and well-being in developing countries", Working Paper No. 8 (Manchester, Chronic Poverty Research Centre).

NLM (National Literacy Mission India) (2001). "Literates and literacy rates, 2001 census", <http://www.nlm.nic.in/literacy01.htm>.

Quisumbing, A.R. (2007). "Investments, bequests, and public policy: Intergenerational transfers and the escape from poverty", Working Paper No. 98 (Manchester, Chronic Poverty Research Centre).

Rao, D.S.P., T.J. Coelli and M. Alauddin (2004). "Agricultural productivity growth, employment and poverty in developing countries, 1970-2000", Employment Strategy Paper No. 2004/9 (Geneva, ILO).

Rao, M.G. (2000). "Fiscal decentralization in Indian federalism" (Bangalore, Institute for Social and Economic Change).

Ravallion, M. and S. Chen (2007). "China's uneven progress against poverty", *Journal of Development Economics,* vol. 82, No. 1, pp. 1-42.

Ravallion, M. and G. Datt (1996). "How important to India's poor is the sectoral composition of economic growth?, *World Bank Economic Review,* vol. 10, pp. 1-26.

_____ (1999). "When is growth pro-poor? Evidence from the diverse experiences of India's states", Policy Research Working Paper No. 2263 (Washington, D.C., World Bank).

_____ (2002). "Why has economic growth been more pro-poor in some states of India than others?", *Journal of Development Economics,* vol. 68, No. 2, pp. 381-400.

Ravi, D.L. (2003) "Operationalizing right to healthcare in India", paper presented at the *10th Canadian Conference on International Health – The Right to Health, Influencing the Global Agenda: How research, advocacy and action can shape our future,* 26-29 October, Ottawa, Canada, <www.cehat.org>.

Rehman, S.A. (1998). "Female functional literacy", paper presented at the *Second Asia Regional Literacy Forum – Innovation and Professionalization in Adult Literacy: A Focus on diversity,* 9-13 February, New Delhi, India, <http://literacy.org/products/ili/webdocs/rehman.html>.

Robilliard, R. and S. Robinson (2006.) "The social impact of a WTO Agreement in Indonesia", in T. Hertel and L.A. Winters (eds.), *Poverty Impacts of a WTO Agreement* (Washington, D.C., World Bank).

SAARC (2005). *Regional Poverty Profile 2005,* Chapter 6 (Kathmandu, SAARC).

Sahay, S. (2007). "Mission e-Choupal", presentation to the *UNESCAP Consultative Meeting for the Establishment of Regional Knowledge Network of Telecentres in Asia-Pacific,* 27-28 September, Bangkok, Thailand, <http://telecentresap.org/meeting/cmap2007/India_Presentation_eChoupal.pdf>.

Sala-i-Martin, X. (2002). "The world distribution of income (estimated from individual country distributions)", *NBER Working Paper Series,* Working Paper No. 8933 (Cambridge, National Bureau of Economic Research).

Salinas, G. and A. Akosoy (2006). "Growth before and after trade liberalisation", Policy Research Working Paper No. 4062 (Washington, D.C., World Bank).

Satyamurthy, L.S. and R.L.N. Murthy (2007). "Indian Telemedicine Programme – Efforts towards integrating the stakeholders for realizing a technology based health care delivery system", paper presented at the *APT Regional Workshop on Telemedicine,* 6-9 February, Chiang Mai, Thailand.

Schiff, M. and A. Valdes (1998). "Agriculture and the macroeconomy", Policy Research Working Paper No. 1967 (Washington, D.C., World Bank).

Sharma, D. (2004). "Farmer's suicides", <http://www.zmag.org/content/showarticle.cfm?ItemID=4871>

Shields, M., P. Frijters and J. Haisken DeNew (2005). "The causal effect of income on health: Evidence from German reunification", *Journal of Health Economics,* vol. 24, No. 5, pp. 997-1017.

Songco, J. (2002). "Do rural infrastructure investment benefit the poor? Evaluating linkages: A global view, A focus on Viet Nam", Policy Research Working Paper No. 2796 (Washington, D.C., World Bank).

Sri Lanka (2007). *Annual Report* (Colombo, Central Bank of Sri Lanka).

Timmer, C.P. (2005). "Agriculture and pro-poor growth: An Asian perspective", Center for Global Development Working Paper No. 63 (Washington, D.C., CGD).

UNIFEM (1998). *Bringing Equality Home: Implementing the Convention on the Elimination of all Forms of Discrimination Against Women* (New York, UNIFEM).

Wang, J., D. Jamison, E. Bos, A. Preker and J. Peabody (1995). "Measuring country performance in health: Selected indication for 115 countries" (Washington, D.C., World Bank).

Washington Post (2007). "Illiteracy jumps in China, despite 50-year campaign to eradicate it", 27 April.

White, H. (2004). "Books, buildings and learning outcome: An impact evaluation of World Bank support the basic education in Ghana" (Washington, D.C., OED, World Bank).

Winters, L.A. (2002). "Trade liberalization and poverty: What are the links?", *World Economy,* vol. 25, No. 9, pp. 1339-1367.

World Bank (2005). "The relative roles of growth and inequality for poverty reduction", <http://siteresources.worldbank.org/EXTLACOFFICEOFCE/Resources/870892-1139877599088/virtuous-circles_ch4.pdf>.

_____ (2006). *World Development Indicators 2006* (CD-ROM) (Washington, D.C., World Bank).

_____ (2007). *World Development Report 2008* (Washington, D.C., World Bank).

Zhang, X. and R. Kanbur (2003). "Spatial inequality in education and health care in China", Centre for Economic Policy Research Discussion Paper No. 4136 (London, CEPR).

Zhung, X. (2006) "Fiscal decentralization and political centralization in China", UNU-WIDER Research Paper No. 2006/93 (Helsenki, UNU-WIDER).

STATISTICAL ANNEX

List of tables

		Page
1.	Real GDP growth rates	158
2.	Gross domestic savings rates	159
3.	Gross domestic investment rates	160
4.	Inflation rates	161
5.	Budget balances	162
6.	Current account balance	163
7.	Change in money supply	164
8.	Merchandise export growth rates	165
9.	Merchandise import growth rates	166
10.	Population, size and dynamics	167
11.	Population, structure	168
12.	International migration	169
13.	Primary education	170
14.	Secondary and tertiary education	171
15.	Life expectancy	172
16.	Health, morbidity	173
17.	Mortality	174
18.	Poverty and malnutrition	175
19.	Gender parity	176
20.	Employment growth, share of total population and productivity	177
21.	Employment, by economic activity	178
22.	Employment, by status	179
23.	Unemployment, by gender and age group	180
24.	Telecommunications	181
25.	Infrastructure and transport	182
26.	Land area and use	183
27.	Energy and water use	184
28.	Pollution and access to water and sanitation	185
Technical notes		186

Table 1. Real GDP growth rates

(Per cent)

	1995	1996	1997	1998	1999	2000	2001	2002	2003	2004	2005	2006	2007
Developing ESCAP economies	7.7	7.2	6.2	1.7	6.0	7.4	4.4	6.5	7.0	7.8	7.7	8.1	8.2
East and North-East Asia	9.7	8.5	7.7	3.4	7.5	8.2	5.6	7.5	7.3	8.4	8.1	8.7	9.0
China	10.9	10.0	9.3	7.8	7.6	8.4	8.3	9.1	10.0	10.1	10.4	11.1	11.4
Hong Kong, China	6.2	4.2	5.1	−5.5	4.0	10.0	0.6	1.8	3.1	8.5	7.1	6.8	6.1
Macao, China	3.3	−0.4	−0.3	−4.6	−2.4	5.7	2.9	10.1	14.2	28.6	6.7	16.6	..
Mongolia	6.3	2.4	4.0	3.5	3.2	1.1	1.1	4.2	6.1	10.8	7.1	8.4	9.0
Republic of Korea	9.2	7.0	4.7	−6.9	9.5	8.5	3.8	7.0	3.1	4.7	4.2	5.0	5.0
North and Central Asia	−4.4	−2.8	1.7	−4.0	6.1	9.6	5.8	5.2	7.5	7.4	7.1	7.6	8.6
Armenia	6.9	5.9	3.3	7.3	3.3	5.9	9.6	13.2	14.0	10.5	13.9	13.3	13.8
Azerbaijan	−11.8	1.3	5.8	10.0	7.4	11.1	9.9	10.6	11.2	10.2	26.4	34.5	25.0
Georgia	2.6	10.5	10.5	3.1	2.9	1.8	4.8	5.5	11.1	5.9	9.6	9.4	12.7[a]
Kazakhstan	−8.2	0.5	1.7	−1.9	2.7	9.8	13.5	9.8	9.3	9.6	9.7	10.6	9.7[a]
Kyrgyzstan	−6.4	7.1	9.9	2.1	3.7	5.4	5.3	0.0	7.0	7.0	−0.2	2.7	8.2
Russian Federation	−4.1	−3.6	1.4	−5.3	6.4	10.0	5.1	4.7	7.3	7.2	6.4	6.7	8.1
Tajikistan	−12.4	−16.8	1.7	5.3	3.7	8.3	9.6	10.8	11.1	10.3	6.7	7.0	7.8
Turkmenistan	−7.2	6.7	−11.4	7.1	16.5	5.5	4.3	0.3	3.3	5.0	9.0	9.0	10.0
Uzbekistan	−0.9	1.7	5.2	4.4	4.4	4.0	4.3	4.2	4.5	7.7	7.0	7.3	9.8[a]
Pacific island economies	−0.4	5.5	−4.0	3.3	8.0	−0.3	2.0	1.9	2.1	3.7	2.8	3.1	2.7
Cook Islands	−4.4	0.0	−2.3	−0.8	2.7	13.9	4.9	2.6	8.2	4.3	0.1	0.8	2.5
Fiji	2.1	4.8	−2.2	1.3	8.8	−1.7	2.0	3.2	1.0	5.3	0.7	3.6	−3.9
French Polynesia	0.5	0.3	1.9	6.2	4.0	4.0	1.3	4.4	4.0	3.5	3.4	3.3	..
Kiribati	5.3	2.9	4.4	14.7	8.3	−0.6	8.4	4.7	0.9	−2.0	2.5	1.1	1.0
Micronesia (Federated States of)	2.3	−3.0	−10.0	5.3	−2.6	4.2	0.4	1.4	3.3	−4.4	1.5	−0.7	1.0
Palau	10.9	10.4	2.3	2.0	−5.4	0.3	1.3	−3.5	−1.3	4.9	5.5	5.7	5.5
Papua New Guinea	−3.3	6.6	−6.3	4.7	10.1	0.0	2.7	2.0	2.0	2.7	3.4	2.6	6.2
Samoa	6.6	7.3	0.8	2.4	1.3	6.8	6.5	1.0	3.5	3.3	6.0	1.8	3.0
Solomon Islands	5.4	1.9	−0.6	1.0	−0.2	−14.2	−8.2	−2.7	6.5	8.0	5.0	6.2	5.4
Tonga	2.9	−0.5	−3.2	4.9	2.3	5.3	1.8	3.2	2.7	1.4	2.3	1.3	−3.5
Tuvalu	−5.0	1.0	10.3	10.5	2.4	−12.8	13.2	5.5	4.0	4.0	2.0	3.0	2.5
Vanuatu	4.7	7.2	4.9	4.3	−3.2	2.7	−2.7	−4.9	2.4	5.5	6.8	5.5	4.7
South and South-West Asia	6.5	7.1	5.0	4.9	3.3	5.2	2.3	5.2	7.2	7.4	8.2	8.0	7.4
Afghanistan	5.0	9.0	10.1	11.9	−5.9	−33.6	−9.4	39.5	14.3	9.4	14.5	7.5	13.0
Bangladesh	4.9	4.6	5.4	5.2	4.9	5.9	5.3	4.4	5.3	6.3	6.0	6.7	6.5
Bhutan	6.8	6.4	5.9	6.1	7.9	7.6	7.2	10.0	7.6	7.5	6.1	5.5	17.6
India	7.3	7.8	4.8	6.5	6.1	4.4	5.8	3.8	8.5	7.5	9.4	9.6	9.0
Iran (Islamic Republic of)	3.2	5.8	3.4	1.6	2.8	5.1	3.3	7.5	6.7	4.8	5.4	6.2	5.8
Maldives	7.1	8.8	11.5	9.3	7.8	4.4	3.3	6.1	9.2	11.3	−4.6	19.1	6.6
Nepal	3.5	5.3	5.3	2.9	4.5	6.1	5.6	0.1	4.0	4.7	3.1	2.8	2.5
Pakistan	5.1	6.6	1.7	3.5	4.2	3.9	1.8	3.1	4.7	7.5	9.0	6.6	7.0
Sri Lanka	5.5	3.8	6.4	4.7	4.3	6.1	−1.4	4.0	5.9	5.4	6.2	7.7	6.7
Turkey	7.2	7.0	7.5	3.1	−4.7	7.4	−7.5	7.9	5.8	8.9	7.4	6.1	5.0
South-East Asia	8.3	7.6	4.6	−6.9	4.0	6.4	2.1	5.0	5.3	6.5	5.6	6.0	6.2
Brunei Darussalam	3.0	3.6	4.1	−0.6	3.1	2.9	2.7	3.9	2.9	0.5	0.4	5.1	0.5
Cambodia	5.9	4.6	5.7	5.0	12.6	8.4	5.5	5.2	7.0	10.0	13.4	10.8	8.5
Indonesia	8.2	7.8	4.7	−13.1	0.8	4.9	3.6	4.5	4.8	5.1	5.7	5.5	6.2
Lao PDR	7.5	6.9	6.9	4.0	7.3	5.8	5.8	5.9	5.8	6.9	7.2	8.3	7.4
Malaysia	9.8	10.0	7.3	−7.4	6.1	8.9	0.3	5.4	5.4	6.8	5.0	5.9	5.7
Myanmar	6.9	6.4	5.7	5.8	10.9	13.7	11.3	12.0	13.8	13.6	13.2	7.0	..
Philippines	4.7	5.8	5.2	−0.6	3.4	4.7	3.0	4.4	4.5	6.4	4.9	5.4	7.0
Singapore	8.0	8.2	8.3	−1.4	7.2	10.0	−2.4	4.2	3.1	8.8	6.6	7.9	7.5
Thailand	9.2	5.9	−1.4	−10.5	4.4	4.8	2.2	5.3	7.1	6.3	4.5	5.1	4.5
Timor-Leste	9.5	10.8	4.1	−2.1	−35.5	13.7	16.5	−6.7	−6.2	0.4	2.2	−1.6	32.1
Viet Nam	9.5	9.3	8.2	5.8	4.8	6.8	6.9	7.1	7.3	7.8	8.4	8.2	8.4
Developed ESCAP economies	2.1	2.7	1.6	−1.4	0.3	2.9	0.4	0.7	1.6	2.8	2.0	2.4	2.0
Australia	3.6	4.3	3.9	5.1	4.4	3.4	2.1	4.1	3.1	3.7	2.8	2.7	4.2
Japan	1.9	2.6	1.4	−2.0	−0.1	2.9	0.2	0.3	1.4	2.7	1.9	2.4	1.8
New Zealand	4.2	3.5	1.5	0.4	5.3	2.1	3.9	4.7	3.6	3.8	2.7	1.8	3.1

Sources: ESCAP, based on United Nations Statistics Division, *National Accounts Main Aggregates Database* at website <http://unstats.un.org/unsd> (online database, January 2008), with updates and estimates from national and local sources.

Notes: Data for 2007 are estimates. The data and estimates for countries relate to fiscal years defined as follows: fiscal year 2005/06 = 2005 for India and the Islamic Republic of Iran; and fiscal year 2004/05 = 2005 for Bangladesh, Nepal and Pakistan.

[a] January-September.

Table 2. Gross domestic savings rates

(Percentage of GDP)

	1995	1996	1997	1998	1999	2000	2001	2002	2003	2004	2005	2006	2007
Developing ESCAP economies													
East and North-East Asia													
China	39.6	38.3	39.0	38.9	38.0	38.0	39.0	40.4	43.0	45.6	47.3	47.3	50.2
Hong Kong, China	29.6	30.1	30.7	29.4	30.1	32.0	29.8	31.1	31.2	30.7	33.0	33.2	33.8
Mongolia	23.4	18.9	25.8	14.3	14.6	10.4	5.7	3.7	8.7	22.4	30.6	38.5	..
Republic of Korea	36.5	35.7	35.8	37.9	35.8	33.9	31.9	31.4	33.0	35.0	33.2	31.7	30.1
North and Central Asia													
Armenia	−19.8	−12.7	−18.9	−14.7	−10.7	−8.5	−0.9	4.9	6.4	10.1	16.7	..	..
Azerbaijan	2.9	0.3	12.9	4.8	8.6	20.4	24.9	24.7	29.6	34.1	49.5	56.3	..
Georgia	−12.8	0.7	−8.5	0.4	3.0	4.7	7.5	8.9	9.9	16.4	13.9	..	..
Kazakhstan	15.3	19.8	17.1	15.9	16.1	26.4	28.7	33.8	34.3	34.9	42.5	44.0	..
Kyrgyzstan	9.3	3.4	14.3	−8.2	1.2	14.2	12.6	13.6	4.5	4.9	4.9	..	..
Russian Federation	28.8	27.9	24.2	21.6	31.9	38.7	34.6	30.8	32.1	33.1	34.5	..	..
Tajikistan	23.9	18.9	13.0	6.4	15.9	9.5	−2.2	0.8	3.0	3.3	..	..	..
Turkmenistan	..	49.3	13.1	7.3	12.3	50.2	37.2	43.2	31.1	25.6	40.3	32.3	..
Uzbekistan	27.1	22.7	18.7	19.9	17.3	19.4	20.0	21.8	26.9	31.2	32.7	30.3	..
Pacific island economies													
Cook Islands	2.7	17.4	13.1	14.8	20.2	21.8	26.7	24.0	21.4	18.1	25.0	21.5	..
Fiji	10.2	11.7	11.6	13.4	10.7	5.0	9.7	17.3	13.7	2.5	1.5	5.9	..
Kiribati	−22.3	−17.6	−10.2	4.2	−0.6	2.8	2.1	1.4	2.1	1.9	1.8	1.9	..
Papua New Guinea	40.2	31.2	22.4	22.6	13.2	23.7	12.6	13.4	24.7	26.2	25.7	25.0	..
Samoa	−5.1	−2.9	−11.9	−6.5	−13.0	−9.2	−14.1	−14.5	−14.0	−14.1	−14.0	−13.9	..
Solomon Islands	18.2	19.1	20.4	19.2	19.5	19.7	19.5	19.6	19.6	19.6	19.6	19.6	..
Tonga	−14.6	−17.2	−13.1	−17.2	−10.2	−9.4	−20.0	−25.5	−24.3	−20.9	−26.3	−26.7	..
Tuvalu	−45.3	−45.3	−45.3	−45.3	−45.3	−45.3	−45.3	−45.3	−45.3	−45.3	−45.3	−45.3	..
Vanuatu	17.0	11.8	20.3	22.4	19.2	19.3	17.9	9.4	12.7	16.4	19.6	..	..
South and South-West Asia													
Bangladesh	13.1	14.9	15.9	17.4	17.7	17.9	18.0	18.2	18.6	19.5	20.0	20.3	19.5
Bhutan	46.1	35.6	23.5	22.9	22.5	29.9	42.2	31.3	27.7	21.2	26.6	19.7	26.4
India	24.4	22.7	23.8	22.3	24.8	23.7	23.5	26.4	29.7	31.1	32.4	33.5	32.3
Iran (Islamic Republic of)	15.7	18.0	20.7	25.5	25.4	26.8	38.4	38.5	38.6	39.6	40.6	41.6	40.7
Maldives	46.8	49.2	45.9	46.7	44.2	44.2	44.9	46.3	49.1	46.2	..	..	..
Nepal	14.8	13.8	14.0	13.8	13.6	15.2	11.7	9.5	8.6	11.7	11.6	7.9	9.4
Pakistan	15.8	14.5	13.2	16.7	14.0	16.0	15.9	18.7	17.3	17.6	15.2	15.3	16.1
Sri Lanka	14.6	15.3	17.3	19.1	19.5	17.4	15.8	14.4	15.9	15.8	17.1	17.0	17.6
Turkey	22.3	20.1	21.8	23.2	21.4	18.4	17.3	19.1	19.1	20.2	20.3	16.9	17.9
South-East Asia													
Brunei Darussalam	36.6	36.1	35.5	29.9	36.9	49.4	44.3	47.2	48.6	51.4	59.1	62.4	..
Cambodia	2.5	−1.0	6.4	2.3	7.6	8.1	11.6	10.5	11.0	10.0	11.4	15.2	..
Indonesia	30.6	30.1	31.5	26.5	19.5	31.8	31.5	25.1	23.7	24.9	23.7	26.6	30.5
Lao PDR	11.5	12.4	9.4	14.8	16.4	15.1	15.4	17.9	17.0	18.2	17.3	18.7	20.0
Malaysia	39.7	42.9	43.9	48.7	47.4	47.3	39.5	39.3	40.2	40.3	39.4	40.1	44.8
Myanmar	13.4	11.5	11.8	11.8	13.0	12.3	11.5	10.2	11.0	12.1	..	..	..
Philippines	14.5	14.6	14.2	12.4	14.3	17.3	17.1	15.9	19.2	18.3	18.5	18.3	20.0
Singapore	50.2	51.1	52.1	53.0	49.0	47.4	44.2	41.0	43.8	46.9	48.5	50.5	48.7
Thailand	34.1	33.8	32.9	33.3	30.7	30.4	29.4	29.3	30.5	31.0	29.5	32.3	33.0
Timor-Leste	..	..	..	..	−13.0	−46.8	−39.7	−30.1	−29.2	−26.5	−17.3	−18.6	..
Viet Nam	18.2	17.2	20.1	21.5	24.6	27.1	28.8	28.7	27.4	28.5	30.2	31.4	31.1
Developed ESCAP economies													
Australia	22.5	23.3	23.0	22.4	22.9	22.2	23.0	22.9	23.2	23.4	24.8	25.4	25.9
Japan	29.8	29.4	29.3	28.1	26.3	26.7	25.5	24.3	24.6	24.6	24.6	25.1	..
New Zealand	24.1	23.4	22.3	20.6	21.5	23.2	24.5	23.5	23.7	23.5	21.9	21.3	..

Sources: ESCAP, based on ADB, *Key Indicators of Developing Asian and Pacific Countries 2007* (Manila, 2007) with updates and estimates from national and local sources.

Notes: Data for 2007 are estimates. Data for Brunei Darussalam refer to gross national savings rates. Data for Islamic Republic of Iran, Lao PDR, Nepal and Turkey are based on national sources. Data for Maldives, Armenia, Georgia, Russian Federation, Tajikistan, Turkmenistan, Australia, Japan and New Zealand are based on World Bank, *World Development Indicators*. Data for Cook Islands, Kiribati, Samoa, Solomon Islands, Timor-Leste and Tuvalu are based on *United Nations Statistics Division Databases*.

Table 3. Gross domestic investment rates

(Percentage of GDP)

	1995	1996	1997	1998	1999	2000	2001	2002	2003	2004	2005	2006	2007
Developing ESCAP economies													
East and North-East Asia													
China	41.9	40.4	37.9	37.1	36.7	35.1	36.3	37.9	41.2	43.3	43.3	44.9	41.8
Hong Kong, China	34.1	31.6	34.0	28.9	24.8	27.5	25.3	22.8	21.9	21.8	20.5	21.6	22.2
Mongolia	31.7	29.9	28.1	35.2	37.0	36.2	36.1	39.6	45.5	42.9	41.5	36.0	..
Republic of Korea	37.7	38.9	36.0	25.0	29.1	31.0	29.3	29.1	30.0	30.4	30.1	29.8	29.2
North and Central Asia													
Armenia	18.4	20.0	19.1	19.1	18.4	18.6	19.8	21.7	24.3	24.9	29.7	32.8	..
Azerbaijan	23.8	29.0	34.2	33.4	26.5	20.7	20.7	34.6	53.2	58.0	41.5	31.6	..
Georgia	4.0	18.7	18.6	19.4	21.8	20.4	20.8	21.1	23.4	27.5	25.9	..	..
Kazakhstan	23.3	16.1	15.6	15.8	17.8	18.1	26.9	27.3	25.7	26.3	31.0	33.0	..
Kyrgyzstan	18.3	25.2	21.7	15.4	18.0	20.0	18.0	17.6	11.8	14.5	16.4	17.4	..
Russian Federation	21.1	20.0	18.3	16.2	14.4	16.9	18.9	17.9	18.4	18.3	18.2	..	..
Tajikistan	21.3	13.3	17.7	13.4	16.6	9.5	9.1	10.7	12.0	13.5	12.8	..	..
Turkmenistan	..	41.9	39.4	45.5	39.7	35.4	32.6	27.6	25.4	23.4	23.0	23.9	..
Uzbekistan	24.2	23.0	18.9	20.9	17.1	19.6	21.1	21.2	20.8	23.9	23.0	..	..
Pacific island economies													
Cook Islands	13.6	11.6	12.2	11.9	11.2	10.9	10.3	10.6	11.0	11.5	10.5	11.0	..
Fiji	13.7	11.3	11.6	15.9	14.3	12.3	14.7	19.7	22.1	19.1	19.0	..	..
Kiribati	53.3	53.3	48.7	42.5	44.9	43.2	43.5	43.9	43.5	43.6	43.7	43.6	..
Papua New Guinea	21.9	22.7	21.1	17.9	16.1	21.3	21.8	19.8	18.1	17.1	18.9	18.3	
Samoa	19.6	18.9	8.8	14.0	14.1	14.2	14.3	13.1	12.3	11.2	10.4	9.8	
Solomon Islands	19.2	19.4	19.9	19.5	19.6	19.6	19.6	19.6	19.6	19.6	19.6	19.6	..
Tonga	20.1	22.6	19.5	19.0	20.2	19.4	18.0	19.7	18.4	18.0	18.5	17.6	..
Tuvalu	56.3	67.6	51.2	54.9	57.9	54.7	55.8	56.1	55.6	55.8	55.8	55.7	..
Vanuatu	23.2	20.2	18.8	17.7	20.3	22.2	20.0	21.1	19.0	20.7	20.5	..	..
South and South-West Asia													
Bangladesh	19.1	20.0	20.7	21.6	22.2	23.0	23.1	23.2	23.4	24.0	24.5	25.0	26.0
Bhutan	46.7	43.0	33.0	35.7	39.7	47.4	58.8	59.6	57.0	59.7	56.0	51.1	52.8
India	26.2	24.0	25.3	23.3	25.9	24.3	22.9	25.2	28.0	31.5	33.8	35.4	35.1
Iran (Islamic Republic of)	14.9	15.3	16.2	24.7	26.0	27.1	32.6	33.9	35.1	35.7	36.2	37.5	39.2
Maldives	31.5	30.5	33.2	30.1	33.6	26.3	28.1	25.5	27.1	35.0	35.0	..	..
Nepal	25.2	27.3	25.3	24.8	20.5	24.3	22.3	20.2	21.4	24.5	26.5	26.0	25.3
Pakistan	18.5	19.0	17.9	17.7	15.6	17.2	17.0	16.6	16.8	16.6	19.1	21.8	23.0
Sri Lanka	24.2	24.2	24.4	25.1	27.3	28.0	22.0	21.2	22.1	24.9	26.3	28.4	29.0
Turkey	25.6	25.0	25.6	24.3	24.0	25.0	15.9	21.4	23.3	26.4	27.4	24.9	25.0
South-East Asia													
Brunei Darussalam	36.7	41.3	35.5	33.8	21.4	13.1	14.4	21.3	15.1	13.5	11.4	10.4	..
Cambodia	12.8	15.2	14.4	12.0	17.0	17.3	21.2	20.1	21.5	18.6	21.5	22.6	22.9
Indonesia	31.9	30.7	31.8	25.4	21.8	21.1	19.2	19.0	19.3	22.4	23.6	24.0	23.7
Lao PDR	24.5	29.0	26.2	24.9	22.7	20.5	21.0	24.0	21.4	21.1	17.5	21.4	22.0
Malaysia	43.6	41.5	43.0	26.7	22.4	27.3	24.4	24.8	22.8	23.0	20.3	20.7	20.6
Myanmar	14.2	12.3	12.5	12.4	13.4	12.4	11.6	10.1	11.0	12.0	..	..	..
Philippines	22.5	24.0	24.8	20.3	18.8	21.2	19.0	17.7	16.8	16.8	14.6	14.3	14.6
Singapore	34.2	35.8	39.2	32.3	32.0	32.5	26.0	23.9	15.7	19.6	19.0	18.8	22.8
Thailand	42.1	41.8	33.7	20.4	20.5	22.8	24.1	23.8	25.0	26.8	31.5	27.9	26.9
Timor-Leste	..	..	..	..	21.0	25.6	30.3	31.5	26.3	19.1	19.1	19.0	..
Viet Nam	27.1	28.1	28.3	29.0	27.6	29.6	31.2	33.2	35.4	35.5	35.6	35.7	37.0
Developed ESCAP economies													
Australia	22.8	22.9	24.0	24.2	24.8	22.0	22.9	24.8	25.3	25.5	26.2	26.7	27.6
Japan	28.0	28.4	27.6	25.9	25.5	25.2	24.7	23.3	22.9	22.9	23.1	23.8	23.3
New Zealand	22.1	22.0	21.1	20.1	20.9	20.4	20.7	21.2	22.6	23.5	23.8	23.0	22.5

Sources: ESCAP, based on ADB, *Key Indicators of Developing Asian and Pacific Countries 2007* (Manila, 2007) with updates and estimates from national and local sources.

Notes: Data for 2007 are estimates. Data for Cambodia, Islamic Republic of Iran, Lao PDR, Turkey are based on national sources. Data for Maldives, Georgia, Russian Federation, Tajikistan, Turkmenistan, Australia, Japan and New Zealand are based on World Bank, *World Development Indicators*. Data for Cook Islands, Kiribati, Samoa, Solomon Islands, Timor-Leste and Tuvalu are based on *United Nations Statistics Division Databases*.

Table 4. Inflation rates

(Per cent)

	1995	1996	1997	1998	1999	2000	2001	2002	2003	2004	2005	2006	2007
Developing ESCAP economies	31.3	14.6	9.3	11.9	10.5	5.6	6.3	4.8	4.3	4.6	4.4	4.4	5.1
East and North-East Asia	12.3	6.9	3.1	1.5	−0.9	0.6	1.2	−0.1	1.3	3.3	2.0	1.6	3.8
China	17.1	8.3	2.8	−0.8	−1.4	0.4	0.7	−0.8	1.2	3.9	1.8	1.5	4.8
Hong Kong, China	9.0	6.3	5.8	2.8	−3.9	−3.7	−1.6	−3.0	−2.6	−0.4	0.9	2.0	1.8
Macao, China	8.6	4.8	3.5	0.2	−3.2	−1.6	−2.0	−2.6	−1.6	1.0	4.4	5.1	5.3[a]
Mongolia	56.8	46.9	36.6	9.4	7.6	11.6	6.3	0.9	5.1	8.2	12.7	5.1	9.0
Republic of Korea	4.5	4.9	4.4	7.5	0.8	2.3	4.1	2.8	3.5	3.6	2.8	2.2	2.6
North and Central Asia	212.1	56.1	17.9	25.3	73.8	19.6	20.0	15.0	12.6	10.2	12.0	9.7	9.4
Armenia	176.7	18.7	14.0	8.7	0.6	−0.8	3.1	1.1	4.7	7.0	0.6	2.9	4.4
Azerbaijan	411.8	19.8	3.7	−0.8	−8.5	1.8	1.5	2.8	2.2	6.8	11.6	8.3	16.7
Georgia	162.7	39.3	7.0	3.6	19.1	4.0	4.7	5.6	4.8	5.7	8.2	9.2	9.2
Kazakhstan	176.3	39.1	17.4	7.3	8.4	13.3	8.4	5.9	6.4	6.9	7.6	8.6	10.8
Kyrgyzstan	43.5	32.0	23.4	10.4	35.9	18.7	6.9	2.1	3.1	4.1	4.4	5.6	10.2
Russian Federation	197.5	47.7	14.8	27.7	85.7	20.8	21.5	15.8	13.7	10.9	12.7	9.7	9.0
Tajikistan	443.0	270.0	72.0	43.0	26.0	24.0	36.5	10.2	17.1	6.8	7.8	11.9	21.5
Turkmenistan	1 005.3	992.4	83.7	16.8	23.5	8.0	11.6	8.8	5.6	5.9	10.7	8.2	6.5
Uzbekistan	304.6	54.0	70.9	29.0	29.1	25.0	27.3	27.3	11.6	6.6	10.0	14.2	12.2
Pacific island economies	9.8	8.3	3.9	9.9	9.2	9.3	7.2	7.7	10.2	3.0	2.6	2.8	2.8
Fiji	0.3	4.9	3.4	5.9	2.0	1.1	4.3	0.8	4.2	2.8	2.4	2.5	4.1
Kiribati	4.1	−1.7	2.1	3.7	1.8	0.4	6.0	3.2	2.5	−1.9	−0.5	−0.2	0.2
Papua New Guinea	17.3	11.6	3.9	13.6	14.9	15.6	9.3	11.8	14.7	2.1	1.7	2.3	1.8
Samoa	−2.9	5.4	6.9	5.4	0.8	−0.2	1.9	7.4	4.3	7.9	7.8	3.3	4.4
Solomon Islands	9.8	11.8	8.0	12.3	8.0	6.9	7.6	9.3	10.0	6.9	7.3	8.1	6.3
Tonga	−0.5	2.7	2.0	3.0	3.9	5.3	6.9	10.4	11.1	11.7	9.7	7.0	5.9
Vanuatu	2.2	0.9	2.8	3.3	2.2	2.5	3.7	2.0	3.0	3.2	0.6	2.6	2.5
South and South-West Asia	31.3	25.6	24.9	27.8	19.2	15.5	15.3	14.0	9.7	6.3	6.6	8.3	7.9
Afghanistan	..	..	..	..	..	..	..	..	24.1	13.2	12.3	5.1	5.9
Bangladesh	..	..	4.0	8.7	7.1	2.8	1.9	2.8	4.4	5.8	6.5	7.2	7.2
Bhutan	8.8	6.5	10.6	6.8	4.0	3.4	2.5	2.1	4.6	5.3	5.0	4.9	
India	10.2	9.0	7.2	13.2	4.7	4.0	3.8	4.3	3.8	3.8	4.4	6.7	5.5
Iran (Islamic Republic of)	49.4	23.2	17.3	18.1	20.1	12.6	11.4	15.8	15.6	15.2	12.1	13.6	17.0
Maldives	5.5	6.2	7.6	−1.4	3.0	−1.2	0.7	0.9	−2.8	6.3	3.3	3.5	7.0
Nepal	7.7	8.1	8.1	8.3	11.4	3.4	2.4	2.9	4.8	4.0	4.5	8.0	6.4
Pakistan	13.0	10.8	11.8	7.8	5.7	3.6	4.4	2.5	3.1	4.6	9.3	7.9	7.8
Sri Lanka	7.7	15.9	9.6	9.4	4.0	6.2	14.2	9.6	6.3	7.6	11.0	10.0	15.8
Turkey	89.6	80.2	85.7	84.7	64.9	55.0	54.2	45.1	25.3	8.6	8.2	9.6	8.6
South-East Asia	7.1	5.6	4.9	21.3	7.9	2.3	5.0	4.7	3.4	4.1	6.0	6.7	3.7
Brunei Darussalam	6.0	2.0	1.7	−0.4	0.0	1.2	0.6	−2.3	0.3	0.9	1.1	0.2	1.2
Cambodia	9.9	7.1	8.0	14.8	4.0	−0.8	0.2	3.3	1.2	3.9	5.8	4.7	3.0
Indonesia	9.4	7.0	6.2	58.0	20.7	3.8	11.5	11.8	6.8	6.2	10.4	13.1	6.3
Lao PDR	19.1	19.1	19.5	90.1	128.4	23.2	9.3	10.6	15.5	10.5	7.2	6.8	4.0
Malaysia	3.2	3.5	2.7	5.3	2.7	1.6	1.4	1.8	1.1	1.4	3.0	3.6	2.0
Myanmar	28.9	20.0	33.9	49.1	10.9	−1.7	34.5	58.1	24.9	3.8	10.7	25.7	..
Philippines	8.5	9.1	5.9	9.7	6.4	4.0	6.8	2.9	3.5	6.0	7.6	6.2	2.7
Singapore	1.7	1.4	2.0	−0.3	0.0	1.3	1.0	−0.4	0.5	1.7	0.4	1.0	1.8
Thailand	5.8	5.9	5.6	8.1	0.3	1.6	1.7	0.6	1.8	2.8	4.5	4.7	2.3
Timor-Leste	..	..	..	..	..	3.0	−0.3	9.5	4.2	1.8	0.9	5.7	5.0
Viet Nam	16.9	5.6	3.1	7.9	4.1	−1.7	−0.4	3.8	3.1	7.8	8.3	7.7	7.9
Developed ESCAP economies	0.3	0.3	1.7	0.6	−0.1	−0.2	−0.2	−0.5	0.0	0.2	0.0	0.6	0.2
Australia	4.6	2.6	0.3	0.9	1.5	4.5	4.4	3.0	2.8	2.3	2.7	3.5	2.4
Japan	−0.1	0.1	1.9	0.6	−0.3	−0.8	−0.7	−0.9	−0.3	0.0	−0.3	0.3	0.0
New Zealand	3.7	2.3	1.2	1.3	−0.1	2.6	2.6	2.6	1.7	2.3	3.0	3.4	2.4

Sources: ESCAP, based on IMF, *World Economic Outlook Database* (Washington, D.C., October 2007) with updates and estimates from national and local sources.

Notes: Data for 2007 are estimates. The data and estimates for countries relate to fiscal years defined as follows: fiscal year 2005/06 = 2005 for India and the Islamic Republic of Iran; and fiscal year 2004/05 = 2005 for Bangladesh, Nepal and Pakistan. Data for Macao, China are based on IMF, *International Financial Statistics*.

[a] January-October compared with the corresponding period of previous year.

Table 5. Budget balances

(Percentage of GDP)

	1995	1996	1997	1998	1999	2000	2001	2002	2003	2004	2005	2006	2007
Developing ESCAP economies													
East and North-East Asia													
China	−1.0	−1.9	−2.0	−2.6	−3.2	−2.8	−2.5	−2.6	−2.2	−1.3	−1.2	−0.7	0.2
Hong Kong, China	−0.3	2.1	6.5	−1.8	0.8	−0.6	−4.9	−4.8	−3.3	1.7	1.0	1.6	1.9
Mongolia	−1.5	−2.6	−9.1	−14.3	−11.6	−7.7	−4.5	−5.8	−4.2	−2.1	2.9	3.9	..
Republic of Korea	0.3	0.2	−1.4	−3.9	−2.5	1.1	1.2	3.3	1.1	0.7	0.4	0.4	0.7
North and Central Asia													
Armenia	−6.0	−4.4	−1.7	−3.8	−5.2	−4.9	−4.3	−2.6	−1.3	−1.7	−2.0	−1.5	−1.5
Azerbaijan	−5.2	−2.9	−2.4	−1.8	−2.4	−1.0	−0.4	−0.4	−0.2	0.1	−0.7	0.5	−2.0
Georgia	−5.9	−7.2	−7.7	−7.6	−4.3	−3.9	−2.2	−1.7	−2.6	3.0	−2.4	−2.8	−2.3
Kazakhstan	−4.0	−2.6	−3.7	−3.9	−3.5	−0.1	−0.4	−0.3	−0.9	−0.3	1.9	0.8	−0.8
Kyrgyzstan	−11.5	−5.4	−5.2	−3.0	−2.5	−2.0	0.4	−1.0	−0.8	−0.5	0.2	−0.2	−2.2
Russian Federation	−4.9	−7.4	−6.4	−4.8	−1.2	2.4	3.1	1.7	2.4	4.8	7.5	7.4	3.0
Tajikistan	−7.4	−5.8	−4.1	−2.7	−2.4	−0.6	0.1	0.7	1.1	0.2	−1.6	0.4	−1.0
Turkmenistan	0.4	0.3	−0.2	−2.6	0.0	−0.3	0.6	0.2	−1.4	0.4	0.9	0.6	0.5
Uzbekistan	−2.9	−2.0	−2.4	−2.0	−1.7	−1.0	0.2	−0.9	−1.3	0.0	−1.0	−1.3	..
Pacific island economies													
Cook Islands	−2.8	−7.8	1.1	−2.5	−2.4	−1.8	1.3	0.2	−0.8	−1.0	2.5	..	..
Fiji	−0.2	−4.7	−6.5	5.0	−0.3	−3.2	−6.5	−5.7	−6.2	−3.2	−3.7	−3.4	0.4
Kiribati	16.2	−11.0	25.7	40.9	17.1	18.7	..	..	..	..	..	..	..
Papua New Guinea	−0.5	0.5	0.2	−1.8	−2.4	−1.8	−3.1	−3.4	−1.0	1.7	0.1	3.1	1.7
Samoa	−7.0	1.4	2.2	2.0	0.3	−0.7	−2.3	−2.1	−0.6	−0.9	0.3	−0.4	−0.5
Solomon Islands	−4.6	−4.3	−3.6	3.0	5.0	−0.6	−7.4	−20.2	−5.8	4.9	−0.9	−4.0	..
Tonga	1.2	0.9	−4.8	−2.4	−0.2	−0.4	−1.5	−1.4	−3.1	0.9	2.4	−3.3	−2.3
Tuvalu	..	..	−31.8	19.1	−3.5	−2.2	−45.7	33.7	..	..	..	..	..
Vanuatu	−2.7	−1.7	−0.5	−9.4	−1.6	−7.0	−3.7	−2.1	−1.8	1.3	1.9	−0.5	−0.5
South and South-West Asia													
Bangladesh	−4.6	−4.7	−3.7	−3.4	−4.6	−6.1	−5.1	−4.7	−4.3	−4.2	−4.4	−3.9	−3.6
Bhutan	0.1	2.2	−2.3	0.9	−1.7	−3.8	−10.5	−3.9	−9.5	1.9	−6.9	−0.8	−3.5
India	−5.1	−4.9	−5.8	−6.5	−5.4	−5.7	−6.2	−5.9	−4.5	−4.0	−4.1	−3.7	−3.3
Iran (Islamic Republic of)	−0.2	−0.2	−1.0	−2.2	−0.2	−0.2	−0.4	−4.1	−3.4	−3.0	−3.7	−7.2	−5.1
Maldives	−6.4	−2.5	−1.3	−1.9	−4.1	−4.4	−4.7	−4.9	−3.4	−1.6	−10.9	−7.1	−27.6
Nepal	−4.8	−5.6	−5.1	−5.9	−5.3	−4.7	−5.5	−5.0	−3.3	−2.9	−3.1	−3.8	−4.1
Pakistan	−5.6	−6.5	−6.4	−7.6	−6.1	−5.4	−4.3	−4.3	−3.7	−2.4	−3.3	−4.2	−4.2
Sri Lanka	−10.1	−9.4	−7.9	−9.1	−7.5	−9.9	−10.8	−8.9	−8.0	−7.9	−8.4	−8.1	−7.2
Turkey	−4.1	−8.4	−7.8	−7.1	−11.7	−10.3	−16.0	−14.4	−11.2	−7.0	−1.7	−0.8	−0.7
South-East Asia													
Cambodia	−7.3	−6.3	−3.8	−5.4	−3.9	−4.8	−6.3	−7.3	−6.3	−3.9	−2.6	−3.3	−3.6
Indonesia	3.0	1.0	0.5	−1.7	−2.5	−1.1	−2.4	−1.3	−1.7	−1.0	−0.6	−1.0	−1.4
Lao PDR	−9.0	−9.1	−8.4	−11.1	−7.6	−6.0	−7.6	−4.5	−7.8	−3.6	−6.2	−5.6	−6.3
Malaysia	0.8	0.7	2.4	−1.8	−3.2	−5.5	−5.2	−5.3	−5.0	−4.1	−3.6	−3.3	−3.2
Myanmar	−3.2	−2.2	−0.9	−5.7	−4.5	−8.4	−5.9	−4.1	−4.5	..	..	..	..
Philippines	0.6	0.3	0.1	−1.9	−3.8	−4.0	−4.0	−5.3	−4.6	−3.8	−2.7	−1.1	−3.2
Singapore	7.8	6.9	3.4	2.5	0.5	2.0	1.6	−1.1	−1.6	−1.1	−0.3	0.6	0.3
Thailand	3.0	0.9	−1.5	−2.8	−3.3	−2.2	−2.4	−1.4	0.4	0.1	−0.6	1.1	−1.9
Timor-Leste	..	..	..	..	..	2.0	1.0	4.0	11.0	77.0	111.0	132.0	158.0
Viet Nam	..	..	−4.8	−2.6	−1.4	−2.4	−4.7	−4.5	−3.3	−4.9	−4.9	−5.0	−5.0
Developed ESCAP economies													
Australia	−2.1	−0.9	0.1	0.8	1.7	1.4	0.1	0.3	1.6	2.0	2.4	1.6	0.8
Japan	−4.7	−5.1	−3.8	−5.6	−7.5	−7.7	−6.4	−8.0	−8.1	−6.2	−4.8	−4.1	−3.9
New Zealand	3.3	2.7	2.2	2.1	1.5	1.2	1.6	1.7	3.4	4.6	5.7	5.0	2.9

Sources: ESCAP, based on national sources; ADB, *Key Indicators of Developing Asian and Pacific Countries 2007* (Manila, 2007); IMF Country Reports; and ESCAP estimates.

Note: Data for 2007 are estimates.

Table 6. Current account balance

(Percentage of GDP)

	1995	1996	1997	1998	1999	2000	2001	2002	2003	2004	2005	2006	2007
Developing ESCAP economies													
East and North-East Asia													
China	0.2	0.8	3.8	3.0	1.9	1.7	1.3	2.4	2.8	3.5	7.1	9.5	10.5
Hong Kong, China	..	..	−4.5	1.5	6.4	4.1	5.9	7.6	10.4	9.5	11.4	10.8	11.1
Mongolia	−6.8	−5.8	−5.5	−7.8	−6.7	−5.7	−7.6	−9.6	−7.5	3.9	4.0	11.4	..
Republic of Korea	−1.7	−4.1	−1.6	11.7	5.5	2.4	1.7	1.0	2.0	4.1	1.9	0.7	0.7
North and Central Asia													
Armenia	−17.0	−18.2	−18.7	−22.1	−16.6	−14.6	−9.4	−6.2	−6.7	−4.5	−3.9	−1.4	−2.5
Azerbaijan	−16.5	−29.3	−23.2	−30.5	−13.0	−3.2	−0.9	−12.3	−27.7	−29.7	1.3	18.6	25.7
Georgia	..	..	−14.7	−7.6	−7.1	−8.8	−6.6	−6.9	−9.6	−8.1	−11.7	−16.1	−15.7
Kazakhstan	−1.2	−3.7	−3.8	−5.8	−1.0	2.0	−6.5	−4.4	−0.9	0.8	−1.8	−2.2	−3.6
Kyrgyzstan	−15.7	−23.3	−7.8	−25.1	−20.1	−9.0	−3.4	−4.9	−5.4	−4.6	−9.3	−14.8	−21.3
Russian Federation	2.2	2.8	0.0	0.1	12.6	18.0	11.1	8.4	8.2	10.1	11.0	9.7	6.3
Tajikistan	−17.9	−7.8	−4.0	−7.3	−0.9	−1.6	−4.9	−3.5	−1.3	−4.0	−2.5	−2.9	−11.6
Turkmenistan	−9.1	0.1	−21.6	−32.7	−14.8	8.2	1.7	6.7	2.7	0.6	5.1	15.3	12.4
Uzbekistan	−0.2	−7.0	−4.0	−0.7	−1.0	1.8	−1.0	1.2	8.7	10.1	13.6	18.8	16.1
Pacific island economies													
Fiji	−0.9	3.1	1.6	−0.3	−3.8	−5.7	−3.3	−1.6	−3.6	−11.0	−11.4	−21.1	−19.6
Kiribati	11.1	−13.5	25.8	40.0	16.5	−1.2	22.0	10.7	12.5	−3.0	−39.9	−37.9	−50.7
Papua New Guinea	18.3	5.6	−5.4	0.9	2.8	8.5	6.5	−1.0	4.5	2.2	3.8	7.4	2.5
Samoa	..	..	..	..	..	..	..	..	..	−1.6	−4.6	−6.1	−8.1
Solomon Islands	3.7	3.1	−5.6	−1.6	4.3	−10.6	−10.9	−10.2	−2.5	3.1	−24.2	−26.5	−40.0
Tonga	−11.3	−6.1	−0.9	−10.9	−0.6	−6.2	−9.5	5.1	−3.1	4.2	−2.6	−8.2	−10.5
Vanuatu	−2.2	−2.3	−1.0	2.5	−4.9	2.0	2.0	−9.7	−10.7	−7.3	−10.0	−8.0	−13.2
South and South-West Asia													
Bangladesh	..	−3.2	−1.3	−1.2	−1.1	−1.0	−2.5	0.3	0.3	0.3	−1.0	0.9	1.4
Bhutan	−11.6	−11.9	−7.6	10.6	2.2	5.4	−5.4	−8.9	−10.7	−10.8	−25.6	−2.0	8.6
India	−1.7	−1.2	−1.4	−1.0	−1.0	−0.6	0.7	1.3	2.4	−0.4	−1.1	−1.1	−1.4
Iran (Islamic Republic of)	..	3.9	1.4	−1.1	12.0	17.5	7.1	3.1	0.6	0.9	8.8	9.1	8.8
Maldives	−4.6	−1.6	−6.8	−4.1	−13.4	−8.2	−9.4	−5.6	−4.5	−15.8	−36.0	−39.8	−45.0
Nepal	−2.3	−5.4	−0.8	−1.0	4.3	3.2	4.5	4.2	2.4	2.7	2.0	2.3	0.5
Pakistan	−2.9	−5.4	−4.7	−2.2	−2.6	−0.3	0.4	3.9	4.9	1.8	−1.4	−4.0	−5.0
Sri Lanka	−6.1	−4.9	−2.6	−1.4	−3.6	−6.5	−1.4	−1.4	−0.4	−3.2	−2.7	−4.7	−4.3
Turkey	−1.4	−1.3	−1.4	1.0	−0.7	−4.9	2.3	−0.8	−3.4	−5.2	−6.2	−8.2	−7.3
South-East Asia													
Cambodia	−3.2	−3.1	0.6	−5.8	−5.1	−2.8	−1.1	−1.5	−3.7	−2.3	−4.3	−2.9	−3.4
Indonesia	−3.2	−3.4	−2.4	4.3	4.1	4.8	4.2	3.9	3.4	0.6	0.1	2.6	2.4
Lao PDR	−19.5	−18.5	−17.5	−11.7	−8.3	−0.5	−4.7	0.3	−2.0	−7.7	−5.7	1.2	−6.8
Malaysia	−9.8	−4.4	−5.9	13.2	15.9	9.4	8.3	8.0	12.1	12.1	14.6	16.3	13.6
Myanmar	−0.2	−0.2	0.0	−0.2	−0.1	−0.1	−0.03	0.01	0.00	0.01	0.03	0.03	..
Philippines	−2.7	−4.8	−5.3	2.4	−3.8	−2.9	−2.4	−0.4	0.4	1.9	2.0	4.3	4.7
Singapore	17.2	15.0	15.6	22.3	17.4	11.6	14.0	13.8	24.2	20.1	24.5	27.5	27.3
Thailand	−7.9	−7.9	−2.1	12.8	10.2	7.6	4.4	3.7	3.3	1.7	−4.4	1.6	4.6
Timor-Leste	..	..	..	..	2.2	11.7	−52.7	−37.3	−25.3	30.4	83.4	115.4	139.6
Viet Nam	−12.8	−9.9	−6.2	−3.9	4.5	2.3	1.6	−1.9	−4.9	−3.5	−0.9	−0.3	−4.8
Developed ESCAP economies													
Australia	−5.2	−3.7	−2.9	−4.8	−5.3	−3.8	−2.0	−3.8	−5.4	−6.0	−5.8	−5.5	−5.8
Japan	2.1	1.4	2.2	3.0	2.6	2.5	2.1	2.9	3.2	3.7	3.6	3.9	4.9
New Zealand	−4.9	−5.8	−6.4	−3.9	−6.1	−5.0	−2.7	−4.1	−4.4	−6.6	−8.9	−9.0	−8.1

Sources: ESCAP, based on IMF, *International Financial Statistcs* (CD-ROM) (Washington D.C., November 2007) with updates and estimates from national and local sources.

Notes: Data for 2007 are estimates. In the case of Timor-Leste, current account includes international assistance.

Table 7. Change in money supply

(Per cent)

	1995	1996	1997	1998	1999	2000	2001	2002	2003	2004	2005	2006	2007
Developing ESCAP economies													
East and North-East Asia													
China	29.5	25.3	20.7	14.9	14.7	12.3	15.0	18.3	19.6	14.4	17.9	16.0	19.2
Hong Kong, China	10.6	12.5	8.7	11.1	8.3	9.3	−0.3	0.5	6.3	7.3	3.5	16.2	10.4
Mongolia	32.6	17.2	42.2	−1.7	31.6	17.6	27.9	42.0	49.6	20.5	37.1	30.8	42.4[a]
Republic of Korea	15.6	15.8	14.1	27.0	27.4	25.4	13.2	11.0	6.7	−0.6	3.1	4.4	5.0
North and Central Asia													
Armenia	64.3	35.1	29.2	36.7	14.0	38.6	4.3	34.0	10.4	22.3	27.8	32.9	43.7[b]
Azerbaijan	25.4	17.1	41.4	−15.2	20.1	73.4	−11.3	14.4	26.8	47.7	23.2	86.9	74.1[b]
Georgia	..	40.2	42.8	−0.8	20.6	39.2	17.6	17.9	22.8	42.4	26.5	39.7	53.1[a]
Kazakhstan	108.2	20.9	24.1	−14.1	84.4	45.0	40.2	30.1	34.2	68.2	26.3	78.1	54.2[b]
Kyrgyzstan	..	14.8	32.2	17.5	33.7	11.7	11.3	33.9	33.4	32.1	10.0	51.5	..
Russian Federation	112.6	29.6	28.8	37.6	56.7	58.0	36.3	33.8	38.5	33.7	36.3	40.5	44.1[b]
Tajikistan	..	78.7	105.1	28.2	24.6	63.3	35.0	40.5	40.9	9.8	25.9	59.7	45.9[b]
Turkmenistan	567.8	247.8	107.2	67.7	75.7	83.3	23.8	1.5	40.9	13.4	27.2	17.7	..
Uzbekistan	151.9	119.0	45.6	27.5	32.7	37.1	54.3	29.7	27.1	47.8	54.2	37.0	..
Pacific island economies													
Cook Islands	..	−3.2	31.2	12.1	16.7	8.1	14.4	3.2	9.9	9.6	−5.2	22.4	..
Fiji	4.5	0.9	−8.7	−0.5	13.6	−1.5	−3.1	7.8	25.1	10.4	15.0	20.2	14.8[c]
Kiribati	..	..	..	..	..	..	..	..	..	..	..	..	..
Papua New Guinea	13.7	30.7	7.7	2.5	9.2	5.0	6.2	7.3	−4.4	14.8	29.5	38.9	23.4[b]
Samoa	24.4	6.3	15.2	2.5	15.7	16.3	6.1	10.2	14.0	8.3	15.6	13.7	13.0[b]
Solomon Islands	9.2	15.3	6.7	2.5	7.0	0.6	−13.6	6.0	25.4	17.5	38.8	26.0	36.7[b]
Tonga	0.7	5.3	7.8	14.7	11.9	18.8	14.9	7.8	14.4	13.2	13.2	13.1	4.4[c]
Tuvalu	..	..	..	..	..	..	..	..	..	..	..	..	..
Vanuatu	13.3	10.1	−0.3	12.6	−9.2	5.5	5.6	−1.7	−0.8	9.8	11.6	7.0	10.4[b]
South and South-West Asia													
Bangladesh	16.1	8.3	10.8	10.2	12.8	18.6	16.6	13.1	15.6	13.8	16.8	19.5	17.0
Bhutan	35.6	9.0	58.9	13.9	32.0	17.4	7.9	26.9	1.8	19.9	11.9	13.0	8.0[c]
India	11.0	18.7	17.7	18.2	17.1	15.2	14.3	16.8	13.0	16.7	15.6	21.6	25.4
Iran (Islamic Republic of)	30.1	32.5	23.7	20.4	21.5	22.4	27.6	24.9	24.5	23.0	22.8	29.1	32.7[d]
Maldives	15.6	26.0	23.1	22.8	3.6	4.1	9.0	19.3	14.6	32.6	11.7	20.6	23.1[b]
Nepal	16.1	14.4	11.9	21.9	20.8	21.8	15.2	4.4	9.8	12.8	8.3	15.6	11.4[b]
Pakistan	13.8	20.1	19.9	7.9	4.3	12.1	11.7	16.8	17.5	20.5	16.5	14.6	15.3
Sri Lanka	35.8	11.3	15.6	13.2	13.4	12.9	13.6	13.4	15.3	19.6	19.1	17.8	16.5
Turkey	104.2	116.5	97.8	89.3	102.0	40.7	87.4	30.6	14.9	21.1	23.6	32.6	18.7[c]
South-East Asia													
Cambodia	44.3	40.4	16.6	15.7	17.3	26.9	20.4	31.1	15.0	30.4	16.1	38.2	26.9
Indonesia	27.6	29.6	23.2	62.3	11.9	16.6	12.8	4.7	8.1	8.1	16.4	14.9	16.4
Lao PDR	16.4	26.7	65.8	113.3	78.4	46.0	13.7	37.6	20.1	21.6	7.9	26.7	43.6[b]
Malaysia	24.0	19.8	22.7	1.5	14.2	5.3	2.3	6.0	11.1	25.2	15.6	17.1	11.4[e]
Myanmar	36.5	38.9	28.8	34.2	29.7	42.4	43.9	34.7	1.4	32.4	27.3	24.6[f]	..
Philippines	23.9	23.7	23.1	8.6	16.9	8.1	3.6	10.4	3.6	9.9	6.4	19.6	22.6
Singapore	8.5	9.8	10.3	30.2	8.5	−2.0	5.9	−0.3	8.1	6.2	6.2	19.4	22.0
Thailand	17.7	10.6	19.6	10.1	3.8	4.9	5.5	3.8	11.0	5.4	5.9	6.7	3.3[b]
Timor-Leste	..	..	..	..	..	..	155.5	6.8	32.4	43.0	32.0	24.3	..
Viet Nam	22.6	25.7	24.3	23.5	66.5	35.4	27.3	13.3	33.1	31.0	30.9	29.7	34.7
Developed ESCAP economies													
Australia	8.5	10.6	7.3	8.4	11.7	3.7	13.2	5.6	13.3	11.7	7.7	15.2	10.1
Japan	4.1	3.8	5.8	3.1	2.8	1.3	−17.0	0.9	1.3	0.3	0.3	−0.7	0.2
New Zealand	9.3	16.1	5.2	1.8	5.0	2.3	6.8	7.7	10.6	5.1	12.2	13.5	8.5

Sources: ESCAP, based on national sources; IMF, *International Financial Statistics* (CD-ROM) (Washington, D.C., November 2007) with updates and estimates from national and local sources.

Notes: Data for 2007 are estimates.

[a] September compared with the corresponding period of previous year.
[b] August compared with the corresponding period of previous year.
[c] July compared with the corresponding period of previous year.
[d] March compared with the corresponding period of previous year.
[e] October compared with the corresponding period of previous year.
[f] August 2006 compared with the corresponding period of previous year.

Table 8. Merchandise export growth rates

(Per cent)

	1995	1996	1997	1998	1999	2000	2001	2002	2003	2004	2005	2006	2007
Developing ESCAP economies													
East and North-East Asia													
China	22.9	1.5	21.0	0.5	6.1	27.9	6.7	22.4	34.6	35.4	28.4	27.2	25.7
Hong Kong, China	14.8	4.0	4.0	−7.5	−0.1	16.1	−5.9	5.4	11.8	15.9	11.6	9.5	8.7
Macao, China	7.2	−0.1	7.6	−0.3	2.8	15.4	−9.4	2.4	9.5	9.0	−11.9	3.3	−6.2[a]
Mongolia	45.9	−10.4	6.4	−23.5	3.8	30.1	11.9	0.5	17.5	41.2	22.4	44.9	31.7[b]
Republic of Korea	30.3	3.7	5.0	−2.8	8.6	19.9	−12.7	8.0	19.3	31.0	12.0	14.5	14.2
North and Central Asia													
Armenia	26.0	7.0	−19.3	−2.1	7.9	25.5	13.9	45.6	35.4	6.0	36.2	1.1	9.1[a]
Azerbaijan	−2.5	5.2	25.5	−16.1	51.2	81.3	11.9	10.9	13.9	42.6	104.4	46.6	23.2[a]
Georgia	−1.3	29.2	20.6	−20.2	10.0	39.1	8.1	21.6	37.8	31.4	34.8	14.8	26.5[a]
Kazakhstan	62.5	15.7	9.6	−14.9	2.0	55.1	−3.9	12.3	32.0	55.7	37.4	37.3	22.9[a]
Kyrgyzstan	20.3	29.8	18.8	−15.2	−13.5	10.4	−6.1	3.8	18.5	24.2	33.3	18.2	38.6[a]
Russian Federation	22.3	8.8	−3.1	−14.3	1.5	39.0	−3.0	5.3	26.7	34.8	32.9	24.8	9.8[a]
Tajikistan	52.2	2.8	−3.1	−20.0	15.4	13.8	−16.8	13.0	8.1	14.8	15.9	53.9	8.9[a]
Turkmenistan	−4.2	−18.9	−55.1	−19.1	93.3	111.1	4.7	9.1	21.2	11.6	27.6	16.9	22.3[c]
Uzbekistan	18.2	1.7	4.6	−21.8	−3.4	5.2	−6.6	−8.4	29.1	31.6	11.6	19.6	16.5[c]
Pacific island economies													
Fiji	3.6	24.1	−23.9	−11.6	19.4	−13.7	0.1	3.6	34.5	−0.7	−6.7	5.6	9.8[d]
Papua New Guinea	13.4	−2.4	−14.8	−16.1	9.1	7.3	−13.7	−9.5	34.4	15.6	28.4	27.3	9.2[d]
Samoa[e]	151.4	14.8	45.5	30.5	..	..	9.7	−8.9	5.2	−18.4	−9.6	−17.0	7.8
Solomon Islands	17.1	−3.5	7.5	−27.6	4.4	−47.4	−5.0	−21.8	38.6	−4.4	6.0	17.5	21.4[f]
Tonga[e]	6.2	−24.8	0.4	−17.8	12.6	−9.9	8.3	50.8	−1.1	−21.6	15.9	−5.6	3.3[f]
Vanuatu	13.2	6.7	16.9	−4.0	−24.2	5.8	−26.8	1.0	32.3	28.6	0.0	2.1	4.1[f]
South and South-West Asia													
Afghanistan[c,e]	..	..	..	..	..	..	−37.7	82.1	46.7	−13.3	−2.6	7.9	..
Bangladesh[e]	..	11.8	13.8	16.8	2.9	8.3	12.4	−7.4	9.4	16.1	13.8	21.6	15.7[g]
Bhutan[e]	10.2	39.7	1.7	12.1	−5.9	9.2	−12.9	4.5	8.7	39.7	34.5	47.2	64.5[c]
India[e]	20.3	5.6	4.5	−3.9	9.5	21.1	1.5	20.3	23.3	28.5	23.4	22.5	24.3[c]
Iran (Islamic Republic of)[e]	−5.5	22.0	−17.9	−28.6	60.3	35.3	−16.0	18.1	20.4	29.0	46.8	16.4	..
Maldives	12.7	−6.0	12.3	6.6	−4.3	18.8	1.4	20.1	14.8	19.1	−10.7	39.4	15.5[f]
Nepal[e]	−9.8	2.3	9.8	12.7	17.4	37.6	4.6	−18.8	4.3	8.9	13.0	2.2	3.6[c]
Pakistan[e]	19.4	7.0	−4.4	3.7	−9.8	10.1	7.4	−0.7	22.2	10.3	16.9	14.3	3.4[c]
Sri Lanka	18.6	7.8	13.3	1.9	−2.6	19.8	−12.8	−2.4	9.2	12.2	10.2	8.4	10.0[f]
Turkey	19.5	33.3	6.3	0.2	4.4	0.1	7.0	16.7	27.6	31.0	14.6	18.9	24.8[h]
South-East Asia													
Brunei Darussalam	11.0	8.9	2.8	−28.7	32.7	54.1	−6.8	1.7	19.4	14.4	23.6	29.4	6.8[f]
Cambodia	74.6	−24.7	14.4	9.0	40.9	23.6	12.5	12.6	17.9	24.1	12.4	26.9	16.8[f]
Indonesia	..	5.8	12.5	−10.5	1.7	27.6	−12.3	3.1	8.4	12.6	22.9	19.0	9.3[f]
Lao PDR	..	..	−1.4	7.7	−10.5	9.5	−3.3	−5.9	11.6	8.3	52.2	59.5	30.0[f]
Malaysia	21.0	7.0	−27.1	32.7	12.1	16.2	−10.4	6.9	11.3	20.8	11.5	18.1	7.4[a]
Myanmar	−4.0	3.6	3.9	9.3	5.6	47.7	39.4	24.1	−5.7	8.0	29.4	20.2	31.6[c]
Philippines	29.4	17.7	22.8	16.9	18.8	8.7	−15.6	9.5	2.9	9.8	3.8	14.6	6.5[c]
Singapore	22.5	5.8	0.0	−12.2	4.4	20.3	−11.8	2.8	27.9	24.2	15.7	18.2	8.5[a]
Thailand	24.8	−1.9	3.8	−6.8	7.4	19.5	−7.1	4.8	18.2	21.6	15.0	17.4	17.2[i]
Timor-Leste	..	..	..	..	..	..	230.8	48.8	21.9	6.4	10.8	−14.1	26.6[f]
Viet Nam	34.4	33.2	26.6	1.9	23.3	25.5	3.8	11.2	20.6	31.4	22.5	22.7	19.4[a]
Developed ESCAP economies													
Australia	11.5	13.6	6.3	−12.7	0.0	13.1	25.7	−9.0	−24.4	−2.9	14.7	18.7	−3.5[d]
Japan	12.1	−7.2	2.3	−8.5	7.9	14.6	−16.4	2.5	13.3	20.4	6.0	8.0	9.0[b]
New Zealand	14.2	5.0	−2.5	−18.0	6.7	3.9	5.8	5.3	15.1	24.6	6.4	3.6	16.2[b]

Sources: ESCAP, calculated from national sources; IMF, *Direction of Trade Statistics* and Country Reports Series; Economist Intelligence Unit, *Country Reports*; and website of Inter-State Statistical Committee of the Commonwealth of Independent States, <www.cisstat.com> (30 January 2008).

[a] Refers to first 9 months of 2007.
[b] Refers to first 10 months of 2007.
[c] Estimate.
[d] Refers to first 6 months of 2007.
[e] Fiscal year data.
[f] Projection.
[g] Provisional.
[h] Refers to first 11 months of 2006.
[i] Preliminary.

Table 9. Merchandise import growth rates

(Per cent)

	1995	1996	1997	1998	1999	2000	2001	2002	2003	2004	2005	2006	2007
Developing ESCAP economies													
East and North-East Asia													
China	14.2	5.1	2.5	−1.5	18.2	24.4	12.6	27.1	39.9	36.0	17.6	19.9	20.8
Hong Kong, China	19.1	3.0	5.1	−11.6	−2.7	18.5	−5.5	3.3	11.7	16.9	10.5	11.7	9.8
Macao, China	−3.8	−2.1	4.1	−6.1	4.4	10.5	5.9	6.0	8.9	26.3	12.5	16.7	15.9[a]
Mongolia	87.3	8.6	3.9	7.5	1.9	19.8	3.8	8.3	16.0	27.5	16.0	25.4	38.3[b]
Republic of Korea	32.0	11.3	−3.8	−35.5	28.4	34.0	−12.1	7.8	17.6	25.5	16.4	18.5	15.3
North and Central Asia													
Armenia	71.1	12.8	4.3	1.6	−10.5	7.2	0.0	14.2	28.0	5.8	33.2	21.6	1.9[a]
Azerbaijan	−14.1	35.8	2.8	25.4	−16.9	7.4	−4.8	24.4	49.4	31.5	21.4	25.0	46.7[a]
Georgia	13.9	78.4	37.4	−14.5	−13.2	12.4	7.8	4.4	34.5	36.7	33.8	47.8	39.4[a]
Kazakhstan	6.9	24.4	8.3	−7.0	−15.4	26.1	11.6	1.2	18.8	44.6	30.1	36.5	45.2[a]
Kyrgyzstan	24.6	47.5	−17.5	17.0	−27.1	−8.0	−11.2	27.1	26.6	24.9	98.7	56.0	50.3[a]
Russian Federation	24.1	8.8	5.7	−19.4	−31.9	13.5	19.8	13.4	24.8	28.0	28.7	39.5	48.1[a]
Tajikistan	48.1	−17.5	12.3	−5.2	−6.8	1.8	1.9	4.8	22.2	56.1	97.0	29.5	35.5[a]
Turkmenistan[c]	−2.7	−6.8	−34.5	−213.2	30.0	20.8	23.3	−3.7	18.1	32.7	9.6	11.5	9.0[d]
Uzbekistan[c]	18.8	30.9	−11.2	−27.9	−4.8	−5.6	4.6	−14.4	10.0	27.3	8.1	13.9	20.4[d]
Pacific island economies													
Fiji	0.6	14.0	−10.1	−19.7	25.3	−7.9	4.8	9.2	39.1	14.6	2.6	20.1	−5.2[e]
Papua New Guinea	7.8	23.3	−1.6	−27.0	−0.1	−7.0	−6.4	14.6	10.3	22.4	4.6	30.5	34.6[e]
Samoa[f]	15.1	7.4	1.2	1.9	..	..	30.9	12.9	−7.6	23.3	24.3	16.6	12.2
Solomon Islands	8.6	−1.9	42.4	−40.8	−13.7	−24.5	−13.0	−19.0	36.3	30.1	52.5	35.4	16.4[g]
Tonga[c,f]	35.4	−8.6	−12.9	18.6	−21.2	12.8	−2.9	0.8	21.0	11.6	27.6	11.7	1.0[g]
Vanuatu[c]	6.4	5.5	−3.5	−5.6	9.3	−7.2	0.8	−4.5	16.4	6.0	16.8	12.5	21.8[g]
South and South-West Asia													
Afghanistan[d,f]	..	..	..	..	..	..	−8.9	52.5	50.9	2.3	9.0	10.1	..
Bangladesh[f]	..	18.8	3.2	5.1	6.5	4.6	11.5	−8.5	13.1	12.9	20.6	12.2	16.3[h]
Bhutan[f]	4.6	14.1	18.4	3.7	19.3	14.0	6.1	−5.2	2.2	29.2	75.5	−5.6	20.6[d]
India[f]	21.6	12.1	4.6	−7.1	16.5	4.6	12.3	14.5	24.1	48.6	33.8	27.8	24.4[d]
Iran (Islamic Republic of)[f]	1.2	17.3	−5.8	1.2	−6.0	12.3	20.2	21.6	34.1	29.2	12.8	15.4	..
Maldives[c]	..	12.6	15.6	1.5	13.6	−3.4	−0.3	1.1	20.2	36.3	16.1	24.4	13.0[g]
Nepal[f]	21.9	6.1	21.2	−11.8	−11.0	22.1	−0.2	−10.6	13.6	10.6	13.8	15.8	13.2[d]
Pakistan[f]	21.4	13.6	0.8	−14.9	−6.8	9.3	4.1	−3.6	18.2	27.6	32.1	38.8	6.9[d]
Sri Lanka	11.4	2.4	7.8	0.4	1.5	22.4	−18.4	2.2	9.3	19.9	10.8	15.7	8.9[g]
Turkey	53.5	13.9	12.9	18.7	−20.0	11.3	−14.7	24.5	34.5	40.7	19.7	19.5	21.5[i]
South-East Asia													
Brunei Darussalam	15.5	19.5	−14.8	−30.6	−4.9	−16.6	−0.7	37.3	−16.9	6.5	5.8	7.6	7.4[g]
Cambodia[c]	59.4	−9.7	−0.7	9.6	36.5	21.6	8.2	12.7	13.0	22.5	20.2	20.9	16.4[g]
Indonesia[c]	..	8.1	4.5	−30.9	−4.2	31.9	−14.1	2.8	10.9	28.0	37.4	6.3	12.3[g]
Lao PDR	..	..	−6.0	−14.7	0.3	−3.4	−4.7	−12.4	3.4	54.2	23.7	20.2	40.0[g]
Malaysia	25.5	2.0	−27.2	5.7	9.1	25.1	−10.0	8.2	4.4	26.4	9.2	18.6	9.4[a]
Myanmar[c]	26.2	9.9	12.7	16.4	−13.7	2.3	19.5	−19.6	−8.1	4.6	−12.0	33.2	33.0[d]
Philippines	24.4	22.2	10.8	−17.5	3.6	12.2	−4.2	18.7	3.1	8.0	8.0	10.6	2.2[d]
Singapore	21.5	5.6	0.8	−23.3	9.4	21.3	−13.9	0.4	17.1	27.4	15.3	19.1	6.7[a]
Thailand	31.9	0.6	−13.4	−33.8	16.9	31.3	−3.0	4.6	17.4	25.7	25.9	7.0	7.1[j]
Timor-Leste	..	..	..	..	..	..	13.5	−16.8	−10.8	−16.1	−16.0	3.4	62.1[g]
Viet Nam	40.0	36.6	4.0	−0.8	2.1	33.2	3.7	21.8	27.9	26.6	15.0	22.1	30.3[a]
Developed ESCAP economies													
Australia	14.7	6.2	2.6	−2.0	7.3	4.1	13.0	1.6	−15.4	−3.4	7.3	13.6	−2.9[e]
Japan	22.6	4.0	−3.0	−18.1	11.5	23.3	−8.4	−4.4	13.3	19.1	17.1	12.3	4.5[b]
New Zealand	15.6	7.0	−1.4	−13.6	14.3	−2.9	−4.2	12.9	22.4	25.0	13.3	0.7	14.8[b]

Sources: ESCAP, calculated from national sources; IMF, *Direction of Trade Statistics*; and Country Reports Series; Economist Intelligence Unit, *Country Reports*; and website of Inter-State Statistical Committee of the Commonwealth of Independent States, <www.cisstat.com> (30 January 2008).

[a] Refers to first 9 months of 2007.
[b] Refers to first 10 months of 2007.
[c] f.o.b. value.
[d] Estimate.
[e] Refers to first 6 months of 2007.
[f] Fiscal year data.
[g] Projection.
[h] Provisional.
[i] Refers to first 11 months of 2006.
[j] Preliminary.

Table 10. Population, size and dynamics

| | Total Population | | | Average annual population growth rate | | | | Total fertility rate | | |
| | Thousands | | | Percentage | | | | Live births per woman | | |
	1990	2000	2006	90-95	95-00	00-05	2006	90-95	95-00	00-05
Developing ESCAP economies										
East and North-East Asia										
China	1 149 069	1 269 962	1 320 864	1.1	0.9	0.7	0.6	1.9	1.8	1.7
DPR Korea	20 143	22 946	23 708	1.5	1.1	0.6	0.4	2.4	2.1	1.9
Hong Kong, China	5 704	6 662	7 132	1.7	1.4	1.2	1.1	1.3	1.1	0.9
Macao, China	372	441	478	2.0	1.4	1.4	0.9	1.6	1.1	0.8
Mongolia	2 216	2 470	2 605	1.5	0.7	0.9	0.9	3.4	2.4	2.1
Republic of Korea	42 869	46 780	48 050	1.0	0.8	0.5	0.4	1.7	1.5	1.2
North and Central Asia										
Armenia	3 545	3 082	3 010	−1.9	−0.9	−0.4	−0.3	2.4	1.8	1.3
Azerbaijan	7 212	8 143	8 406	1.5	0.9	0.5	0.6	2.9	2.2	1.7
Georgia	5 460	4 720	4 433	−1.6	−1.3	−1.1	−0.9	2.0	1.6	1.5
Kazakhstan	16 530	14 954	15 314	−0.8	−1.3	0.3	0.7	2.6	2.0	2.0
Kyrgyzstan	4 395	4 946	5 259	0.9	1.5	1.0	1.1	3.6	3.0	2.5
Russian Federation	148 615	147 423	143 221	0.1	−0.2	−0.5	−0.5	1.5	1.2	1.3
Tajikistan	5 303	6 173	6 640	1.7	1.3	1.2	1.4	4.9	4.3	3.8
Turkmenistan	3 668	4 502	4 899	2.7	1.4	1.4	1.4	4.0	3.0	2.8
Uzbekistan	20 515	24 724	26 981	2.2	1.5	1.5	1.5	3.9	3.0	2.7
Pacific island economies										
American Samoa	47	57	65	2.2	1.6	2.3	2.2			
Cook Islands	18	16	14	0.3	−2.5	−2.7	−2.5			
Fiji	724	802	833	1.2	0.9	0.6	0.6	3.4	3.2	3.0
French Polynesia	195	236	259	2.0	1.8	1.6	1.4	3.1	2.6	2.4
Guam	134	155	171	1.7	1.3	1.7	1.5	3.1	3.0	2.7
Kiribati	72	84	94	1.5	1.7	1.8	1.7			
Marshall Islands	47	52	58	1.5	0.4	1.7	2.2			
Micronesia (Federated States of)	96	107	111	2.1	0.0	0.5	0.5	4.8	4.5	4.2
Nauru	9	10	10	1.7	0.1	0.1	0.2			
New Caledonia	171	215	238	2.4	2.2	1.7	1.6	2.9	2.6	2.2
Niue	2	2	2	−0.1	−3.6	−2.8	−2.1			
Northern Mariana Islands	44	69	82	5.5	3.6	3.0	2.3			
Palau	15	19	20	2.7	2.4	0.9	0.5			
Papua New Guinea	4 131	5 381	6 202	2.6	2.7	2.4	2.2	4.7	4.6	4.3
Samoa	161	177	185	0.8	1.1	0.7	0.8	4.7	4.7	4.4
Solomon Islands	314	415	484	2.9	2.8	2.6	2.5	5.5	4.9	4.4
Tonga	95	98	100	0.6	0.1	0.3	0.5	4.5	4.0	3.7
Tuvalu	9	10	10	0.8	0.7	0.5	0.4			
Vanuatu	149	190	221	2.8	1.9	2.5	2.5	4.8	4.6	4.2
South and South-West Asia										
Afghanistan	12 659	20 737	26 088	7.3	2.5	3.8	4.1	8.0	8.0	7.5
Bangladesh	113 049	139 434	155 991	2.2	2.0	1.9	1.8	4.1	3.5	3.2
Bhutan	547	559	649	−1.5	1.9	2.6	1.8	5.4	4.2	2.9
India	860 195	1 046 235	1 151 751	2.1	1.8	1.6	1.5	3.9	3.5	3.1
Iran (Islamic Republic of)	56 674	66 125	70 270	1.9	1.2	1.0	1.2	4.3	2.5	2.1
Maldives	216	273	300	2.8	1.9	1.6	1.7	5.6	3.8	2.8
Nepal	19 114	24 419	27 641	2.5	2.4	2.1	2.0	5.0	4.4	3.7
Pakistan	112 991	144 360	160 943	2.5	2.4	1.8	1.8	5.8	5.0	4.0
Sri Lanka	17 114	18 714	19 207	1.1	0.7	0.4	0.5	2.5	2.2	2.0
Turkey	57 345	68 158	73 922	1.8	1.7	1.4	1.3	2.9	2.6	2.2
South-East Asia										
Brunei Darussalam	257	333	382	2.8	2.5	2.3	2.2	3.1	2.7	2.5
Cambodia	9 698	12 780	14 197	3.2	2.3	1.8	1.7	5.5	4.5	3.6
Indonesia	182 847	211 693	228 864	1.5	1.4	1.3	1.2	2.9	2.6	2.4
Lao PDR	4 076	5 224	5 759	2.8	2.1	1.6	1.7	5.9	4.7	3.6
Malaysia	18 103	23 274	26 114	2.6	2.4	1.9	1.8	3.5	3.1	2.9
Myanmar	40 147	45 884	48 379	1.4	1.2	0.9	0.9	3.1	2.7	2.2
Philippines	61 226	76 213	86 264	2.3	2.1	2.1	2.0	4.1	3.7	3.5
Singapore	3 016	4 017	4 382	2.8	2.9	1.5	1.3	1.8	1.6	1.4
Thailand	54 291	60 666	63 444	1.2	1.1	0.8	0.7	2.0	1.9	1.8
Timor-Leste	740	819	1 114	2.8	−0.8	5.3	4.4	5.7	7.0	7.0
Viet Nam	66 173	79 094	86 206	2.1	1.5	1.4	1.4	3.3	2.5	2.3
Developed ESCAP economies										
Australia	16 873	19 139	20 530	1.4	1.1	1.2	1.1	1.9	1.8	1.8
Japan	123 537	127 034	127 953	0.3	0.2	0.1	0.0	1.5	1.4	1.3
New Zealand	3 411	3 854	4 140	1.5	1.0	1.2	1.0	2.1	2.0	2.0

Source: United Nations Department of Economic and Social Affairs, *World Population Prospects, The 2006 Revision Population Database,* <http://esa.un.org/unpp/> (June 2007).

Table 11. Population, structure

	Proportion of children in total population			Proportion of elderly in total population			Population sex ratio			Urbanization rate		
	Percentage			Percentage			Women per 100 men			% of total population		
	1990	2000	2006	1990	2000	2006	1990	2000	2006	1990	2000	2006
Developing ESCAP economies												
East and North-East Asia												
China	27.7	24.9	21.1	5.4	6.8	7.8	94	94	94	27.4	35.8	41.3
DPR Korea	26.2	25.9	23.6	4.7	6.9	8.8	104	104	103	58.4	60.2	61.9
Hong Kong, China	21.5	16.9	14.8	8.5	11.0	12.1	95	107	108	99.5	100.0	100.0
Macao, China	25.7	22.4	15.2	6.5	7.4	7.5	106	108	109	99.8	100.0	100.0
Mongolia	41.7	34.5	28.0	4.0	3.9	4.0	100	100	101	57.0	56.6	56.8
Republic of Korea	25.8	20.8	18.1	5.0	7.4	9.8	99	100	100	73.8	79.6	81.0
North and Central Asia												
Armenia	30.4	25.9	20.0	5.6	10.0	12.1	106	113	115	67.5	65.1	63.9
Azerbaijan	34.3	31.0	24.2	4.2	5.9	7.2	104	105	106	53.7	50.9	51.5
Georgia	24.6	21.6	18.4	9.3	12.5	14.4	110	111	112	55.2	52.7	52.3
Kazakhstan	31.5	27.6	23.9	5.9	6.8	8.0	107	109	109	56.3	56.3	57.6
Kyrgyzstan	37.6	34.9	30.4	5.0	5.5	5.8	104	103	103	37.8	35.4	35.9
Russian Federation	23.0	18.1	14.9	10.0	12.3	13.7	113	114	116	73.4	73.4	72.9
Tajikistan	43.2	42.4	38.7	3.8	3.5	3.9	101	100	102	31.5	25.9	24.5
Turkmenistan	40.5	36.2	30.9	3.8	4.4	4.6	103	103	103	45.1	45.1	46.6
Uzbekistan	40.9	37.2	32.4	4.0	4.3	4.7	102	101	101	40.1	37.3	36.7
Pacific island economies												
American Samoa							95	96	96			
Cook Islands							92	94	94			
Fiji	37.9	34.0	32.6	3.1	3.5	4.3	97	97	97	41.6	48.3	51.3
French Polynesia	35.3	31.5	26.9	3.2	4.3	5.3	92	94	95	55.9	52.4	51.6
Guam	30.2	30.5	29.0	3.9	5.4	6.7	88	96	96	90.8	93.2	94.2
Kiribati							103	103	103			
Marshall Islands							96	95	96			
Micronesia (Federated States of)	44.1	40.1	38.3	3.6	3.7	3.8	96	98	97	25.8	22.3	22.4
Nauru							101	101	102			
New Caledonia	32.3	29.7	26.6	4.6	5.6	6.8	96	97	99	59.6	61.9	64.0
Niue							102	103	104			
Northern Mariana Islands							91	118	130			
Palau							85	83	86			
Papua New Guinea	41.7	41.3	40.3	2.2	2.2	2.4	93	96	97	13.1	13.2	13.5
Samoa	40.9	40.9	40.5	3.9	4.4	4.6	90	92	92	21.2	21.9	22.6
Solomon Islands	45.3	42.0	40.1	3.0	2.9	3.0	93	93	93	13.7	15.7	17.3
Tonga	39.4	38.3	37.2	4.5	5.6	6.5	98	97	96	22.7	23.2	24.2
Tuvalu							104	108	111			
Vanuatu	43.9	42.1	39.3	3.6	3.3	3.3	94	95	96	18.7	21.7	23.8
South and South-West Asia												
Afghanistan	46.2	47.3	46.9	2.3	2.2	2.2	93	93	93	18.3	21.3	23.3
Bangladesh	40.7	37.2	34.7	3.0	3.3	3.6	94	95	95	19.8	23.2	25.5
Bhutan	42.6	40.2	31.7	3.3	4.4	4.7	95	97	89	7.2	9.6	11.4
India	37.8	35.0	32.5	3.9	4.6	5.0	92	93	93	25.5	27.7	29.0
Iran (Islamic Republic of)	44.7	35.1	27.8	3.5	4.5	4.5	95	97	97	56.3	64.2	67.5
Maldives	46.5	40.3	32.9	3.3	3.7	3.8	95	95	95	25.8	27.5	30.1
Nepal	41.9	40.9	38.5	3.4	3.5	3.7	98	101	102	8.9	13.4	16.2
Pakistan	44.0	41.8	36.4	3.3	3.7	3.9	94	94	94	30.6	33.1	35.2
Sri Lanka	32.0	26.8	23.7	5.4	6.5	6.6	98	100	103	17.2	15.7	15.1
Turkey	35.7	30.5	27.9	4.0	5.2	5.7	98	98	99	59.2	64.7	67.8
South-East Asia												
Brunei Darussalam	34.5	31.3	29.2	2.7	2.9	3.2	89	92	93	65.8	71.1	74.0
Cambodia	44.7	41.9	36.7	2.7	2.9	3.2	110	106	105	12.6	16.9	20.3
Indonesia	35.8	30.3	28.0	3.8	4.9	5.6	100	100	100	30.6	42.0	49.3
Lao PDR	44.7	43.4	38.9	3.4	3.4	3.5	100	100	101	15.4	18.9	21.0
Malaysia	37.4	33.5	31.0	3.7	3.9	4.4	97	97	97	49.8	61.8	68.3
Myanmar	35.6	30.2	26.7	4.9	5.5	5.6	101	101	102	24.9	28.0	31.3
Philippines	40.9	37.8	35.8	3.2	3.5	3.9	99	99	99	48.8	58.5	63.5
Singapore	21.5	21.8	18.8	5.6	7.2	8.8	99	99	99	100.0	100.0	100.0
Thailand	28.5	23.6	21.4	4.9	6.7	8.0	102	104	105	29.4	31.1	32.6
Timor-Leste	39.9	49.4	44.7	2.0	2.5	2.7	94	96	97	20.8	24.5	26.9
Viet Nam	38.9	33.5	28.9	4.9	5.5	5.6	101	100	100	20.3	24.3	26.9
Developed ESCAP economies												
Australia	21.9	20.7	19.3	11.2	12.4	13.3	100	101	101	85.4	87.2	88.4
Japan	18.4	14.6	13.8	12.0	17.2	20.3	104	104	105	63.1	65.2	66.0
New Zealand	23.4	22.7	21.2	11.1	11.8	12.3	103	104	103	84.7	85.7	86.3

Source: United Nations Department of Economic and Social Affairs, *World Population Prospects, The 2006 Revision Population Database,* <http://esa.un.org/unpp/> (June 2007).

Table 12. International migration

	Stock of foreign population			Stock of foreign population as share in total population			Crude net migration rate		
	Thousands			Percentage			Per 1 000 population		
	1990	2000	2005	1990	2000	2005	90-95	95-00	00-05
Developing ESCAP economies									
East and North-East Asia									
China	380	513	596	0.03	0.04	0.05	−0.2	−0.2	−0.3
DPR Korea	34	36	37	0.17	0.17	0.16			
Hong Kong, China	2 218	2 701	2 999	38.89	40.69	42.59	10.1	9.3	8.7
Macao, China	204	240	257	54.86	54.18	55.91	7.8	7.1	10.9
Mongolia	7	8	9	0.30	0.33	0.34	−5.2	−7.4	−4.0
Republic of Korea	572	568	551	1.33	1.21	1.15	−0.5	−0.3	−0.3
North and Central Asia									
Armenia	659	314	235	18.58	10.19	7.80	−29.5	−14.3	−6.6
Azerbaijan	361	160	182	5.00	1.97	2.16	−3.1	−3.2	−2.4
Georgia	338	219	191	6.20	4.63	4.27	−21.3	−14.4	−10.8
Kazakhstan	3,619	2 871	2 502	21.93	19.10	16.88	−18.6	−17.1	−2.7
Kyrgyzstan	623	372	288	14.18	7.52	5.47	−12.2	−1.1	−3.0
Russian Federation	11 525	11 892	12 080	7.77	8.11	8.44	3.0	3.0	1.3
Tajikistan	426	330	306	8.03	5.36	4.71	−11.3	−11.6	−10.8
Turkmenistan	307	241	224	8.36	5.35	4.63	2.5	−2.3	−0.4
Uzbekistan	1 653	1 367	1 268	8.06	5.53	4.77	−3.1	−3.4	−2.3
Pacific island economies									
American Samoa	21	21	20	44.97	35.73	31.42			
Cook Islands	3	3	3	14.09	15.34	17.00			
Fiji	14	16	17	1.89	1.96	2.03	−9.3	−10.7	−10.3
French Polynesia	26	31	34	13.22	13.03	13.08	−0.5	1.4	1.5
Guam	70	97	113	52.43	62.20	66.85	−4.6	−6.4	1.0
Kiribati	2	2	3	3.03	2.71	2.59			
Marshall Islands									
Micronesia (Federated States of)	3	3	4	3.18	3.24	3.22	−4.4	−25.4	−17.9
Nauru	4	5	5	41.49	37.41	36.09			
New Caledonia	37	41	43	21.40	18.97	18.22	5.8	5.5	4.3
Niue	0	0	0	11.44	8.70	7.61			
Northern Mariana Islands	5	5	5	10.95	7.33	6.48			
Palau	2	3	3	12.66	13.53	15.22			
Papua New Guinea	33	26	25	0.80	0.50	0.43			
Samoa	6	8	9	3.64	4.46	4.97	−15.8	−16.2	−16.6
Solomon Islands	4	4	3	1.28	0.84	0.69			
Tonga	3	2	1	3.19	1.59	1.14	−18.0	−19.5	−16.1
Tuvalu	0	0	0	3.23	3.12	3.12			
Vanuatu	2	1	1	1.44	0.69	0.49	−1.1	−7.9	
South and South-West Asia									
Afghanistan							42.9	−4.1	9.7
Bangladesh	882	988	1 032	0.85	0.77	0.73	−0.4	−0.5	−0.7
Bhutan	8	9	10	0.51	0.47	0.45	−38.3	0.1	11.7
India	7 493	6 271	5 700	0.88	0.61	0.52	−0.2	−0.3	−0.2
Iran (Islamic Republic of)	3 809	2 321	1 959	6.72	3.50	2.82	−5.3	−1.7	−3.7
Maldives	3	3	3	1.23	1.08	1.02			
Nepal	413	718	819	2.16	2.94	3.02	−1.0	−0.9	−0.8
Pakistan	6 556	4 243	3 254	5.87	2.97	2.06	−4.3	−0.1	−1.6
Sri Lanka	461	397	368	2.59	2.00	1.78	−2.9	−4.3	−4.7
Turkey	1 150	1 259	1 328	2.01	1.85	1.81	0.4	0.3	−0.1
South-East Asia									
Brunei Darussalam	73	104	124	28.48	31.23	33.22	2.6	2.2	2.0
Cambodia	38	237	304	0.39	1.86	2.16	2.8	1.3	0.2
Indonesia	466	330	160	0.26	0.16	0.07	−0.8	−0.9	−0.9
Lao PDR	23	24	25	0.55	0.46	0.42	−1.4	−3.5	−4.2
Malaysia	1 014	1 392	1 639	5.68	6.05	6.47	3.0	4.5	1.2
Myanmar	101	115	117	0.25	0.24	0.23	−0.6	0.0	−0.4
Philippines	164	322	374	0.27	0.43	0.45	−2.8	−2.5	−2.2
Singapore	727	1 352	1 843	24.11	33.65	42.61	15.4	19.6	9.6
Thailand	391	844	1 050	0.72	1.37	1.64	0.6	1.7	0.7
Timor-Leste	5	5	6	0.72	0.73	0.65		−40.8	21.2
Viet Nam	28	28	21	0.04	0.04	0.03	−0.7	−0.5	−0.5
Developed ESCAP economies									
Australia	3 984	4 072	4 097	23.61	21.35	20.33	5.9	5.0	6.0
Japan	877	1 620	2 048	0.71	1.28	1.60	0.4	0.4	0.4
New Zealand	529	708	642	15.52	18.54	15.94	5.3	2.1	5.1

Source: United Nations Department of Economic and Social Affairs, *World Population Prospects, The 2006 Revision Population Database,* <http://esa.un.org/unpp/> (June 2007).

Table 13. Primary education

| | Net enrolment rate (%) | | Girls to boys ratio | | Completion rate (%) | | | | | |
| | | | | | Both sexes | | Girls | | Boys | |
	1991	2005	1991	2005	1991	2005	1991	2005	1991	2005
Developing ESCAP economies										
East and North-East Asia										
China	98.0		0.93	1.00 (04)	103.3					
DPR Korea										
Hong Kong, China		97.0			102.2	109.6		106.7		112.4
Macao, China	81.3	90.9				96.3		96.3		96.3
Mongolia	95.7	88.0	1.02	1.02		94.5		97.0		92.2
Republic of Korea	99.7	99.6	1.01	0.99	103.3	101.0 (06)	98.3	100.1	97.6	101.9 (06)
North and Central Asia										
Armenia		86.2		1.04		90.7		92.5		89.1
Azerbaijan	88.8	84.6	0.99	0.98		94.1		93.4		94.8
Georgia	97.1	93.1 (04)	1.00	1.01		86.7				86.5
Kazakhstan	89.3	99.0	0.99	0.99		114.1		113.3		114.8
Kyrgyzstan	92.3	94.6		0.99		97.5		97.8		97.2
Russian Federation	98.6	92.2	1.00	1.00						
Tajikistan	76.7	97.4	0.98	0.96		102.1		100.0		104.2
Turkmenistan										
Uzbekistan	78.2		0.98	0.99 (04)						
Pacific island economies										
American Samoa										
Cook Islands	86.3 (99)	78.8 (00)								
Fiji	99.4	98.7	1.00	0.98		104.1		104.3		103.9
French Polynesia										
Guam										
Kiribati	99.2 (99)	99.7 (02)		1.02		128.7		125.0		132.4
Marshall Islands		91.7 (03)		0.96						
Micronesia (Federated States of)				0.97						
Nauru				0.99 (04)						
New Caledonia										
Niue	98.5 (99)									
Northern Mariana Islands										
Palau	96.8 (99)	96.4 (00)		0.93		115.4				
Papua New Guinea			0.88		47.4		42.5		52.2	
Samoa	94.2 (99)	99.1 (04)	1.02	1.00						
Solomon Islands		63.4 (03)	0.86	0.95	71.6					
Tonga	90.9 (99)	98.1	0.97	0.95	102.6		98.4		106.7	
Tuvalu										
Vanuatu	90.9 (99)	95.1	0.96	0.97		87.3				
South and South-West Asia										
Afghanistan			0.55	0.59		32.3		17.7		45.8
Bangladesh	93.0 (99)	97.6 (04)		1.03 (04)						
Bhutan										
India		94.6	0.76	0.93	68.2	89.8	54.9	85.7	80.6	93.8
Iran (Islamic Republic of)	92.4	95.4	0.90	1.22	91.2	95.7	85.2	100.3	96.9	91.4
Maldives	97.7 (99)	79.7		0.98		127.3				129.0
Nepal	66.9 (99)	80.1 (04)	0.63	0.91	50.9	76.0 (06)		72.3 (06)		79.6 (06)
Pakistan		68.1		0.76		63.2		52.5		73.4
Sri Lanka		97.1 (04)	0.95			97.0		96.4		97.6
Turkey	90.4	89.4	0.92	0.95	89.7	87.2	86.0	83.0	93.2	91.2
South-East Asia										
Brunei Darussalam	92.7	96.9			100.0	106.9		111.0		103.1
Cambodia	69.5	98.9	0.81	0.92		92.3		90.4		94.2
Indonesia	97.3	98.3	0.98	0.96	90.7	101.1		101.7		100.5
Lao PDR	62.8	83.6	0.79	0.88		75.9		71.5		80.1
Malaysia	97.8 (99)	95.4 (04)	1.00	1.00 (04)	91.4		91.5		91.4	
Myanmar	98.1	90.2				79.0		80.3		77.6
Philippines	96.5	94.4	0.99	0.99		96.6		100.4		92.9
Singapore			0.97	1.00						
Thailand	75.8	93.1 (06)	0.96	0.95						
Timor-Leste		97.8		0.92						
Viet Nam	90.2	87.8	0.93	0.94		93.5				
Developed ESCAP economies										
Australia	99.3	96.8	0.99	0.99						
Japan	99.7	99.8	1.00	1.00	101.4		101.6		101.3	
New Zealand	97.8	99.4	0.99	1.00				98.7		100.6

Source: United Nations Department of Economic and Social Affairs, *Millennium Development Goals Indicators*, <http://mdgs.un.org/unsd/mdg/Default.aspx> (September 2007).

Table 14. Secondary and tertiary education

	Secondary level				Tertiary level			
	Net enrolment rate (%)		Girls to boys ratio		Gross enrolment rate (%)		Women to men ratio	
	1999	2005	1991	2005	1999	2005	1991	2005
Developing ESCAP economies								
East and North-East Asia								
China			0.75	1.00 (04)	6	19 (04)	0.52	0.85 (04)
DPR Korea								
Hong Kong, China	74 (01)	78 (04)	1.05		28 (01)	32 (04)		
Macao, China	62	77 (04)	1.11		27	69 (04)		
Mongolia	55	82 (04)	1.14	1.14	26	39 (04)	1.89	1.62
Republic of Korea	97	90	0.97	1.00	66	90	0.49	0.62
North and Central Asia								
Armenia	85 (00)	84 (04)	0.98 (00)	1.03	24	26 (04)	1.11 (99)	1.22
Azerbaijan	73	77 (04)	1.01	0.96	15	15 (04)	0.67	0.90
Georgia	77	81 (04)	0.97	1.01	36	41 (04)	1.18	1.04
Kazakhstan	85 (00)	92 (04)	1.04	0.97	25	48 (04)	1.16 (99)	1.42
Kyrgyzstan		80	1.02	1.01	29	40 (04)	1.04 (99)	1.25
Russian Federation			1.06	0.99	65 (03)	68 (04)	1.27	1.36
Tajikistan	66	79 (04)	0.86 (99)	0.83	14	16 (04)	0.62	0.35
Turkmenistan								
Uzbekistan			0.91	0.97 (04)	15 (02)	15 (04)	0.80 (02)	0.80 (04)
Pacific island economies								
American Samoa								
Cook Islands	59	57 (00)						
Fiji	79	83 (04)	0.95	1.07	15 (03)	15 (04)	1.20 (03)	1.20
French Polynesia								
Guam								
Kiribati	71 (03)	70 (04)	1.18 (99)	1.13				
Marshall Islands	74 (02)	74 (03)	1.06 (99)	1.05	17 (01)	17 (03)	1.29 (01)	1.30 (03)
Micronesia (Federated States of)			1.04 (04)	1.07	14	14 (00)		
Nauru			1.21 (00)	1.07 (04)				
New Caledonia								
Niue	93 (99)							
Northern Mariana Islands								
Palau			1.07 (99)	1.08	41 (00)	40 (02)	2.35 (00)	2.15 (02)
Papua New Guinea			0.61	0.79 (03)	2		0.55 (99)	0.55 (99)
Samoa	72	66 (04)	1.96	1.12	12	7 (01)	1.04 (99)	0.93 (01)
Solomon Islands	22	26 (03)	0.61	0.83				
Tonga	71 (99)	68 (04)	1.03	1.08 (04)	3	6 (04)	1.27 (99)	1.67 (04)
Tuvalu				0.93 (01)				
Vanuatu	29 (99)	39 (04)	0.80	0.86 (04)	4	5 (04)	0.56 (02)	0.58 (04)
South and South-West Asia								
Afghanistan			0.51	0.33	1 (03)	1 (04)	0.28 (03)	0.28 (04)
Bangladesh	46	48 (03)	1.01 (99)	1.03 (04)	6	7 (03)	0.51 (99)	0.53 (04)
Bhutan								
India			0.60	0.81	10 (00)	12 (04)	0.54	0.70
Iran (Islamic Republic of)	78 (04)	78 (04)	0.75	0.94	19	22 (04)	0.48	1.09
Maldives	32	51 (02)	1.07 (99)	1.14 (04)			2.37 (03)	2.37 (04)
Nepal			0.46	0.86	4 (00)	6 (04)	0.33	0.40 (04)
Pakistan		21	0.48	0.74	3 (02)	3 (04)	0.58	0.88
Sri Lanka			1.08	1.00 (04)			0.55	0.55 (91)
Turkey		67	0.63	0.82	22	29 (04)	0.53	0.74
South-East Asia								
Brunei Darussalam		87			10	15		
Cambodia	15	26 (04)	0.43	0.69 (04)	2 (00)	3 (04)	0.33 (00)	0.46
Indonesia	49 (00)	57 (04)	0.83	0.99	14 (01)	17 (04)	0.76 (01)	0.79
Lao PDR	27	37 (04)	0.62	0.76	2	6 (04)	0.49 (99)	0.72
Malaysia	69	76 (03)	1.05	1.14 (04)	23	32 (03)	1.04 (99)	1.31 (04)
Myanmar	31	37			7	11 (02)		
Philippines	51	61 (04)	1.04	1.12	29	29 (04)	1.42	1.23
Singapore			0.93	1.03			0.71	0.71 (91)
Thailand			0.94	1.03	32	43	1.16 (99)	1.11
Timor-Leste	20 (01)		0.99 (04)	1.00	10 (02)		1.48 (02)	
Viet Nam	59 (99)	65 (02)	0.90 (99)	0.97	11	10 (04)	0.76 (99)	
Developed ESCAP economies								
Australia	89 (00)	85 (04)	1.03	0.95	66	72 (04)	1.19	1.25
Japan	99	100 (04)	1.02	1.00	45	54 (04)	0.65	0.89
New Zealand	91 (02)	95 (04)	1.02	1.07	67	63 (04)	0.11	1.50

Sources: United Nations Department of Economic and Social Affairs, *Millennium Development Goals Indicators*, <http://mdgs.un.org/unsd/mdg/Default.aspx> (September 2007); and UNESCO Institute for Statistics, Data Centre (online database, August 2007).

Table 15. Life expectancy

	Life expectancy								
	Years								
	Total			Female			Male		
	90-95	95-00	00-05	90-95	95-00	00-05	90-95	95-00	00-05
Developing ESCAP economies									
East and North-East Asia									
China	68.7	70.4	72.0	70.3	72.0	73.7	67.4	69.0	70.5
DPR Korea	70.0	67.7	66.7	73.7	71.0	68.8	66.1	64.0	64.2
Hong Kong, China	77.6	80.0	81.5	81.0	83.0	84.5	75.5	77.2	78.6
Macao, China	77.3	78.8	80.0	79.8	80.9	82.2	75.2	76.5	77.6
Mongolia	61.3	63.6	65.0	63.2	66.3	68.4	59.4	61.1	61.9
Republic of Korea	72.2	74.7	77.1	76.5	78.5	80.6	68.5	70.9	73.5
North and Central Asia									
Armenia	68.7	70.4	71.4	72.1	73.7	74.6	65.3	66.9	67.9
Azerbaijan	65.6	66.3	66.8	69.5	70.0	70.5	62.2	62.6	63.2
Georgia	70.5	70.5	70.5	74.3	74.3	74.3	66.5	66.5	66.5
Kazakhstan	65.4	63.0	64.9	70.3	68.9	70.6	60.5	57.5	59.5
Kyrgyzstan	66.1	65.0	65.4	70.1	69.0	69.4	62.1	61.0	61.4
Russian Federation	66.4	65.7	64.8	72.6	72.2	71.8	60.5	59.6	58.5
Tajikistan	63.4	64.3	65.9	65.9	66.9	68.6	60.8	61.7	63.4
Turkmenistan	63.3	62.9	62.4	67.6	67.2	66.7	59.2	58.8	58.2
Uzbekistan	66.2	66.5	66.5	69.4	69.7	69.7	63.0	63.3	63.3
Pacific island economies									
American Samoa									
Cook Island									
Fiji	66.6	66.8	67.8	68.8	69.1	70.1	64.6	64.8	65.7
French Polynesia	70.2	71.8	73.0	72.8	74.6	75.8	67.9	69.5	70.6
Guam	72.5	73.6	74.6	75.0	76.0	77.0	70.4	71.4	72.4
Kiribati									
Marshall Islands									
Micronesia (Federated States of)	66.4	67.1	67.6	67.0	67.6	68.2	65.9	66.5	66.9
Nauru									
New Caledonia	71.5	72.7	75.1	74.5	76.1	78.7	69.2	69.8	71.9
Niue									
Northern Mariana Islands									
Palau									
Papua New Guinea	55.2	56.2	56.7	58.5	59.5	59.9	53.0	53.7	54.1
Samoa	66.0	68.4	70.0	69.7	71.9	73.5	63.1	65.4	67.1
Solomon Islands	58.3	60.7	62.3	58.8	61.3	63.0	57.9	60.3	61.6
Tonga	70.0	71.1	72.3	71.4	72.2	73.3	69.0	70.2	71.3
Tuvalu									
Vanuatu	65.1	66.5	68.4	65.9	68.3	70.4	62.9	65.0	66.8
South and South-West Asia									
Afghanistan	41.7	41.8	42.1	41.7	41.8	42.1	41.7	41.8	42.2
Bangladesh	56.0	59.4	62.0	56.7	59.9	62.8	55.5	59.0	61.3
Bhutan	54.5	58.9	63.5	56.3	60.8	65.2	53.0	57.3	61.8
India	60.2	61.8	62.9	60.8	62.7	64.2	59.9	61.0	61.7
Iran (Islamic Republic of)	65.7	68.0	69.5	67.1	69.3	71.0	64.7	66.9	68.0
Maldives	61.0	63.4	65.6	59.8	62.6	65.6	62.3	64.3	65.6
Nepal	55.7	59.4	61.3	55.6	59.6	61.6	55.8	59.1	61.0
Pakistan	60.8	61.8	63.6	61.4	62.2	63.9	60.5	61.4	63.3
Sri Lanka	70.4	70.5	70.8	74.0	74.3	75.0	67.5	66.9	67.0
Turkey	66.2	68.8	70.8	68.5	71.2	73.3	64.0	66.6	68.5
South-East Asia									
Brunei Darussalam	74.5	75.5	76.3	77.1	78.1	78.9	72.4	73.4	74.2
Cambodia	55.8	56.5	56.8	57.3	58.4	59.5	54.1	54.4	53.7
Indonesia	62.7	66.0	68.6	64.5	67.9	70.5	61.1	64.2	66.7
Lao PDR	56.0	59.5	61.9	57.3	60.7	63.1	54.9	58.2	60.7
Malaysia	70.7	71.9	73.0	73.1	74.5	75.5	68.7	69.6	70.8
Myanmar	59.3	60.3	59.9	61.6	63.0	63.4	57.3	57.8	56.7
Philippines	66.5	68.6	70.3	68.7	70.7	72.5	64.5	66.5	68.2
Singapore	75.8	77.2	78.8	78.3	79.3	80.8	73.9	75.1	76.8
Thailand	67.3	67.5	68.6	71.2	72.8	74.0	64.0	62.8	63.7
Timor-Leste	49.2	54.4	58.3	50.1	55.2	59.1	48.5	53.6	57.5
Viet Nam	67.7	70.7	73.0	69.6	72.4	74.9	66.1	69.0	71.2
Developed ESCAP economies									
Australia	77.6	78.7	80.4	80.6	81.5	82.9	74.7	75.9	77.9
Japan	79.5	80.5	81.9	82.4	83.8	85.2	76.2	77.1	78.3
New Zealand	76.1	77.6	79.2	78.9	80.1	81.3	73.3	75.0	77.0

Source: United Nations Department of Economic and Social Affairs, *World Population Prospects, The 2006 Revision Population Database*, <http://esa.un.org/unpp/> (June 2007).

Table 16. Health, morbidity

	HIV/AIDS			Malaria incidence			Tuberculosis			
	Number of adults aged 15 and above living with HIV/AIDS	Prevalence rate, aged 15-49	Number of cases			Inci-dence	Prevalence			
	Female	Total	Percentage	Per 100 000 population				Per 100 000 population		
	2005	2005	2005	1990	2000	2005	2005	1990	2000	2005
Developing ESCAP economies										
East and North-East Asia										
China	180 000	650 000	0.10	8	1	2	100	325	271	208
DPR Korea					321	28	178	428	368	179
Hong Kong, China						0		138	87	77
Macao, China						0		123	87	87
Mongolia	100	500	0.10			0	191	566	285	206
Republic of Korea	1 400	13 000	0.10	0	9	3	96	123	142	135
North and Central Asia										
Armenia	1 000	2 900	0.10	0	5	0	71	53	96	79
Azerbaijan	1 000	5 400	0.10	0	19	3	76	58	113	85
Georgia	1 000	5 600	0.20	0	5	3	83	52	98	86
Kazakhstan	6 800	12 000	0.10			0	144	96	145	155
Kyrgyzstan	1 000	4 000	0.10	0	0	4	121	90	157	133
Russian Federation	210 000	940 000	1.10			0	119	82	190	150
Tajikistan	500	4 900	0.10	3	309	35	198	196	193	297
Turkmenistan		500	0.10	0	1	0	70	106	130	90
Uzbekistan	4 100	31 000	0.20	0	1	0	113	115	140	139
Pacific island economies										
American Samoa								27	15	9
Cook Islands							16	49	26	26
Fiji	500	1 000	0.10				23	62	38	30
French Polynesia								167	51	32
Guam								116	58	39
Kiribati							380	1 157	559	426
Marshall Islands							224	682	430	269
Micronesia (Federated States of)							105	311	171	123
Nauru							108	328	206	156
New Caledonia								145	48	30
Niue							44	133	96	87
Northern Mariana Islands								232	84	92
Palau							52	88	115	61
Papua New Guinea	34 000	57 000	1.80	2 539	1 509	1 627	250	789	637	475
Samoa							20	44	27	27
Solomon Islands				37 149	16 341	16 249	142	658	289	201
Tonga							25	53	34	32
Tuvalu							305	1 146	723	495
Vanuatu				19 274	3 385	4 566	60	212	87	84
South and South-West Asia										
Afghanistan	100	1 000	0.10	2 508	983	266	168	607	449	288
Bangladesh	1 400	11 000	0.10	48	40	31	227	630	494	406
Bhutan	100	500	0.10	1 735	1 063	286	103	374	218	174
India		2 500 000	0.36	235	194	160	168	570	457	299
Iran (Islamic Republic of)	11 000	66 000	0.20	137	30	27	23	50	40	30
Maldives				7	7		47	151	90	53
Nepal	16 000	74 000	0.50	120	31	18	180	621	310	244
Pakistan	14 000	84 000	0.10	71	57	81	181	429	416	297
Sri Lanka	1 000	5 000	0.10	1 679	1 122	9	60	109	109	80
Turkey				15	17	3	29	83	49	44
South-East Asia										
Brunei Darussalam	100	100	0.10				54	113	56	63
Cambodia	59 000	130 000	1.60	1 277	489	354	506	951	806	703
Indonesia	29 000	170 000	0.10	94	116	192	239	440	327	262
Lao PDR	1 000	3 600	0.10	541	766		155	472	346	306
Malaysia	17 000	67 000	0.50	279	55	22	102	195	139	131
Myanmar	110 000	350 000	1.30	2 464	1 291	316	171	417	287	170
Philippines	3 400	12 000	0.10	141	48	55	291	820	554	450
Singapore	1 500	5 500	0.30			4	29	52	39	28
Thailand	220 000	560 000	1.40	504	135	47	142	355	252	204
Timor-Leste					6 089	3 669	556	1 200	1 111	713
Viet Nam	84 000	250 000	0.50	187	79	23	175	470	251	235
Developed ESCAP economies										
Australia	1 000	16 000	0.10				6	7	6	6
Japan	9 900	17 000	0.10				28	70	45	38
New Zealand		1 400	0.10				9	10	11	9

Sources: UNAIDS/WHO, *Report on the Global AIDS Epidemic,* <http://www.who.int> (Geneva, UNAIDS/WHO, 2006); United Nations Department of Economic and Social Affairs, *Millennium Development Goals Indicators,* <http://mdgs.un.org> (online database, September 2007); and WHO, *World Malaria Report 2005* (Geneva, WHO, 2006), <http://www.who.int> (November 2007).

Table 17. Mortality

	Infant mortality rate			Children under 5 mortality rate			Children 1 yr old immunized against measles			Maternal mortality rate	
	Deaths per 1 000 live births			Deaths per 1 000 live births			Percentage			Number	Deaths per 100 000 live births
	1990	2000	2005	1990	2000	2005	1990	2000	2005	2000	2000
Developing ESCAP economies											
East and North-East Asia											
China	38	33	23	49	41	27	98	85	86	10,404	56
DPR Korea	42	42	42	55	55	55	98	78	96	260	67
Hong Kong, China											
Macao, China											
Mongolia	78	50	39	108	65	49	92	94	99	54	110
Republic of Korea	8	5	5	9	5	5	93	95	99	111	20
North and Central Asia											
Armenia	46	32	26	54	36	29		92	94	20	55
Azerbaijan	84	77	74	105	93	89		99	98	122	94
Georgia	43	41	41	47	45	45		73	92	17	32
Kazakhstan	53	63	63	63	73	73		99	99	505	210
Kyrgyzstan	68	60	58	80	70	67		98	99	120	110
Russian Federation	21	19	14	27	24	18		97	99	907	67
Tajikistan	91	75	59	115	93	71		87	84	190	100
Turkmenistan	80	77	81	97	99	104		97	99	33	31
Uzbekistan	65	59	57	79	71	68		99	99	143	24
Pacific island economies											
American Samoa											
Cook Islands	26	20	17	32	24	20	67	76	99		
Fiji	19	16	16	22	18	18	84	85	70	15	75
French Polynesia										1	20
Guam										0	12
Kiribati	65	52	48	88	70	65	75	80	56		
Marshall Islands	63	55	51	92	68	58	52	94	86		
Micronesia (Federated States of)	45	37	34	58	47	42	81	82	96		
Nauru		25	25		30	30		8	80		
New Caledonia										0	10
Niue							99	99	99		
Northern Mariana Islands											
Palau	18	13	10	21	14	11	98	83	98		
Papua New Guinea	69	60	55	94	80	74	67	62	60	577	300
Samoa	40	28	24	50	34	29	89	93	57	1	15
Solomon Islands	31	26	24	38	32	29	70	87	72	19	130
Tonga	26	22	20	32	26	24	86	95	99		
Tuvalu	42	35	31	54	43	38	95	81	62		
Vanuatu	48	38	31	62	48	38	66	94	70	2	32
South and South-West Asia											
Afghanistan	168	165	165	260	257	257	20	35	64	20 457	1 900
Bangladesh	100	66	54	149	92	73	65	76	81	15 160	380
Bhutan	107	77	65	166	100	75	93	76	93	60	420
India	84	69	56	123	94	74	56	56	58	148 968	540
Iran (Islamic Republic of)	54	36	31	72	44	36	85	99	94	922	76
Maldives	79	45	33	111	60	42	96	99	97	7	110
Nepal	100	69	56	145	95	74	57	71	74	5 823	740
Pakistan	100	85	79	130	108	99	50	56	78	21 524	500
Sri Lanka	26	16	12	32	19	14	80	99	99	295	92
Turkey	67	38	26	82	44	29	78	86	91	995	70
South-East Asia											
Brunei Darussalam	10	8	8	11	9	9	99	99	97	3	37
Cambodia	80	95	98	115	135	143	34	65	79	1 675	450
Indonesia	60	36	28	91	48	36	58	72	72	10 383	230
Lao PDR	120	77	62	163	101	79	32	42	41	1 052	650
Malaysia	16	11	10	22	14	12	70	88	90	225	41
Myanmar	91	78	75	130	110	105	90	84	72	3 412	360
Philippines	41	30	25	62	40	33	85	81	80	4 363	200
Singapore	7	3	3	9	4	3	84	96	96	14	30
Thailand	31	19	18	37	22	21	80	94	96	430	44
Timor-Leste	133	85	52	177	107	61			48	253	660
Viet Nam	38	23	16	53	30	19	88	97	95	2 103	130
Developed ESCAP economies											
Australia	8	6	5	10	6	6	86	91	94	20	8
Japan	5	3	3	6	5	4	73	96	99	118	10
New Zealand	8	6	5	11	8	6	90	85	82	4	7

Source: United Nations Department of Economic and Social Affairs, *Millennium Development Goals Indicators,* <http://mdgs.un.org> (online database, September 2007).

Table 18. Poverty and malnutrition

	Share of population below $1 [1993 PPP] per day (%)		Share of population below the national poverty line (%)		Gini coefficient of income distribution		Children under 5 moderately or severely underweight (%)	
	Earliest	Latest	Earliest	Latest	Earliest	Latest	Earliest	Latest
Developing ESCAP economies								
East and North-East Asia								
China	33.0 (90)	9.9 (04)	6.0 (96)	4.6 (98)		46.9 (04)	19.1 (90)	7.8 (02)
DPR Korea							27.9 (00)	23.9 (04)
Hong Kong, China					43.4 (96)			
Macao, China								
Mongolia	13.9 (95)	10.8 (02)	36.3 (95)	36.1 (02)	33.2 (95)	32.8 (02)	12.3 (92)	6.7 (04)
Republic of Korea		2.0 (98)				31.6 (98)		
North and Central Asia								
Armenia	6.7 (96)	2.0 (03)		50.9 (01)	44.4 (96)	33.8 (03)		4.0 (05)
Azerbaijan	10.9 (95)	3.7 (01)	68.1 (95)	49.6 (01)	36.0 (95)	36.5 (01)	2.6 (00)	6.8 (01)
Georgia	2.0 (96)	6.5 (03)		54.5 (03)	37.1 (96)	40.4 (03)		3.1 (99)
Kazakhstan	2.0 (93)	2.0 (03)	34.6 (96)		32.7 (93)	33.9 (03)		4.2 (03)
Kyrgyzstan	8.0 (93)	2.0 (03)		41.0 (03)	53.7 (93)	30.3 (03)		11.0 (97)
Russian Federation	7.0 (96)	2.0 (02)	30.9 (94)		46.2 (96)	39.9 (02)	3.0 (95)	
Tajikistan		7.4 (03)				32.6 (03)		
Turkmenistan	20.7 (93)				35.4 (93)	40.8 (98)		12.0 (00)
Uzbekistan	3.3 (93)	2.0 (03)		27.5 (00)	33.3 (93)	36.8 (03)		7.9 (02)
Pacific island economies								
American Samoa								
Cook Islands								
Fiji							7.9 (93)	
French Polynesia								
Guam								
Kiribati								
Marshall Islands								
Micronesia (Federated States of)								
Nauru								
New Caledonia								
Niue								
Northern Mariana Islands								
Palau								
Papua New Guinea			37.5 (96)		50.9 (96)			
Samoa								
Solomon Islands								
Tonga								
Tuvalu								
Vanuatu								
South and South-West Asia								
Afghanistan							48.0 (97)	39.3 (04)
Bangladesh	35.9 (92)	41.3 (00)	51.0 (96)	49.8 (00)	28.3 (92)	33.4 (00)	65.8 (90)	47.5 (04)
Bhutan								18.7 (99)
India	41.8 (93)	34.3 (04)	36.0 (94)	28.6 (00)		36.8 (04)	53.4 (93)	48.5 (99)
Iran (Islamic Republic of)	2.0 (90)	2.0 (98)			43.6 (90)	43.0 (98)		10.9 (98)
Maldives							38.9 (94)	30.4 (01)
Nepal	34.4 (96)	24.1 (04)	41.8 (96)	30.9 (04)	37.7 (96)	47.2 (04)		48.3 (01)
Pakistan		17.0 (02)	28.6 (93)	32.9 (99)		30.6 (02)	40.4 (91)	37.8 (02)
Sri Lanka	3.8 (90)	5.6 (02)	20.0 (91)		30.1 (90)	40.2 (02)		29.4 (00)
Turkey	2.4 (94)	3.4 (03)	28.3 (94)	27.0 (02)	41.5 (94)	43.6 (03)	10.4 (93)	3.9 (03)
South-East Asia								
Brunei Darussalam								
Cambodia		34.1 (97)		35 (04)	40.4 (97)	41.7 (04)	39.8 (94)	45.2 (00)
Indonesia	17.4 (93)	7.5 (02)	15.7 (96)	27.1 (99)	34.4 (93)	34.3 (02)	26.4 (99)	28.2 (03)
Lao PDR	18.6 (92)	27.0 (02)	45.0 (93)	38.6 (98)	30.4 (92)	34.6 (02)	44.0 (93)	40.0 (00)
Malaysia	2.0 (92)	2.0 (97)			47.7 (92)		23.3 (93)	10.6 (03)
Myanmar							32.4 (90)	31.8 (03)
Philippines	19.8 (91)	14.8 (03)	40.6 (94)	36.8 (97)	43.8 (91)	44.5 (03)	33.5 (90)	27.6 (03)
Singapore						42.5 (98)		3.4 (00)
Thailand	6.0 (92)	2.0 (02)	9.8 (94)	13.6 (98)	46.2 (92)	42.0 (02)	18.6 (93)	17.6 (95)
Timor-Leste							42.6 (02)	45.8 (03)
Viet Nam				28.9 (02)	35.7 (93)	34.4 (04)	33.1 (00)	26.6 (04)
Developed ESCAP economies								
Australia					35.2 (94)			
Japan					24.9 (93)			
New Zealand					36.2 (97)			

Sources: United Nations Department of Economic and Social Affairs, *Millennium Development Goals Indicators,* <http://mdgs.un.org> (online database, September 2007); and World Bank, *World Development Indicators,* <http://devdata.worldbank.org> (online database, September 2007).

Table 19. Gender parity

	Women wage employment in non-agricultural sector, as a share of total non-agricultural employees (%)			Women to men employers (%)			Difference between women and men employment to population ratios (%)				Woment in parliamentary seats, as a share of total parliamentarians (%)		
	1990	2000	2005	1990	2000	2005	1991	2000	2005	2006	1990	2000	2006
Developing ESCAP economies													
East and North-East Asia													
China	37.7						−10.1	−11.4	−12.0	−12.2	21.3	21.8	20.3
DPR Korea	40.7						−28.5	−27.8	−28.3	−28.1	21.1	20.1	20.1
Hong Kong, China	41.2	44.8	47.8		16.8	21.9	−30.3	−21.9	−15.4	−14.9			
Macao, China	42.7	48.9	49.5		13.8	22.1	−25.7	−16.3	−14.3	−13.2			
Mongolia		50.4	53.1		38.9		−19.2	−22.0	−24.1	−24.5	24.9	7.9	6.7
Republic of Korea		40.1	41.8	37.5	22.0	25.3	−25.8	−22.8	−22.7	−22.5	2.0	3.7	13.4
North and Central Asia													
Armenia		45.5					−13.3	−14.1	−11.8	−11.6	35.6	3.1	5.3
Azerbaijan		43.6	49.1				−13.1	−13.5	−12.0	−11.4		12.0	13.0
Georgia			48.6		13.6	23.2	−2.9	−17.4	−21.9	−22.5		7.2	9.4
Kazakhstan							−17.5	−14.0	−11.4	−11.0		10.4	10.4
Kyrgyzstan		45.8	51.9				−15.7	−17.8	−18.4	−18.3		1.4	0
Russian Federation		50.4	50.9		40.3	66.2	−13.3	−13.5	−13.2	−13.3		7.7	9.8
Tajikistan							−19.0	−15.7	−14.2	−14.1		2.8	17.5
Turkmenistan	41.8						−11.5	−13.2	−11.2	−11.3	26.0	26.0	16.0
Uzbekistan							−15.2	−14.8	−14.2	−13.9		6.8	17.5
Pacific island economies													
American Samoa	41.3												
Cook Islands	38.4												
Fiji	29.9						−29.2	−28.2	−27.5	−27.2		11.3	8.5
French Polynesia		42.4											
Guam			44.6										
Kiribati		37.4									0	4.9	4.8
Marshall Islands			33.2										3.0
Micronesia (Federated States of)												0	0
Nauru											5.6	0	0
New Caledonia													
Niue													
Northern Mariana Islands													
Palau												0	0
Papua New Guinea	20.3	32.1					−3.2	−2.3	−3.0	−3.1	0	1.8	0.9
Samoa											0	8.2	6.1
Solomon Islands							−24.0	−25.1	−26.6	−27.0	0	2.0	0
Tonga											0		3.4
Tuvalu											7.7	0	0
Vanuatu											4.3	0	3.8
South and South-West Asia													
Afghanistan	17.8						−49.7	−49.5	−47.4	−47.2	3.7		27.3
Bangladesh	17.6	22.9			12.8		−25.5	−30.9	−32.4	−32.5	10.3	9.1	14.8
Bhutan							−50.2	−44.6	−35.0	−31.9	2.0	2.0	9.3
India	12.7	16.6					−26.1	−28.3	−29.2	−29.4	5.0	9.0	8.3
Iran (Islamic Republic of)							−54.7	−40.5	−34.7	−33.7	1.5	4.9	4.1
Maldives		36.7			12.5		−55.4	−35.0	−23.7	−21.8	6.3		12.0
Nepal							−31.6	−29.8	−29.1	−29.0	6.1	5.9	5.9
Pakistan	6.6	7.4	9.7		2.1	1.6	−58.4	−54.4	−49.0	−48.4	10.1		21.3
Sri Lanka	39.1	46.0					−37.0	−38.8	−40.8	−40.6	4.9	4.9	4.9
Turkey		19.1	20.3		4.0	4.7	−41.9	−44.0	−43.4	−43.3	1.3	4.2	4.4
South-East Asia													
Brunei Darussalam		30.3					−34.1	−33.3	−33.9	−34.5			
Cambodia		51.9			11.7		−7.5	−5.9	−5.8	−5.8		8.2	9.8
Indonesia	29.2	31.7					−31.5	−32.9	−33.3	−33.1	12.4		11.3
Lao PDR							−25.3	−25.7	−25.6	−25.6	6.3	21.2	22.9
Malaysia	37.8	36.7			11.1		−36.3	−35.0	−33.6	−33.1	5.1		9.1
Myanmar	40.6						−17.7	−17.6	−17.4	−17.3			
Philippines		41.1	41.9			25.5	−34.2	−29.7	−26.3	−25.3	9.1	12.4	15.7
Singapore					24.5		−28.8	−25.1	−25.2	−24.7	4.9	4.3	16.0
Thailand	45.3	46.1	47.9	28.3	30.3		−14.3	−16.5	−15.3	−14.9	2.8	5.6	10.6
Timor-Leste	19.0						−29.0	−26.8	−26.4	−26.4			25.3
Viet Nam		48.2			55.4		−7.2	−6.1	−6.4	−6.4	17.7	26.0	27.3
Developed ESCAP economies													
Australia	44.6	48.1	48.9	46.5	50.0	50.6	−20.0	−16.5	−14.4	−13.4	6.1	22.4	24.7
Japan		40.0	41.3	20.6	22.1	21.6	−26.6	−26.2	−24.7	−24.5	1.4	4.6	9.0
New Zealand	43.9	47.3	47.4		40.8	44.0	−16.9	−16.1	−14.2	−13.1	14.4	29.2	32.2

Sources: United Nations Department of Economic and Social Affairs, *Millennium Development Goals Indicators*, <http://mdgs.un.org/unsd/mdg/Default.aspx> (online database, 2007); and International Labour Organization, *Key Indicators of the Labour Market, Fifth Edition* (September 2007).

Table 20. Employment growth, share of total population and productivity

	Average annual employment growth rate				Employment to population ratio (%, population aged 15 and above)					Average annual labour productivity growth rate		
	Percentage				Percentage					% (1990 PPP dollars)		
	91-95	95-00	00-95	2006	1991	1995	2000	2005	2006	91-95	95-00	00-05
Developing ESCAP economies												
East and North-East Asia												
China	1.4	1.0	1.0	0.9	74.9	74.5	72.9	70.9	70.6	10.0	3.4	10.4
DPR Korea	1.2	0.4	0.8	0.9	63.7	63.0	59.9	59.1	58.9			
Hong Kong, China	1.1	1.5	1.6	2.0	62.6	58.5	56.5	56.2	56.4	4.1	1.4	3.1
Macao, China	2.4	3.3	4.4	3.1	56.5	57.0	59.3	63.4	64.0			
Mongolia	6.5	1.4	3.3	3.6	49.5	57.5	55.4	57.6	58.4			
Republic of Korea	2.2	0.6	1.6	1.1	59.0	59.9	57.4	58.7	58.7	5.0	3.6	2.9
North and Central Asia												
Armenia	-5.7	-2.1	-0.1	0.3	67.6	56.4	50.5	47.8	47.5	-8.4	8.2	15.9
Azerbaijan	1.3	2.2	2.7	3.0	58.5	57.0	58.3	60.0	60.5	-18.8	7.0	19.4
Georgia	-2.0	-1.6	-1.5	-1.0	60.4	57.7	55.5	52.2	51.7	-15.0	5.3	8.5
Kazakhstan	-1.0	-0.8	2.4	1.5	62.8	60.2	60.1	63.6	63.8	-5.3	3.5	6.8
Kyrgyzstan	0.7	2.2	2.5	2.3	58.7	57.5	57.2	57.9	58.1	-12.5	4.1	0.7
Russian Federation	-0.8	0.0	1.0	0.5	58.4	54.1	52.6	54.5	54.8	-7.7	2.2	5.3
Tajikistan	0.2	0.9	1.6	2.2	54.4	51.2	49.1	47.7	47.5	-18.2	-0.2	6.8
Turkmenistan	3.3	3.2	2.6	2.8	57.6	57.6	59.6	59.0	59.0	-12.8	2.7	1.7
Uzbekistan	2.0	3.1	3.1	3.2	55.9	54.3	55.7	56.8	57.0	-5.5	2.7	2.9
Pacific island economies												
American Samoa												
Cook Islands												
Fiji	2.1	1.4	1.3	1.7	60.7	60.7	60.7	61.7	62.0			
French Polynesia												
Guam												
Kiribati												
Marshall Islands												
Micronesia (Federated States of)												
Nauru												
New Caledonia												
Niue												
Northern Mariana Islands												
Palau												
Papua New Guinea	2.2	3.1	2.9	2.8	70.7	69.1	70.2	71.0	71.1			
Samoa												
Solomon Islands	3.6	3.1	3.3	3.2	65.8	65.8	64.8	65.4	65.5			
Tonga												
Tuvalu												
Vanuatu												
South and South-West Asia												
Afghanistan	7.6	2.5	5.0	3.5	55.8	55.8	55.8	58.6	58.2			
Bangladesh	1.8	2.2	2.0	2.3	73.4	70.6	68.5	66.4	66.3	2.8	2.9	3.3
Bhutan	-2.4	3.4	6.6	7.2	54.6	53.6	54.1	58.3	60.2			
India	2.0	2.1	1.9	2.0	58.6	57.2	56.3	55.2	55.1	4.9	4.0	4.9
Iran (Islamic Republic of)	2.2	4.6	4.1	4.0	46.1	44.9	46.8	49.7	50.4	-1.0	-0.7	3.0
Maldives	4.4	4.7	5.3	6.1	49.6	51.3	53.7	58.1	59.6			
Nepal	2.3	2.8	2.6	2.8	59.0	57.9	58.0	57.4	57.4			
Pakistan	2.3	3.1	3.7	5.4	54.4	53.9	53.0	53.7	54.9	2.3	1.1	1.9
Sri Lanka	0.3	2.9	0.7	2.0	51.6	48.1	51.6	50.4	50.9	3.9	1.6	0.4
Turkey	1.5	0.9	1.8	2.0	53.0	50.3	46.8	46.4	46.5	2.2	2.6	3.9
South-East Asia												
Brunei Darussalam	2.9	2.8	2.2	2.6	62.5	61.3	60.7	58.9	58.8			
Cambodia	2.4	3.5	3.2	2.9	78.7	77.5	75.6	75.7	75.5	-1.0	5.7	-1.2
Indonesia	2.2	2.5	1.0	1.5	63.1	62.1	63.0	60.4	60.2	6.3	-1.6	3.5
Lao PDR	2.9	2.7	3.0	3.2	65.3	64.9	65.1	65.5	65.6			
Malaysia	3.1	3.6	2.6	2.7	60.9	60.6	61.3	61.4	61.5	6.6	0.8	2.8
Myanmar	2.2	2.1	1.7	1.4	74.6	73.7	73.7	73.6	73.5	5.0	5.3	8.5
Philippines	3.4	2.0	4.4	3.3	59.1	60.2	58.0	63.3	63.8	0.0	2.3	0.9
Singapore	2.0	3.0	1.5	1.5	64.4	61.8	61.5	59.6	59.2	6.4	2.0	2.3
Thailand	0.8	1.0	1.4	1.0	77.4	73.5	70.8	71.0	70.9	7.4	0.2	3.0
Timor-Leste	1.7	-3.2	8.5	5.9	61.9	61.2	62.1	65.9	66.5			
Viet Nam	2.6	2.4	2.4	2.4	75.4	74.2	73.2	72.4	72.3	6.3	4.2	4.8
Developed ESCAP economies												
Australia	1.9	1.8	1.7	1.5	56.7	56.0	57.1	57.3	57.3	2.3	2.1	1.1
Japan	0.4	-0.1	-0.2	-0.2	62.5	59.2	56.9	54.8	54.5	0.7	1.0	1.6
New Zealand	3.1	1.3	2.6	1.6	56.9	58.5	59.1	62.0	62.1	1.4	1.3	0.7

Source: International Labour Organization, *Key Indicators of the Labour Market, Fifth Edition* (online database, accessed in September 2007).

Table 21. Employment, by economic activity

| | Share of total employment (%) | | | | | | | | | | | |
| | Agriculture | | | | Industry | | | | Services | | | |
	1990	1995	2000	2005	1990	1995	2000	2005	1990	1995	2000	2005
Developing ESCAP economies												
East and North-East Asia												
China	64.9	59.3	60.6		23.1	25.7	22.7		12.1	15.0	16.7	
DPR Korea												
Hong Kong, China	0.9	0.6	0.3	0.3	36.7	27.0	20.3	15.2	62.4	72.4	79.4	84.5
Macao, China	0.2	0.2	0.2	0.1	42.6	32.1	28.2	25.2	57.3	67.7	71.6	74.7
Mongolia		46.1	48.6	39.9		17.9	14.1	16.8		35.9	37.2	43.3
Republic of Korea	17.9	12.4	10.6	7.9	35.4	33.3	28.2	26.9	46.7	54.3	61.2	65.2
North and Central Asia												
Armenia												
Azerbaijan	36.4	36.5	41.0	39.3	26.9	21.1	10.9	12.1	36.6	42.4	48.1	48.6
Georgia			52.2	54.4			9.8	9.3			38.0	36.2
Kazakhstan												
Kyrgyzstan	32.7	47.2	53.1	48.0	27.9	16.7	10.5	12.5	39.4	36.1	36.5	39.5
Russian Federation			14.5	10.2			28.4	29.8			57.1	60.0
Tajikistan	82.1	61.4			0.0	16.1			17.9	22.5		
Turkmenistan												
Uzbekistan		43.3				20.1				36.6		
Pacific island economies												
American Samoa												
Cook Islands												
Fiji												
French Polynesia												
Guam												
Kiribati												
Marshall Islands												
Micronesia (Federated States of)												
Nauru												
New Caledonia												
Niue												
Northern Mariana Islands												
Palau												
Papua New Guinea			73.3				3.7				23.0	
Samoa												
Solomon Islands												
Tonga												
Tuvalu												
Vanuatu												
South and South-West Asia												
Afghanistan												
Bangladesh	69.5		64.8		13.6		10.7		16.9		24.5	
Bhutan												
India	69.1	66.7			13.6	12.9			17.3	20.3		
Iran (Islamic Republic of)	26.4	22.1		25.0	28.3	31.4		30.4	45.3	46.5		44.6
Maldives		23.0	16.5			24.8	22.9			52.2	60.6	
Nepal	83.9	74.8			2.4	5.2			13.8	20.0		
Pakistan	51.2	46.8	48.4	43.1	19.8	18.5	18.0	20.3	29.0	34.6	33.5	36.6
Sri Lanka	48.6	39.6			20.9	24.8			30.5	35.6		
Turkey	46.9	43.4	36.0	29.5	20.7	22.3	24.0	24.7	32.4	34.3	40.0	45.8
South-East Asia												
Brunei Darussalam												
Cambodia			73.8				8.4				17.7	
Indonesia	56.0	44.0	45.1	44.0	13.8	18.4	17.5	18.0	30.3	37.6	37.3	38.0
Lao PDR		85.4				3.5				11.1		
Malaysia	26.0	20.0	18.4		27.5	32.3	32.2		46.5	47.7	49.5	
Myanmar	69.7				9.2				21.0			
Philippines	45.2	44.1	37.5	37.0	15.0	15.6	16.0	14.9	39.7	40.3	46.5	48.1
Singapore		0.2	0.0	0.0		31.2	34.0	29.8		68.5	66.0	70.2
Thailand	64.0	52.0	48.8	42.6	14.0	19.8	19.0	20.3	22.0	28.3	32.2	37.1
Timor-Leste												
Viet Nam			65.3				12.4				22.3	
Developed ESCAP economies												
Australia	5.6	5.0	5.0	3.7	25.1	22.8	21.7	21.1	69.3	72.2	73.3	75.2
Japan	7.3	5.7	5.1	4.5	34.2	33.7	31.4	28.3	58.5	60.6	63.5	67.2
New Zealand	10.6	9.7	8.7	7.2	24.7	25.1	23.3	22.1	64.7	65.2	68.0	70.8

Source: International Labour Organization, *Key Indicators of the Labour Market, Fifth Edition* (online database, accessed in September 2007).

Table 22. Employment, by status

	Share of total sex-specific employment (%)											
	Employees				Employers				Other self-employed			
	Women		Men		Women		Men		Women		Men	
	1990	2005	1990	2005	1990	2005	1990	2005	1990	2005	1990	2005
Developing ESCAP economies												
East and North-East Asia												
China												
DPR Korea												
Hong Kong, China	94.7 (93)	93.3	85.0 (93)	83.2	1.7 (93)	1.8	8.4 (93)	6.8	3.6 (93)	4.9	6.6 (93)	10.0
Macao, China	93.0 (96)	93.4	86.2 (96)	86.0	1.0 (96)	1.5	5.4 (96)	6.2	6.0 (96)	5.1	8.4 (96)	7.8
Mongolia	43.6 (00)	41.9 (03)	39.3 (00)	37.2 (03)	0.8 (00)	0.4 (03)	1.7 (00)	0.7 (03)	55.4 (00)	57.5 (03)	58.4 (00)	62.0 (03)
Republic of Korea	56.8	67.1	63.1	66.0	18.7	3.5	34.4	10.0	24.5	29.4	2.5	24.1
North and Central Asia												
Armenia		87.2 (01)		77.4 (01)				2.2 (01)		12.7 (01)		19.9 (01)
Azerbaijan												
Georgia	43.5 (98)	34.5	42.9 (98)	34.3	0.4 (98)	0.4	2.6 (98)	1.6	55.4 (98)	64.8	53.6 (98)	63.8
Kazakhstan	54.1 (02)	60.2 (04)	61.0 (02)	64.1 (04)	0.5 (02)	0.6 (04)	1.2 (02)	1.6 (04)	45.4 (02)	39.1 (04)	37.8 (02)	34.3 (04)
Kyrgyzstan	44.1 (02)	48.7 (04)	41.7 (02)	48.4 (04)	1.0 (02)	0.8 (04)	2.0 (02)	1.2 (04)	54.9 (02)	50.5 (04)	56.3 (02)	50.4 (04)
Russian Federation	94.4 (92)	92.7	89.9 (92)	91.7	0.0 (92)	1.0	0.2 (92)	1.5	5.6 (92)	6.2	10.0 (92)	6.7
Tajikistan												
Turkmenistan												
Uzbekistan												
Pacific island economies												
American Samoa												
Cook Islands												
Fiji												
French Polynesia												
Guam												
Kiribati												
Marshall Islands												
Micronesia (Federated States of)												
Nauru												
New Caledonia	89.1 (96)		80.5 (96)		10.4 (96)		19.3 (96)		0.5 (96)		0.3 (96)	
Niue												
Northern Mariana Islands												
Palau												
Papua New Guinea												
Samoa												
Solomon Islands												
Tonga												
Tuvalu												
Vanuatu												
South and South-West Asia												
Afghanistan												
Bangladesh	8.7 (96)	13.3 (03)	14.7 (96)	13.8 (03)	0.1 (96)	0.2 (03)	0.3 (96)	0.4 (03)	85.0 (96)	82.2 (03)	59.8 (96)	83.4 (03)
Bhutan												
India												
Iran (Islamic Republic of)	53.7 (96)		51.4 (96)		0.9 (96)		4.0 (96)		40.9 (96)		4.6 (96)	
Maldives	43.9 (95)	28.8 (00)	33.9 (95)	21.3 (00)	2.3 (95)	1.1 (00)	5.7 (95)	4.5 (00)	48.4 (95)	39.7 (00)	55.9 (95)	66.2 (00)
Nepal												
Pakistan	24.8 (95)	31.2	35.4 (95)	39.2	0.3 (95)	0.1	1.1 (95)	1.0	74.9 (95)	68.7	63.5 (95)	59.7
Sri Lanka		59.6 (03)		57.9 (03)		0.9 (03)		3.6 (03)		39.5 (03)		38.6 (03)
Turkey	23.8	43.8	78.1	57.8	0.8 (98)	0.9	8.1 (98)	6.6	76.2	55.3	21.9	35.6
South-East Asia												
Brunei Darussalam												
Cambodia		13.6 (01)		19.1 (01)		0.1 (01)		0.2 (01)		86.2 (01)		80.7 (01)
Indonesia												
Lao PDR	5.4 (95)		14.3 (95)		0.1 (95)		0.4 (95)		94.5 (95)		85.4 (95)	
Malaysia	72.9 (95)	77.5 (03)	72.5 (95)	75.5 (03)	0.7 (95)	1.2 (03)	3.4 (95)	4.6 (03)	26.3 (95)	21.1 (03)	24.2 (95)	19.9 (03)
Myanmar												
Philippines	47.9 (01)	49.7	49.8 (01)	50.8	3.3 (01)	2.4	7.7 (01)	5.9	48.8 (01)	47.9	42.6 (01)	43.4
Singapore	92.4 (91)	91.9 (04)	82.8 (91)	81.2 (04)	2.0 (91)	2.2 (04)	7.4 (91)	7.0 (04)	5.5 (91)	5.9 (04)	9.8 (91)	11.8 (04)
Thailand	25.6	42.9 (04)	31.0	44.5 (04)	0.6	1.5 (04)	1.8	4.3 (04)	73.9	55.5 (04)	67.2	51.2 (04)
Timor-Leste												
Viet Nam	13.5 (96)	21.2 (04)	20.1 (96)	29.8 (04)	0.4 (96)	0.3 (04)	1.1 (96)	0.7 (04)	85.7 (96)	78.5 (04)	78.4 (96)	69.5 (04)
Developed ESCAP economies												
Australia	87.8	90.1	82.8	84.4	3.7	2.4	5.6	3.8	8.5	7.5	11.6	11.8
Japan	72.3	84.6	80.8	85.0	1.3	1.1	4.3	3.6	26.1	13.8	14.5	10.9
New Zealand	97.8	86.6	99.0	77.0	4.8 (91)	4.3	10.2 (91)	8.4	2.2	9.1	1.0	14.5

Source: International Labour Organization, *Key Indicators of the Labour Market, Fifth Edition* (online database, accessed in September 2007).

Table 23. Unemployment, by gender and age group

| | Unemployment rate % of labour force | | | Women to men ratio | | | Youth unemployment rate % of labour force aged 15-24 | | | |
| | | | | | | | Women | | Men | |
	1990	2000	2005	1990	2000	2005	1990	2005	1990	2005
Developing ESCAP economies										
East and North-East Asia										
China	2.5	3.1	4.2				1.0		0.7	
DPR Korea										
Hong Kong, China	1.3	4.9	5.6	0.6	0.5	0.5	3.3	8.0	3.6	13.8
Macao, China	3.0	6.5	4.0	1.5	0.4	0.7		5.8		10.8
Mongolia		17.5			0.8					
Republic of Korea	2.5	4.4	3.7	0.4	0.5	0.6	5.5	9.0	9.5	12.3
North and Central Asia										
Armenia										
Azerbaijan			8.6			1.1				
Georgia		10.8	13.8		0.8	0.8		30.6		26.8
Kazakhstan		12.8								
Kyrgyzstan										
Russian Federation		9.8			0.9					
Tajikistan										
Turkmenistan										
Uzbekistan										
Pacific island economies										
American Samoa										
Cook Islands										
Fiji	6.4									
French Polynesia										
Guam	2.2									
Kiribati										
Marshall Islands			50.0							
Micronesia (Federated States of)										
Nauru										
New Caledonia										
Niue										
Northern Mariana Islands										
Palau										
Papua New Guinea	7.7	2.9		0.5	0.3					
Samoa										
Solomon Islands										
Tonga										
Tuvalu										
Vanuatu										
South and South-West Asia										
Afghanistan			8.5			1.1				
Bangladesh		3.3			0.6					
Bhutan										
India		4.3			0.4					
Iran (Islamic Republic of)		11.5			0.4			32.1		20.3
Maldives		2.3			1.0					
Nepal										
Pakistan	2.6	7.2	7.7	0.0	0.5	0.4	1.3		5.7	
Sri Lanka	14.4	7.4	7.6	1.5	1.0	1.1	46.9	37.1	22.8	20.1
Turkey	8.0	6.5	10.3	0.5	0.3	0.3	15.0	19.3	16.6	19.3
South-East Asia										
Brunei Darussalam										
Cambodia		2.5			1.4					
Indonesia		6.1	10.3		1.0					
Lao PDR			1.4			1.0				
Malaysia	4.7	3.0			0.6					
Myanmar	6.0			0.9						
Philippines	8.1	10.1	7.4	0.8	0.6	0.6	19.2	18.9	13.1	14.9
Singapore	1.7		4.2	0.4	0.8	1.0		6.3		4.1
Thailand	2.2	2.4	1.3	1.0	0.8	0.7	4.2	4.6	4.3	4.9
Timor-Leste										
Viet Nam		2.3			0.9					
Developed ESCAP economies										
Australia	6.9	6.3	5.1	0.8	0.7	0.9	12.4	10.0	13.9	11.0
Japan	2.1	4.8	4.4	0.7	0.6	0.6	4.1	7.4	4.5	9.9
New Zealand	7.8	5.9	3.7	0.7	0.8	1.0	13.2	9.8	14.8	9.1

Sources: International Labour Organization, *Key Indicators of the Labour Market, Fifth Edition* (online database, accessed in September 2007); and United Nations Department of Economic and Social Affairs, *Millennium Development Goals Indicators,* <http://mdgs.un.org/unsd/mdg/Default.aspx> (September 2007).

Table 24. Telecommunications

	Personal computers			Internet users			Telephone subscribers					
							Land lines			Mobile cellular		
	Per 100 population						Per 100 population					
	2000	2004	2005	2000	2005	2006	2000	2005	2006	2000	2005	2006
Developing ESCAP economies												
East and North-East Asia												
China	1.6	4.1	4.2	1.8	8.4	10.4	11.4	26.6	27.8	6.7	29.9	34.8
DPR Korea							2.3	4.4	4.4			
Hong Kong, China	40.2	60.6	59.3	27.8	50.1	53.0	58.9	53.9	54.1	81.7	123.5	131.5
Macao, China	16.2	29.0	34.8	13.9	37.0	43.2	40.9	37.9	38.1	32.7	115.8	137.4
Mongolia	1.4	11.9	12.8	1.3	10.1	10.1	5.0	5.9	5.9	6.5	21.1	21.1
Republic of Korea	40.5	50.5	53.2	41.4	68.4	71.1	56.2	55.9	56.0	58.3	79.4	83.8
North and Central Asia												
Armenia	0.8	6.6	9.9	1.3	5.3	5.8	17.3	19.7	19.7	0.6	10.5	10.5
Azerbaijan		1.8	2.3	0.2	8.1	9.8	9.8	13.0	14.0	5.2	26.7	39.2
Georgia	2.4	4.3	4.7	0.5	6.1	7.5	10.8	12.7	12.5	4.1	26.3	38.4
Kazakhstan				0.7	4.1	8.4	12.2	18.3	19.8	1.3	36.4	52.9
Kyrgyzstan	0.5	1.7	1.9	1.1	5.3	5.6	7.7	8.4	8.4	0.2	10.3	10.3
Russian Federation	6.4	10.4	12.1	2.0	15.2	18.0	21.9	27.9	27.9	2.2	83.6	83.6
Tajikistan		0.3	1.3	0.1	0.3	0.3	3.6	4.3	4.3	0.0	4.1	4.1
Turkmenistan		2.3	7.2	0.1	1.0	1.3	8.2	8.2	8.2	0.2	2.2	2.2
Uzbekistan		2.2	2.8	0.5	3.3	6.3	6.7	6.7	6.7	0.2	2.7	2.7
Pacific island economies												
American Samoa							17.9	16.7	16.7	3.5	3.6	3.6
Cook Islands												
Fiji	4.4	5.2	5.9	1.5	8.3	9.4	10.7	13.3	13.3	6.8	24.2	24.2
French Polynesia	6.3	9.9	10.9	6.3	21.5	25.0	22.6	20.8	20.7	16.8	46.8	58.5
Guam				16.2	38.5	38.5	48.0	50.9		17.6	59.4	59.4
Kiribati	0.9	1.1	1.1	1.8	2.2	2.2	4.0	5.1	5.1	0.4	0.7	0.7
Marshall Islands	3.9	8.8	8.8	1.6			7.8	8.3	8.3	0.9		1.1
Micronesia (Federated States of)				3.7	12.6	14.4	9.0	11.2	11.2		12.7	12.7
Nauru					2.6		15.7	16.0		10.5	13.0	
New Caledonia		2.2	2.5	14.0	32.1	33.2	23.8	23.3	23.3	23.3	56.7	56.7
Niue												
Northern Mariana Islands							30.3			4.3	27.3	27.3
Palau												
Papua New Guinea	5.5	6.3	6.6	0.9	1.8	1.8	1.3	1.1	1.1	0.2	1.3	1.3
Samoa	0.6	1.6	2.0	0.6	3.4	4.5	4.9	10.9	10.9	1.4	13.4	13.4
Solomon Islands	3.8	4.1	4.6	0.5	0.8	1.6	1.8	1.6	1.6	0.3	1.3	1.3
Tonga	1.3	5.0	6.0	2.4	3.0	3.0	9.8	13.7	13.7	0.2	29.8	29.8
Tuvalu				5.3	16.2	16.2	7.0	8.5	8.5		12.4	12.4
Vanuatu	1.3	1.4	1.4	2.1	3.5	3.5	3.5	3.2	3.2	0.2	5.9	5.9
South and South-West Asia												
Afghanistan			0.3		1.0	1.7	0.1	0.3	0.5		4.0	8.1
Bangladesh	0.2	1.2	1.6	0.1	0.3	0.3	0.4	0.8	0.8	0.2	6.4	13.3
Bhutan	0.8	1.4	1.6	0.3	3.1		2.2	4.0			4.7	
India	0.5	1.2	1.5	0.5	5.4	5.4	3.2	4.6	3.6	0.4	8.2	14.8
Iran (Islamic Republic of)				1.0	10.9	25.5	14.9	27.3	31.2	1.5	10.4	19.4
Maldives	3.7	11.0		2.2			9.1		10.9	2.8		87.9
Nepal	0.3	0.5	0.5	0.2	0.8	0.9	1.2	1.8	2.2	0.1	0.8	3.8
Pakistan	0.4	0.5	0.5	0.2	6.8	7.6	2.2	3.4	3.3	0.2	8.3	22.0
Sri Lanka	0.7	2.7	3.5	0.7	1.7	2.1	4.2	6.0	9.0	2.3	16.2	25.9
Turkey	3.7	5.1	5.6	3.7	15.3	16.6	27.0	25.9	25.4	23.6	59.6	71.0
South-East Asia												
Brunei Darussalam	6.9	8.7	8.8	9.0	36.1	43.4	24.3	22.4	21.0	28.6	62.3	66.5
Cambodia	0.1	0.3	0.3	0.1	0.3	0.3	0.2	0.2	0.2	1.0	7.6	7.9
Indonesia	1.0	1.4	1.5	0.9	7.2	7.2	3.2	5.7	6.6	1.8	21.1	28.3
Lao PDR	0.3	0.4	1.7	0.1	0.4	0.4	0.8	1.3	1.3	0.2	10.8	10.8
Malaysia	9.5	19.2	21.5	21.4	42.4	43.8	19.9	16.8	16.8	22.0	75.2	75.5
Myanmar	0.2	0.6	0.7		0.1	0.2	0.5	0.9	0.9	0.0	0.2	0.4
Philippines	1.9	4.5	5.4	2.0	5.5	5.5	4.0	4.0	4.3	8.4	41.3	50.8
Singapore	48.3	65.7	68.0	32.4	39.8	39.2	48.4	42.4	42.3	68.4	100.8	109.3
Thailand	2.8	5.8	6.9	3.7	11.3	13.1	9.1	11.0	10.9	5.0	48.5	63.0
Timor-Leste					0.1	0.1		0.3	0.3		3.5	4.9
Viet Nam	0.8	1.3	1.4	0.3	12.7	17.2	3.2	18.8	18.8	1.0	11.4	18.2
Developed ESCAP economies												
Australia	47.0	68.9	76.6	34.5	70.4	75.1	52.5	50.2	48.8	44.7	91.4	97.0
Japan	31.5	54.2	67.5	29.9	66.6	68.3	48.8	45.3	43.0	52.6	75.3	79.3
New Zealand	35.8	48.2	51.6	39.3	68.4	78.8	47.5	42.9	42.9	40.0	87.6	87.6

Source: International Telecommunication Union, *ICT Statistics Database*, <http://www.itu.int> (August 2007).

Table 25. Infrastructure and transport

	Roads density Km per 1 000 km²		Paved roads % of total roads		Railway density Km per 1 000 km²			Passenger cars in use Per 1 000 population		
	1990	2004	1990	2004	1990	2000	2005	1990	2000	2004
Developing ESCAP economies										
East and North-East Asia										
China	127	201		81	6	6	7	1.4	6.7	13.3
DPR Korea	231									
Hong Kong, China	1 499	1 850	100	100				37.7	52.5	52.0
Macao, China		12 929	100	100				67.2	111.1	130.4
Mongolia	27		10		1	1	1			
Republic of Korea	574	1 016	72	87	31	32	34	48.4	172.8	222.7
North and Central Asia										
Armenia			99			30	26			
Azerbaijan		715		49			26	36.1	40.8	48.6
Georgia		291	94	39		22	19	88.3	51.9	83.5
Kazakhstan		33	55	93		5	5	49.0	66.9	79.7
Kyrgyzstan			90				2	44.4	38.4	38.0
Russian Federation			74			5	5	60.3	137.3	166.5
Tajikistan			72				4		19.0	
Turkmenistan			74				5			
Uzbekistan			79			9	9			
Pacific island economies										
American Samoa								84.9		
Cook Islands										
Fiji	167		44				33	55.3	76.1	98.4
French Polynesia										
Guam								530.2	418.9	
Kiribati										
Marshall Islands										
Micronesia (Federated States of)			16							
Nauru										
New Caledonia								315.7	404.6	
Niue										
Northern Mariana Islands										
Palau										
Papua New Guinea	41		3						4.6	
Samoa										
Solomon Islands	43		2							
Tonga								21.2	51.0	
Tuvalu										
Vanuatu			22					26.8	15.8	
South and South-West Asia										
Afghanistan	32	53	13	24				2.4	0.3	
Bangladesh	1 444				21	21	22	0.4		
Bhutan	50		77							
India	673				21	21	21	3.1	5.9	
Iran (Islamic Republic of)	80				3	4	4	27.5	17.2	
Maldives								4.6	7.3	6.9
Nepal	48	122	38	30			0	1.1	2.0	
Pakistan	219	335	54	65	11	10	10	4.9	7.4	8.8
Sri Lanka	1 439				22			10.2	17.9	26.6
Turkey	477	555			11	11	11	28.8	64.9	75.0
South-East Asia										
Brunei Darussalam	192		31	78				416.3	548.8	618.0
Cambodia	203	217	8	6	3	3	4	0.5	0.6	
Indonesia	159		45					7.2	14.4	
Lao PDR	61		24							
Malaysia	262	300	70	81	5	5	5	8.6	15.0	19.1
Myanmar	38		11		5			1.9	3.8	4.0
Philippines	538				2			17.5	28.3	14.8
Singapore	4 176	4 627	97	100				95.1	103.1	102.5
Thailand	141		55		8	8		22.5	43.9	47.8
Timor-Leste										
Viet Nam	295	717	24		9	10	9			
Developed ESCAP economies										
Australia	105		35		1	1	1	454.7		529.3
Japan	3 057		69		56	55	55	282.7	415.1	438.2
New Zealand	346		57		15			440.1	494.5	530.3

Sources: World Bank, *World Development Indicators*, <http://devdata.worldbank.org/data-query> (September 2007); United Nations Department of Economic and Social Affairs, Statistics Division, United Nations Common Database, <http://unstats.un.org/unsd/cdb/cdb_help/cdb_quick_start.asp> (September 2007); and Food and Agriculture Organization of the United Nations FAOSTAT database, <http://faostat.fao.org/site/348/default.aspx> (September 2007).

Table 26. Land area and use

	Surface area km²	Population density Persons per km²	Forested land area as a share of land area (%)			Protected area as a share of land area (%)		
	2006	2006	1990	2000	2005	1990	2000	2005
Developing ESCAP economies								
East and North-East Asia								
China	9 598 060	138	16.8	19.0	21.2	11.6	13.7	14.9
DPR Korea	120 540	197	68.1	56.6	51.4	2.4	2.4	2.4
Hong Kong, China	1 092	6 531						
Macao, China	28	16 934						
Mongolia	1 566 500	2	7.3	6.8	6.5	4.1	13.9	13.9
Republic of Korea	99 260	484	64.5	63.8	63.5	3.8	3.9	3.9
North and Central Asia								
Armenia	29 800	101	12.3	10.8	10.0	9.1	9.1	10.0
Azerbaijan	86 600	97	11.3	11.3	11.3	6.1	6.6	7.3
Georgia	69,700	64	39.7	39.7	39.7	3.0	4.0	4.0
Kazakhstan	2 724 900	6	1.3	1.2	1.2	2.5	2.9	2.9
Kyrgyzstan	199 900	26	4.4	4.5	4.5	2.9	3.6	3.6
Russian Federation	17 098 240	8	47.9	47.9	47.9	7.5	8.8	8.8
Tajikistan	142 550	47	2.9	2.9	2.9	6.8	18.2	18.2
Turkmenistan	488 100	10	8.8	8.8	8.8	4.0	4.1	4.1
Uzbekistan	447 400	60	7.4	7.8	8.0	2.0	4.6	4.6
Pacific island economies								
American Samoa	200	327	91.9	90.3	89.4			
Cook Islands	240	57	63.9	66.5	66.5			
Fiji	18 270	46	53.6	54.7	54.7	0.2	0.3	0.3
French Polynesia	4 000	65	28.7	28.7	28.7			
Guam	550	311	47.1	47.1	47.1			
Kiribati	730	128	3.0	3.0	3.0	0.8	1.5	1.5
Marshall Islands	180	322						
Micronesia (Federated States of)	700	158						
Nauru	20	507						
New Caledonia	18 580	13	39.2	39.2	39.2			
Niue	260	6	66.2	58.1	54.2			
Northern Mariana Islands	477	172						
Palau	460	44	82.9	86.1	87.6		0.3	0.4
Papua New Guinea	462 840	13	69.6	66.5	65.0	3.3	3.6	3.6
Samoa	2 840	65	45.9	60.4	60.4	0.8	1.6	1.8
Solomon Islands	28 900	17	98.9	84.7	77.6		0.1	0.2
Tonga	750	133	5.0	5.0	5.0	0.1	27.6	27.8
Tuvalu	30	350						
Vanuatu	12 190	18	36.1	36.1	36.1	0.1	0.2	0.2
South and South-West Asia								
Afghanistan	652 090	40	2.0	1.6	1.3	0.3	0.3	0.3
Bangladesh	144 000	1 083	6.8	6.8	6.7	0.4	1.2	1.3
Bhutan	47 000	14	64.6	66.8	68.0		26.4	26.4
India	3 287 260	350	21.5	22.7	22.8	4.8	5.4	5.4
Iran (Islamic Republic of)	1 648 200	43	6.8	6.8	6.8	4.7	5.4	6.6
Maldives	300	1 001	3.0	3.0	3.0			
Nepal	147 180	188	33.7	27.3	25.4	6.8	16.0	16.3
Pakistan	796 100	202	3.3	2.7	2.5	9.0	9.1	9.1
Sri Lanka	65 610	293	36.4	32.2	29.9	15.5	17.1	17.2
Turkey	783 560	94	12.6	13.1	13.2	2.6	3.9	3.9
South-East Asia								
Brunei Darussalam	5 770	66	59.4	54.6	52.8	32.9	38.3	38.3
Cambodia	181 040	78	73.3	65.4	59.2	0.1	21.6	21.6
Indonesia	1 904 570	120	64.3	54.0	48.8	6.6	8.8	9.1
Lao PDR	236 800	24	75.0	71.6	69.9	0.9	16.0	16.0
Malaysia	329 740	79	68.1	65.7	63.6	15.9	17.2	17.3
Myanmar	676 580	72	59.6	52.5	49.0	1.2	2.6	4.6
Philippines	300 000	288	35.5	26.7	24.0	4.0	6.4	6.5
Singapore	699	6 269	3.4	3.4	3.4	2.1	2.1	2.2
Thailand	513 120	124	31.2	29.0	28.4	13.0	18.8	19.0
Timor-Leste	14 870	75	65.0	57.4	53.7		1.2	1.2
Viet Nam	329 310	262	28.8	36.0	39.7	0.9	3.1	3.6
Developed ESCAP economiesa								
Australia	7 741 220	3	21.9	21.4	21.3	9.1	15.0	17.5
Japan	377 910	339	68.4	68.2	68.2	8.0	8.5	8.6
New Zealand	270 530	15	28.8	30.7	31.0	16.3	17.9	19.6

Sources: World Bank, *World Development Indicators,* <http://devdata.worldbank.org/data-query> (September 2007); United Nations Department of Economic and Social Affairs, Statistics Division, United Nations Common Database, <http://unstats.un.org/unsd/cdb/cdb_help/cdb_quick_start.asp> (September 2007); United Nations Department of Economic and Social Affairs, Population Division, *World Population Prospects, The 2006 Revision,* <http://esa.un.org/unpp/> (June 2007); and Food and Agriculture Organization of the United Nations, FAOSTAT database, <http://faostat.fao.org/site/348/default.aspx> (September 2007).

Table 27. Energy and water use

	Consumption of electricity for domestic purposes		Energy use per $1 000 [2000 PPP] GDP			Water withdrawal					
						Share of total renewable water resources (%)			Withdrawal for domestic purposes cubic metres per capita		
	kilowatt-hrs. per capita		kgs. of oil equivalent								
	2000	2004	1990	2000	2004	88-92	93-97	98-02	1990	1995	2000
Developing ESCAP economies											
East and North-East Asia											
China	132	189	470	226	226	17.7	18.6	22.3	30.5	21.2 (93)	32.7
DPR Korea								11.7			78.0
Hong Kong, China	1 344	1 358	95	88	85						
Macao, China	1 186	1 037									
Mongolia	124	222					1.2	1.3		36.4 (93)	36.4
Republic of Korea	793	1 020	220	251	234			26.7		139.0 (94)	141.5
North and Central Asia											
Armenia	506	543	427	278	183	33.3	27.8	28.0	273.1	268.1	285.5
Azerbaijan	1 385	1 433	539	578	436	51.4	54.6	57.0	102.2	99.9	101.9
Georgia	564	625		307	231	5.5		5.7	133.3		152.5
Kazakhstan	395	389		614	568	33.4	30.7	31.9	38.3	36.6	39.5
Kyrgyzstan	475	483		332	313	53.4	49.0	49.0	62.6	66.2 (94)	64.7
Russian Federation	955	990		599	494	1.8	1.7	1.7	98.6	95.8 (94)	97.5
Tajikistan	527	478		581	456	75.2	74.3	74.8	91.5	72.4 (94)	71.3
Turkmenistan	272	279		942		100.1	96.2	99.7	52.1	85.1 (94)	93.3
Uzbekistan	292	292	1 359	1 203		124.0	115.2	115.7	100.0	114.9 (94)	112.0
Pacific island economies											
American Samoa											
Cook Islands											
Fiji	119	134						0.2			12.5
French Polynesia											
Guam	3 478	2 987									
Kiribati											
Marshall Islands											
Micronesia (Federated States of)											
Nauru											
New Caledonia											
Niue	1 598	1 795									
Northern Mariana Islands											
Palau											
Papua New Guinea	23	21						0.0			7.4
Samoa	225	258									
Solomon Islands											
Tonga											
Tuvalu											
Vanuatu											
South and South-West Asia											
Afghanistan	5	5						35.8			20.3
Bangladesh	39	55	103	94	93			6.6	15.0	32.5 (94)	18.1
Bhutan	54	69						0.4			35.8
India	72	86	257	213	186	26.4		34.1	29.1		49.9
Iran (Islamic Republic of)	473	591	268	321	315		50.9	53.0		72.9 (93)	75.0
Maldives	161	231									
Nepal	22	26	293	252	249			4.8		11.6 (94)	12.3
Pakistan	149	178	246	246	242	69.9		76.1			22.7
Sri Lanka	93	116	138	121	124	19.5		25.2	11.4		16.0
Turkey	350	383	173	177	163	14.8		17.6			81.6
South-East Asia											
Brunei Darussalam	2 420	3 167				0.9	1.1				
Cambodia								0.9			4.7
Indonesia	144	143	246	244	244	2.6		2.9	25.9		31.3
Lao PDR								0.9			24.9
Malaysia	487	609	228	248	243	1.7		1.6	45.2	65.2	65.3
Myanmar	28	45						3.2			8.9
Philippines	169	192	116	139	122		5.8	6.0		62.2	62.1
Singapore	1 425	1 527	293	235	237						
Thailand	321	395	175	192	204			21.2	27.6		35.8
Timor-Leste											
Viet Nam	139	217	319	236	240	6.1		8.0	30.2		70.0
Developed ESCAP economies											
Australia	2 548	2 834	254	225	207			4.9			183.9
Japan	2 030	2 143	152	160	154	21.3		20.6	136.7 (92)		137.0
New Zealand	2 941	3 026	238	227	197			0.6			264.7

Sources: United Nations Department of Economic and Social Affairs, Statistics Division, *Energy Statistics Yearbook,* <http://unstats.un.org/unsd/energy/yearbook/default.htm> (September 2007); Food and Agriculture Organization of the United Nations, AQUASTAT database, <http://www.fao.org/AG/AGL/aglw/aquastat/dbases/index.stm>(September 2007); and United Nations Department of Economic and Social Affairs, Statistics Division, *Millennium Development Goals Indicators,* <http://mdgs.un.org/unsd/mdg/Default.aspx> (September 2007).

Table 28. Pollution and access to water and sanitation

| | CO_2 emissions | | Ozone-depleting substances use | | Share of population with access to improved drinking water sources (%) | | | | Share of population with access to improved sanitation (%) | | | |
| | Tons per capita | | kgs per 1 000 pop. | | Rural | | Urban | | Rural | | Urban | |
	1990	2004	1990	2005	1990	2004	1990	2004	1990	2004	1990	2004
Developing ESCAP economies												
East and North-East Asia												
China	2.1	3.8	51.9	23.6	59	67	99	93	7	28	64	69
DPR Korea	12.2	3.4		12.0	100	100	100	100		60		58
Hong Kong, China	4.6	5.4										
Macao, China	2.8	4.7										
Mongolia	4.5	3.3		1.5	30	30	87	87		37		75
Republic of Korea	5.6	9.8		111.5		71	97	97				
North and Central Asia												
Armenia		1.2		28.8		80	99	99		61	96	96
Azerbaijan		3.8		2.6	51	59	82	95		36		73
Georgia		0.9		7.6	67	67	91	96	94	91	99	96
Kazakhstan		13.3	142.5	2.6	73	73	97	97	52	52	87	87
Kyrgyzstan		1.1		3.1	66	66	98	98	51	51	75	75
Russian Federation		10.5	878.6	5.4	86	88	97	100	70	70	93	93
Tajikistan		0.8		0.5		48		92		45		70
Turkmenistan		8.8	39.6	5.6		54		93		50		77
Uzbekistan		5.3		0.2	91	75	99	95	39	61	69	78
Pacific island economies												
American Samoa												
Cook Islands	1.2	2.0			87	88	99	98	91	100	100	100
Fiji	1.1	1.3	57.8	7.2		51		43	55	55	87	87
French Polynesia	3.1	2.7			100	100	100	100	97	99	99	97
Guam					100	100	100	100	98	99	99	98
Kiribati	0.3	0.3			33	53	76	77	21	22	33	59
Marshall Islands				26.2	97	96	95	82	51	58	88	93
Micronesia (Federated States of)				9.1	86	94	93	95	20	14	54	61
Nauru	14.4	14.2										
New Caledonia	9.4	11.2										
Niue	1.6	2.2			100	100	100	100	100	100	100	100
Northern Mariana Islands					100	97	98	98	78	94	85	96
Palau	15.7	11.9			98	94	73	79	54	52	76	96
Papua New Guinea	0.6	0.4		3.1	32	32	88	88	41	41	67	67
Samoa	0.8	0.8			89	87	99	90	98	100	100	100
Solomon Islands	0.5	0.4	6.6	2.1		65		94		18	98	98
Tonga	0.8	1.2			100	100	100	100	96	96	98	98
Tuvalu					89	92	92	94	74	84	83	93
Vanuatu	0.4	0.4			53	52	93	86		42		78
South and South-West Asia												
Afghanistan	0.2	0.0		5.8	3	31	10	63	2	29	7	49
Bangladesh	0.1	0.2	1.8	1.8	69	72	83	82	12	35	55	51
Bhutan	0.2	0.7				60		86		70		65
India	0.8	1.2		3.8	64	83	89	95	3	22	45	59
Iran (Islamic Republic of)	3.9	6.3	24.6	35.3	84	84	99	99	78		86	
Maldives	0.7	2.5	20.9	10.2	95	76	100	98		42	100	100
Nepal	0.0	0.1			67	89	95	96	7	30	48	62
Pakistan	0.6	0.8	12.9	3.8	78	89	95	96	17	41	82	92
Sri Lanka	0.2	0.6	12.7	8.6	62	74	91	98	64	89	89	98
Turkey	2.6	3.1	76.0	10.9	74	93	92	98	70	72	96	96
South-East Asia												
Brunei Darussalam	22.7	24.1		112.4								
Cambodia	0.0	0.0		3.7		35		64		8		53
Indonesia	1.2	1.7		12.1	63	69	92	87	37	40	65	73
Lao PDR	0.1	0.2		3.7		43		79		20		67
Malaysia	3.1	7.0	231.7	26.2	96	96	100	100		93	95	95
Myanmar	0.1	0.2		0.3	47	77	86	80	16	72	48	88
Philippines	0.7	1.0	56.8	14.6	80	82	95	87	48	59	66	80
Singapore	15.0	12.2	1 609.6	34.9			100	100			100	100
Thailand	1.8	4.3	128.6	36.8	94	100	98	98	74	99	95	98
Timor-Leste		0.2				56		77		33		66
Viet Nam	0.3	1.2		5.4	59	80	90	99	30	50	58	92
Developed ESCAP economies												
Australia	16.5	16.3	440.6	8.3	100	100	100	100	100	100	100	100
Japan	8.7	9.8	972.0	8.4	100	100	100	100	100	100	100	100
New Zealand	6.6	7.8	350.5	10.3	82		100	100	88			

Sources: United Nations Department of Economic and Social Affairs, Statistics Division, *Millennium Development Goals Indicators,* <http://mdgs.un.org/unsd/mdg/Default.aspx> (September 2007); and United Nations Department of Economic and Social Affairs, Population Division, *World Population Prospects, The 2006 Revision* <http://esa.un.org/unpp> (June 2007).

Technical notes

Table 1. Real GDP growth rates

GDP growth rate at constant prices. The real (at constant market prices) annual percentage changes in GDP in national currencies are reported in this table. Most countries use constant market price values. The growth rates of some countries are at factor cost, including Fiji, India, the Islamic Republic of Iran and Pakistan, while Bhutan is at purchasers' prices and Nepal at producers' prices. The table contains historical data from 1995 to 2006. Historical data are based on United Nations Statistics Division, *National Accounts Main Aggregates Database* with updates from national and local sources. The data for 2007 are generally ESCAP estimates and calculations, although some projections are in line with the economic programmes/ projections of the governments concerned.

Tables 2 and 3. Gross domestic savings and investment rates

Gross domestic savings (GDS) and investment (GDI). Gross domestic savings are calculated as the difference between GDP and total consumption expenditure in the national accounts statistics. Gross domestic investment (GDI) is the sum of gross fixed capital formation and changes in inventories. Gross fixed capital formation is measured by the total value of a producer's acquisitions, minus disposals of fixed assets in a given accounting period. Additions to the value of non-produced assets, e.g. land, form part of gross fixed capital formation. Inventories are stocks of goods held by institutional units to meet temporary or unexpected fluctuations in production and sales. All figures used in computing the GDS and GDI as a percentage of GDP are in current prices. Historical data are mostly based on ADB, *Key indicators of Developing Asian and Pacific Countries 2007* and updated with national and local sources and input provided by country authorities. The 2007 data are obtained from input supplied by national authorities and ESCAP calculations and estimates.

Table 4. Inflation rates

Inflation rates. Rates of inflation in this table refer to changes in the consumer price index (CPI) and reflect changes in the cost of acquiring a fixed basket of goods and services by an average consumer. Historical data are based on IMF, *World Economic Outlook Database,* October 2007, with updates and estimates from national and local sources, statistical publications, secondary publications and documents from IMF. The figures for 2007 are generally estimates and based on ESCAP calculations. The projections/estimates are also provided by country authorities. For India, data refer to the industrial workers index. Consumer price inflation for the following countries are for a given city or group of consumers: Cambodia is for Phnom Penh; Sri Lanka is for Colombo; Timor-Leste is for Dili and the data for Nepal is for national urban consumers.

Table 5. Budget balance

Government surplus or deficit, as share of GDP. The government fiscal balance (surplus/deficit) is the difference between total revenues and total expenditures as a percentage of GDP. This provides a picture of the changes in the government's financial position each year. When the difference is positive, the fiscal position is in surplus; otherwise, it is in deficit. Government revenue is the sum of current and capital revenues. Current revenue is the revenue accruing from taxes, as well as all current non-tax revenues, except for transfers received from other (foreign or domestic) governments and international institutions. Major items of non-tax revenue include receipts from government enterprises, rents and royalties, fees and fines,

forfeits, private donations and repayments of loans properly defined as components of net lending. Capital revenue is the proceeds from the sale of non-financial capital assets. As for government expenditure, it is the sum of current and capital expenditure. Current expenditure comprises purchases of goods and services by the central government, transfers to non-central government units and to households, subsidies to producers and the interest on public debt. Capital expenditures, on the other hand, cover outlays for the acquisition or construction of capital assets and for the purchase of land and intangible assets, as well as capital transfers to domestic and foreign recipients. Loans and advances for capital purposes are also included. In most countries, the budget surplus/deficit is the balance and excludes grants. In the case of Armenia, Azerbaijan, Bhutan, Cook Islands, Fiji, Georgia, India, Kazakhstan, Kyrgyzstan, Maldives, Mongolia, Myanmar, Nepal, Papua New Guinea, Philippines, Russian Federation, Samoa, Solomon Islands, Tajikistan, Timor-Leste, Tonga, Turkey, Tuvalu, Uzbekistan, Vanuatu and Viet Nam, the budget balance includes grants. The budget surplus/deficit of Singapore is computed from government operating revenue minus government operating expenditure and minus government development expenditure; while the budget balance of Thailand refers to a government cash balance comprising the budgetary balance and non-budgetary balance. For developed ESCAP member countries, the budget balance refers to general government fiscal balance. In the case of Australia, budget balance also refers to data on a cash basis, and in the case of New Zealand, the government balance comprises revenue minus expenditure plus the balance of State-owned enterprises, excluding privatization receipts.

Table 6. Current account balance

Current account balance, as share of GDP. The current account balance refers to the net difference between credit and debit flows from goods, services and income. It also includes current transfers crossing national borders. In contrast, transactions in financial assets and liabilities are recorded in the capital account. A positive (a negative) balance shows that the foreign currencies flow into (out of) the domestic economy. The figures are reported as a percentage of GDP (current prices, national currency) to allow for cross-country comparisons. Historical data are mainly based on *International Financial Statistics* (IMF) with updates and estimates from national and local sources. The 2007 data are derived from projections supplied by national authorities and ESCAP estimates.

Table 7. Changes in money supply

Growth of money supply. The annual growth rates of board money supply (at the end of a given period) as represented by M2. M2 is defined as the sum of currency in circulation plus demand deposits (M1) and quasi-money, which consists of time and savings deposits, including foreign currency deposits. Historical data for M2 are mainly obtained from IMF publications with updates and estimates from national and local sources. The data for 2007 are computed by ESCAP on the basis of IMF data and estimates based on national sources.

Tables 8 and 9. Growth rates of merchandise exports and imports

Growth rates of exports and imports. The annual growth rates of exports and imports, in terms of merchandise goods only, are shown in these tables. Data are in millions of United States dollars primarily obtained from the balance-of-payments accounts of each country. Exports in general are reported on a free-on-board (f.o.b.) basis. In this case, exports are valued at the customs frontier of the exporting country; export duties are levied along with the costs of loading the goods onto the carriers unless the latter is borne by the carrier. It excludes the cost of freight and insurance beyond the customs frontier. As for imports, data are reported either on an f.o.b. or c.i.f. (cost, insurance, freight) basis. On a c.i.f. basis, the value of imports includes the cost of international freight and insurance up to the customs frontier of the importing country. It excludes the cost of unloading the goods from the carrier unless this cost is borne by the carrier.

Historical data on exports and imports are mainly obtained from country sources, statistical publications, and secondary publications. The figures for 2007 are generally estimates based on country sources and calculations by ESCAP and are also provided by national consultants.

Table 10 – Population, size and dynamics

Total population. De facto mid-year population, covering all residents, regardless of legal status or citizenship, except for refugees not permanently settled in the country of asylum.

Average annual population growth rate. The average annual rate of change in the total population over a five-year period, starting and ending in the middle of the years indicated.

Total fertility rate. The number of children a woman would have by the end of her reproductive period if she experienced the current prevailing age-specific fertility rates throughout her childbearing life. Reported as annual averages for five-year periods starting and ending in the middle of the indicated years.

Table 11 – Population, structure

Proportion of children in total population. The proportion of children aged 0-14 in the total population.

Proportion of elderly in total population. The proportion of people aged 65 or older in the total population.

Population sex ratio. The number of women divided by the number of men in the total population, expressed per 100 men.

Urbanization rate. Population living in areas classified as urban according to the administrative criteria used by each country or area, as a percentage of the total population.

Table 12 – International migration

Stock of foreign population. Estimated number of international immigrants, male and female, in the middle of the year indicated. Generally represents the number of persons born in a country other than where they live.

Stock of foreign population as a share of total population. The number of international immigrants divided by the total population. Expressed as a percentage in the middle of the year indicated. Where data on the place of birth was unavailable, the number of non-citizens was used as a proxy for the number of international immigrants. In either case, the migrant stock includes refugees, some of whom may not be foreign-born.

Crude net migration rate. The number of international immigrants minus the number of emigrants over a period, divided by the person-years lived by the population of the receiving country over that period. Expressed as the net number of migrants per 1,000 population.

Table 13 – Primary education

Net primary enrolment rate. The net primary education enrolment rate is the number of children of official primary school age (as defined by the national educational system) who are enrolled in primary school divided by the total population of children of official primary school age.

Country notes

India: projected at the national level (593 districts) on the basis of data by age collected for International Standard Classification of Education (ISCED) level 1 in a sample of 193 districts under the District Information System on Education.

Cook Islands, Kiribati, Marshall Islands, Niue, Palau: national population data were used to calculate enrolment ratios.

Russian Federation: the most common structure is three grades of primary education starting at age 7. However, there is also a four-grade structure, in which about one third of primary pupils are enrolled. Gross enrolment ratios may therefore be overestimated.

China: children enter primary school at age 6 or 7. As the most common entrance age is 7 years, enrolment ratios were calculated using the 7-11 age group for both enrolment and population.

Ratio of girls to boys. This is the ratio of the female gross enrolment rate in primary school to the male gross enrolment rate.

Country notes: Refer to the country notes for the "net [primary] enrolment rate" indicator.

Completion rate is the percentage of students completing the last year of primary school. It is calculated by taking the total number of students in the last grade of primary school, minus the number of repeaters in that grade, divided by the total number of children of official graduation age. The primary completion rate reflects the primary cycle as defined by the International Standard Classification of Education (ISCED), ranging from three or four years of primary education (in a very small number of countries) to five or six years (in most countries) and seven (in a small number of countries). Because curricula and standards for school completion vary across countries, a high rate of primary completion does not necessarily mean high levels of student learning.

Country notes

Cook Islands, Kiribati, Marshall Islands, Nauru, Palau and Tuvalu: national population data were used to calculate enrolment ratios.

Table 14 – Secondary and tertiary education

Net [secondary] education enrolment rate. The net secondary enrolment rate is the ratio of the number of children of official secondary school age (as defined by the national educational system) who are enrolled in secondary school to the total population of children of official secondary school age.

Ratio of girls to boys, secondary level enrolment. This is the ratio of female gross enrolment rate in secondary school to the male gross enrolment rate.

Gross [tertiary] education enrolment rate. Gross tertiary enrolment ratio refers to the number of students enrolled in the tertiary level of education, regardless of age, as a percentage of the total population of official school age for that level. The gross enrolment ratio can be greater than 100% as a result of grade repetition and entry at ages younger or older than the typical age at that grade level.

Ratio of women to men (tertiary level enrolment). The ratio of women to men in tertiary education is the number of female students enrolled at the tertiary level in public and private schools divided by the number of male students. When analysing the data, one needs to bear in mind that the sex ratio at birth is significantly unbalanced in some countries. This imbalance, of course, then influences the ratio of women to men in education.

Country notes

Marshall Islands and Palau: national population data were used to calculate enrolment ratios.

Table 15 – Life expectancy

Life expectancy. The number of years a newborn infant would live if prevailing patterns of age-specific mortality rates at the time of birth were to stay the same throughout the child's life.

Table 16 – Health, morbidity

Number of adults aged 15 and above living with HIV/AIDS. The estimated number of adults aged 15 and above who are infected or living with HIV/AIDS at a given point in time. Data for both sexes combined and for female adults only are reported.

HIV prevalence rate, ages 15-49. The proportion of the population aged 15-49 living with HIV/AIDS at a given point in time in the total population.

Malaria incidence, reported cases. The number of new cases of malaria reported in a given time period, expressed per 100,000 population.

Tuberculosis incidence. Refers to the estimated number of new TB cases that arise during the given time period, i.e. 2004 (expressed as a per capita rate). A tuberculosis case is defined as a patient in whom tuberculosis has been bacteriologically confirmed or diagnosed by a clinician. All forms of TB are included, as are cases of people infected with HIV.

Tuberculosis prevalence. The number of people living with tuberculosis per 100,000 population.

Table 17 – Mortality

Infant mortality rate. Typically defined as the number of infants dying before reaching the age of one year per 1,000 live births in a given year.

Children under 5 mortality rate. The probability (expressed as a rate per 1,000 live births) of a child born in a specified year dying before reaching the age of five if subject to current age-specific mortality rates.

Children 1 yr old immunized against measles. The proportion of one-year-old children who have received at least one dose of the measles vaccine.

Maternal mortality, number. The number of deaths of women from pregnancy-related causes, while pregnant or within 42 days of termination of pregnancy, during a specified year.

Maternal mortality ratio. The maternal mortality ratio refers to the number of maternal deaths per 100,000 live births during a specified time period, usually one year. The maternal mortality ratio can be calculated directly from data collected through vital registration sys-

tems, household surveys or other sources. However, those sources all have data quality problems, particularly as regards the underreporting and misclassification of maternal deaths. The World Health Organization, the United Nations Children's Fund and the United Nations Population Fund have developed a method to adjust existing data in order to take into account these data quality issues. The method involves a dual approach whereby existing data are adjusted for underreporting and misclassification of deaths and model-based estimates are made for countries with no reliable national-level data.

Table 18 – Poverty and malnutrition

Share of population below $1 (1993 PPP) per day. The percentage of the population living on less than $1.08 a day at 1993 international prices. The $1 a day poverty line is compared with consumption or income per person and includes consumption from the person's own production and income in kind. Because this poverty line has fixed purchasing power across countries or areas, the $1 a day poverty line is often called an "absolute poverty line".

Country notes

The value of 2 per cent indicates that the actual headcount is less than or equal to 2 per cent and should be treated with caution. This is the case for Armenia, Georgia, the Islamic Republic of Iran, Kazakhstan, Kyrgyzstan, Malaysia, the Russian Federation and Thailand.

Share of population below the national poverty line. This indicator describes the proportion of the population whose incomes are below the official threshold (or thresholds) set by the national government. National poverty lines are usually set for households of various compositions to allow for different family sizes. Where there are no official poverty lines, they may be defined as the level of income required to have only sufficient food or food plus other necessities for survival.

Gini coefficient of income distribution. The Gini coefficient measures the extent to which the distribution of income (or consumption) among individuals or households within a country deviates from a perfectly equal distribution. A Gini coefficient of 0 represents perfect equality, while a coefficient of 1 represents perfect inequality.

Children under 5 moderately or severely underweight. The proportion of children aged 0-59 months who fall below by more than three standard deviations from the median weight for age of the NCHS/WHO standard reference population. In a normally distributed population, only 0.13 per cent of children would be expected to be severely underweight.

Table 19 – Gender parity

Women in wage employment in the non-agricultural sector, a as share of total non-agricultural employees. This indicator refers to the share of female workers in wage employment in the non-agricultural sector expressed as a percentage of total wage employment in the sector. The non-agricultural sector includes industry and services. Employment refers to people above a certain minimum age who worked or held a job during a reference period. Employment data include both full-time and part-time workers whose remuneration is determined on the basis of hours worked or number of items produced and is independent of profits or expectation of profits.

Percentage of female to male employers. The number of female employers divided by the number the male employers, expressed as a percentage.

Percentage difference in the employment of women and men compared with population ratios. The ratio of employed women aged 15 and above divided by the population of women in the same age group minus the ratio of employed men aged 15 and above divided by the population of men in the same age group.

Women in parliamentary seats, as a share of the total number of parliamentarians. This refers to the number of seats held by women in national parliaments expressed as a percentage of all occupied seats.

Table 20 – Employment growth, share of total population and productivity

Average annual employment growth rate. The average annual increment in the number of employed persons during a five-year interval is calculated on the basis of the geometric growth model with annual compounding (see statistical methods).

Country notes

Primary sources of data of countries as reported in Laborsta are Labour Force Surveys (LFS) except for the following: population censuses for American Samoa, Brunei Darussalam, Islamic Republic of Iran (1996), Lao People's Democratic Republic, Maldives, Marshall Islands (1999) and New Caledonia; official estimates for Armenia, Azerbaijan, China, Kazakhstan (years prior to 2001), Kyrgyzstan, Mongolia, Myanmar, Tajikistan and Uzbekistan.

Employment to population ratio. Refers to the number of employed persons aged 15 and above divided by the total population in the same age group.

Average annual labour productivity growth rate. The output (measured as value added in 1990 PPP dollars) divided by the total number of employed persons, expressed as the average annual rate of change.

Table 21 – Employment, by economic activity

Share of total employment – agriculture, industry and services. Refers to the share of agriculture, industry, and services in total employment. All persons working in a given establishment are classified under the same economic activity irrespective of their particular occupations.

Table 22 – Employment, by status

Share of total sex-specific employment – employees, employers and other self-employed. Employment by status refers to the share of each status group in total employment. Status refers to job classifications with respect to the type of explicit or implicit contract of employment the person has with other persons or organizations. The basic criteria used to define groups are the type of economic risk and the type of authority over establishments and other workers which the job incumbent has (or will have). The International Classification of Status in Employment (ICSE) recognizes five groups: employers, own-account workers, employees, members of producers' cooperatives and contributing family workers. Due to space constraints, own-account workers, members of producers' cooperatives, and contributing family workers are grouped together in this publication under "Other self-employed".

Table 23 – Unemployment, by gender and age group

Unemployment rate. The unemployment rate is calculated by dividing the number of persons who are unemployed during the reference period by the total number of employed and unemployed persons during the same period. The unemployed comprise all persons above a specified age who were not employed during a specified reference period but were available for work and had taken concrete steps to seek paid employment or self-employment. National definitions of unemployment may differ from this recommended international standard definition. Beyond the question of definition, measuring employ-

ment remains a challenge, particularly in countries with large informal and agricultural sectors underreporting is common, especially in the case of women.

Ratio of women to men. Refers to the female unemployment rate divided by the male unemployment rate. A ratio above 1 indicates, for example, that there were more women than men unemployed during the reference period.

Youth unemployment rate (percentage of labour force aged 15-24). The number of young persons aged 15-24 who are without work, currently available for work and seeking work divided by the total labour force of that age group. The table shows data on the youth unemployment rate disaggregated by sex.

Table 24 – Telecommunications

Personal computers per 100 population. Personal computers (PCs) are computers designed to be used by a single user at a time.

Internet users per 100 population. The Internet is a linked global network of computers in which users at one computer, if they have permission, receive information from other computers in the network.

Telephone subscribers, land lines per 100 population. This refers to the number of land lines connecting equipment to the public switched network and that have a dedicated port in the telephone exchange equipment.

Telephone subscribers, mobile cellular per 100 population. This refers to users of mobile telephones who subscribe to an automatic public mobile telephone service that provides access to the public switched telephone network using cellular technology.

Table 25 – Infrastructure and transport

Roads density. The total road network divided by the land area. Total road network includes motorways, highways, and main or national roads, secondary or regional roads, and all other roads measured in kilometres in a country.

Paved roads. The share of roads surfaced with crushed stone (macadam) and hydrocarbon binder or bituminized agents, concrete, or cobblestones, expressed as a percentage of the length of all roads.

Railway density. The length of rail lines divided by the land area expressed in 1,000 km^2. Rail lines are the length of railway route available for train service measured in kilometres, irrespective of the number of parallel tracks.

Passenger cars in use. The number of passenger cars, expressed per 1,000 population. Covers road motor vehicles designed for the conveyance of passengers and seating not more than nine persons, including the driver. Taxis, jeep-type vehicles and station wagons are included. Special-purpose vehicles, such as two-wheeled or three-wheeled cycles or motorcycles, trams, trolley-buses, ambulances, hearses, and military vehicles operated by police or other governmental security organizations, are excluded.

Table 26 – Land area and use

Surface area. Total surface area comprises total land area plus water area. Total land area comprises agricultural land, forest and other wooded land, built-up and related land (excluding scattered farm buildings), wet open land, dry open land with special vegetation cover and open land without, or with insignificant, vegetation cover. Water area comprises inland waters and tidal waters. Land and water area should cover the total area of a country.

Population density. Number of people per square kilometre of surface area. Total surface area comprises total land area, inland and tidal water area.

Forested land area, as a share of land area. This indicator gives the forested land area as a percentage of total land area. Forested land or forests and woodland as indicated by FAO refer to land under natural or planted stands of trees, whether productive or not. This category includes land from which forests have been cleared but which will be reforested in the foreseeable future, and excludes woodland or forest used only for recreation purposes. Data on forested land may be incomplete as there is no data available for the category of shrub land/savannah since 1995.

Protected area, as a share of land area. This indicator gives the area protected to maintain biological diversity as a percentage of the total surface area of a country. The generally accepted IUCN-World Conservation Union definition of a protected area is an area of land or sea dedicated to the protection and maintenance of biological diversity and of natural and associated cultural resources and managed through legal or other effective means. Protected areas, both terrestrial and marine, are totalled and expressed as a percentage of the total surface area of the country. The total surface area of the country includes terrestrial area plus any territorial sea area (up to 12 nautical miles).

Table 27 – Energy and water use

Consumption of electricity for domestic purposes. Refers to total annual electricity consumption by households given in the energy database of the United Nations Statistics Division. The indicator is calculated by dividing the annual household electricity consumption by the population and is expressed in kilowatt-hours per capita per year.

Energy use per $1,000 (2000 PPP) GDP. Apparent consumption of commercial energy measured in units of oil equivalent per $1,000 of GDP converted from national currencies using purchasing power parity conversion factors, expressed as kilograms of oil equivalent per $1,000 of GDP measured in 2000 PPP.

Water withdrawal (share of total renewable water resources). The gross amount of water extracted in a day from any source either permanently or temporarily. Water sources can be either withdrawn from surface water or groundwater or produced (non-conventional water sources), for example reused treated wastewater and desalinated water.

Water withdrawal for domestic purposes. Domestic water withdrawal per capita (cubic metres per year). Drinking water plus water withdrawn for homes, municipalities, commercial establishments, and public services, divided by the population.

Table 28 – Pollution and access to water and sanitation

Carbon dioxide (CO_2) emissions. The estimated quantity of carbon dioxide emissions (tons of carbon dioxide per capita) divided by the total population.

Use of ozone-depleting substances. The sum of the national annual consumption in weighted tons of the individual substances in the group of ozone-depleting substances multiplied by their ozone-depleting potential. Ozone-depleting substances are any substance containing chlorine or bromine that destroys the stratospheric ozone layer. Expressed as ODP kilograms per 1,000 population.

Share of [rural/urban] population with access to improved drinking water sources. The proportion of the rural population, or the urban population, as appropriate, with sustainable access to an improved water source is the percentage of the population in rural areas that uses any of the following types of water supply for drinking: piped water, public tap, borehole or pump, protected well, protected spring or rainwater. Improved water sources do not include vendor-provided water, bottled water, tanker trucks or unprotected wells and springs. The *Global Water Supply and Assessment 2000 Report* defines reasonable access as "the availability of 20 litres per capita per day at a distance no longer than 1,000 meters." However, access and volume of drinking water are difficult to measure, and so sources of drinking water that are thought to provide safe water are used as a proxy.

Share of [rural/urban] population with access to improved sanitation. The proportion of the rural population, or the urban population, as appropriate, with access to improved sanitation refers to the percentage of the population in rural areas with access to facilities that hygienically separate human excreta from human, animal and insect contact. Facilities such as sewers or septic tanks, poor-flush latrines and simple pit or ventilated improved pit latrines are assumed to be adequate, provided that they are not public, according to the *Global Water Supply and Sanitation Assessment 2000 Report*. To be effective, facilities must be correctly constructed and properly maintained.

Statistical methods

Exponential growth rate. The average annual growth rate between two points in time for certain demographic data, notably labour force and population, is calculated from the equation

$$r = \left(\frac{\ln P_n / P_1}{n} \right).100$$

where P_n and P_1 are the last and first observations in the period, n is the number of years in the period, and ln is the natural logarithm operator. The growth rate is based on an exponential growth model between two points in time using continuous compounding. Note that it does not take into account the intermediate values of the series.

The **geometric growth rate** uses discrete compounding instead of continuous compounding. Therefore, it is applicable to capture compound growth over discrete periods. Although continuous growth, as modeled by the exponential growth rate, may be more realistic, many economic phenomena are measured only on an annual basis, in which case the annual compound model is appropriate. If the underlying data are levels, the formula for the average annual percentage change over n periods is

$$r = \left[\exp \left(\frac{\ln P_n / P_1}{n} \right) - 1 \right].100$$

Note that it does not take into account the intermediate values of the series. However, if the underlying data are already reported as annual changes, the formula becomes

$$r = \{[(1 + g_0)(1 + g_1)...(1 + g_n)]^{1/n} - 1\}.100,$$

where $g_0, g_1, ..., g_n$ denote the annual changes from the year 1 to n.